PENGUIN ENGLISH POETS

GENERAL EDITOR: CHRISTOPHER RICKS

GEORGE HERBERT: THE COMPLETE ENGLISH POEMS

GEORGE HERBERT was born in 1593, the fifth son of Richard Herbert of Montgomery and Magdalene Herbert, to whom John Donne dedicated his elegy 'Autumnal Beauty'. He was educated at Westminster School and Trinity College, Cambridge, where he was appointed Reader in Rhetoric in 1618 and Public Orator in 1620. Herbert was an excellent Greek and Latin scholar and was fluent in Italian, Spanish and French; he was also an accomplished amateur musician. He seemed destined for a great public career and attracted the attention of two powerful and influential figures, the Duke of Richmond and the Marquess of Hamilton, and, when they met, King James I took a liking to him. However, when his two aristocratic patrons, and then, in 1625, King James, all died, any hope of immediate preferment was dashed. In 1626 he resigned his seat in Parliament and took holy orders, becoming Rector of Bemerton, a tiny rural parish on Salisbury Plain, in 1630. In the previous year he had married Jane Danvers after a courtship of only three days, and their marriage was a happy one. Herbert died of consumption at the age of forty on 1 March 1633.

Early in 1633 Herbert, aware of his imminent death, sent a copy of his book *The Temple* to his friend Nicholas Ferrar, requesting him to burn it or print it as he saw fit, and two editions were published before the end of that year. *The Temple* comprises almost all his surviving English poems, and it is upon this volume that his reputation rests. His other surviving work includes a set of Latin poems, *Memoriae Matris Sacrum*, written in memory of his mother; a handful of short occasional poems; two sets of sacred poems, *Lucus* and *Passio Discerpta*; and *Musae Responsoriae*, a defence of the Church of England against Andrew Melville's *Anti-Tami-Cami-Categoria*. Of his prose, *A Priest*

to the Temple, notes on *The Hundred and Ten Considerations* by Juan de Valdés, the translation of Luigi Cornaro's *Treatise of Temperance and Sobrietie*, some of his Latin letters and orations, and a portion of his private correspondence have survived. Thirteen editions of *The Temple* were published between 1633 and 1679; after that his reputation began to wane. However, the 1799 edition of *The Temple* heralded a revival, to which Coleridge's appreciation in *Biographia Literaria* gave a considerable boost: 'George Herbert is a true poet, but a poet *sui generis*, the merits of whose poems will never be felt, without a sympathy with the mind and character of the man.'

JOHN TOBIN has studied at Boston College, the University of Toronto (MA, Ph.D.), and King's College, London, as a Fulbright Scholar. His work on the sources of Renaissance poetry and drama has appeared in numerous journals and *Festschriften*, as well as in his study of Apuleius in the Renaissance, *Shakespeare's Favorite Novel*. He has taught at Boston College, York University, in Canada and at Clark University in Massachusetts. He is currently a Professor of English Literature at the University of Massachusetts at Boston.

GEORGE HERBERT

The Complete English Poems

Edited by JOHN TOBIN

PENGUIN BOOKS

PENGUIN BOOKS

Published by the Penguin Group
Penguin Books Ltd, 80 Strand, London WC2R ORL, England
Penguin Group (USA) Inc., 375 Hudson Street, New York, New York 10014, USA
Penguin Books Australia Ltd, 250 Camberwell Road, Camberwell, Victoria 3124, Australia
Penguin Books Canada Ltd, 10 Alcorn Avenue, Toronto, Ontario, Canada M4V 3B2
Penguin Books India (P) Ltd, 11 Community Centre, Panchsheel Park, New Delhi – 110 017, India
Penguin Group (NZ), cnr Airborne and Rosedale Roads, Albany, Auckland 1310, New Zealand
Penguin Books (South Africa) (Pty) Ltd, 24 Sturdee Avenue, Rosebank 2196, South Africa

Penguin Books Ltd, Registered Offices: 80 Strand, London WC2R ORL, England

www.penguin.com

This edition first published 1991
Reprinted with a new Introduction and corrections 2004
1

Printed in England by Clays Ltd, St Ives plc
Set in Monophoto Sabon

CONTENTS

INTRODUCTION

George Herbert is either our most major minor poet in English literature or he is the most modestly exquisite of our major poets. The modesty of his poems is both attitudinal and structural, sweetly charming in the literal etymological sense of charming, and limited in size if not number. The more than one hundred and seventy poems that make up *The Church*, the central section of *The Temple*, are briefer than the songs of complaint, praise, penitence and thanksgiving that make up the Book of Psalms of the sweetly singing David, but are more numerous. Valued over the centuries by discriminating readers, Herbert remains a much-loved and much-studied poet even in the largely secular twenty-first century. There are several explanations for the popularity of his poetry, or, if popularity is too strong a term, widespread and often deep appreciation, respect and affection. First, there are still many readers who share Herbert's belief in a Christian God of salvation and love. The poems which so often reflect what Herbert himself said are, according to Izaak Walton, his first biographer, 'the many spiritual conflicts that have passed betwixt God and my soul, before I could subject mine to the will of Jesus my Master, in whose service I have now found perfect freedom' speak to the religious, moral and psychological tribulations and joys of such devout and devoted readers. Second, there are the readers who once shared the faith of Herbert, but who no longer believe in the story he tells as a participant, yet, out of a feeling of nostalgia, find pleasure, perhaps comfort, in the momentary suspension of disbelief in the poet's ordered world. Third, there are the academic readers of Herbert who find scholarly pleasure in the observation of the poet's creative manipulation of his sources, not only from the Bible but also from his immediate English predecessors –

Spenser, Sidney, Shakespeare, and most especially Donne – and in the additional appreciation of Herbert's images, rhythms and phrases being reworked in such nineteenth- and twentieth-century poets as Emily Dickinson, Gerard Manley Hopkins, Thomas Hardy and Elizabeth Bishop. Fourth, there are the great many lovers of poetry who are not necessarily Christian, nostalgic or academic but who find pleasures in the works of someone whose combination of formal artistry and clear enthusiasm for his subjects is attractive in itself.

The first three classes of reader, especially the third, will want to fix Herbert in an exact position on the sectarian spectrum of early seventeenth-century Protestant Christianity. Alas, for all his precision of wording, Herbert frustrates the desire for such certitude. The best that we can say is that he is not 'High' church or, to use the term anachronistically, 'Anglo-Catholic' or Laudian, but he does prefer ceremony over barrenness and is drawn frequently and powerfully to the image and role of the Eucharistic sacrament. The church windows in his poem with that title, if not in his own little church in Bemerton, have some stained glass in them, while the longest poem in *The Church*, 'The Sacrifice', offers a medieval, quite Catholic image of Christ's sufferings, though it is admittedly a good deal less gruesomely detailed than that of some recent cinematic versions. While such a carnal display goes further than Puritan Calvinists of Herbert's day could or would tolerate, there are on the other hand signs that the poet was Calvinist (and we know that not all Calvinists were Puritan, however that pejorative is defined), especially in terms of the central and vexed issue of election, the notion that God has chosen only some people for salvation, quite independent of works or merit. Yet Herbert's pervasive charity conflicts with such a harsh doctrine, and clearly he worried at times, or more properly the speaker in his poetry has given voice to the fitful anxiety that the only apparently universally offered sacrifice by Christ is meant to include the speaker ('O spiteful bitter thought', 'Assurance'). These moments of doubt make Herbert easier to appreciate by modern readers with our own uncertainties.

In terms of religion, Herbert is close to centre of that Protestant spectrum. However much Chillingworth's dictum that 'the Bible only is the religion of Protestants' was true for many, Herbert's additional embrace of the church with its rituals, however modified, and its calendar balances book and building, scripture and temple. Socially, he is also pushed and pulled between the goal of secular advancement and the obligation of religious calling, between the satisfying of pride and ambition and the yielding to priestly humility. We remember that Herbert was the fifth of seven sons in a family of ten children, a family of considerable military prominence in the past, that his mother, Magdalene, was a culturally significant woman who was the patroness of, among others, John Donne, and that his eldest brother, Edward Herbert, the author of *Autobiography*, one of the most extraordinarily eccentric self-portraits ever written, was for a time King James's ambassador to France as well as the author of the first English philosophical treatise arguing for what we now call deism. Further, in terms of status, George Herbert's cousins included Mary Sidney, Countess of Pembroke, the sister of the late Sir Philip Sidney, and William and Philip Herbert, the Earls of Pembroke and Montgomery, described in the dedication of the 1623 Folio of Shakespeare as the two 'most noble and incomparable of brethren'. On his own merits George was a gifted student at Westminster School, where he was noticed by the foremost classical and biblical scholar of the day Lancelot Andrews (whose distinctive preaching style with the analysis of the smallest units of the text, 'the crumbling a text into small parts', was nevertheless not influential on Herbert in his own preaching). He was even more noticeably successful at Cambridge, where he became Public Orator, a post from which promotion at court and political influence were common. Clearly, in spite of what we believe to be his delicate health ('for he had a body apt to a consumption, and to fevers and other infirmities') (Walton's *Life*, p. 280), he was on the road to worldly success. He was even a member of parliament in King James's last parliament, 1624, the one which raised money for war in spite of the pacific political nature of James himself. For all Herbert's earned success and expected promotion, his all-but-realised court career was, in the homely phrase he uses in other contexts in his poetry, 'nipped in the bud', probably by the elevation of the Duke of Buckingham, James's favourite, at the expense of William Herbert, the poet's kinsman and patron. Of course, we should remember that Herbert's sense of vocation in the ministry, a sense of his being called, may only seem to parallel the politically ambitious Donne's delayed vocation, one that took place only after King James had pronounced, 'I will prefer Mr. Donne in the Church and in no way else'. Herbert entered the ministry six years after his parliamentary experience and the surpassing of Pembroke by Buckingham. The scepticism, which may already have led us to be unjust to Donne, should not create the *post-hoc-ergo-propter hoc*[1] fallacy that after Herbert lost the chance for secular advancement he therefore chose to be a priest.

Certain it is that Herbert was a very able younger son of a prominent family, one whose personal physical vulnerability never deprived him of an inner confidence, a sense of social entitlement, that shines through his writings whether in *The County Parson*, where he refuses to have the church and its ministries condescended to by the upper classes, or in the many poems of dialogue with God where, however humble the guilty speaker in the poem may be, he is confident of being a worthy member of the dialogue. We believe that Herbert was truly honest when he viewed himself as the 'Less than the least of God's mercies' ('The Printers to the Reader', p. 4). There is, nevertheless, a paradox contained within that statement, at least as the world goes now, for there is vanity, that mild subspecies of pride, in being first, even and perhaps especially being first among the last; it is a most prominent position.

Whatever the force and depth of Herbert's social, political and psychological tensions, he entered the ministry of a religion which in its essential tenets was fraught with its own overt tensions in the form of paradoxes, doctrinal oxymora ripe for the delicate handling by a true believer with a most subtle creative imagination. After all, Christianity offers a god who becomes a man, a man whose death gives life, a defeat that is highest victory, a humility that is triumphant, flesh that is bread and blood that is wine.

Herbert, by church affiliation, by social status, by religious

1 'after this, therefore because of this.'

belief, was always already in the middle of a paradoxical universe. With his classical education and religious commitment, he was Janus-faced in the Anglican *via media*.[2] It is not surprising with all this integrating of doubleness, not double binds but twofold natures, that Herbert should be as a writer so intriguing a punster, finding in non-comic wordplay a device to illustrate the fused unions of so many of the truths he believed in. We know that some gifted critics seem to need to pun in order to think. Herbert seems equally to need wordplay in order to allow him to ring the changes on the basic score of the Christian story. He tells us directly in 'The Son' that 'I like our language/How neatly do we give one only name/To parents' issue and the sun's bright star' The number of creative puns in Herbert is extraordinarily large, and it must be said that these puns are not only English puns but also macaronic, that is, they involve wordplay between two languages. We don't think of Herbert as a Milton, reliant on Latinate diction, but he really does play creatively with the language of Virgil and the Vulgate Bible.

For example, Matthias Bauer has shown there is subtle wordplay in 'The Pulley' on the English 'rest', the Latin '*restis*', the rope that is essential to the pulley, and '*ampullae*', the plural of the Latin for 'jar' or 'flask' from which liquids (or graces) are poured, pronounced a little differently from our customary first declension 'eye' sound for the ending in the plural with an 'e' sound equalling 'ampull*ey*'.[3] And there are the 'ac*cords*', of 'A True Hymn' in 'when the soul unto the lines ac*cords*' (line 10) and 'whereas if th' heart be moved' (line 16) and 'As when th' heart sayes' (line 19): the Latin '*cor/cordis*' means heart, the stem of Herbert's favourite word, '*cord*ial(s).' Non-macaronic but elegant is the pun in 'Jordan (2)' where 'penned' means both 'written' and 'contained'. These are but a few of the very many instances of serious wordplay by a poet whose very name suggests a life fragrant of many virtues.

Herbert the secular rhetorician at Cambridge as Public Orator

2 'the middle way' (that is, between Roman Catholicism and Presbyterianism).

3 '"A title strange yet true": Toward an Explanation of Herbert's Titles', in *George Herbert: Sacred and Profane*, ed. Helen Wilcox and Richard Todd (Amsterdam: VU University Press, 1995).

has become the religious rhetorician who uses subtle rhetorical tactics beyond paronomasia.

For all his integrity, Herbert does practise tricks against our expectations, as in the absent, but we would think necessary, verb in 'Prayer (1)', an absence that speaks loudly of the impossibility of limiting the mystery of one-sided prayer by an exhaustive definition; as in the imperfect or broken rhyme of 'Denial' where the non-rhyming 'disorder' of line 5 establishes the speaker's spiritual confusion; and as in the poem-length delayed chiasmus, the rhetorical crossing, of 'The Bag', where Christ the messenger, the container, is so because of his death upon the cross. There are further the bold-faced acrostics of 'Colossians 3:3' and the peeling-off of the letters in the final words of each three-line stanza in 'Paradise', such that the still-surviving letters are meaningful terms. In 'Jesu' there is the Lancelot Andrews-like creative parcelling out, the crumbling of the name of Christ in order to have both 'Jesu' and 'I ease you' drawn out in the carving of the holy name letter by letter in the speaker's heart, and the only slightly less subtle play on the letters '*J* and *C*' annealed on grapes in 'Love-Joy' (where one sees and hears also a pun on 'annealed' 'aneled' as 'burnt in' and 'oiled' as in baptism). There is further the well-known anagram on 'army' 'Mary' in 'Anagram', and the subtler variations in vowel quality, for example, 'loved' as a rhyme for 'moved' and 'approved' in 'A True Hymn'. Each instance of formal cleverness startles the reader into attentiveness with a heightened appreciation of a content that is fundamentally simple.

Whatever the tactical subtleties, there is essentially in Herbert a simplicity and thematic straightforwardness, the kind of right-angled exactitude we find illustrated in his many images of security, with boxes, cabinets, drawers of closure throughout the canon, for 'Life is straight, Straight as a line' ('A Wreath'). Curlings, curves, indirection, jaggedness, winding stairs and writhings are negatives, with the exception of the twice-heaven-associated 'twist' in 'The Pearl' (line. 38) and 'Providence' (lines 58–60).

In all of these poems, Herbert's frequent use of the word 'fain' meaning 'gladly' indicates his genial acceptance of the divine plan and his place in it. His choice of 'pro*fane*' and 'pro*fan*ation', with the Latin *fanum* meaning 'temple', reminds us that throughout *The Temple* the sacred and the secular, the holy and the unholy have their locus in that fleshly temple, the human heart. Lastly, not to crack the wind of the poor phrase, Herbert is as honest a poet in his themes and attitudes as there is. He does not feign, cannot fake it. There is, finally, no feigning in content or form. No seeking out 'quaint words and trim invention', only plain-speaking of what is the whispered sweetness always already within.

Great writers have a binocular view of reality, with one lens focused on the passing scene and the other on what their literary predecessors have written about the same aspects of life. In the case of Herbert, apart from the Bible and Sir Philip Sidney in his work on the Psalms and the role of candour in expression, the most note-worthy influences come from Shakespeare and Donne. Herbert read carefully Shakespeare's plays, and among the most important of those in terms of influence upon the lyrics in *The Temple* is *Richard II*. This is a play we know with near certainty that Herbert's frequent model John Donne had actually seen rather than merely read and, more importantly, it is the play whose protagonist identifies himself, however hubristically, with Christ. We note at least three clear instances of creative borrowing where Herbert evokes the poignancy but not the vanity of the Shakespearean protagonist: 'Justice (2)', with its glass and scales like buckets, is indebted to the phrasing of Richard's request for a glass (mirror) and his use of scales as buckets in IV, i; 'The British Church', with its John of Gaunt-influenced double moat of grace from II, i; and 'Church-Music', with its echo of the sitting down to tell the sad story of the death of kings, which derives from III, ii. Less ironic is another Shakespearean borrowing which occurs in 'Bitter-Sweet'. This poem, with its opening expression 'Ah my dear', affected Gerard Manley Hopkins in his most famous poem, 'The Windhover', and refers primarily to the apple eaten by Adam, bittersweet because it led to the Fall of man but also to the sweet gift of the Incarnation. There is a secondary allusion to *King Lear*, the greatest drama of lamentation and love, in the Fool's lesson to his Lord about the difference 'between a *bitter* fool and a *sweet* fool' (I.iv). Of course, the First Folio did not include Shakespeare's

Sonnets, but Herbert had read from the 1609 Quarto edition at least Sonnet 30, with its theme of the compulsively repeated memory of pain, 'the sad account of fore-bemoaned moan,/Which I new pay as if not paid before' (lines 11–12), which weaves its way into 'The Discharge' (lines 47–50).

Shakespeare is not the only Elizabethan dramatist that Herbert shows a clear knowledge of. In 'The Size', Herbert writes of a modest sphere of activity: 'A Christian's state and case/Is not a corpulent, but a thin and spare' (lines 31–2), 'Modest and moderate joys . . . are *passing brave*' (lines 2, 4), where the contrast between a proper religious humility and a secular pride is underscored by the clear allusion to Marlowe's Tamburlaine, the conqueror of Persia, 'Is it not *passing brave* to be a king,/And ride in triumph through Persepolis (*Tamburlaine the Great, Part I*, II, v, lines 53–4).

As for that great frequenter of playhouses Donne himself, his poems and sermons have had their effect on at least thirty of Herbert's lyrics. Herbert echoes most frequently 'A Valediction: forbidding Mourning', 'The Ecstasy' and 'The Sun Rising', as well as Holy Sonnets 7, 10 and 14. More important than the very many verbal borrowings of individual words and whole phrases is Herbert's realising the dramatic nature of Donne's lyrics. This dramatic quality is modified or toned down throughout *The Temple* when one compares the borrowings with the Donnean originals, but it is present clearly enough in spite of the poet's even temper and modest level of energy. For example, we sometimes overlook the fact that a poem such as 'The Forerunners' is itself a forerunner of the dramatic monologue which we associate with nineteenth-century poets like Tennyson and Browning or early twentieth-century writers like T. S. Eliot. 'The Forerunners' plays with a central Herbertian thematic tension between the outside and the inside, with the former being trivial and the latter essential. Herbert qualifies that issue with the idea of aging, of external decay and paradoxically of internal energising. We can speculate that Herbert himself was prematurely grey ('White is their colour, and behold my head') or suppress that possibility and instead stress Herbert's imaginative gift for putting himself dramatically in another's position, as he had done in 'The Sacrifice', a striking example of negative capability. Herbert here is anticipating the 24-year-old Tennyson's creating an aged hero in *Ulysses*, and even the only slightly older T. S. Eliot producing a speaker with a bald spot in the middle of his hair in 'The Love Song of J. Alfred Prufrock'. Whether we agree that Herbert is imaginatively projecting or autobiographically confessing, his speaker is willing to lose the enchantingly embellished language of the young and the secular in favour of gaining a discourse mature, simple and religious. Like a less-troubled Tennyson, who clearly had absorbed not only 'Love (1)' but also 'The Temper' in the fabric of the Prologue to *In Memoriam*, Herbert introduces moments of doubt into his verses, verses which nevertheless flourish ultimately the comforting theme of divine love.

Perhaps no poem illustrates better Herbert's flourishing the theme of inside/outside than 'Aaron'. The artistry is especially impressive from the poem's opening stanza of definition as to what constitutes the true dress of Aaron, the archetypal priest of the Jewish testament, to the concluding line of priestly command which opens the poem to the congregation who are welcomed by the now-ready celebrant. At the heart of the poem is the paradoxical situation of the speaker's having put on Christ, the ultimate priest, typologically anticipated by Aaron, while simultaneously having Christ within himself; thus we have three priests in one person, Aaron, Christ and the speaker, a unity that is no sacrilege, but a sacerdotal trinity, in a movement from individual 'defect' (line 7) to communal 'perfect' (line 22) – and 'perfect' designedly echoes the '*perfectus*' of Matthew 5:48 in the Vulgate, the quality the believer shares according to the Gospel with his Father in heaven. Each stanza has a musical bridging note, 'Harmonious bells', (line 3), 'A noise of passions', (line 8), where 'noise' is both cacophony and the group of imperfect musicians who make the sound, to 'Another music' (line 13), 'My only music' (line 18), to the doctrine finely and finally 'tuned by Christ' (line 23). The pronouns in the prepositional phrases carry the paradox: Christ 'lives in me' (line 24), even as 'In him I am well dressed' (line 15). Herbert/the speaker is the descendant of both Aaron and the new Aaron, Christ.

While Herbert never rises to the generic heights of epic, he contains within his many lyrics implied narrative, drama, pastoral, even proverbial expressions honed to epigram, as well as in 'Humility' a little dream vision, 'I saw the Virtues sitting hand in hand', together with a beast fable with its personifications and exemplary animals. He even writes some eighteen sonnets, many of them quite Shakespearean in structure and rhyme scheme. Some of the most successful of these lyrics are those that may be said to have two voices, one that is the speaker/Herbert, and the other, God, as in 'The Collar', 'Redemption', 'Jordan (2)', 'Dialogue', 'Love Unknown', 'Artillery', 'A True Hymn', 'Love (3)'. And it is a God Herbert continually praises.

Lyrics, unlike the larger forms of narrative and drama, are more easily abstracted from their social and political contexts, but even when such abstractions are made, the quality or attitudinal practices belonging to the original context are still operative. In the case of Herbert, it is the combination of humble gratitude (both absolute and yet with thanks for favour(s) yet to come) and direct praise to a patron, the King in Heaven, which replicates the mode of address proper to a courtier at Whitehall in the reigns of James and Charles. Critical agnostics frown upon such self-abnegation, even self-abasement, but, for most readers, Herbert has within the rules of both games secular and sacred struck just the right note. Now, flattery is still flattery at court and in society even when the praise is based on the truth, and even or especially when the recipient is a figure of power and influence. Certainly there is no figure of greater power than Herbert's God. But inasmuch as that God is no respecter of persons, looking as he does straight into the human heart, the praise of Him is never enough. In Herbert's poetry of praise, flattery is logically impossible; there is no pretending.

Part of the attractiveness of Herbert's lyrics for some readers is the quality of security, of faith guaranteed of reward. Yes, there are many poems which introduce the issues of doubt and anxiety, but tonally there is precious little fear within the framework of assured love and forgiveness. A good way to calculate, if calculation is possible in matters of tone and feeling, the difference between the attitudes of Herbert in regard to doubt and faith and the greater degree of anxiety in the posture of a later poet who knew Herbert's work is to compare and contrast Herbert and Hopkins, or Herbert and Tennyson, the Tennyson who reworks the Immortal Love of 'Love (I)' in the 'Strong son of God, Immortal Love' of the Prologue to *In Memoriam*.

Herbert's world is so neatly bounded that the universe seems for all its sinfulness ultimately manageable. It can be said that in spite of Herbert's Christian discipline, Herbert appears at bottom as a religious Epicurean, finding pleasure in the exercise of virtue as the prudent Greek philosopher Epicurus (342–270 BC) wishes, believing that gentle motion is best. The low energy and circumscribed vocation, together with a risk-averse attitude make him so unlike his charismatically energetic literary predecessors like the murdered Marlowe or the flamboyant Donne or, subsequently, the nearly executed Milton that we sometimes forget that poetry need not be explosive or hyperbolical, that litotes, understatement, has its subtle claims upon us.

We think of Herbert as a master of subtle rhythms, elegant antitheses and clever rhymes, assonances and alliteration. He is a supremely musical poet, yet one who can also depict discrete narrative and even dramatic scenes. Nevertheless beyond this quite proper appreciation of Herbert's musical, narrative and dramatic skills, there is the quintessential Herbertian virtue of tact. He has an aristocratic sense of the right form of address, the confidence and poise that makes his poetry neither banal nor overwhelming, an aesthetic middle way that parallels his sectarian position in the religious options of his time.

If Ben Jonson was right on the mark about the correspondence between speech and the essential self, 'Speak that I may know thee', then we have a strong sense of the man Herbert behind and within the lyrics, however much we may theoretically understand that the speaker in the poem need not be a direct version of the poet. We do note that the remarkable consistency of voice in *The Temple*, even if Herbert has only adopted that voice, suggests in its ubiquity a good deal of how it is that custom has become second nature.

Manners maketh the man, and the decorum that Herbert maintains as he fine-tunes the bells of accepted doctrine makes us appreciate the artist and the man we think we see behind the art. Herbert becomes or always already was the model rhetorician, the good man expert in speaking (or writing), the '*vir bonus peritus dicendi*'[4] Because we think we know the man behind the work and think that man admirable, we value even more the work itself.

The Temple concludes in the 'L'Envoy' with a reference to sheep, thereby reminding us that his Christ is both King and Good Shepherd. The world of the shepherd, the pastoral world, for all its black and white and vulnerable sheep, is in its literary form a world of conversation, of dialogue, of pastors divine and human. While we never know how a true conversation will develop and end, in Herbert, as we sit down and read, we are uncertain only of how the conversation with God will develop; we always know how it will end.

4 'a good man expert in speaking.'

ACKNOWLEDGEMENTS

A number of friends, colleagues and lovers of Herbert's poetry have provided me with texts, information and insights. Foremost among them I wish to thank my wife, Professor Rosemary Barton Tobin, for sharing with me her profound knowledge both of Christian doctrine and of Renaissance Latin; my friends Professors Gwynne Evans and Vincent Petronella, who each read the manuscript and made a number of valuable suggestions; and the General Editor, Christopher Ricks, for his support and detailed criticism.

I am grateful for additional assistance from colleagues and friends, Professors Neal Bruss, Mordechai Feingold and John Klause, and Mr Steven Praeger. Caroline Lamb has been not only an eagle-eyed copy editor but also the source of a number of suggestions for quite useful scriptural and lexical glosses. I owe a debt to the expert librarians at the Bodleian Library, the Cambridge University Library, Dr Williams's Library, London, the Manuscript Room of the British Library, and the Houghton Library, Harvard University. I wish to thank the Faculty Committee on Educational Needs and Dean Richard Freeland of the College of Arts and Sciences, University of Massachusetts at Boston, for a grant to defray in part the cost of travel. I am grateful to my former student, Mr Haixin Xu, MA, for his assistance, and to Mr Howard Davies for his proofreading. Professor Ted-Larry Pebworth and the editors of *ELR* were kind enough to grant permission to use the edition of the texts from 'George Herbert's Poems to the Queen of Bohemia: A Rediscovered Text and a New Edition', *ELR* 9 (1973).

My special thanks go to Sara Praeger, my research assistant and most knowledgeable Herbertian, who prepared with great skill and good humour the many versions of the complete manuscript.

No one but myself is responsible for any errors that may have survived, certainly not Susannah Barton Tobin who generously helped with the pagination.

TABLE OF DATES

1593	Born 3 April, Montgomeryshire, fifth son and seventh of ten children of Richard and Magdalene Herbert (née Newport).
1596	Richard Herbert (father) dies.
1599	Herbert family moves to Oxford. Donne makes the acquaintance of Magdalene Herbert, the subject of 'The Autumnal': 'No spring, nor summer beauty hath such grace,/As I have seen in one autumnal face' (lines 1–2).
1601	Herbert family moves to London.
1604–9	At Westminster School, where in his first year he would have profited from the occasional tutelage of Lancelot Andrewes, then Dean of Westminster; as early as 1604 he writes *Musae Responsoriae* (published 1620), lightly satiric Latin verses against the Presbyterian controversialist Andrew Melville.
1609	Magdalene Herbert marries Sir John Danvers, aged twenty, who will prove a benign and generous stepfather to Herbert.
1609–13	At Trinity College, Cambridge.
1613	Proceeded BA.
1614	Minor Fellow of Trinity College.
1616	Proceeded MA; Shakespeare dies.
1618	Praelector in Rhetoric, Cambridge University.
1619	Elected Public Orator of Cambridge University. Eldest brother Edward Herbert appointed Ambassador to France.
1621	Henry Vaughan born.

1622 Is one of two dedicatees (along with William Boswell) of Edward Herbert's philosophical treatise *De Veritate*.

1623 First Folio of Shakespeare's plays published, dedicated 'to the most noble and incomparable pair of brethren', William and Philip Herbert, Earls of Pembroke and Montgomery, respectively, kinsmen of George Herbert.

1623–4 Member of Parliament for Montgomeryshire. Another MP is Nicholas Ferrar, who had been Herbert's Cambridge contemporary while at Clare Hall.

1624 Ordained deacon.

1625 King James dies.

1626 Installed as a canon of Lincoln Cathedral and receives the living of Leighton Bromswold. Bacon dies. Lancelot Andrewes dies.

1627 Death of Magdalene Herbert. Donne preaches her funeral sermon.

1628 Sir John Danvers remarries.

1628–9 Herbert lives at the home of the Earl of Danby in Wiltshire.

1629 5 March: marries Jane Danvers, a cousin of Sir John Danvers.

1630 Receives the living of Fugglestone with Bemerton; installed 26 April. 19 September: ordained priest in Salisbury Cathedral.

1631 Donne dies.

1633 1 March: Herbert dies in the rectory at Bemerton. *The Temple* published at Cambridge.

1634 Herbert's English translation of the Jesuit Leonard Lessius's Latin version of Luigi Cornaro's *Trattato de la vita sobria* (*A Treatise of Temperance and Sobriety*) published.

1637 Nicholas Ferrar dies.

1638 Ferrar's English translation from the Italian version of the Spanish text of Juan de Valdés, *The Divine Considerations of John Valdesso*, published; it contains a letter and notes by Herbert.

1640 *Outlandish Proverbs, Selected by Mr G. H.*, published; the first of the proverbs is 'Man proposeth, God disposeth'.

1652 *Herbert's Remains*, ed. B. Oley, published; includes a life, *A Priest to the Temple*, *Jacula Prudentum* (expanded list of proverbs), *Prayer Before and After Sermon*, Latin poems to Bacon and to Donne, with additional aphorisms.

1670 First edition of Izaak Walton's *The Life of Mr George Herbert*.

1671 Second edition of *A Priest to the Temple*, the first separate edition.

FURTHER READING

EDITIONS

Palmer, G. H. (ed.), *The English Works of George Herbert*, 3 vols., Houghton Mifflin, 1905. Still of value in spite of its eccentric grouping of the poems.

Hutchinson, F. E. (ed.), *The Works of George Herbert*, Clarendon Press, 1941. Revised 1945. The standard text.

Patrides, C. A. (ed.), *The English Poems of George Herbert*, J. M. Dent, 1974. Reprinted with corrections 1977, 1978, 1981 and 1984. Follows the 1633 edition and includes valuable notes and useful bibliography.

Charles, Amy B. (ed.), *The Williams Manuscript of George Herbert's Poems: A Facsimile Reproduction*, Scholars' Facsimiles & Reprints, 1977.

Wall, John N., Jr (ed.), *George Herbert: The Country Parson, The Temple*, Paulist Press, 1981. Reprinted with corrections 1985. Modernised texts with useful introduction, especially on spiritual background.

Charles, Amy B., and Mario Di Cesare (eds.), *The Bodleian Manuscript of George Herbert's Poems*, Scholars' Facsimiles & Reprints, 1984

McCloskey, Mark, and Paul R. Murphy (trans.), *The Latin Poetry of George Herbert, a Bilingual Edition*, Ohio University Press, 1965

CONCORDANCE

Di Cesare, Mario A., and Rigo Mignani (eds.), *A Concordance to the Complete Writings of George Herbert*, Cornell University Press, 1977

BIOGRAPHY

Novarr, David, *The Making of Walton's Lives*, Cornell University Press, 1958

Reiter, Robert E., 'George Herbert and His Biographers', *Cithara* 9 (1970)

Charles, Amy M., *A Life of George Herbert*, Cornell University Press, 1977

CRITICAL STUDIES

Asals, Heather A. R., *Equivocal Predication: George Herbert's Way to God*, University of Toronto Press, 1981

Austin, Francis, *The Language of the Metaphysical Poets*, St Martin's Press, 1992

Benet, Diana, *Secretary of Praise: The Poetic Vocation of George Herbert*, University of Missouri Press, 1984

Bennett, J. A. W., *Poetry of the Passion*, Clarendon Press, 1982

Bennett, Joan, *Five Metaphysical Poets*, Cambridge University Press, 1963

Bienz, John, 'Images and Ceremonial in *The Temple*: Herbert's Solution to a Reformation Controversy', *SEL* 26 (1986)

Bloch, Chana, *Spelling the Word: George Herbert and the Bible*, University of California Press, 1985

Bottrall, Margaret, *George Herbert*, John Murray, 1954

Clark, Ira, *Christ Revealed: The History of the Neotypological Lyric in the English Renaissance*, University Presses of Florida, 1982

Clements, Arthur L., *Poetry of Contemplation: John Donne, George Herbert, Henry Vaughan, and the Modern Period*, State University of New York Press, 1990

Cooley, Ronald W., '"Untill the Book Grow to a Compleat Pastorall": Re-Reading *The Country Parson*', *English Studies in Canada* 18 (1992)

Edgecombe, Rodney, *'Sweetnesse Readie Penn'd': Imagery, Syntax and Metrics in the Poetry of George Herbert*, Salzburg: Institut, 1980

Eggert, Paul and Margaret Sankey, *The Editorial Gaze: Meditating Texts in Literature and the Arts*, Garland Publishing, 1998

Eliot, T. S., *George Herbert*, Longmans, 1962

Ferry, Anne, 'Titles in George Herbert's "little Book"', *English Literary Renaissance* 23 (1993)

Festugiere, A. J., *George Herbert, poete, saint, anglican*, J. Vrin, 1971

Fish, Stanley, *The Living Temple: George Herbert and Catechising*, University of California Press, 1978

Flesch, William, *Generosity and the Limits of Authority: Shakespeare, Herbert, Milton*, Cornell University Press, 1992

Freeman, Rosemary, *English Emblem Books*, Chatto & Windus, 1948

Freer, Coburn, *Music for a King: George Herbert's Style and the Metrical Psalms*, Johns Hopkins University Press, 1972

Gardner, Helen, *Religion and Literature*, Oxford University Press, 1971

Gottlieb, Sidney, *The George Herbert Journal*, published at Sacred Heart University, Connecticut, 1978–

— (ed.), *Approaches to Teaching the Metaphysical Poets*, The Modern Language Association of America, 1990

Grant, Patrick, *The Transformation of Sin: Studies in Donne, Herbert, Vaughan and Traherne*, McGill–Queen's University Press/University of Massachusetts Press, 1974

Guernsey, Julia Carolyn, *The Pulse of Praise*, Associated University Presses, 1999

Guibbory, Achsah, *Ceremony and Community from Herbert to Milton: Literature, Religion, and Cultural Conflict in Seventeenth-century England*, Cambridge University Press, 1998

Halewood, William H., *The Poetry of Grace: Reformation Themes and Structures in English Seventeenth-century Poetry*, Yale University Press, 1970

Harman, Barbara Leah, *Costly Monuments: Representations of the Self in George Herbert's Poetry*, Harvard University Press, 1982

Harvey, Elizabeth D., and Katherine Eisaman Maus (eds.), *Soliciting Interpretation: Literary Theory and Seventeenth-*

century English Poetry, University of Chicago Press, 1990

Heissler, John Martin (ed.), 'Mr Herbert's Temple and Church Militant Explained and Improved By a Discourse Upon Each Poem Critical and Practical by George Ryley: A Critical Edition', Ph.D. dissertation, University of Illinois, 1960

Hodgkins, Christopher, *Authority, Church and Society in George Herbert: Return to the Middle Way*, University of Missouri Press, 1993

Johnson, Bruce A., 'Theological Inconsistency and Its Uses in George Herbert's Poetry', *George Herbert Journal* 15, ii (1992)

Johnson, Jeffrey S., 'Recreating the Word: Typology in Herbert's "The Altar"', *Christianity and Literature* 37, i (1987)

Jones, Nicholas R., 'Texts and Contexts: Two Languages in George Herbert's Poetry', *SP* 79 (1982)

Klause, John L., 'George Herbert, *Kenosis* and the Whole Truth', in Morton W. Bloomfield (ed.), *Allegory, Myth and Symbol*, Harvard English Studies 9, Harvard University Press, 1981

Knights, L. C., 'George Herbert' in *Explorations*, Chatto & Windus, 1946

Kyne, Mary Theresa, *Country Parsons, Country Poets: George Herbert and Gerard Manley Hopkins as Spiritual Autobiographers*, Eadmer Press, 1992

Leimberg, Inge, 'Annotating Baroque Poetry: George Herbert's "A Dialogue Anthem"', *George Herbert Journal* 15, i (1991)

Leishman, J. B., *The Metaphysical Poets*, Clarendon Press, 1934

Lewalski, Barbara Kiefer, *Protestant Poetics and the Seventeenth-century Religious Lyric*, Princeton University Press, 1979, especially chapter 9

Low, Anthony, *Love's Architecture: Devotional Modes in Seventeenth-century English Poetry*, New York University Press, 1978

Lull, Janis, *The Poem in Time: Reading George Herbert's Revisions of 'The Church'*, Associated University Presses, 1990

Lynch, Katherine, '*The Temple*: "These Parts Vied and Multiplied"', *SEL 29 (1989)*

McLeod, Randall, *Crisis in Editing Texts of the English Renaissance*, AMS Press, 1994

Mahood, M. M., 'Something Understood: The Nature of Herbert's Wit' in Malcolm Bradbury and David Palmer (eds.), *Metaphysical Poetry*, Stratford-upon-Avon Studies 11, Edward Arnold, 1970

Malcolmson, *Heart-Work: George Herbert and the Protestant Ethic*, Stanford University Press, 1999

Martin, Jessica, *Walton's Lives: Conformist Confirmations and the Rise of Biography*, Oxford University Press, 2001

Martz, Louis L., *The Poetry of Meditation*, Yale University Press, 1954; second edition, revised, 1962

Miller, Edmund, *Drudgerie Divine: The Rhetoric of God and Man in George Herbert*, Salzburg: Institut, 1979

Mulder, John R., *The Temple of the Mind: Education and Literary Taste in Seventeenth-century England*, Pegasus, 1969

Nuttall, A. D., *Overheard by God: Fiction and Prayer in Herbert, Milton, Dante and St John*, Methuen, 1980

Patrides, C. A. (ed.), *George Herbert: The Critical Heritage*, Routledge & Kegan Paul, 1983

Pearlman, E., 'George Herbert's God', *ELR 13 (1983)*

Piret, Michael, 'Herbert and Proverbs', *The Cambridge Quarterly* 17 (1988)

Post, Jonathan F. S., 'Reforming *The Temple*: Recent Criticism of George Herbert', *John Donne Journal* 3 (1984)

— *English Lyric Poetry: The Early Seventeenth Century*, Routledge, 1999

Powers-Beck, Jeffrey, *Writing the Flesh: The Herbert Family Dialogue*, Duquesne University Press, 1998

Ray, Robert H, *A George Herbert Companion*, Garland Publishing, 1995

Rickey, Mary Ellen, *Utmost Art: Complexity in the Verse of George Herbert*, University of Kentucky Press, 1966

Roberts, John R., *Essential Articles for the Study of George Herbert's Poetry*, Anchor Books, 1979

— *George Herbert: An Annotated Bibliography of Modern Criticism*, 1905–1984, revised edition, University of Missouri Press, 1988

Schoenfeldt, Michael C., '"Subject to Ev'ry Mounters Bended

Knee"' in Heather Dubrow and Richard Strier (eds.), *The Historical Renaissance: New Essays on Tudor and Stuart Literature and Culture*, University of Chicago Press, 1988

— *Prayer and Power: George Herbert and Renaissance Courtship*, University of Chicago Press, 1991

— *Bodies and Selves in Early Modern England: Physiology and Inwardness in Spenser, Shakespeare, Herbert, and Milton*, Cambridge University Press, 1999

Shaw, Robert B., *The Call of God: The Theme of Vocation in the Poetry of Donne and Herbert*, Cowley, 1981

Sherwood, Terry G., 'Tasting and Telling Sweetness in George Herbert's Poetry', *ELR 12 (1982)*

— *Herbert's Prayerful Art*, University of Toronto Press, 1989

Singleton, Marion White, *God's Courtier: Configuring a Different Grace in George Herbert's 'Temple'*, Cambridge University Press, 1987

Slights, Camille Wells, *The Casuistical Tradition in Shakespeare, Donne, Herbert and Milton*, Princeton University Press, 1981

Stanwood, P. G., *Izaak Walton*, Twayne Publishers, 1998

Stein, Arnold, *George Herbert's Lyrics*, Johns Hopkins University Press, 1968

Stewart, Stanley, 'Herbert and the "Harmonies" of Little Gidding', *Cithara* 24 (1984)

— *George Herbert*, Twayne, 1986

Strier, Richard, *Love Known: Theology and Experience in George Herbert's Poetry*, University of Chicago Press, 1983

— *Resistant Structures: Particularity, Radicalism, and Renaissance Texts*, University of California Press, 1995

Summers, Claude J., and Ted-Larry Pebworth (eds.), *'Too Rich to Clothe the Sunne': Essays on George Herbert*, University of Pittsburg Press, 1980

Summers, Joseph H., *George Herbert: His Religion and Art*, Chatto & Windus/Harvard University Press, 1954

Targoff, Ramie, *Common Prayer: The Language of Public Devotion in Early Modern England*, University of Chicago Press, 2001

Taylor, Mark, *The Soul in Paraphrase: George Herbert's Poetics*, Mouton, 1974

Sister Thekla, *George Herbert, Idea and Image: A Study of 'The Temple'*, The Greek Orthodox Monastery of the Assumption, Filgrave, Newport Pagnell, 1974

Thorpe, Douglas, '"Delight into Scripture": Resting in Herbert's *Temple*', *SEL 26 (1986)*

Todd, Richard, *The Opacity of Signs: Acts of Interpretation in George Herbert's 'The Temple'*, University of Missouri Press, 1986

Toliver, Harold, 'Herbert's Interim and Final Places', *SEL* 24 (1984)

— *George Herbert's Christian Narrative*, Pennsylvania State University Press, 1993

Tuve, Rosemond, *A Reading of George Herbert*, University of Chicago Press/Faber & Faber, 1952

van Wengen-Shute, Rosemary Margaret, *George Herbert and the Liturgy of the Church of England*, Oegstgeest: Drukkerij de Kempenaer, 1981

Veith, Gene Edward, Jr, *Reformation Spirituality: The Religion of George Herbert*, Bucknell/Associated University Presses, 1985

Vendler, Helen, *The Poetry of George Herbert*, Harvard University Press, 1975

Wall, John N., *Transformations of the Word: Spenser, Herbert, Vaughan*, University of Georgia Press, 1988

Watson, Robert N., *The Rest is Silence: Death as Annihilation in the English Renaissance*, University of California Press, 1994

Westerweel, Bart, *Patterns of Patterning: A Study of Four Poems by George Herbert*, *Costerus*, n.s. 41. Amsterdam: Rodopi, 1984

White, Helen C., *The Metaphysical Poets: A Study in Religious Experience*, Macmillan, 1936

Wolberg, Kristine, 'All Possible Art: *The Country Parson* and Courtesy', *John Donne Journal* 8 (1989)

Young, R.V., *Doctrine and Devotion in Seventeenth-century Poetry: Studies in Donne, Herbert, Crashaw, and Vaughan*. D.S. Brewer, 2000

Extracts from the poetry of John Donne are from:
John Donne: The Complete English Poems, ed. A. J. Smith, Harmondsworth: Penguin, 1970

References to Shakespeare are to:
The Riverside Shakespeare second edition, eds. G. B. Evans and J. J. M. Tobin, Boston: Houghton Mifflin, 1997

A NOTE ON THE TEXTS

This text of *The Temple* is a modernised spelling version of the first edition of 1633 (hereafter referred to as 1633). Notes indicate significant variants found in Bodleian MS Tanner 307 (MSB), thought to be a copy of the 'little book' that Herbert on his deathbed had conveyed to Nicholas Ferrar, and MS Jones B 62 in Dr Williams's Library, London (MSW), an early version of sixty-nine of the one hundred and sixty-four poems of *The Temple*, as well as six poems not included in 1633 or MSB. Izaak Walton's *The Life of Mr George Herbert* (1670) provides three additional poems. Further, the two poems to the Queen of Bohemia and the poem to the Lord Chancellor Bacon are included as canonical on the basis of recent scholarship as indicated in the notes.

Added to *The Temple* are Herbert's *A Priest to the Temple*, first published in 1652, itself a useful commentary on many of the poems, and Walton's *The Life of Mr George Herbert*, the 1675 edition, the last corrected by the author, as well as an appendix of selected Latin poems that display further aspects of Herbert's wit and versatility.

In the matter of punctuation of *The Temple* I have followed the general policy of this series in preserving the pointing of the original, except for the silent expansion of *d* to *ed* in preterites and past participles and in rare instances where a printer's error has led to the violation of logic or grammatical sense. Such corrections are noted. In the prose works I have not hesitated in the interest of clarity to adjust the punctuation in favour of modern expectations, especially in the case of Walton's use of the colon, where today a comma, semi-colon or full stop is required. Initial capitals that serve rhetorical as well as grammatical functions have been retained; all others have been reduced to lower case.

The first edition of *The Temple* is the work of Thomas Buck, a careful printer given to particularly heavy punctuation and a regularised layout of lines and stanzas, stanzas sometimes unnecessarily subdivided, here restored to their integrity. Supporters of MSB argue that the lighter, if occasionally eccentric, punctuation and the variable line placement of that manuscript (for which there now exists a critically valuable facsimile edition) better reflect the subtlety and complexity of Herbert's expression. Herbert made corrections in his own hand of poems in MSW. He died without seeing either MSB or 1633.

Scripture is cited from the Authorised Version of 1611, the King James Bible, except for passages from the Psalms, which are from the Book of Common Prayer, the text Herbert himself used.

A NOTE ON METRE

The reader will see and hear that in the midst of an astonishing variety of stanzaic forms, some unusual in the history of English verse, and inventive shifts in form within a single poem, Herbert's rhythm within a line is exact and regular. Apart from some notable exceptions in trochaic metre, like 'The Invitation', 'The Banquet', and 'Discipline', Herbert's poems are consistently iambic. This iambic rhythm requires that two truths of seventeenth-century pronunciation be kept in mind and upon lip: first, that some words spelled as of today, charming false friends so to speak, have their main stress placed on a syllable other than the one that the modern reader expects; and, second, that the participal ending '-ed' is often, but not always, sounded as a separate syllable. The nearly fifty instances of such sounded, metrically stressed syllables are made clear to the reader by the very regular rhythm of the line, with the need of a stressed syllable in order to fill out or complete a tetrameter or pentameter, and sometimes by both the rhythm and the need for rhyme, for example 'purchasèd' ('*Perirrhanterium*', line 172, and *The Church Militant*, line 128), and 'borrowèd' ('The Pearl', line 3).

Important instances of words with seventeenth century accentuation include 'cóntemptible' ('*Perirrhanterium*', line 156), 'pérspective' ('Sin (2)', line 10), 'cément' ('The Church-Floor', line 10), 'cóntribute' ('Avarice', line 5), 'commérce' ('Giddiness', line 22, and 'The Odour', line 29), 'triúmph' ('Church-Rents and Schisms', line 2), 'aspéct' ('The Glance', line 22), and 'persévér' ('Heaven', line 19).

In addition to the repeated 'purchasèd', among the stressed participal '-ed' instances, there are the two examples of 'cleansed' ('The Church-Floor', line 15, and 'Love' in MSW, line 12) and the many instances of 'blessed' ('The Altar', line 15, 'Sepulchre', line 1, 'Easter', line 17, 'Anagram', line 9, 'Prayer (2)', line 2, 'The British Church', line 28, 'Mary Magdalene', line 1, and 'L'Envoy', lines 1 and 2). Non-repeated and perhaps not immediately perceived accentuated final '-ed' examples occur as 'Usèd' and 'wishèd' ('The Sacrifice', line 10), 'Wreathèd', 'deservèd' and 'deservèd' ('A Wreath', lines 1 and 2), and 'grievèd' and 'grievèd' ('Ephesians 4:30', lines 1 and 4), but 'grieved' (no terminal stress, line 5), 'calcinèd' ('Easter', line 5), 'owèd' ('Faith', line 13), 'short-brièfed' ('Repentance', line 14), 'reversèd' ('Prayer' (1), line 6), 'pressèd' ('The Bunch of Grapes', line 28). Some instances may allow for debate, as one person's seventeenth-century shift in stress is another person's trochee, but Herbert's careful keeping of accent points to each need for added emphasis in metres that are the simple frames within which the poet's voice provides a rich and complicated variety of emphases in sense.

THE TEMPLE

SACRED POEMS
AND PRIVATE EJACULATIONS

The Printers to the Reader

The dedication of this work having been made by the author to the Divine Majesty only, how should we now presume to interest any mortal man in the patronage of it? Much less think we it meet to seek the recommendation of the Muses, for that which himself was confident to have been inspired by a diviner breath than flows from Helicon. The world therefore shall receive it in that naked simplicity with which he left it, without any addition either of support or ornament more than is included in itself. We leave it free and unforestalled to every man's judgement, and to the benefit that he shall find by perusal. Only for the clearing of some passages we have thought it not unfit to make the common Reader privy to some few particularities of condition and disposition of the Person.

Being nobly born, and as eminently endued with gifts of the mind, and having by industry and happy education perfected them to that great height of excellency, whereof his fellowship of Trinity College in Cambridge, and his Oratorship in the University, together with that knowledge which the King's Court had taken of him, could make relation far above ordinary. Quitting both his deserts and all the opportunities that he had for worldly preferment, he betook himself to the Sanctuary and Temple of God, choosing rather to serve at God's Altar, than to seek the honour of State employments. As for those inward enforcements to this course (for outward there was none) which many of these ensuing verses bear witness of, they detract not from the freedom but add to the honour of this resolution in him. As God had enabled him, so he accounted him meet not only to be called but to be compelled to this service: wherein his faithful discharge was such as may make him justly a companion to the primitive Saints, and a pattern or more for the age he lived in.

To testify his independency upon all others and to quicken his diligence in this kind, he used in his ordinary speech, when he made mention of the blessed name of our Lord and Saviour Jesus Christ, to add, *My Master*.

Next God, he loved that which God himself has magnified above all things, that is, his Word: so as he has been heard to make solemn protestation, that he would not part with one leaf thereof for the whole world, if it were offered him in exchange.

His obedience and conformity to the Church and the discipline thereof was singularly remarkable. Though he abounded in private devotions, yet went he every morning and evening with his family to the Church; and by his example, exhortations and encouragements drew the greater part of his parishioners to accompany him daily in the public celebration of Divine Service.

As for worldly matters, his love and esteem to them was so little, as no man can more ambitiously seek than he did earnestly endeavour the resignation of the Ecclesiastical dignity, which he was possessor of. But God permitted not the accomplishment of this desire, having ordained him his instrument for re-edifying of the Church belonging thereunto that had lain ruinated almost twenty years. The reparation whereof, having been uneffectually attempted by public collections, was in the end by his own and some few others' private free-will offerings successfully effected. With the remembrance whereof, as of an especial good work, when a friend went about to comfort him on his deathbed, he made answer, *It is a good work, if it be sprinkled with the blood of Christ*: otherwise than in this respect he could find nothing to glory or comfort himself with, neither in this nor in any other thing.

And these are but a few of many that might be said, which we have chosen to premise as a glance to some parts of the ensuing book, and for an example to the Reader. We conclude all with his own Motto, with which he used to conclude all things that might seem to tend any way to his own honour:

Less than the least of God's mercies.

The Dedication

Lord, my first fruits present themselves to thee;
Yet not mine neither: for from thee they came,
And must return. Accept of them and me,
And make us strive, who shall sing best thy name.
Turn their eyes hither, who shall make a gain:
Theirs, who shall hurt themselves or me, refrain.

THE CHURCH-PORCH

Perirrhanterium

1

Thou, whose sweet youth and early hopes enhance
Thy rate and price, and mark thee for a treasure;
Harken unto a Verser, who may chance
Rhyme thee to good, and make a bait of pleasure.
  A verse may find him, who a sermon flies,
  And turn delight into a sacrifice.

2

Beware of lust: it doth pollute and foul
Whom God in Baptism washed with his own blood.
It blots thy lesson written in thy soul;
The holy lines cannot be understood.
  How dare those eyes upon a Bible look,
  Much less towards God, whose lust is all their book?

3

Abstain wholly, or wed. Thy bounteous Lord
Allows thee choice of paths: take no byways;
But gladly welcome what he doth afford;
Not grudging, that thy lust hath bounds and stays.
  Continence hath his joy: weigh both; and so
  If rottenness have more, let Heaven go.

4

If God had laid all common, certainly
Man would have been th' incloser: but since now
God hath impaled us, on the contrary
Man breaks the fence, and every ground will plough.
O what were man, might he himself misplace!
Sure to be cross he would shift feet and face.

5

Drink not the third glass, which thou canst not tame,
When once it is within thee; but before
Mayst rule it, as thou list; and pour the shame,
Which it would pour on thee, upon the floor.
It is most just to throw that on the ground,
Which would throw me there, if I keep the round.

6

He that is drunken, may his mother kill
Big with his sister; he hath lost the reins,
Is outlawed by himself: all kind of ill
Did with his liquor slide into his veins.
The drunkard forfeits Man, and doth devest
All worldly right, save what he hath by beast.

7

Shall I, to please another's wine-sprung mind,
Lose all mine own? God hath giv'n me a measure
Short of his can, and body; must I find
A pain in that, wherein he finds a pleasure?
Stay at the third glass: if thou lose thy hold,
Then thou art modest, and the wine grows bold.

8

If reason move not gallants, quit the room,
(All in a shipwrack shift their several way)
Let not a common ruin thee entomb:
Be not a beast in courtesy; but stay,
Stay at the third cup, or forgo the place.
Wine above all things doth God's stamp deface.

9

Yet, if thou sin in wine or wantonness,
Boast not thereof; nor make thy shame thy glory.
Frailty gets pardon by submissiveness;
But he that boasts, shuts that out of his story.
He makes flat war with God, and doth defy
With his poor clod of earth the spacious sky.

10

Take not his name, who made thy mouth, in vain:
It gets thee nothing, and hath no excuse.
Lust and wine plead a pleasure, avarice gain:
But the cheap swearer through his open sluice
Lets his soul run for nought, as little fearing.
Were I an *Epicure*, I could bate swearing.

11

When thou dost tell another's jest, therein
Omit the oaths, which true wit cannot need:
Pick out of tales the mirth, but not the sin.
He pares his apple, that will cleanly feed.
Play not away the virtue of that name,
Which is thy best stake, when griefs make thee tame.

12

The cheapest sins most dearly punished are;
Because to shun them also is so cheap:
For we have wit to mark them, and to spare.
O crumble not away thy soul's fair heap.
If thou wilt die, the gates of hell are broad:
Pride and full sins have made the way a road.

13

Lie not; but let thy heart be true to God,
Thy mouth to it, thy actions to them both:
Cowards tell lies, and those that fear the rod;
The stormy working soul spits lies and froth.
Dare to be true. Nothing can need a lie:
A fault, which needs it most, grows two thereby.

14

Fly idleness, which yet thou canst not fly
By dressing, mistressing, and compliment.
If those take up thy day, the sun will cry
Against thee: for his light was only lent.
  God gave thy soul brave wings; put not those feathers
  Into a bed, to sleep out all ill weathers.

15

Art thou a magistrate? then be severe:
If studious; copy fair, what time hath blurred;
Redeem truth from his jaws: if soldier,
Chase brave employments with a naked sword
  Throughout the world. Fool not: for all may have,
  If they dare try, a glorious life, or grave.

16

O England! full of sin, but most of sloth;
Spit out thy phlegm, and fill thy breast with glory:
Thy gentry bleats, as if thy native cloth
Transfused a sheepishness into thy story:
  Not that they all are so; but that the most
  Are gone to grass, and in the pasture lost.

17

This loss springs chiefly from our education.
Some till their ground, but let weeds choke their son:
Some mark a partridge, never their child's fashion:
Some ship them over, and the thing is done.
  Study this art, make it thy great design;
  And if God's image move thee not, let thine.

18

Some great estates provide, but do not breed
A mast'ring mind; so both are lost thereby:
Or else they breed them tender, make them need
All that they leave: this is flat poverty.
  For he, that needs five thousand pound to live,
  Is full as poor as he, that needs but five.

19

The way to make thy son rich, is to fill
His mind with rest, before his trunk with riches:
For wealth without contentment, climbs a hill
To feel those tempests, which fly over ditches.
But if thy son can make ten pound his measure,
Then all thou addest may be called his treasure.

20

When thou dost purpose ought (within thy power),
Be sure to do it, though it be but small:
Constancy knits the bones, and makes us stour,
When wanton pleasures beckon us to thrall.
Who breaks his own bond, forfeiteth himself:
What nature made a ship, he makes a shelf.

21

Do all things like a man, not sneakingly:
Think the king sees thee still; for his King does.
Simp'ring is but a lay-hypocrisy:
Give it a corner, and the clue undoes.
Who fears to do ill, sets himself to task:
Who fears to do well, sure should wear a mask.

22

Look to thy mouth; diseases enter there.
Thou hast two sconces, if thy stomach call;
Carve, or discourse; do not a famine fear.
Who carves, is kind to two; who talks, to all.
Look on meat, think it dirt, then eat a bit;
And say withal, Earth to earth I commit.

23

Slight those who say amidst their sickly healths,
Thou liv'st by rule. What doth not so, but man?
Houses are built by rule, and common-wealths.
Entice the trusty sun, if that you can,
From his Ecliptic line: beckon the sky.
Who lives by rule then, keeps good company.

24

Who keeps no guard upon himself, is slack,
And rots to nothing at the next great thaw.
Man is a shop of rules, a well trussed pack,
Whose every parcel underwrites a law.
  Lose not thyself, nor give thy humours way:
  God gave them to thee under lock and key.

25

By all means use sometimes to be alone.
Salute thyself: see what thy soul doth wear.
Dare to look in thy chest; for 'tis thine own:
And tumble up and down what thou find'st there.
  Who cannot rest till he good fellows find,
  He breaks up house, turns out of doors his mind.

26

Be thrifty, but not covetous: therefore give
Thy need, thine honour, and thy friend his due.
Never was scraper brave man. Get to live;
Then live, and use it: else, it is not true
  That thou hast gotten. Surely use alone
  Makes money not a contemptible stone.

27

Never exceed thy income. Youth may make
Ev'n with the year: but age, if it will hit,
Shoots a bow short, and lessens still his stake,
As the day lessens, and his life with it.
  Thy children, kindred, friends upon thee call;
  Before thy journey fairly part with all.

28

Yet in thy thriving still misdoubt some evil;
Lest gaining gain on thee, and make thee dim
To all things else. Wealth is the conjurer's devil;
Whom when he thinks he hath, the devil hath him.
  Gold thou mayst safely touch; but if it stick
  Unto thy hands, it woundeth to the quick.

29

What skills it, if a bag of stones or gold
About thy neck do drown thee? raise thy head;
Take stars for money; stars not to be told
By any art, yet to be purchased.
None is so wasteful as the scraping dame.
She loseth three for one; her soul, rest, fame.

30

By no means run in debt: take thine own measure.
Who cannot live on twenty pound a year,
Cannot on forty: he's a man of pleasure,
A kind of thing that's for itself too dear.
The curious unthrift makes his cloth too wide,
And spares himself, but would his tailor chide.

31

Spend not on hopes. They that by pleading clothes
Do fortunes seek, when worth and service fail,
Would have their tale believed for their oaths,
And are like empty vessels under sail.
Old courtiers know this; therefore set out so,
As all the day thou mayst hold out to go.

32

In clothes, cheap handsomeness doth bear the bell.
Wisdom's a trimmer thing, than shop e'er gave.
Say not then, This with that lace will do well;
But, This with my discretion will be brave.
Much curiousness is a perpetual wooing
Nothing with labour; folly long a-doing.

33

Play not for gain, but sport. Who plays for more,
Than he can lose with pleasure, stakes his heart;
Perhaps his wife's too, and whom she hath bore;
Servants and churches also play their part.
Only a herald, who that way doth pass,
Finds his cracked name at length in the church glass.

34

If yet thou love game at so dear a rate,
Learn this, that hath old gamesters dearly cost:
Dost lose? rise up: dost win? rise in that state.
Who strive to sit out losing hands, are lost.
Game is a civil gunpowder, in peace
Blowing up houses with their whole increase.

35

In conversation boldness now bears sway.
But know, that nothing can so foolish be,
As empty boldness: therefore first assay
To stuff thy mind with solid bravery;
Then march on gallant: get substantial worth.
Boldness gilds finely, and will set it forth.

36

Be sweet to all. Is thy complexion sour?
Then keep such company; make them thy allay:
Get a sharp wife, a servant that will lour.
A stumbler stumbles least in rugged way.
Command thyself in chief. He life's war knows,
Whom all his passions follow, as he goes.

37

Catch not at quarrels. He that dares not speak
Plainly and home, is coward of the two.
Think not thy fame at ev'ry twitch will break:
By great deeds show, that thou canst little do;
And do them not: that shall thy wisdom be;
And change thy temperance into bravery.

38

If that thy fame with ev'ry toy be posed,
'Tis a thin web, which poisonous fancies make:
But the great soldier's honour was composed
Of thicker stuff, which would endure a shake.
Wisdom picks friends; civility plays the rest.
A toy shunned cleanly passeth with the best.

39

Laugh not too much: the witty man laughs least:
For wit is news only to ignorance.
Less at thine own things laugh; lest in the jest
Thy person share, and the conceit advance.
  Make not thy sport, abuses: for the fly
  That feeds on dung, is coloured thereby.

40

Pick out of mirth, like stones out of thy ground,
Profaneness, filthiness, abusiveness.
These are the scum, with which coarse wits abound:
The fine may spare these well, yet not go less.
  All things are big with jest: nothing that's plain,
  But may be witty, if thou hast the vein.

41

Wit's an unruly engine, wildly striking
Sometimes a friend, sometimes the engineer.
Hast thou the knack? pamper it not with liking:
But, if thou want it, buy it not too dear.
  Many, affecting wit beyond their power,
  Have got to be a dear fool for an hour.

42

A sad wise valour is the brave complexion,
That leads the van, and swallows up the cities.
The giggler is a milk-maid, whom infection,
Or a fir'd beacon frighteth from his ditties.
  Then he's the sport: the mirth then in him rests,
  And the sad man is cock of all his jests.

43

Towards great persons use respective boldness:
That temper gives them theirs, and yet doth take
Nothing from thine: in service, care or coldness
Doth rateably thy fortunes mar or make.
  Feed no man in his sins: for adulation
  Doth make thee parcel-devil in damnation.

44

Envy not greatness: for thou mak'st thereby
Thyself the worse, and so the distance greater.
Be not thine own worm: yet such jealousy,
As hurts not others, but may make thee better,
  Is a good spur. Correct thy passions' spite;
  Then may the beasts draw thee to happy light.

45

When baseness is exalted, do not bate
The place its honour, for the person's sake.
The shrine is that which thou dost venerate;
And not the beast, that bears it on his back.
  I care not though the cloth of state should be
  Not of rich arras, but mean tapestry.

46

Thy friend put in thy bosom: wear his eyes
Still in thy heart, that he may see what's there.
If cause require, thou art his sacrifice;
Thy drops of blood must pay down all his fear:
  But love is lost, the way of friendship's gone,
  Though *David* had his *Jonathan*, *Christ* his *John*.

47

Yet be not surety, if thou be a father.
Love is a personal debt. I cannot give
My children's right, nor ought he take it: rather
Both friends should die, than hinder them to live.
  Fathers first enter bonds to nature's ends;
  And are her sureties, ere they are a friend's.

48

If thou be single, all thy goods and ground
Submit to love; but yet not more than all.
Give one estate, as one life. None is bound
To work for two, who brought himself to thrall.
  God made me one man; love makes me no more,
  Till labour come, and make my weakness score.

49

In thy discourse, if thou desire to please:
All such is courteous, useful, new, or witty.
Usefulness comes by labour, wit by ease;
Courtesy grows in court; news in the city.
Get a good stock of these, then draw the card
That suits him best, of whom thy speech is heard.

50

Entice all neatly to what they know best;
For so thou dost thyself and him a pleasure:
(But a proud ignorance will lose his rest,
Rather than show his cards) steal from his treasure
What to ask further. Doubts well raised do lock
The speaker to thee, and preserve thy stock.

51

If thou be Master-gunner, spend not all
That thou canst speak, at once; but husband it,
And give men turns of speech: do not forestall
By lavishness thine own, and others' wit,
As if thou mad'st thy will. A civil guest
Will no more talk all, than eat all the feast.

52

Be calm in arguing: for fierceness makes
Error a fault, and truth discourtesy.
Why should I feel another man's mistakes
More than his sicknesses or poverty?
In love I should: but anger is not love,
Nor wisdom neither: therefore gently move.

53

Calmness is great advantage: he that lets
Another chafe, may warm him at his fire:
Mark all his wand'rings, and enjoy his frets;
As cunning fencers suffer heat to tire.
Truth dwells not in the clouds: the bow that's there,
Doth often aim at, never hit the sphere.

54

Mark what another says: for many are
Full of themselves, and answer their own notion.
Take all into thee; then with equal care
  Balance each dram of reason, like a potion.
    If truth be with thy friend, be with them both:
    Share in the conquest, and confess a troth.

55

Be useful where thou livest, that they may
Both want, and wish thy pleasing presence still.
Kindness, good parts, great places are the way
To compass this. Find out men's wants and will,
    And meet them there. All worldly joys go less
    To the one joy of doing kindnesses.

56

Pitch thy behaviour low, thy projects high;
So shalt thou humble and magnanimous be:
Sink not in spirit: who aimeth at the sky,
Shoots higher much than he that means a tree.
    A grain of glory mixed with humbleness
    Cures both a fever and lethargicness.

57

Let thy mind still be bent, still plotting where,
And when, and how the business may be done.
Slackness breeds worms; but the sure traveller,
Though he alight sometimes, still goeth on.
    Active and stirring spirits live alone.
    Write on the others, Here lies such a one.

58

Slight not the smallest loss, whether it be
In love or honour: take account of all;
Shine like the sun in every corner: see
Whether thy stock of credit swell or fall.
    Who say, I care not, those I give for lost;
    And to instruct them, 'twill not quit the cost.

59

Scorn no man's love, though of a mean degree;
(Love is a present for a mighty king).
Much less make anyone thy enemy.
As guns destroy, so may a little sling.
  The cunning workman never doth refuse
  The meanest tool, that he may chance to use.

60

All foreign wisdom doth amount to this,
To take all that is given; whether wealth,
Or love, or language; nothing comes amiss:
A good digestion turneth all to health:
  And then as far as fair behaviour may,
  Strike off all scores; none are so clear as they.

61

Keep all thy native good, and naturalise
All foreign of that name; but scorn their ill:
Embrace their activeness, not vanities.
Who follows all things, forfeiteth his will.
  If thou observest strangers in each fit,
  In time they'll run thee out of all thy wit.

62

Affect in things about thee cleanliness,
That all may gladly board thee, as a flower.
Slovens take up their stock of noisomeness
Beforehand, and anticipate their last hour.
  Let thy mind's sweetness have his operation
  Upon thy body, clothes, and habitation.

63

In Alms regard thy means, and others' merit.
Think heav'n a better bargain, than to give
Only thy single market-money for it.
Join hands with God to make a man to live.
  Give to all something; to a good poor man,
  Till thou change names, and be where he began.

64

Man is God's image; but a poor man is
Christ's stamp to boot: both images regard.
God reckons for him, counts the favour his:
Write, So much giv'n to God; thou shalt be heard.
  Let thy alms go before, and keep heav'n's gate
  Open for thee; or both may come too late.

65

Restore to God his due in tithe and time:
A tithe purloined cankers the whole estate.
Sundays observe: think when the bells do chime,
'Tis angels' music; therefore come not late.
  God then deals blessings: If a king did so,
  Who would not haste, nay give, to see the show?

66

Twice on the day his due is understood;
For all the week thy food so oft he gave thee.
Thy cheer is mended; bate not of the food,
Because 'tis better, and perhaps may save thee.
  Thwart not th' Almighty God: O be not cross.
  Fast when thou wilt; but then 'tis gain, not loss.

67

Though private prayer be a brave design,
Yet public hath more promises, more love:
And love's a weight to hearts, to eyes a sign.
We all are but cold suitors; let us move
  Where it is warmest. Leave thy six and seven;
  Pray with the most: for where most pray, is heaven.

68

When once thy foot enters the church, be bare.
God is more there, than thou: for thou art there
Only by his permission. Then beware,
And make thyself all reverence and fear.
  Kneeling ne'er spoil'd silk stocking: quit thy state.
  All equal are within the church's gate.

69

Resort to sermons, but to prayers most:
Praying's the end of preaching. O be dressed;
Stay not for th' other pin: why thou hast lost
A joy for it worth worlds. Thus hell doth jest
Away thy blessings, and extremely flout thee,
Thy clothes being fast, but thy soul loose about thee.

70

In time of service seal up both thine eyes,
And send them to thine heart; that spying sin,
They may weep out the stains by them did rise:
Those doors being shut, all by the ear comes in.
Who marks in church-time others' symmetry,
Makes all their beauty his deformity.

71

Let vain or busy thoughts have there no part:
Bring not thy plough, thy plots, thy pleasures thither.
Christ purged his temple; so must thou thy heart.
All worldly thoughts are but thieves met together
To cozen thee. Look to thy actions well:
For churches are either our heav'n or hell.

72

Judge not the preacher; for he is thy Judge:
If thou mislike him, thou conceiv'st him not.
God calleth preaching folly. Do not grudge
To pick out treasures from an earthen pot.
The worst speak something good: if all want sense,
God takes a text, and preacheth patience.

73

He that gets patience, and the blessing which
Preachers conclude with, hath not lost his pains.
He that by being at church escapes the ditch,
Which he might fall in by companions, gains.
He that loves God's abode, and to combine
With saints on earth, shall one day with them shine.

74

Jest not at preacher's language, or expression:
How know'st thou, but thy sins made him miscarry?
Then turn thy faults and his into confession:
God sent him, whatso'er he be: O tarry,
  And love him for his Master: his condition,
  Though it be ill, makes him no ill Physician.

75

None shall in hell such bitter pangs endure,
As those, who mock at God's way of salvation.
Whom oil and balsams kill, what salve can cure?
They drink with greediness a full damnation.
  The Jews refused thunder; and we, folly.
  Though God do hedge us in, yet who is holy?

76

Sum up at night, what thou hast done by day;
And in the morning, what thou hast to do.
Dress and undress thy soul: mark the decay
And growth of it: if with thy watch, that too
  Be down, then wind up both; since we shall be
  Most surely judged, make thy accounts agree.

77

In brief, acquit thee bravely; play the man.
Look not on pleasures as they come, but go.
Defer not the least virtue: life's poor span
Make not an ell, by trifling in thy woe.
  If thou do ill; the joy fades, not the pains:
  If well; the pain doth fade, the joy remains.

Superliminare

Thou, whom the former precepts have
Sprinkled and taught, how to behave
Thyself in church; approach, and taste
The church's mystical repast.

Avoid profaneness; come not here:
Nothing but holy, pure, and clear,
Or that which groaneth to be so,
May at his peril further go.

THE CHURCH

The Altar

A broken ALTAR, Lord, thy servant rears,
Made of a heart, and cemented with tears:
Whose parts are as thy hand did frame;
No workman's tool hath touched the same.
A HEART alone
Is such a stone,
As nothing but
Thy pow'r doth cut.
Wherefore each part
Of my hard heart
Meets in this frame,
To praise thy name:
That if I chance to hold my peace,
These stones to praise thee may not cease.
O let thy blessed SACRIFICE be mine,
And sanctify this ALTAR to be thine.

The Sacrifice

O, *all ye*, who pass by, whose eyes and mind
To worldly things are sharp, but to me blind;
To me, who took eyes that I might you find:
Was ever grief like mine?

The Princes of my people make a head
Against their Maker: they do wish me dead,
Who cannot wish, except I give them bread:
Was ever grief like mine?

Without me each one, who doth now me brave,
Had to this day been an Egyptian slave.
They use that power against me, which I gave:
Was ever grief like mine?

Mine own Apostle, who the bag did bear,
Though he had all I had, did not forbear
To sell me also, and to put me there:
Was ever grief like mine?

For thirty pence he did my death devise,
Who at three hundred did the ointment prize,
Not half so sweet as my sweet sacrifice:
Was ever grief like mine?

Therefore my soul melts, and my heart's dear treasure
Drops blood (the only beads) my words to measure:
O let this cup pass, if it be thy pleasure:
Was ever grief like mine?

These drops being tempered with a sinner's tears,
A Balsam are for both the Hemispheres:
Curing all wounds, but mine; all, but my fears:
Was ever grief like mine?

Yet my Disciples sleep: I cannot gain
One hour of watching; but their drowsy brain
Comforts not me, and doth my doctrine stain:
Was ever grief like mine?

Arise, arise, they come. Look how they run.
Alas! what haste they make to be undone!
How with their lanterns do they seek the sun!
Was ever grief like mine?

With clubs and staves they seek me, as a thief,
Who am the way of truth, the true relief;
Most true to those, who are my greatest grief:
Was ever grief like mine?

Judas, dost thou betray me with a kiss?
Canst thou find hell about my lips? and miss

Of life, just at the gates of life and bliss?
Was ever grief like mine?

See, they lay hold on me, not with the hands
Of faith, but fury: yet at their commands
I suffer binding, who have loosed their bands:
Was ever grief like mine?

All my Disciples fly; fear puts a bar
Betwixt my friends and me. They leave the star,
That brought the wise men of the East from far.
Was ever grief like mine?

Then from one ruler to another bound
They lead me; urging, that it was not sound
What I taught: Comments would the text confound.
Was ever grief like mine?

The Priest and rulers all false witness seek
'Gainst him, who seeks not life, but is the meek
And ready Paschal Lamb of this great week:
Was ever grief like mine?

Then they accuse me of great blasphemy,
That I did thrust into the Deity,
Who never thought that any robbery:
Was ever grief like mine?

Some said, that I the Temple to the floor
In three days razed, and raised as before.
Why, he that built the world can do much more:
Was ever grief like mine?

Then they condemn me all with that same breath,
Which I do give them daily, unto death.
Thus *Adam* my first breathing rendereth:
Was ever grief like mine?

They bind, and lead me unto *Herod*: he
Sends me to *Pilate*. This makes them agree;
But yet their friendship is my enmity:
Was ever grief like mine?

Herod and all his bands do set me light,
Who teach all hands to war, fingers to fight,
And only am the Lord of hosts and might:
Was ever grief like mine?

Herod in judgement sits, while I do stand;
Examines me with a censorious hand:
I him obey, who all things else command:
Was ever grief like mine?

The *Jews* accuse me with despitefulness;
And vying malice with my gentleness,
Pick quarrels with their only happiness:
Was ever grief like mine?

I answer nothing, but with patience prove
If stony hearts will melt with gentle love.
But who does hawk at eagles with a dove?
Was ever grief like mine?

My silence rather doth augment their cry;
My dove doth back into my bosom fly,
Because the raging waters still are high:
Was ever grief like mine?

Hark how they cry aloud still, *Crucify*:
It is not fit he live a day, they cry,
Who cannot live less than eternally:
Was ever grief like mine?

Pilate a stranger holdeth off; but they,
Mine own dear people, cry, *Away, away*,
With noises confused frighting the day:
Was ever grief like mine?

Yet still they shout, and cry, and stop their ears,
Putting my life among their sins and fears,
And therefore wish *my blood on them and theirs*:
Was ever grief like mine?

See how spite cankers things. These words aright
Used, and wished, are the whole world's light:
But honey is their gall, brightness their night:
Was ever grief like minc?

They choose a murderer, and all agree
In him to do themselves a courtesy:
For it was their own cause who killed me:
Was ever grief like mine?

And a seditious murderer he was:
But I the Prince of peace; peace that doth pass
All understanding, more than heav'n doth glass:
Was ever grief like mine?

Why, Caesar is their only King, not I:
He clave the stony rock, when they were dry;
But surely not their hearts, as I well try:
Was ever grief like mine?

Ah! how they scourge me! yet my tenderness
Doubles each lash: and yet their bitterness
Winds up my grief to a mysteriousness:
Was ever grief like mine?

They buffet me, and box me as they list,
Who grasp the earth and heaven with my fist,
And never yet, whom I would punish, missed:
Was ever grief like mine?

Behold, they spit on me in scornful wise,
Who by my spittle gave the blind man eyes,
Leaving his blindness to mine enemies:
Was ever grief like mine?

My face they cover, though it be divine.
As *Moses'* face was veiled, so is mine,
Lest on their double-dark souls either shine:
Was ever grief like mine?

Servants and abjects flout me; they are witty:
Now prophesy who strikes thee, is their ditty.
So they in me deny themselves all pity:
Was ever grief like mine?

And now I am delivered unto death,
Which each one calls for so with utmost breath,
That he before me well nigh suffereth:
Was ever grief like mine?

Weep not, dear friends, since I for both have wept
When all my tears were blood, the while you slept:
Your tears for your own fortunes should be kept:
Was ever grief like mine?

The soldiers lead me to the common hall;
There they deride me, they abuse me all:
Yet for twelve heav'nly legions I could call:
Was ever grief like mine?

Then with a scarlet robe they me array;
Which shows my blood to be the only way,
And cordial left to repair man's decay:
Was ever grief like mine?

Then on my head a crown of thorns I wear:
For these are all the grapes *Sion* doth bear,
Though I my vine planted and wat'red there:
Was ever grief like mine?

So sits the earth's great curse in *Adam's* fall
Upon my head: so I remove it all
From th' earth unto my brows, and bear the thrall;
Was ever grief like mine?

Then with the reed they gave to me before,
They strike my head, the rock from whence all store
Of heav'nly blessings issue evermore:
Was ever grief like mine?

They bow their knees to me, and cry, *Hail king*:
Whatever scoffs or scornfulness can bring,
I am the floor, the sink, where they it fling:
Was ever grief like mine?

Yet since man's sceptres are as frail as reeds,
And thorny all their crowns, bloody their weeds;
I, who am Truth, turn into truth their deeds:
Was ever grief like mine?

The soldiers also spit upon that face,
Which Angels did desire to have the grace
And Prophets once to see, but found no place:
Was ever grief like mine?

Thus trimmed forth they bring me to the rout,
Who *Crucify him*, cry with one strong shout.
God holds his peace at man, and man cries out:
Was ever grief like mine?

They lead me in once more, and putting then
Mine own clothes on, they lead me out again.
Whom devils fly, thus is he tossed of men:
Was ever grief like mine?

And now weary of sport, glad to engross
All spite in one, counting my life their loss,
They carry me to my most bitter cross:
Was ever grief like mine?

My cross I bear myself, until I faint:
Then Simon bears it for me by constraint,
The decreed burden of each mortal Saint:
Was ever grief like mine?

O all ye who pass by, behold and see;
Man stole the fruit, but I must climb the tree;
The tree of life to all, but only me:
Was ever grief like mine?

Lo, here I hang, charged with a world of sin,
The greater world o' th' two; for that came in
By words, but this by sorrow I must win:
Was ever grief like mine?

Such sorrow, as if sinful man could feel,
Or feel his part, he would not cease to kneel
Till all were melted, though he were all steel:
Was ever grief like mine?

But, *O my God, my God!* why leav'st thou me,
The son, in whom thou dost delight to be?
My God, my God –
Never was grief like mine.

Shame tears my soul, my body many a wound;
Sharp nails pierce this, but sharper that confound;
Reproaches, which are free, while I am bound.
Was ever grief like mine?

Now heal thyself, Physician; now come down.
Alas! I did so, when I left my crown
And father's smile for you, to feel his frown:
Was ever grief like mine?

In healing not myself, there doth consist
All that salvation, which ye now resist;
Your safety in my sickness doth subsist:
Was ever grief like mine?

Betwixt two thieves I spend my utmost breath,
As he that for some robbery suffereth.
Alas! what have I stolen from you? death:
Was ever grief like mine?

A king my title is, prefixed on high;
Yet by my subjects am condemned to die
A servile death in servile company:
Was ever grief like mine?

They gave me vinegar mingled with gall,
But more with malice: yet, when they did call,
With Manna, Angel's food, I fed them all:
Was ever grief like mine?

They part my garments, and by lot dispose
My coat, the type of love, which once cured those
Who sought for help, never malicious foes:
Was ever grief like mine?

Nay, after death their spite shall further go;
For they will pierce my side, I full well know;
That as sin came, so Sacraments might flow:
Was ever grief like mine?

But now I die; now all is finished.
My woe, man's weal: and now I bow my head.
Only let others say, when I am dead,
Never was grief like mine.

The Thanksgiving

O King of grief! (a title strange, yet true,
To thee of all kings only due)
O King of wounds! how shall I grieve for thee,
Who in all grief preventest me?
Shall I weep blood? why, thou hast wept such store
That all thy body was one door.
Shall I be scourged, flouted, boxed, sold?
'Tis but to tell the tale is told.
My God, my God, why dost thou part from me?
Was such a grief as cannot be.
Shall I then sing, skipping thy doleful story,
And side with thy triumphant glory?
Shall thy strokes be my stroking? thorns, my flower?
Thy rod, my posy? cross, my bower?
But how then shall I imitate thee, and
Copy thy fair, though bloody hand?

Surely I will revenge me on thy love,
And try who shall victorious prove.
If thou dost give me wealth, I will restore
All back unto thee by the poor.
If thou dost give me honour, men shall see,
The honour doth belong to thee.
I will not marry; or, if she be mine,
She and her children shall be thine.
My bosom friend, if he blaspheme thy name,
I will tear thence his love and fame.
One half of me being gone, the rest I give
Unto some Chapel, die or live.
As for thy passion – But of that anon,
When with the other I have done.
For thy predestination I'll contrive,
That three years hence, if I survive,
I'll build a spittle, or mend common ways,
But mend mine own without delays.
Then I will use the works of thy creation,
As if I used them but for fashion.
The world and I will quarrel; and the year
Shall not perceive, that I am here.
My music shall find thee, and ev'ry string
Shall have his attribute to sing;
That all together may accord in thee,
And prove one God, one harmony.
If thou shalt give me wit, it shall appear,
If thou hast giv'n it me, 'tis here.
Nay, I will read thy book, and never move
Till I have found therein thy love;
Thy art of love, which I'll turn back on thee,
O my dear Saviour, Victory!
Then for thy passion – I will do for that –
Alas, my God, I know not what.

The Reprisal

I have considered it, and find
There is no dealing with thy mighty passion:
For though I die for thee, I am behind;
My sins deserve the condemnation.

O make me innocent, that I
May give a disentangled state and free:
And yet thy wounds still my attempts defy,
For by thy death I die for thee.

Ah! was it not enough that thou
By thy eternal glory didst outgo me?
Couldst thou not grief's sad conquests me allow,
But in all vict'ries overthrow me?

Yet by confession will I come
Into the conquest. Though I can do nought
Against thee, in these I will overcome
The man, who once against thee fought.

The Agony

Philosophers have measured mountains,
Fathomed the depths of seas, of states, and kings,
Walked with a staff to heav'n, and traced fountains:
But there are two vast, spacious things,
The which to measure it doth more behove:
Yet few there are that sound them; Sin and Love.

Who would know Sin, let him repair
Unto Mount Olivet; there shall he see
A man so wrung with pains, that all his hair,
His skin, his garments bloody be.
Sin is that press and vice, which forceth pain
To hunt his cruel food through ev'ry vein.

Who knows not Love, let him assay
And taste that juice, which on the cross a pike
Did set again abroach; then let him say
If ever he did taste the like.
Love is that liquor sweet and most divine,
Which my God feels as blood; but I, as wine.

The Sinner

Lord, how I am all ague, when I seek
What I have treasured in my memory!
Since, if my soul make even with the week,
Each seventh note by right is due to thee.
I find there quarries of piled vanities,
But shreds of holiness, that dare not venture
To show their face, since cross to thy decrees:
There the circumference earth is, heav'n the centre.
In so much dregs the quintessence is small:
The spirit and good extract of my heart
Comes to about the many hundredth part.
Yet Lord restore thine image, hear my call:
And though my hard heart scarce to thee can groan,
Remember that thou once didst write in stone.

Good Friday

O my chief good,
How shall I measure out thy blood?
How shall I count what thee befell,
And each grief tell?

Shall I thy woes
Number according to thy foes?
Or, since one star showed thy first breath,
Shall all thy death?

Or shall each leaf,
Which falls in Autumn, score a grief?
Or cannot leaves, but fruit, be sign
Of the true vine?

Then let each hour
Of my whole life one grief devour;
That thy distress through all may run,
And be my sun.

Or rather let
My several sins their sorrows get;
That as each beast his cure doth know,
Each sin may so.

Since blood is fittest, Lord, to write
Thy sorrows in, and bloody fight;
My heart hath store, write there, wherein
One box doth lie both ink and sin:

That when sin spies so many foes,
Thy whips, thy nails, thy wounds, thy woes,
All come to lodge there, sin may say,
No room for me, and fly away.

Sin being gone, O fill the place,
And keep possession with thy grace;
Lest sin take courage and return,
And all the writings blot or burn.

Redemption

Having been tenant long to a rich Lord,
Not thriving, I resolved to be bold,
And make a suit unto him, to afford
A new small-rented lease, and cancel th' old.
In heaven at his manor I him sought:
They told me there, that he was lately gone

About some land, which he had dearly bought
Long since on earth, to take possession.
I straight returned, and knowing his great birth,
Sought him accordingly in great resorts;
In cities, theatres, gardens, parks, and courts:
At length I heard a ragged noise and mirth
Of thieves and murderers: there I him espied,
Who straight, *Your suit is granted*, said, and died.

Sepulchre

O blessed body! Whither art thou thrown?
No lodging for thee, but a cold hard stone?
So many hearts on earth, and yet not one
Receive thee?
Sure there is room within our hearts good store;
For they can lodge transgressions by the score:
Thousands of toys dwell there, yet out of door
They leave thee.

But that which shows them large, shows them unfit.
Whatever sin did this pure rock commit,
Which holds thee now? Who hath indicted it
Of murder?
Where our hard hearts have took up stones to brain thee,
And missing this, most falsely did arraign thee;
Only these stones in quiet entertain thee,
And order.

And as of old, the law by heav'nly art
Was writ in stone; so thou, which also art
The letter of the word, find'st no fit heart
To hold thee.
Yet do we still persist as we began,
And so should perish, but that nothing can,
Though it be cold, hard, foul, from loving man
Withhold thee.

Easter

Rise heart; thy Lord is risen. Sing his praise
Without delays,
Who takes thee by the hand, that thou likewise
With him mayst rise:
That, as his death calcined thee to dust,
His life may make thee gold, and much more just.

Awake, my lute, and struggle for thy part
With all thy art.
The cross taught all wood to resound his name,
Who bore the same.
His stretched sinews taught all strings, what key
Is best to celebrate this most high day.

Consort both heart and lute, and twist a song
Pleasant and long:
Or since all music is but three parts vied
And multiplied;
O let thy blessed Spirit bear a part,
And make up our defects with his sweet art.

I got me flowers to straw thy way;
I got me boughs off many a tree:
But thou wast up by break of day,
And brought'st thy sweets along with thee.

The Sun arising in the East,
Though he give light, and th' East perfume;
If they should offer to contest
With thy arising, they presume.

Can there be any day but this,
Though many suns to shine endeavour?
We count three hundred, but we miss:
There is but one, and that one ever.

Easter-Wings

Lord, who createdst man in wealth and store,
Though foolishly he lost the same,
Decaying more and more,
Till he became
Most poor:
With thee
O let me rise
As larks, harmoniously,
And sing this day thy victories:
Then shall the fall further the flight in me.

My tender age in sorrow did begin:
And still with sicknesses and shame
Thou didst so punish sin,
That I became
Most thin.
With thee
Let me combine,
And feel this day thy victory:
For, if I imp my wing on thine,
Affliction shall advance the flight in me.

Holy Baptism (1)

As he that sees a dark and shady grove,
Stays not, but looks beyond it on the sky;
So when I view my sins, mine eyes remove
More backward still, and to that water fly,
Which is above the heav'ns, whose spring and rent
Is in my dear Redeemer's pierced side.
O blessed streams! either ye do prevent
And stop our sins from growing thick and wide,
Or else give tears to drown them, as they grow.
In you Redemption measures all my time,
And spreads the plaster equal to the crime:
You taught the Book of Life my name, that so
Whatever future sins should me miscall,
Your first acquaintance might discredit all.

Holy Baptism (2)

Since, Lord, to thee
A narrow way and little gate
Is all the passage, on my infancy
Thou didst lay hold, and antedate
My faith in me.

O let me still
Write thee great God, and me a child:
Let me be soft and supple to thy will,
Small to myself, to others mild,
Behither ill.

Although by stealth
My flesh get on; yet let her sister
My soul bid nothing, but preserve her wealth:
The growth of flesh is but a blister;
Childhood is health.

Nature

Full of rebellion, I would die,
Or fight, or travel, or deny
That thou hast ought to do with me.
O tame my heart;
It is thy highest art
To captivate strong holds to thee.

If thou shalt let this venom lurk,
And in suggestions fume and work,
My soul will turn to bubbles straight,
And thence by kind
Vanish into a wind,
Making thy workmanship deceit.

O smooth my rugged heart, and there
Engrave thy rev'rend law and fear;
Or make a new one, since the old
Is sapless grown,
And a much fitter stone
To hide my dust, than thee to hold.

Sin (1)

Lord, with what care hast thou begirt us round!
Parents first season us: then schoolmasters
Deliver us to laws; they send us bound
To rules of reason, holy messengers,
Pulpits and Sundays, sorrow dogging sin,
Afflictions sorted, anguish of all sizes,
Fine nets and stratagems to catch us in,
Bibles laid open, millions of surprises,
Blessings beforehand, ties of gratefulness,
The sound of glory ringing in our ears:
Without, our shame; within, our consciences;
Angels and grace, eternal hopes and fears.
Yet all these fences and their whole array
One cunning bosom-sin blows quite away.

Affliction (I)

When first thou didst entice to thee my heart,
I thought the service brave:
So many joys I writ down for my part,
Besides what I might have
Out of my stock of natural delights,
Augmented with thy gracious benefits.

I looked on thy furniture so fine,
And made it fine to me:
Thy glorious household-stuff did me entwine,
And 'tice me unto thee.
Such stars I counted mine: both heav'n and earth
Paid me my wages in a world of mirth.

What pleasures could I want, whose King I served?
Where joys my fellows were.
Thus argued into hopes, my thoughts reserved
No place for grief or fear.
Therefore my sudden soul caught at the place,
And made her youth and fierceness seek thy face,

At first thou gav'st me milk and sweetnesses;
I had my wish and way:
My days were strawed with flow'rs and happiness;
There was no month but May.
But with my years sorrow did twist and grow,
And made a party unawares for woe.

My flesh began unto my soul in pain,
Sicknesses cleave my bones;
Consuming agues dwell in ev'ry vein,
And tune my breath to groans.
Sorrow was all my soul; I scarce believed,
Till grief did tell me roundly, that I lived.

When I got health, thou took'st away my life,
And more; for my friends die:
My mirth and edge was lost; a blunted knife
Was of more use than I.
Thus thin and lean without a fence or friend,
I was blown through with ev'ry storm and wind.

Whereas my birth and spirit rather took
The way that takes the town;
Thou didst betray me to a ling'ring book,
And wrap me in a gown.
I was entangled in the world of strife,
Before I had the power to change my life.

Yet, for I threat'ned oft the siege to raise,
Not simp'ring all mine age,
Thou often didst with academic praise
Melt and dissolve my rage.
I took thy sweet'ned pill, till I came where
I could not go away, nor persevere.

Yet lest perchance I should too happy be
In my unhappiness,
Turning my purge to food, thou throwest me
Into more sicknesses.
Thus doth thy power cross-bias me, not making
Thine own gift good, yet me from my ways taking.

Now I am here, what thou wilt do with me
None of my books will show:
I read, and sigh, and wish I were a tree;
For sure then I should grow
To fruit or shade: at least some bird would trust
Her household to me, and I should be just.

Yet, though thou troublest me, I must be meek;
In weakness must be stout.
Well, I will change the service, and go seek
Some other master out.

Ah my dear God! though I am clean forgot,
Let me not love thee, if I love thee not.

Repentance

Lord, I confess my sin is great;
Great is my sin. O! gently treat
With thy quick flow'r, thy momentary bloom;
Whose life still pressing
Is one undressing,
A steady aiming at a tomb.

Man's age is two hours' work, or three:
Each day doth round about us see.
Thus are we to delights: but we are all
To sorrows old,
If life be told
From what life feeleth, Adam's fall.

O let thy height of mercy then
Compassionate short-breathed men.
Cut me not off for my most foul transgression:
I do confess
My foolishness;
My God, accept of my confession.

Sweeten at length this bitter bowl,
Which thou hast poured into my soul;
Thy wormwood turn to health, winds to fair weather:
For if thou stay,
I and this day,
As we did rise, we die together.

When thou for sin rebukest man,
Forthwith he waxeth woe and wan:
Bitterness fills our bowels; all our hearts

Pine, and decay,
And drop away,
And carry with them th' other parts.

But thou wilt sin and grief destroy;
That so the broken bones may joy,
And tune together in a well-set song,
Full of his praises,
Who dead men raises.
Fractures well cured make us more strong.

Faith

Lord, how couldst thou so much appease
Thy wrath for sin as, when man's sight was dim,
And could see little, to regard his ease,
And bring by Faith all things to him?

Hungry I was, and had no meat:
I did conceit a most delicious feast;
I had it straight, and did as truly eat,
As ever did a welcome guest.

There is a rare outlandish root,
Which when I could not get, I thought it here:
That apprehension cured so well my foot,
That I can walk to heav'n well near.

I owed thousands and much more:
I did believe that I did nothing owe,
And lived accordingly; my creditor
Believes so too, and lets me go.

Faith makes me anything, or all
That I believe is in the sacred story:
And where sin placeth me in Adam's fall,
Faith sets me higher in his glory.

If I go lower in the book,
What can be lower than the common manger?

Faith puts me there with him, who sweetly took
Our flesh and frailty, death and danger.

If bliss had lien in art or strength,
None but the wise or strong had gained it:
Where now by Faith all arms are of a length;
One size doth all conditions fit.

A peasant may believe as much
As a great clerk, and reach the highest stature.
Thus dost thou make proud knowledge bend and crouch
While grace fills up uneven nature.

When creatures had no real light
Inherent in them, thou didst make the sun,
Impute a lustre, and allow them bright;
And in this show, what Christ hath done.

That which before was dark'ned clean
With bushy groves, pricking the looker's eye,
Vanished away, when Faith did change the scene:
And then appeared a glorious sky.

What though my body run to dust?
Faith cleaves unto it, counting ev'ry grain
With an exact and most particular trust,
Reserving all for flesh again.

Prayer (I)

Prayer the Church's banquet, Angels' age,
God's breath in man returning to his birth,
The soul in paraphrase, heart in pilgrimage,
The Christian plummet sounding heav'n and earth;
Engine against th' Almighty, sinners' tower,
Reversed thunder, Christ-side-piercing spear,
The six-days world-transposing in an hour,
A kind of tune, which all things hear and fear;

Softness, and peace, and joy, and love, and bliss,
Exalted Manna, gladness of the best,
Heaven in ordinary, man well dressed,
The milky way, the bird of Paradise,
Church-bells beyond the stars heard, the soul's blood,
The land of spices; something understood.

The Holy Communion

Not in rich furniture, or fine array,
Nor in a wedge of gold,
Thou, who from me wast sold,
To me dost now thyself convey;
For so thou shouldst without me still have been,
Leaving within me sin:

But by the way of nourishment and strength
Thou creep'st into my breast;
Making thy way my rest,
And thy small quantities my length;
Which spread their forces into every part,
Meeting sin's force and art.

Yet can these not get over to my soul,
Leaping the wall that parts
Our souls and fleshly hearts;
But as th' outworks, they may control
My rebel-flesh, and carrying thy name,
Affright both sin and shame.

Only thy grace, which with these elements comes,
Knoweth the ready way,
And hath the privy key,
Op'ning the soul's most subtle rooms;
While those to spirits refined, at door attend
Dispatches from their friend.

Give me my captive soul, or take
My body also thither.
Another lift like this will make
Them both to be together.

Before that sin turned flesh to stone,
And all our lump to leaven;
A fervent sigh might well have blown
Our innocent earth to heaven.

For sure when Adam did not know
To sin, or sin to smother;
He might to heav'n from Paradise go,
As from one room t'another.

Thou hast restored us to this ease
By this thy heav'nly blood;
Which I can go to, when I please,
And leave th' earth to their food.

Antiphon (I)

Chorus Let all the world in ev'ry corner sing,
My God and King.

Verse The heav'ns are not too high,
His praise may thither fly:
The earth is not too low,
His praises there may grow.

Chorus Let all the world in ev'ry corner sing,
My God and King.

Verse The church with psalms must shout,
No door can keep them out:
But above all, the heart
Must bear the longest part.

Chorus Let all the world in ev'ry corner sing,
My God and King.

Love (1)

Immortal Love, author of this great frame,
Sprung from that beauty which can never fade;
How hath man parcelled out thy glorious name,
And thrown it on that dust which thou hast made,
While mortal love doth all the title gain!
Which siding with invention, they together
Bear all the sway, possessing heart and brain
(Thy workmanship), and give thee share in neither.
Wit fancies beauty, beauty raiseth wit:
The world is theirs; they two play out the game,
Thou standing by: and though thy glorious name
Wrought our deliverance from th' infernal pit,
Who sings thy praise? only a scarf or glove
Doth warm our hands, and make them write of love.

Love (2)

Immortal Heat, O let thy greater flame
Attract the lesser to it: let those fires,
Which shall consume the world, first make it tame;
And kindle in our hearts such true desires,
As may consume our lusts, and make thee way.
Then shall our hearts pant thee; then shall our brain
All her invention on thine Altar lay,
And there in hymns send back thy fire again:
Our eyes shall see thee, which before saw dust;
Dust blown by wit, till that they both were blind:
Thou shalt recover all thy goods in kind,
Who wert disseised by usurping lust:
All knees shall bow to thee; all wits shall rise,
And praise him who did make and mend our eyes.

The Temper (I)

How should I praise thee, Lord! how should my rhymes
Gladly engrave thy love in steel,
If what my soul doth feel sometimes,
My soul might ever feel!

Although there were some forty heav'ns, or more,
Sometimes I peer above them all;
Sometimes I hardly reach a score,
Sometimes to hell I fall.

O rack me not to such a vast extent;
Those distances belong to thee:
The world's too little for thy tent,
A grave too big for me.

Wilt thou meet arms with man, that thou dost stretch
A crumb of dust from heav'n to hell?
Will great God measure with a wretch?
Shall he thy stature spell?

O let me, when thy roof my soul hath hid,
O let me roost and nestle there:
Then of a sinner thou art rid,
And I of hope and fear.

Yet take thy way; for sure thy way is best:
Stretch or contract me thy poor debtor:
This is but tuning of my breast,
To make the music better.

Whether I fly with angels, fall with dust,
Thy hands made both, and I am there:
Thy power and love, my love and trust
Make one place ev'ry where.

The Temper (2)

It cannot be. Where is that mighty joy,
  Which just now took up all my heart?
  Lord, if thou must needs use thy dart,
Save that, and me; or sin for both destroy.

The grosser world stands to thy word and art;
  But thy diviner world of grace
  Thou suddenly dost raise and race,
And ev'ry day a new Creator art.

O fix thy chair of grace, that all my powers
  May also fix their reverence:
  For when thou dost depart from hence,
They grow unruly, and sit in thy bowers.

Scatter, or bind them all to bend to thee:
  Though elements change, and heaven move,
  Let not thy higher Court remove,
But keep a standing Majesty in me.

Jordan (1)

Who says that fictions only and false hair
Become a verse? Is there in truth no beauty?
Is all good structure in a winding stair?
May no lines pass, except they do their duty
  Not to a true, but painted chair?

Is it no verse, except enchanted groves
And sudden arbours shadow coarse-spun lines?
Must purling streams refresh a lover's loves?
Must all be veiled, while he that reads, divines,
  Catching the sense at two removes?

Shepherds are honest people; let them sing:
Riddle who list, for me, and pull for Prime:
I envy no man's nightingale or spring;
Nor let them punish me with loss of rhyme,
Who plainly say, *My God, My King*.

Employment (I)

If as a flower doth spread and die,
Thou wouldst extend me to some good,
Before I were by frost's extremity
Nipped in the bud;

The sweetness and the praise were thine;
But the extension and the room,
Which in thy garland I should fill, were mine
At thy great doom.

For as thou dost impart thy grace,
The greater shall our glory be.
The measure of our joys is in this place,
The stuff with thee.

Let me not languish then, and spend
A life as barren to thy praise,
As is the dust, to which that life doth tend,
But with delays.

All things are busy; only I
Neither bring honey with the bees,
Nor flow'rs to make that, nor the husbandry
To water these.

I am no link of thy great chain,
But all my company is a weed.
Lord place me in thy consort; give one strain
To my poor reed.

The Holy Scriptures (1)

O Book! infinite sweetness! let my heart
    Suck ev'ry letter, and a honey gain,
    Precious for any grief in any part;
To clear the breast, to mollify all pain.
Thou art all health, health thriving till it make
    A full eternity: thou art a mass
    Of strange delights, where we may wish and take.
Ladies, look here; this is the thankful glass,
That mends the looker's eyes: this is the well
    That washes what it shows. Who can endear
    Thy praise too much? thou art heav'n's lidger here,
Working against the states of death and hell.
    Thou art joy's handsel: heav'n lies flat in thee,
    Subject to ev'ry mounter's bended knee.

The Holy Scriptures (2)

O that I knew how all thy lights combine,
    And the configurations of their glory!
    Seeing not only how each verse doth shine,
But all the constellations of the story.
This verse marks that, and both do make a motion
    Unto a third, that ten leaves off doth lie:
    Then as dispersed herbs do watch a potion,
These three make up some Christian's destiny:
Such are thy secrets, which my life makes good,
    And comments on thee: for in ev'rything
    Thy words do find me out, and parallels bring,
And in another make me understood.
    Stars are poor books, and oftentimes do miss:
    This book of stars lights to eternal bliss.

Whitsunday

Listen sweet Dove unto my song,
And spread thy golden wings in me;
Hatching my tender heart so long,
Till it get wing, and fly away with thee.

Where is that fire which once descended
On thy Apostles? thou didst then
Keep open house, richly attended,
Feasting all comers by twelve chosen men.

Such glorious gifts thou didst bestow,
That th' earth did like a heav'n appear:
The stars were coming down to know
If they might mend their wages, and serve here.

The sun, which once did shine alone,
Hung down his head, and wished for night,
When he beheld twelve suns for one
Going about the world, and giving light.

But since those pipes of gold, which brought
That cordial water to our ground,
Were cut and martyred by the fault
Of those, who did themselves through their side wound,

Thou shut'st the door, and keep'st within;
Scarce a good joy creeps through the chink:
And if the braves of conqu'ring sin
Did not excite thee, we should wholly sink.

Lord, though we change, thou art the same;
The same sweet God of love and light:
Restore this day, for thy great name,
Unto his ancient and miraculous right.

Grace

My stock lies dead, and no increase
Doth my dull husbandry improve:
O let thy graces without cease
Drop from above!

If still the sun should hide his face,
Thy house would but a dungeon prove,
Thy works night's captives: O let grace
Drop from above!

The dew doth ev'ry morning fall;
And shall the dew out-strip thy Dove?
The dew, for which grass cannot call,
Drop from above.

Death is still working like a mole,
And digs my grave at each remove:
Let grace work too, and on my soul
Drop from above.

Sin is still hammering my heart
Unto a hardness, void of love:
Let suppling grace, to cross his art,
Drop from above.

O come! for thou dost know the way.
Or if to me thou wilt not move,
Remove me, where I need not say,
Drop from above.

Praise (1)

To write a verse or two, is all the praise,
That I can raise:
Mend my estate in any ways,
Thou shalt have more.

I go to Church; help me to wings, and I
Will thither fly;
Or, if I mount unto the sky,
I will do more.

Man is all weakness; there is no such thing
As Prince or King:
His arm is short; yet with a sling
He may do more.

An herb distilled, and drunk, may dwell next door,
On the same floor,
To a brave soul: Exalt the poor,
They can do more.

O raise me then! Poor bees, that work all day,
Sting my delay,
Who have a work, as well as they,
And much, much more.

Affliction (2)

Kill me not ev'ry day,
Thou Lord of life; since thy one death for me
Is more than all my deaths can be,
Though I in broken pay
Die over each hour of Methusalem's stay.

If all men's tears were let
Into one common sewer, sea, and brine;
What were they all, compared to thine?
Wherein if they were set,
They would discolour thy most bloody sweat.

Thou art my grief alone,
Thou Lord conceal it not: and as thou art
All my delight, so all my smart:
Thy cross took up in one,
By way of imprest, all my future moan.

Matins

I cannot ope mine eyes,
But thou art ready there to catch
My morning-soul and sacrifice:
Then we must needs for that day make a match.

My God, what is a heart?
Silver, or gold, or precious stone,
Or star, or rainbow, or a part
Of all these things, or all of them in one?

My God, what is a heart,
That thou shouldst it so eye, and woo,
Pouring upon it all thy art,
As if that thou hadst nothing else to do?

Indeed man's whole estate
Amounts (and richly) to serve thee:
He did not heav'n and earth create,
Yet studies them, not him by whom they be.

Teach me thy love to know;
That this new light, which now I see,
May both the work and workman show:
Then by a sunbeam I will climb to thee.

Sin (2)

O that I could a sin once see!
We paint the devil foul, yet he
Hath some good in him, all agree.
Sin is flat opposite to th' Almighty, seeing
It wants the good of *virtue*, and of *being*.

But God more care of us hath had:
If apparitions make us sad,
By sight of sin we should grow mad.
Yet as in sleep we see foul death, and live:
So devils are our sins in perspective.

Evensong (1)

Blest be the God of love,
Who gave me eyes, and light, and power this day,
Both to be busy, and to play.
But much more blest be God above,
Who gave me sight alone,
Which to himself he did deny:
For when he sees my ways, I die:
But I have got his son, and he hath none.
What have I brought thee home
For this thy love? have I discharged the debt,
Which this day's favour did beget?
I ran; but all I brought, was foam.
Thy diet, care, and cost
Do end in bubbles, balls of wind;
Of wind to thee whom I have crossed,
But balls of wild-fire to my troubled mind.
Yet still thou goest on.
And now with darkness closest weary eyes,

Saying to man, *It doth suffice:*
Henceforth repose; your work is done.
Thus in thy Ebony box
Thou dost enclose us, till the day
Put our amendment in our way,
And give new wheels to our disordered clocks.

I muse, which shows more love,
The day or night: that is the gale, this th' harbour;
That is the walk, and this the arbour;
Or that the garden, this the grove.
My God, thou art all love.
Not one poor minute 'scapes thy breast,
But brings a favour from above;
And in this love, more than in bed, I rest.

Church-Monuments

While that my soul repairs to her devotion,
Here I intomb my flesh, that it betimes
May take acquaintance of this heap of dust;
To which the blast of death's incessant motion,
Fed with the exhalation of our crimes,
Drives all at last. Therefore I gladly trust

My body to this school, that it may learn
To spell his elements, and find his birth
Written in dusty heraldry and lines:
Which dissolution sure doth best discern,
Comparing dust with dust, and earth with earth.
These laugh at Jet and Marble put for signs,

To sever the good fellowship of dust,
And spoil the meeting. What shall point out them,
When they shall bow, and kneel, and fall down flat
To kiss those heaps, which now they have in trust?

Dear flesh, while I do pray, learn here thy stem
And true descent; that when thou shalt grow fat,

And wanton in thy cravings, thou mayst know,
That flesh is but the glass, which holds the dust
That measures all our time; which also shall
Be crumbled into dust. Mark here below
How tame these ashes are, how free from lust,
That thou mayst fit thyself against thy fall.

Church-Music

Sweetest of sweets, I thank you: when displeasure
Did through my body wound my mind,
You took me thence, and in your house of pleasure
A dainty lodging me assigned.

Now I in you without a body move,
Rising and falling with your wings:
We both together sweetly live and love,
Yet say sometimes, *God help poor Kings*.

Comfort, I'll die; for if you post from me,
Sure I shall do so, and much more:
But if I travel in your company,
You know the way to heaven's door.

Church-Lock and Key

I know it is my sin, which locks thine ears,
And binds thy hands,
Out-crying my requests, drowning my tears;
Or else the chillness of my faint demands.

But as cold hands are angry with the fire,
And mend it still;

So I do lay the want of my desire,
Not on my sins, or coldness, but thy will.

Yet hear, O God, only for his blood's sake
Which pleads for me:
For though sins plead too, yet like stones they make
His blood's sweet current much more loud to be.

The Church-Floor

Mark you the floor? that square and speckled stone,
Which looks so firm and strong,
Is *Patience*:

And th' other black and grave, wherewith each one
Is checkered all along,
Humility:

The gentle rising, which on either hand
Leads to the Choir above,
Is *Confidence*:

But the sweet cement, which in one sure band
Ties the whole frame, is *Love*
And *Charity*.

Hither sometimes Sin steals, and stains
The marble's neat and curious veins:
But all is cleansed when the marble weeps.
Sometimes Death, puffing at the door,
Blows all the dust about the floor:
But while he thinks to spoil the room, he sweeps.
Blessed be the *Architect*, whose art
Could build so strong in a weak heart.

The Windows

Lord, how can man preach thy eternal word?
He is a brittle crazy glass:
Yet in thy temple thou dost him afford
This glorious and transcendent place,
To be a window, through thy grace.

But when thou dost anneal in glass thy story,
Making thy life to shine within
The holy Preacher's; then the light and glory
More rev'rend grows, and more doth win:
Which else shows wat'rish, bleak, and thin.

Doctrine and life, colours and light, in one
When they combine and mingle, bring
A strong regard and awe: but speech alone
Doth vanish like a flaring thing,
And in the ear, not conscience ring.

Trinity Sunday

Lord, who hast formed me out of mud,
And hast redeemed me through thy blood,
And sanctified me to do good;

Purge all my sins done heretofore:
For I confess my heavy score,
And I will strive to sin no more.

Enrich my heart, mouth, hands in me,
With faith, with hope, with charity;
That I may run, rise, rest with thee.

Content

Peace mutt'ring thoughts, and do not grudge to keep
Within the walls of your own breast:
Who cannot on his own bed sweetly sleep,
Can on another's hardly rest.

Gad not abroad at ev'ry quest and call
Of an untrained hope or passion.
To court each place or fortune that doth fall,
Is wantonness in contemplation.

Mark how the fire in flints doth quiet lie,
Content and warm t' itself alone:
But when it would appear to other's eye,
Without a knock it never shone.

Give me the pliant mind, whose gentle measure
Complies and suits with all estates;
Which can let loose to a crown, and yet with pleasure
Take up within a cloister's gates.

This soul doth span the world, and hang content
From either pole unto the centre:
Where in each room of the well-furnished tent
He lies warm, and without adventure.

The brags of life are but a nine days' wonder;
And after death the fumes that spring
From private bodies make as big a thunder,
As those which rise from a huge King.

Only thy Chronicle is lost; and yet
Better by worms be all once spent,
Than to have hellish moths still gnaw and fret
Thy name in books, which may not rent:

When all thy deeds, whose brunt thou feel'st alone,
Are chawed by others' pens and tongue;
And as their wit is, their digestion,
Thy nourished fame is weak or strong.

Then cease discoursing soul, till thine own ground,
Do not thyself or friends importune.
He that by seeking hath himself once found,
Hath ever found a happy fortune.

The Quiddity

My God, a verse is not a crown,
No point of honour, or gay suit,
No hawk, or banquet, or renown,
Nor a good sword, nor yet a lute:

It cannot vault, or dance, or play;
It never was in *France* or *Spain*;
Nor can it entertain the day
With a great stable or demesne:

It is no office, art, or news,
Nor the Exchange, or busy Hall;
But it is that which while I use
I am with thee, and *Most take all*.

Humility

I saw the Virtues sitting hand in hand
In sev'ral ranks upon an azure throne,
Where all the beasts and fowls by their command
Presented tokens of submission.
Humility, who sat the lowest there
To execute their call,
When by the beasts the presents tendered were,
Gave them about to all.

The angry Lion did present his paw,
Which by consent was giv'n to Mansuetude.
The fearful Hare her ears, which by their law
Humility did reach to Fortitude.
The jealous Turkey brought his coral-chain;
That went to Temperance.
On Justice was bestowed the Fox's brain,
Kill'd in the way by chance.

At length the Crow bringing the Peacock's plume
(For he would not), as they beheld the grace
Of that brave gift, each one began to fume,
And challenge it, as proper to his place,
Till they fell out: which when the beasts espied,
They leapt upon the throne;
And if the Fox had lived to rule their side,
They had deposed each one.

Humility, who held the plume, at this
Did weep so fast, that the tears trickling down
Spoiled all the train: then saying *Here it is*
For which ye wrangle, made them turn their frown
Against the beasts: so jointly bandying,
They drive them soon away;
And then amerced them, double gifts to bring
At the next Session-day.

Frailty

Lord, in my silence how do I despise
What upon trust
Is styled *honour*, *riches*, or *fair eyes*;
But is *fair dust*!
I surname them *gilded clay*,
Dear earth, *fine grass*, or *hay*;
In all, I think my foot doth ever tread
Upon their head.

But when I view abroad both Regiments;
The world's and thine:
Thine clad with simpleness, and sad events;
The other fine,
Full of glory and gay weeds,
Brave language, braver deeds:
That which was dust before, doth quickly rise,
And prick mine eyes.

O brook not this, lest if what even now
My foot did tread,
Affront those joys, wherewith thou didst endow,
And long since wed
My poor soul, ev'n sick of love:
It may a Babel prove
Commodious to conquer heav'n and thee
Planted in me.

Constancy

Who is the honest man?
He that doth still and strongly good pursue,
To God, his neighbour, and himself most true:
Whom neither force nor fawning can
Unpin, or wrench from giving all their due.

Whose honesty is not
So loose or easy, that a ruffling wind
Can blow away, or glittering look it blind:
Who rides his sure and even trot,
While the world now rides by, now lags behind.

Who, when great trials come,
Nor seeks, nor shuns them; but doth calmly stay,
Till he the thing and the example weigh:
All being brought into a sum,
What place or person calls for, he doth pay.

Whom none can work or woo
To use in anything a trick or sleight;
For above all things he abhors deceit:
His words and works and fashion too
All of a piece, and all are clear and straight.

Who never melts or thaws
At close tentations: when the day is done,
His goodness sets not, but in dark can run:
The sun to others writeth laws,
And is their virtue; Virtue is his Sun.

Who, when he is to treat
With sick folks, women, those whom passions sway,
Allows for that, and keeps his constant way:
Whom others' faults do not defeat;
But though men fail him, yet his part doth play.

Whom nothing can procure,
When the wide world runs bias from his will,
To writhe his limbs, and share, not mend the ill.
This is the Mark-man, safe and sure,
Who still is right, and prays to be so still.

Affliction (3)

My heart did heave, and there came forth, *O God!*
By that I knew that thou wast in the grief,
To guide and govern it to my relief,
Making a sceptre of the rod:
Hadst thou not had thy part,
Sure the unruly sigh had broke my heart.

But since thy breath gave me both life and shape,
Thou know'st my tallies; and when there's assigned
So much breath to a sigh, what's then behind?

Or if some years with it escape,
The sigh then only is
A gale to bring me sooner to my bliss.

Thy life on earth was grief, and thou art still
Constant unto it, making it to be
A point of honour, now to grieve in me,
And in thy members suffer ill.
They who lament one cross,
Thou dying daily, praise thee to thy loss.

The Star

Bright spark, shot from a brighter place,
Where beams surround my Saviour's face,
Canst thou be any where
So well as there?

Yet, if thou wilt from thence depart,
Take a bad lodging in my heart;
For thou canst make a debtor,
And make it better.

First with thy fire-work burn to dust
Folly, and worse than folly, lust:
Then with thy light refine,
And make it shine:

So disengaged from sin and sickness,
Touch it with thy celestial quickness,
That it may hang and move
After thy love.

Then with our trinity of light,
Motion, and heat, let's take our flight
Unto the place where thou
Before didst bow.

Get me a standing there, and place
  Among the beams, which crown the face
      Of him, who died to part
        Sin and my heart:

That so among the rest I may
  Glitter, and curl, and wind as they:
      That winding is their fashion
        Of adoration.

Sure thou wilt joy, by gaining me
  To fly home like a laden bee
      Unto that hive of beams
        And garland-streams.

Sunday

      O day most calm, most bright,
The fruit of this, the next world's bud,
Th' endorsement of supreme delight,
Writ by a friend, and with his blood;
The couch of time; care's balm and bay:
The week were dark, but for thy light:
      Thy torch doth show the way.

      The other days and thou
Make up one man; whose face thou art,
Knocking at heaven with thy brow:
The worky-days are the back-part;
The burden of the week lies there,
Making the whole to stoop and bow,
      Till thy release appear.

      Man had straight forward gone
To endless death: but thou dost pull
And turn us round to look on one,
Whom, if we were not very dull,
We could not choose but look on still;

Since there is no place so alone,
The which he doth not fill.

Sundays the pillars are,
On which heav'n's palace arched lies:
The other days fill up the spare
And hollow room with vanities.
They are the fruitful beds and borders
In God's rich garden: that is bare,
Which parts their ranks and orders.

The Sundays of man's life,
Threaded together on time's string,
Make bracelets to adorn the wife
Of the eternal glorious King.
On Sunday heaven's gate stands ope;
Blessings are plentiful and rife,
More plentiful than hope.

This day my Saviour rose,
And did inclose this light for his:
That, as each beast his manger knows,
Man might not of his fodder miss.
Christ hath took in this piece of ground,
And made a garden there for those
Who want herbs for their wound.

The rest of our Creation
Our great Redeemer did remove
With the same shake, which at his passion
Did th' earth and all things with it move.
As Samson bore the doors away,
Christ's hands, though nailed, wrought our salvation,
And did unhinge that day.

The brightness of that day
We sullied by our foul offence:
Wherefore that robe we cast away,
Having a new at his expense,

Whose drops of blood paid the full price,
That was required to make us gay,
And fit for Paradise.

Thou art a day of mirth:
And where the week-days trail on ground,
Thy flight is higher, as thy birth.
O let me take thee at the bound,
Leaping with thee from sev'n to sev'n,
Till that we both, being tossed from earth,
Fly hand in hand to heav'n!

Avarice

Money, thou bane of bliss, and source of woe,
Whence com'st thou, that thou art so fresh and fine?
I know thy parentage is base and low:
Man found thee poor and dirty in a mine.
Surely thou didst so little contribute
To this great kingdom, which thou now hast got,
That he was fain, when thou wert destitute,
To dig thee out of thy dark cave and grot:
Then forcing thee, by fire he made thee bright:
Nay, thou hast got the face of man; for we
Have with our stamp and seal transferred our right:
Thou art the man, and man but dross to thee.
Man calleth thee his wealth, who made thee rich;
And while he digs out thee, falls in the ditch.

Ana-{Mary / Army}gram

How well her name an *Army* doth present,
In whom the *Lord of Hosts* did pitch his tent!

To All Angels and Saints

O glorious spirits, who after all your bands
See the smooth face of God, without a frown
Or strict commands;
Where ev'ry one is king, and hath his crown,
If not upon his head, yet in his hands:

Not out of envy or maliciousness
Do I forbear to crave your special aid:
I would address
My vows to thee most gladly, blessed Maid,
And Mother of my God, in my distress.

Thou art the holy mine, whence came the gold,
The great restorative for all decay
In young and old;
Thou art the cabinet where the jewel lay:
Chiefly to thee would I my soul unfold:

But now (alas!) I dare not; for our King,
Whom we do all jointly adore and praise,
Bids no such thing:
And where his pleasure no injunction lays,
('Tis your own case) ye never move a wing.

All worship is prerogative, and a flower
Of his rich crown, from whom lies no appeal
At the last hour:
Therefore we dare not from his garland steal,
To make a posy for inferior power.

Although then others court you, if ye know
What's done on earth, we shall not fare the worse,
Who do not so;
Since we are ever ready to disburse,
If any one our Master's hand can show.

Employment (2)

He that is weary, let him sit.
My soul would stir
And trade in courtesies and wit,
Quitting the fur
To cold complexions needing it.

Man is no star, but a quick coal
Of mortal fire:
Who blows it not, nor doth control
A faint desire,
Lets his own ashes choke his soul.

When th' elements did for place contest
With him, whose will
Ordain'd the highest to be best;
The earth sat still,
And by the others is oppressed.

Life is a business, not good cheer;
Ever in wars.
The sun still shineth there or here,
Whereas the stars
Watch an advantage to appear.

O that I were an Orange-tree,
That busy plant!
Then should I ever laden be,
And never want
Some fruit for him that dressed me.

But we are still too young or old;
The man is gone,
Before we do our wares unfold:
So we freeze on,
Until the grave increase our cold.

Denial

When my devotions could not pierce
Thy silent ears;
Then was my heart broken, as was my verse:
My breast was full of fears
And disorder:

My bent thoughts, like a brittle bow,
Did fly asunder:
Each took his way; some would to pleasures go,
Some to the wars and thunder
Of alarms.

As good go anywhere, they say,
As to benumb
Both knees and heart, in crying night and day,
Come, come my God, O come,
But no hearing.

O that thou shouldst give dust a tongue
To cry to thee,
And then not hear it crying! all day long
My heart was in my knee,
But no hearing.

Therefore my soul lay out of sight,
Untuned, unstrung:
My feeble spirit, unable to look right,
Like a nipped blossom, hung
Discontented.

O cheer and tune my heartless breast,
Defer no time;
That so thy favours granting my request,
They and my mind may chime,
And mend my rhyme.

Christmas

All after pleasures as I rid one day,
My horse and I, both tired, body and mind,
With full cry of affections, quite astray;
I took up in the next inn I could find.
There when I came, whom found I but my dear,
My dearest Lord, expecting till the grief
Of pleasures brought me to him, ready there
To be all passengers' most sweet relief?
O Thou, whose glorious, yet contracted light,
Wrapped in night's mantle, stole into a manger;
Since my dark soul and brutish is thy right,
To Man of all beasts be not thou a stranger:
Furnish and deck my soul, that thou mayst have
A better lodging, than a rack, or grave.

The shepherds sing; and shall I silent be?
My God, no hymn for thee?
My soul's a shepherd too; a flock it feeds
Of thoughts, and words, and deeds.
The pasture is thy word: the streams, thy grace
Enriching all the place.

Shepherd and flock shall sing, and all my powers
Out-sing the day-light hours.
Then we will chide the sun for letting night
Take up his place and right:
We sing one common Lord; wherefore he should
Himself the candle hold.
I will go searching, till I find a sun
Shall stay, till we have done;
A willing shiner, that shall shine as gladly,
As frost-nipped suns look sadly.
Then we will sing, and shine all our own day,
And one another pay:
His beams shall cheer my breast, and both so twine,
Till ev'n his beams sing, and my music shine.

Ungratefulness

Lord, with what bounty and rare clemency
Hast thou redeemed us from the grave!
If thou hadst let us run,
Gladly had man adored the sun,
And thought his god most brave;
Where now we shall be better gods than he.

Thou hast but two rare cabinets full of treasure,
The *Trinity*, and *Incarnation*:
Thou hast unlocked them both,
And made them jewels to betroth
The work of thy creation
Unto thyself in everlasting pleasure.

The statelier cabinet is the *Trinity*,
Whose sparkling light access denies:
Therefore thou dost not show
This fully to us, till death blow
The dust into our eyes:
For by that powder thou wilt make us see.

But all thy sweets are packed up in the other;
Thy mercies thither flock and flow:
That as the first affrights,
This may allure us with delights;
Because this box we know;
For we have all of us just such another.

But man is close, reserved, and dark to thee:
When thou demandest but a heart,
He cavils instantly.
In his poor cabinet of bone
Sins have their box apart,
Defrauding thee, who gavest two for one.

Sighs and Groans

O do not use me
After my sins! look not on my desert,
But on thy glory! then thou wilt reform
And not refuse me: for thou only art
The mighty God, but I a silly worm;
O do not bruise me!

O do not urge me!
For what account can thy ill steward make?
I have abused thy stock, destroyed thy woods,
Sucked all thy magazines: my head did ache,
Till it found out how to consume thy goods:
O do not scourge me!

O do not blind me!
I have deserved that an Egyptian night
Should thicken all my powers; because my lust
Hath still sewed fig-leaves to exclude thy light:
But I am frailty, and already dust;
O do not grind me!

O do not fill me
With the turned vial of thy bitter wrath!
For thou hast other vessels full of blood,
A part whereof my Saviour emptied hath,
Ev'n unto death: since he died for my good,
O do not kill me!

But O reprieve me!
For thou hast *life* and *death* at thy command;
Thou art both *Judge* and *Saviour*, *feast* and *rod*,
Cordial and *Corrosive*: put not thy hand
Into the bitter box; but O my God,
My God, relieve me!

The World

Love built a stately house; where *Fortune* came,
And spinning fancies, she was heard to say,
That her fine cobwebs did support the frame,
Whereas they were supported by the same:
But *Wisdom* quickly swept them all away.

Then *Pleasure* came, who liking not the fashion,
Began to make *Balconies*, *Terraces*,
Till she had weak'ned all by alteration:
But rev'rend *laws*, and many a *proclamation*
Reformed all at length with menaces.

Then entered *Sin*, and with that Sycamore,
Whose leaves first sheltered man from drought and dew,
Working and winding slyly evermore,
The inward walls and Sommers cleft and tore:
But *Grace* shored these, and cut that as it grew.

Then *Sin* combined with *Death* in a firm band
To raze the building to the very floor:
Which they effected, none could them withstand.
But *Love* and *Grace* took *Glory* by the hand,
And built a braver Palace than before.

Colossians 3:3

Our life is hid with Christ in God.

My words and thoughts do both express this notion,
That ***Life*** hath with the sun a double motion.
The first ***Is*** straight, and our diurnal friend,
The other ***Hid*** and doth obliquely bend.
One life is wrapped ***In*** flesh, and tends to earth:
The other winds towards ***Him***, whose happy birth
Taught me to live here so, ***That*** still one eye
Should aim and shoot at that which ***Is*** on high:
Quitting with daily labour all ***My*** pleasure,
To gain at harvest an eternal ***Treasure***.

Vanity (1)

The fleet Astronomer can bore,
And thread the spheres with his quick-piercing mind:
He views their stations, walks from door to door,
Surveys, as if he had designed
To make a purchase there: he sees their dances,
And knoweth long before,
Both their full-eyed aspects, and secret glances.

The nimble Diver with his side
Cuts through the working waves, that he may fetch
His dearly-earned pearl, which God did hide
On purpose from the vent'rous wretch;
That he might save his life, and also hers,
Who with excessive pride
Her own destruction and his danger wears.

The subtle Chymick can divest
And strip the creature naked, till he find
The callow principles within their nest:
There he imparts to them his mind,
Admitted to their bed-chamber, before
They appear trim and dressed
To ordinary suitors at the door.

What hath not man sought out and found,
But his dear God? who yet his glorious law
Embosoms in us, mellowing the ground
With show'rs and frosts, with love and awe,
So that we need not say, Where's this command?
Poor man, thou searchest round
To find out *death*, but missest *life* at hand.

Lent

Welcome dear feast of Lent: who loves not thee,
He loves not Temperance, or Authority,
But is composed of passion.
The Scriptures bid us *fast*; the Church says, *now*:
Give to thy Mother, what thou wouldst allow
To ev'ry Corporation.

The humble soul composed of love and fear
Begins at home, and lays the burden there,
When doctrines disagree.
He says, in things which use hath justly got,
I am a scandal to the Church, and not
The Church is so to me.

True Christians should be glad of an occasion
To use their temperance, seeking no evasion,
When good is seasonable;
Unless Authority, which should increase
The obligation in us, make it less,
And Power itself disable.

Besides the cleanness of sweet abstinence,
Quick thoughts and motions at a small expense,
A face not fearing light:
Whereas in fullness there are sluttish fumes,
Sour exhalations, and dishonest rheums,
Revenging the delight.

Then those same pendant profits, which the spring
And Easter intimate, enlarge the thing,
And goodness of the deed.
Neither ought other men's abuse of Lent
Spoil the good use; lest by that argument
We forfeit all our Creed.

It's true, we cannot reach Christ's forti'th day;
Yet to go part of that religious way,
Is better than to rest:
We cannot reach our Saviour's purity;
Yet are we bid, *Be holy ev'n as he.*
In both let's do our best.

Who goeth in the way which Christ hath gone,
Is much more sure to meet with him, than one
That travelleth by-ways:
Perhaps my God, though he be far before,
May turn, and take me by the hand, and more
May strengthen my decays.

Yet Lord instruct us to improve our fast
By starving sin and taking such repast
As may our faults control:
That ev'ry man may revel at his door,
Not in his parlour; banqueting the poor,
And among those his soul.

Virtue

Sweet day, so cool, so calm, so bright,
The bridal of the earth and sky:

The dew shall weep thy fall tonight;
For thou must die.

Sweet rose, whose hue angry and brave
Bids thc rash gazer wipe his eye:
Thy root is ever in its grave,
And thou must die.

Sweet spring, full of sweet days and roses,
A box where sweets compacted lie;
My music shows ye have your closes,
And all must die.

Only a sweet and virtuous soul,
Like seasoned timber, never gives;
But though the whole world turn to coal,
Then chiefly lives.

The Pearl. Matthew 13:45

I know the ways of learning; both the head
And pipes that feed the press, and make it run;
What reason hath from nature borrowed,
Or of itself, like a good huswife, spun
In laws and policy; what the stars conspire,
What willing nature speaks, what forc'd by fire;
Both th' old discoveries, and the new-found seas,
The stock and surplus, cause and history:
All these stand open, or I have the keys:
Yet I love thee.

I know the ways of honour, what maintains
The quick returns of courtesy and wit:
In vies of favours whether party gains,
When glory swells the heart, and mouldeth it
To all expressions both of hand and eye,
Which on the world a true-love-knot may tie,
And bear the bundle, wheresoe'er it goes:

How many drams of spirit there must be
To sell my life unto my friends or foes:
Yet I love thee.

I know the ways of pleasure, the sweet strains,
The lullings and the relishes of it;
The propositions of hot blood and brains;
What mirth and music mean; what love and wit
Have done these twenty hundred years, and more:
I know the projects of unbridled store:
My stuff is flesh, not brass; my senses live,
And grumble oft, that they have more in me
Than he that curbs them, being but one to five:
Yet I love thee.

I know all these, and have them in my hand:
Therefore not sealed, but with open eyes
I fly to thee, and fully understand
Both the main sale, and the commodities;
And at what rate and price I have thy love;
With all the circumstances that may move:
Yet through the labyrinths, not my grovelling wit,
But thy silk twist let down from heaven to me;
Did both conduct, and teach me, how by it
To climb to thee.

Affliction (4)

Broken in pieces all asunder,
Lord, hunt me not,
A thing forgot,
Once a poor creature, now a wonder,
A wonder tortured in the space
Betwixt this world and that of grace.

My thoughts are all a case of knives,
Wounding my heart

With scattered smart,
As wat'ring pots give flowers their lives.
Nothing their fury can control,
While they do wound and prick my soul.

All my attendants are at strife,
Quitting their place
Unto my face:
Nothing performs the task of life:
The elements are let loose to fight,
And while I live, try out their right.

O help, my God! let not their plot
Kill them and me,
And also thee,
Who art my life: dissolve the knot,
As the sun scatters by his light
All the rebellions of the night.

Then shall those powers, which work for grief,
Enter thy pay,
And day by day
Labour thy praise, and my relief:
With care and courage building me,
Till I reach heav'n, and much more, thee.

Man

My God, I heard this day,
That none doth build a stately habitation,
But he that means to dwell therein.
What house more stately hath there been,
Or can be, than is Man? to whose creation
All things are in decay.

For Man is ev'ry thing,
And more: He is a tree, yet bears no fruit;
A beast, yet is, or should be more:

Reason and speech we only bring.
Parrots may thank us, if they are not mute,
They go upon the score.

Man is all symmetry,
Full of proportions, one limb to another,
And all to all the world besides:
Each part may call the farthest, brother:
For head with foot hath private amity,
And both with moons and tides.

Nothing hath got so far,
But Man hath caught and kept it, as his prey.
His eyes dismount the highest star:
He is in little all the sphere.
Herbs gladly cure our flesh; because that they
Find their acquaintance there.

For us the winds do blow,
The earth doth rest, heav'n move, and fountains flow.
Nothing we see, but means our good,
As our *delight*, or as our *treasure*:
The whole is, either our cupboard of *food*,
Or cabinet of *pleasure*.

The stars have us to bed;
Night draws the curtain, which the sun withdraws;
Music and light attend our head.
All things unto our *flesh* are kind
In their *descent* and *being*; to our *mind*
In their *ascent* and *cause*.

Each thing is full of duty:
Waters united are our navigation;
Distinguished, our habitation;
Below, our drink; above, our meat;
Both are our cleanliness. Hath one such beauty?
Then how are all things neat?

More servants wait on Man,
Than he'll take notice of: in ev'ry path
He treads down that which doth befriend him,
When sickness makes him pale and wan.
O mighty love! Man is one world, and hath
Another to attend him.

Since then, my God, thou hast
So brave a Palace built; O dwell in it,
That it may dwell with thee at last!
Till then, afford us so much wit;
That, as the world serves us, we may serve thee,
And both thy servants be.

Antiphon (2)

Chorus Praised be the God of love,
Men Here below,
Angels And here above:
Chorus Who hath dealt his mercies so,
Angels To his friend,
Men And to his foe;

Chorus That both grace and glory tend
Angels Us of old,
Men And us in th' end.
Chorus The great shepherd of the fold
Angels Us did make,
Men For us was sold.

Chorus He our foes in pieces brake;
Angels Him we touch;
Men And him we take.
Chorus Wherefore since that he is such,
Angels We adore,
Men And we do crouch.

Chorus Lord, thy praises should be more.
Men We have none,
Angels And we no store.
Chorus Praised be the God alone,
Who hath made of two folds one.

Unkindness

Lord, make me coy and tender to offend:
In friendship, first I think, if that agree,
Which I intend,
Unto my friend's intent and end.
I would not use a friend, as I use Thee.

If any touch my friend, or his good name;
It is my honour and my love to free
His blasted fame
From the least spot or thought of blame.
I could not use a friend, as I use Thee.

My friend may spit upon my curious floor:
Would he have gold? I lend it instantly;
But let the poor,
And thou within them, starve at door.
I cannot use a friend, as I use Thee.

When that my friend pretendeth to a place,
I quit my interest, and leave it free:
But when thy grace
Sues for my heart, I thee displace,
Nor would I use a friend, as I use Thee.

Yet can a friend what thou hast done fulfil?
O write in brass, *My God upon a tree*
His blood did spill
Only to purchase my good-will:
Yet use I not my foes, as I use thee.

Life

I made a posy, while the day ran by;
Here will I smell my remnant out, and tie
My life within this band.
But time did beckon to the flowers, and they
By noon most cunningly did steal away,
And withered in my hand.

My hand was next to them, and then my heart:
I took, without more thinking, in good part
Time's gentle admonition:
Who did so sweetly death's sad taste convey,
Making my mind to smell my fatal day;
Yet sug'ring the suspicion.

Farewell dear flowers, sweetly your time ye spent,
Fit, while ye lived, for smell or ornament,
And after death for cures.
I follow straight without complaints or grief,
Since if my scent be good, I care not, if
It be as short as yours.

Submission

But that thou art my wisdom, Lord,
And both mine eyes are thine,
My mind would be extremely stirred
For missing my design.

Were it not better to bestow
Some place and power on me?
Then should thy praises with me grow,
And share in my degree.

But when I thus dispute and grieve,
I do resume my sight,
And pilf'ring what I once did give,
Disseise thee of thy right.

How know I, if thou shouldst me raise,
That I should then raise thee?
Perhaps great places and thy praise
Do not so well agree.

Wherefore unto my gift I stand;
I will no more advise:
Only do thou lend me a hand,
Since thou hast both mine eyes.

Justice (I)

I cannot skill of these thy ways.
Lord, thou didst make me, yet thou woundest me;
Lord, thou dost wound me, yet thou dost relieve me:
Lord, thou relievest, yet I die by thee:
Lord, thou dost kill me, yet thou dost reprieve me.

But when I mark my life and praise,
Thy justice me most fitly pays:
For, *I do praise thee, yet I praise thee not:*
My prayers mean thee, yet my prayers stray:
I would do well, yet sin the hand hath got:
My soul doth love thee, yet it loves delay.
I cannot skill of these my ways.

Charms and Knots

Who read a chapter when they rise,
Shall ne'er be troubled with ill eyes.

A poor man's rod, when thou dost ride,
Is both a weapon and a guide.

Who shuts his hand, hath lost his gold:
Who opens it, hath it twice told.

Who goes to bed and doth not pray,
Maketh two nights to ev'ry day.

Who by aspersions throws a stone
At th' head of others, hit their own.

Who looks on ground with humble eyes,
Finds himself there, and seeks to rise.

When th' hair is sweet through pride or lust,
The powder doth forget the dust.

Take one from ten, and what remains?
Ten still, if sermons go for gains.

In shallow water heav'n doth show;
But who drinks on, to hell may go.

Affliction (5)

My God, I read this day,
That planted Paradise was not so firm,
As was and is thy floating Ark; whose stay
And anchor thou art only, to confirm
And strengthen it in ev'ry age,
When waves do rise, and tempests rage.

At first we lived in pleasure;
Thine own delights thou didst to us impart:
When we grew wanton, thou didst use displeasure
To make us thine: yet that we might not part,
As we at first did board with thee,
Now thou wouldst taste our misery.

There is but joy and grief;
If either will convert us, we are thine:
Some Angels used the first; if our relief
Take up the second, then thy double line
And sev'ral baits in either kind
Furnish thy table to thy mind.

Affliction then is ours;
We are the trees, whom shaking fastens more,
While blust'ring winds destroy the wanton bow'rs,
And ruffle all their curious knots and store.
My God, so temper joy and woe,
That thy bright beams may tame thy bow.

Mortification

How soon doth man decay!
When clothes are taken from a chest of sweets
To swaddle infants, whose young breath
Scarce knows the way;
Those clouts are little winding sheets,
Which do consign and send them unto death.

When boys go first to bed,
They step into their voluntary graves,
Sleep binds them fast; only their breath
Makes them not dead:
Successive nights, like rolling waves,
Convey them quickly, who are bound for death.

When youth is frank and free,
And calls for music, while his veins do swell,
All day exchanging mirth and breath
In company;
That music summons to the knell,
Which shall befriend him at the house of death.

When man grows staid and wise,
Getting a house and home, where he may move

Within the circle of his breath,
Schooling his eyes;
That dumb inclosure maketh love
Unto the coffin, that attends his death.

When age grows low and weak,
Marking his grave, and thawing ev'ry year,
Till all do melt, and drown his breath
When he would speak;
A chair or litter shows the bier,
Which shall convey him to the house of death.

Man, ere he is aware,
Hath put together a solemnity,
And dressed his hearse, while he has breath
As yet to spare:
Yet Lord, instruct us so to die,
That all these dyings may be life in death.

Decay

Sweet were the days, when thou didst lodge with Lot,
Struggle with Jacob, sit with Gideon,
Advise with Abraham, when thy power could not
Encounter Moses' strong complaints and moan:
Thy words were then, *Let me alone.*

One might have sought and found thee presently
At some fair oak, or bush, or cave, or well:
Is my God this way? No, they would reply:
He is to Sinai gone, as we heard tell:
List, ye may hear great Aaron's bell.

But now thou dost thyself immure and close
In some one corner of a feeble heart:
Where yet both Sin and Satan, thy old foes,
Do pinch and straiten thee, and use much art
To gain thy thirds and little part.

I see the world grows old, when as the heat
Of thy great love once spread, as in an urn
Doth closet up itself, and still retreat,
Cold sin still forcing it, till it return,
And calling Justice, all things burn.

Misery

Lord, let the Angels praise thy name.
Man is a foolish thing, a foolish thing,
Folly and Sin play all his game.
His house still burns, and yet he still doth sing,
Man is but grass,
He knows it, fill the glass.

How canst thou brook his foolishness?
Why he'll not lose a cup of drink for thee:
Bid him but temper his excess;
Not he: he knows, where he can better be,
As he will swear,
Than to serve thee in fear.

What strange pollutions doth he wed,
And make his own? as if none knew, but he.
No man shall beat into his head,
That thou within his curtains drawn canst see:
They are of cloth,
Where never yet came moth.

The best of men, turn but thy hand
For one poor minute, stumble at a pin:
They would not have their actions scanned,
Nor any sorrow tell them that they sin,
Though it be small,
And measure not their fall.

They quarrel thee, and would give over
The bargain made to serve thee: but thy love
Holds them unto it, and doth cover
Their follies with the wing of thy mild Dove,
Not suff'ring those
Who would, to be thy foes.

My God, Man cannot praise thy name:
Thou art all brightness, perfect purity;
The sun holds down his head for shame,
Dead with eclipses, when we speak of thee:
How shall infection
Presume on thy perfection?

As dirty hands foul all they touch,
And those things most, which are most pure and fine:
So our clay hearts, ev'n when we crouch
To sing thy praises, make them less divine.
Yet either this,
Or none, thy portion is.

Man cannot serve thee; let him go,
And serve the swine: there, there is his delight:
He doth not like this virtue, no;
Give him his dirt to wallow in all night:
These Preachers make
His head to shoot and ache.

O foolish man! where are thine eyes?
How hast thou lost them in a crowd of cares?
Thou pull'st the rug, and wilt not rise,
No, not to purchase the whole pack of stars:
There let them shine,
Thou must go sleep, or dine.

The bird that sees a dainty bow'r
Made in the tree, where she was wont to sit,
Wonders and sings, but not his power
Who made the arbour: this exceeds her wit.

But Man doth know
The spring, whence all things flow:

And yet as though he knew it not,
His knowledge winks, and lets his humours reign;
They make his life a constant blot,
And all the blood of God to run in vain.
Ah wretch! what verse
Can thy strange ways rehearse?

Indeed at first Man was a treasure,
A box of jewels, shop of rarities,
A ring, whose posy was, *My pleasure*:
He was a garden in a Paradise:
Glory and grace
Did crown his heart and face.

But sin hath fooled him. Now he is
A lump of flesh, without a foot or wing
To raise him to the glimpse of bliss:
A sick tossed vessel, dashing on each thing;
Nay, his own shelf:
My God, I mean myself.

Jordan (2)

When first my lines of heav'nly joys made mention,
Such was their lustre, they did so excel,
That I sought out quaint words, and trim invention;
My thoughts began to burnish, sprout, and swell,
Curling with metaphors a plain intention,
Decking the sense, as if it were to sell.

Thousands of notions in my brain did run,
Off'ring their service, if I were not sped:
I often blotted what I had begun;
This was not quick enough, and that was dead.
Nothing could seem too rich to clothe the sun,
Much less those joys which trample on his head.

As flames do work and wind, when they ascend,
So did I weave my self into the sense.
But while I bustled, I might hear a friend
Whisper, *How wide is all this long pretence!*
There is in love a sweetness ready penned:
Copy out only that, and save expense.

Prayer (2)

Of what an easy quick access,
My blessed Lord, art thou! how suddenly
May our requests thine ear invade!
To show that state dislikes not easiness,
If I but lift mine eyes, my suit is made:
Thou canst no more not hear, than thou canst die.

Of what supreme almighty power
Is thy great arm which spans the east and west,
And tacks the centre to the sphere!
By it do all things live their measured hour:
We cannot ask the thing, which is not there,
Blaming the shallowness of our request.

Of what unmeasurable love
Art thou possessed, who, when thou couldst not die,
Wert fain to take our flesh and curse,
And for our sakes in person sin reprove,
That by destroying that which tied thy purse,
Thou mightst make way for liberality!

Since then these three wait on thy throne,
Ease, Power, and *Love*; I value prayer so,
That were I to leave all but one,
Wealth, fame, endowments, virtues, all should go;
I and dear prayer would together dwell,
And quickly gain, for each inch lost, an ell.

Obedience

My God, if writings may
Convey a Lordship any way
Whither the buyer and the seller please;
Let it not thee displease,
If this poor paper do as much as they.

On it my heart doth bleed
As many lines as there doth need
To pass itself and all it hath to thee.
To which I do agree,
And here present it as my special deed.

If that hereafter Pleasure
Cavil, and claim her part and measure,
As if this passed with a reservation,
Or some such words in fashion;
I here exclude the wrangler from thy treasure.

O let thy sacred will
All thy delight in me fulfil!
Let me not think an action mine own way,
But as thy love shall sway,
Resigning up the rudder to thy skill.

Lord, what is man to thee,
That thou shouldst mind a rotten tree?
Yet since thou canst not choose but see my actions;
So great are thy perfections,
Thou mayst as well my actions guide, as see.

Besides, thy death and blood
Showed a strange love to all our good:
Thy sorrows were in earnest, no faint proffer,
Or superficial offer
Of what we might not take, or be withstood.

Wherefore I all forgo:
To one word only I say, No:
Where in the deed there was an intimation
Of a *gift* or *donation*,
Lord, let it now by way of *purchase* go.

He that will pass his land,
As I have mine, may set his hand
And heart unto this deed, when he hath read;
And make the purchase spread
To both our goods, if he to it will stand.

How happy were my part,
If some kind man would thrust his heart
Into these lines; till in heav'n's Court of Rolls
They were by winged souls
Ent'red for both, far above their desert!

Conscience

Peace prattler, do not lour:
Not a fair look, but thou dost call it foul:
Not a sweet dish, but thou dost call it sour:
Music to thee doth howl.
By listening to thy chatting fears
I have both lost mine eyes and ears.

Prattler, no more, I say:
My thoughts must work, but like a noiseless sphere;
Harmonious peace must rock them all the day:
No room for prattlers there.
If thou persistest, I will tell thee,
That I have physic to expel thee.

And the receipt shall be
My Saviour's blood: whenever at his board
I do but taste it, straight it cleanseth me,
And leaves thee not a word;

No, not a tooth or nail to scratch,
And at my actions carp, or catch.

Yet if thou talkest still,
Besides my physic, know there's some for thee:
Some wood and nails to make a staff or bill
For those that trouble me:
The bloody cross of my dear Lord
Is both my physic and my sword.

Sion

Lord, with what glory wast thou served of old,
When Solomon's temple stood and flourished!
Where most things were of purest gold;
The wood was all embellished
With flowers and carvings, mystical and rare:
All showed the builder's, craved the seer's care.

Yet all this glory, all this pomp and state
Did not affect thee much, was not thy aim;
Something there was, that sowed debate:
Wherefore thou quitt'st thy ancient claim:
And now thy Architecture meets with sin;
For all thy frame and fabric is within.

There thou art struggling with a peevish heart,
Which sometimes crosseth thee, thou sometimes it:
The fight is hard on either part.
Great God doth fight, he doth submit.
All Solomon's sea of brass and world of stone
Is not so dear to thee as one good groan.

And truly brass and stones are heavy things,
Tombs for the dead, not temples fit for thee:
But groans are quick, and full of wings,
And all their motions upward be;
And ever as they mount, like larks they sing;
The note is sad, yet music for a king.

Home

Come Lord, my head doth burn, my heart is sick,
While thou dost ever, ever stay:
Thy long deferrings wound me to the quick,
My spirit gaspeth night and day.
O show thyself to me,
Or take me up to thee!

How canst thou stay, considering the pace
The blood did make, which thou didst waste?
When I behold it trickling down thy face,
I never saw thing make such haste.
O show thyself to me,
Or take me up to thee!

When man was lost, thy pity looked about
To see what help in th' earth or sky:
But there was none; at least no help without;
The help did in thy bosom lie.
O show thyself to me,
Or take me up to thee!

There lay thy son: and must he leave that nest,
That hive of sweetness, to remove
Thraldom from those, who would not at a feast
Leave one poor apple for thy love?
O show thyself to me,
Or take me up to thee!

He did, he came: O my Redeemer dear,
After all this canst thou be strange?
So many years baptised, and not appear?
As if thy love could fail or change.
O show thyself to me,
Or take me up to thee!

Yet if thou stayest still, why must I stay?
        My God, what is this world to me?
This world of woe? hence all ye clouds, away,
        Away; I must get up and see.
                O show thyself to me,
                Or take me up to thee!

What is this weary world; this meat and drink,
        That chains us by the teeth so fast?
What is this woman-kind, which I can wink
        Into a blackness and distaste?
                O show thyself to me,
                Or take me up to thee!

With one small sigh thou gav'st me th' other day
        I blasted all the joys about me:
And scowling on them as they pined away,
        Now come again, said I, and flout me.
                O show thyself to me,
                Or take me up to thee!

Nothing but drought and dearth, but bush and brake,
        Which way soe'er I look, I see.
Some may dream merrily, but when they wake,
        They dress themselves and come to thee.
                O show thyself to me,
                Or take me up to thee!

We talk of harvests; there are no such things,
        But when we leave our corn and hay:
There is no fruitful year, but that which brings
        The last and loved, though dreadful day.
                O show thyself to me,
                Or take me up to thee!

O loose this frame, this knot of man untie!
        That my free soul may use her wing,
Which now is pinioned with mortality,
        As an entangled, hampered thing.

O show thyself to me,
Or take me up to thee!

What have I left, that I should stay and groan?
The most of me to heav'n is fled:
My thoughts and joys are all packed up and gone,
And for their old acquaintance plead.
O show thyself to me,
Or take me up to thee!

Come dearest Lord, pass not this holy season,
My flesh and bones and joints do pray:
And ev'n my verse, when by the rhyme and reason
The word is, *Stay*, says ever, *Come*.
O show thyself to me,
Or take me up to thee!

The British Church

I joy, dear Mother, when I view
Thy perfect lineaments, and hue
Both sweet and bright.
Beauty in thee takes up her place,
And dates her letters from thy face,
When she doth write.

A fine aspect in fit array,
Neither too mean, nor yet too gay,
Shows who is best.
Outlandish looks may not compare:
For all they either painted are,
Or else undressed.

She on the hills, which wantonly
Allureth all in hope to be
By her preferr'd,
Hath kissed so long her painted shrines,
That ev'n her face by kissing shines,
For her reward.

She in the valley is so shy
Of dressing that her hair doth lie
About her ears:
While she avoids her neighbour's pride,
She wholly goes on th' other side,
And nothing wears.

But dearest Mother, (what those miss)
The mean thy praise and glory is,
And long may be.
Blessed be God, whose love it was
To double-moat thee with his grace,
And none but thee.

The Quip

The merry world did on a day
With his train-bands and mates agree
To meet together, where I lay,
And all in sport to jeer at me.

First, Beauty crept into a rose,
Which when I plucked not, Sir, said she,
Tell me, I pray, Whose hands are those?
But thou shalt answer, Lord, for me.

Then Money came, and chinking still,
What tune is this, poor man? said he:
I heard in Music you had skill.
But thou shalt answer, Lord, for me.

Then came brave Glory puffing by
In silks that whistled, who but he?
He scarce allowed me half an eye.
But thou shalt answer, Lord, for me.

Then came quick Wit and Conversation,
And he would needs a comfort be,
And, to be short, make an oration.
But thou shalt answer, Lord, for me.

Yet when the hour of thy design
To answer these fine things shall come;
Speak not at large, say, I am thine:
And then they have their answer home.

Vanity (2)

Poor silly soul, whose hope and head lies low;
Whose flat delights on earth do creep and grow:
To whom the stars shine not so fair, as eyes;
Nor solid work, as false embroideries;
Hark and beware, lest what you now do measure
And write for sweet, prove a most sour displeasure.

O hear betimes, lest thy relenting
May come too late!
To purchase heaven for repenting,
Is no hard rate.
If souls be made of earthly mould,
Let them love gold;
If born on high,
Let them unto their kindred fly:
For they can never be at rest,
Till they regain their ancient nest.
Then silly soul take heed; for earthly joy
Is but a bubble, and makes thee a boy.

The Dawning

Awake sad heart, whom sorrow ever drowns;
Take up thine eyes, which feed on earth;
Unfold thy forehead gathered into frowns:
Thy Saviour comes, and with him mirth:
Awake, awake:
And with a thankful heart his comforts take.
But thou dost still lament, and pine, and cry;
And feel his death, but not his victory.

Arise sad heart; if thou dost not withstand,
Christ's resurrection thine may be:
Do not by hanging down break from the hand,
Which as it riseth, raiseth thee:
Arise, arise;
And with his burial-linen dry thine eyes:
Christ left his grave-clothes, that we might, when grief
Draws tears, or blood, not want an handkerchief.

Jesu

JESU is in my heart, his sacred name
Is deeply carved there: but th' other week
A great affliction broke the little frame,
Ev'n all to pieces: which I went to seek:
And first I found the corner, where was *J*,
After, where *ES*, and next where *U* was graved.
When I had got these parcels, instantly
I sat me down to spell them, and perceived
That to my broken heart he was *I ease you*,
And to my whole is *JESU*.

Business

Canst be idle? canst thou play,
Foolish soul who sinned today?

Rivers run, and springs each one
Know their home, and get them gone:
Hast thou tears, or hast thou none?

If, poor soul, thou hast no tears;
Would thou hadst no faults or fears!
Who hath these, those ill forbears.

Winds still work: it is their plot,
Be the season cold, or hot:
Hast thou sighs, or hast thou not?

If thou hast no sighs or groans,
Would thou hadst no flesh and bones!
Lesser pains scape greater ones.

But if yet thou idle be,
Foolish soul, Who died for thee?

Who did leave his Father's throne,
To assume thy flesh and bone;
Had he life, or had he none?

If he had not lived for thee,
Thou hadst died most wretchedly;
And two deaths had been thy fee.

He so far thy good did plot,
That his own self he forgot.
Did he die, or did he not?

If he had not died for thee,
Thou hadst lived in misery.
Two lives worse than ten deaths be.

And hath any space of breath
'Twixt his sins and Saviour's death?

He that loseth gold, though dross,
Tells to all he meets, his cross:
He that sins, hath he no loss?

He that finds a silver vein,
Thinks on it, and thinks again:
Brings thy Saviour's death no gain?

Who in heart not ever kneels,
Neither sin nor Saviour feels.

Dialogue

Sweetest Saviour, if my soul
Were but worth the having,
Quickly should I then control
Any thought of waiving.
But when all my care and pains
Cannot give the name of gains
To thy wretch so full of stains;
What delights or hope remains?

What (child) is the balance thine,
Thine the poise and measure?
If I say, Thou shalt be mine;
Finger not my treasure.
What the gains in having thee
Do amount to, only he,
Who for man was sold, can see;
That transferred th' accounts to me.

But as I can see no merit,
Leading to this favour:
So the way to fit me for it,
Is beyond my savour.
As the reason then is thine;
So the way is none of mine:

I disclaim the whole design:
Sin disclaims and I resign.

That is all, if that I could
Get without repining;
And my clay my creature would
Follow my resigning.
That as I did freely part
With my glory and desert,
Left all joys to feel all smart – –
Ah! no more: thou break'st my heart.

Dullness

Why do I languish thus, drooping and dull,
As if I were all earth?
O give me quickness, that I may with mirth
Praise thee brimfull!

The wanton lover in a curious strain
Can praise his fairest fair;
And with quaint metaphors her curlèd hair
Curl o'er again.

Thou art my loveliness, my life, my light,
Beauty alone to me:
Thy bloody death and undeserved, makes thee
Pure red and white.

When all perfections as but one appear,
That those thy form doth show,
The very dust, where thou dost tread and go,
Makes beauties here;

Where are my lines then? my approaches? views?
Where are my window-songs?
Lovers are still pretending, and ev'n wrongs
Sharpen their Muse:

But I am lost in flesh, whose sugared lies
Still mock me, and grow bold:
Sure thou didst put a mind there, if I could
Find where it lies.

Lord, clear thy gift, that with a constant wit
I may but look towards thee:
Look only; for to *love* thee, who can be,
What angel fit?

Love-Joy

As on a window late I cast mine eye,
I saw a vine drop grapes with *J* and *C*
Annealed on every bunch. One standing by
Asked what it meant. I (who am never loath
To spend my judgement) said, It seemed to me
To be the body and the letters both
Of *Joy* and *Charity*. Sir, you have not missed,
The man replied; it figures *JESUS CHRIST*.

Providence

O sacred Providence, who from end to end
Strongly and sweetly movest! shall I write,
And not of thee, through whom my fingers bend
To hold my quill? shall they not do thee right?

Of all the creatures both in sea and land
Only to Man thou hast made known thy ways,
And put the pen alone into his hand,
And made him Secretary of thy praise.

Beasts fain would sing; birds ditty to their notes;
Trees would be tuning on their native lute
To thy renown: but all their hands and throats
Are brought to Man, while they are lame and mute.

Man is the world's high Priest: he doth present
The sacrifice for all; while they below
Unto the service mutter an assent,
Such as springs use that fall, and winds that blow.

He that to praise and laud thee doth refrain,
Doth not refrain unto himself alone,
But robs a thousand who would praise thee fain,
And doth commit a world of sin in one.

The beasts say, Eat me: but, if beasts must teach,
The tongue is yours to eat, but mine to praise.
The trees say, Pull me: but the hand you stretch,
Is mine to write, as it is yours to raise.

Wherefore, most sacred Spirit, I here present
For me and all my fellows praise to thee:
And just it is that I should pay the rent,
Because the benefit accrues to me.

We all acknowledge both thy power and love
To be exact, transcendent, and divine;
Who dost so strongly and so sweetly move,
While all things have their will, yet none but thine.

For either thy *command*, or thy *permission*
Lay hands on all: they are thy *right* and *left*.
The first puts on with speed and expedition;
The other curbs sin's stealing pace and theft.

Nothing escapes them both; all must appear,
And be disposed, and dressed, and tuned by thee,
Who sweetly temper'st all. If we could hear
Thy skill and art, what music would it be!

Thou art in small things great, not small in any:
Thy even praise can neither rise, nor fall.
Thou art in all things one, in each thing many:
For thou art infinite in one and all.

Tempests are calm to thee; they know thy hand,
And hold it fast, as children do their father's,
Which cry and follow. Thou hast made poor sand
Check the proud sea, ev'n when it swells and gathers.

Thy cupboard serves the world: the meat is set,
Where all may reach: no beast but knows his feed.
Birds teach us hawking; fishes have their net:
The great prey on the less, they on some weed.

Nothing engend'red doth prevent his meat:
Flies have their table spread, ere they appear.
Some creatures have in winter what to eat;
Others do sleep, and envy not their cheer.

How finely dost thou times and seasons spin,
And make a twist chequered with night and day!
Which as it lengthens winds, and winds us in,
As bowls go on, but turning all the way.

Each creature hath a wisdom for his good.
The pigeons feed their tender offspring, crying,
When they are callow; but withdraw their food
When they are fledge, that need may teach them flying.

Bees work for man; and yet they never bruise
Their master's flower, but leave it, having done,
As fair as ever, and as fit to use;
So both the flower doth stay, and honey run.

Sheep eat the grass, and dung the ground for more:
Trees after bearing drop their leaves for soil:
Springs vent their streams, and by expense get store:
Clouds cool by heat, and baths by cooling boil.

Who hath the virtue to express the rare
And curious virtues both of herbs and stones?
Is there an herb for that? O that thy care
Would show a root, that gives expressions!

And if an herb hath power, what have the stars?
A rose, besides his beauty, is a cure.
Doubtless our plagues and plenty, peace and wars
Are there much surer than our art is sure.

Thou hast hid metals: man may take them thence;
But at his peril: when he digs the place,
He makes a grave; as if the thing had sense,
And threat'ned man, that he should fill the space.

Ev'n poisons praise thee. Should a thing be lost?
Should creatures want for want of heed their due?
Since where are poisons, antidotes are most:
The help stands close, and keeps the fear in view.

The sea, which seems to stop the traveller,
Is by a ship the speedier passage made.
The winds, who think they rule the mariner,
Are ruled by him, and taught to serve his trade.

And as thy house is full, so I adore
Thy curious art in marshalling thy goods.
The hills with health abound; the vales with store;
The South with marble; North with furs and woods.

Hard things are glorious; easy things good cheap.
The common all men have; that which is rare,
Men therefore seek to have, and care to keep.
The healthy frosts with summer-fruits compare.

Light without wind is glass: warm without weight
Is wool and furs: cool without closeness, shade:
Speed without pains, a horse: tall without height,
A servile hawk: low without loss, a spade.

All countries have enough to serve their need:
If they seek fine things, thou dost make them run
For their offence; and then dost turn their speed
To be commerce and trade from sun to sun.

Nothing wears clothes, but Man; nothing doth need
But he to wear them. Nothing useth fire,
But Man alone, to show his heav'nly breed:
And only he hath fuel in desire.

When th' earth was dry, thou mad'st a sea of wet:
When that lay gathered, thou didst broach the mountains:
When yet some places could no moisture get,
The winds grew gard'ners, and the clouds good fountains.

Rain, do not hurt my flowers; but gently spend
Your honey drops: press not to smell them here:
When they are ripe, their odour will ascend,
And at your lodging with their thanks appear.

How harsh are thorns to pears! and yet they make
A better hedge, and need less reparation.
How smooth are silks compared with a stake,
Or with a stone! yet make no good foundation.

Sometimes thou dost divide thy gifts to man,
Sometimes unite. The Indian nut alone
Is clothing, meat and trencher, drink and can,
Boat, cable, sail and needle, all in one.

Most herbs that grow in brooks, are hot and dry.
Cold fruits warm kernels help against the wind.
The lemon's juice and rind cure mutually.
The whey of milk doth loose, the milk doth bind.

Thy creatures leap not, but express a feast,
Where all the guests sit close, and nothing wants.
Frogs marry fish and flesh; bats, bird and beast;
Sponges, non-sense and sense; mines, th' earth and plants.

To show thou art not bound, as if thy lot
Were worse than ours; sometimes thou shiftest hands.
Most things move th' under-jaw; the Crocodile not.
Most things sleep lying; th' Elephant leans or stands.

But who hath praise enough? nay who hath any?
None can express thy works, but he that knows them:
And none can know thy works, which are so many,
And so complete, but only he that owes them.

All things that are, though they have sev'ral ways,
Yet in their being join in one advice
To honour thee: and so I give thee praise
In all my other hymns, but in this twice.

Each thing that is, although in use and name
It go for one, hath many ways in store
To honour thee; and so each hymn thy fame
Extolleth many ways, yet this one more.

Hope

I gave to Hope a watch of mine: but he
    An anchor gave to me.
Then an old prayer-book I did present:
    And he an optic sent.
With that I gave a vial full of tears:
    But he a few green ears:
Ah Loiterer! I'll no more, no more I'll bring:
    I did expect a ring.

Sin's Round

Sorry I am, my God, sorry I am,
That my offences course it in a ring.
My thoughts are working like a busy flame,
Until their cockatrice they hatch and bring:
And when they once have perfected their draughts,
My words take fire from my inflamèd thoughts.

My words take fire from my inflamèd thoughts,
Which spit it forth like the Sicilian hill.

They vent the wares, and pass them with their faults,
And by their breathing ventilate the ill.
But words suffice not, where are lewd intentions:
My hands do join to finish the inventions.

My hands do join to finish the inventions:
And so my sins ascend three stories high,
As Babel grew, before there were dissensions.
Yet ill deeds loiter not: for they supply
New thoughts of sinning: wherefore, to my shame,
Sorry I am, my God, sorry I am.

Time

Meeting with Time, slack thing, said I,
Thy scythe is dull; whet it for shame.
No marvel Sir, he did reply,
If it at length deserve some blame:
    But where one man would have me grind it,
    Twenty for one too sharp do find it.

Perhaps some such of old did pass,
Who above all things loved this life;
To whom thy scythe a hatchet was,
Which now is but a pruning-knife.
    Christ's coming hath made man thy debtor,
    Since by thy cutting he grows better.

And in his blessing thou art blessed;
For where thou only wert before
An executioner at best;
Thou art a gard'ner now, and more,
    An usher to convey our souls
    Beyond the utmost stars and poles.

And this is that makes life so long,
While it detains us from our God.
Ev'n pleasures here increase the wrong,

And length of days lengthen the rod.
Who wants the place, where God doth dwell,
Partakes already half of hell.

Of what strange length must that needs be,
Which ev'n eternity excludes!
Thus far Time heard me patiently:
Then chafing said, This man deludes:
What do I here before his door?
He doth not crave less time, but more.

Gratefulness

Thou that hast giv'n so much to me,
Give one thing more, a grateful heart.
See how thy beggar works on thee
By art.

He makes thy gifts occasion more,
And says, If he in this be crossed,
All thou hast giv'n him heretofore
Is lost.

But thou didst reckon, when at first
Thy word our hearts and hands did crave,
What it would come to at the worst
To save.

Perpetual knockings at thy door,
Tears sullying thy transparent rooms,
Gift upon gift, much would have more,
And comes.

This not withstanding, thou wentst on,
And didst allow us all our noise:
Nay thou hast made a sigh and groan
Thy joys.

Not that thou hast not still above
Much better tunes, than groans can make;
But that these country-airs thy love
Did take.

Wherefore I cry, and cry again;
And in no quiet canst thou be,
Till I a thankful heart obtain
Of thee:

Not thankful, when it pleaseth me;
As if thy blessings had spare days:
But such a heart, whose pulse may be
Thy praise.

Peace

Sweet Peace, where dost thou dwell? I humbly crave,
Let me once know.
I sought thee in a secret cave,
And asked, if Peace were there.
A hollow wind did seem to answer, No:
Go seek elsewhere.

I did; and going did a rainbow note:
Surely, thought I,
This is the lace of Peace's coat:
I will search out the matter.
But while I looked, the clouds immediately
Did break and scatter.

Then went I to a garden, and did spy
A gallant flower,
The Crown Imperial: Sure, said I,
Peace at the root must dwell.
But when I digged, I saw a worm devour
What showed so well.

At length I met a rev'rend good old man,
Whom when for Peace
I did demand, he thus began:
There was a Prince of old
At Salem dwelt, who lived with good increase
Of flock and fold.

He sweetly lived; yet sweetness did not save
His life from foes.
But after death out of his grave
There sprang twelve stalks of wheat:
Which many wond'ring at, got some of those
To plant and set.

It prospered strangely, and did soon disperse
Through all the earth:
For they that taste it do rehearse,
That virtue lies therein,
A secret virtue bringing peace and mirth
By flight of sin.

Take of this grain, which in my garden grows,
And grows for you;
Make bread of it: and that repose
And peace which ev'rywhere
With so much earnestness you do pursue,
Is only there.

Confession

O what a cunning guest
Is this same grief! within my heart I made
Closets; and in them many a chest;
And like a master in my trade,
In those chests, boxes; in each box, a till:
Yet grief knows all, and enters when he will.

No screw, no piercer can
Into a piece of timber work and wind,
As God's afflictions into man,
When he a torture hath designed.
They are too subtle for the subtlest hearts;
And fall, like rheums, upon the tend'rest parts.

We are the earth; and they,
Like moles within us, heave, and cast about:
And till they foot and clutch their prey,
They never cool, much less give out.
No smith can make such locks, but they have keys:
Closets are halls to them; and hearts, high-ways.

Only an open breast
Doth shut them out, so that they cannot enter;
Or, if they enter, cannot rest,
But quickly seek some new adventure.
Smooth open hearts no fast'ning have; but fiction
Doth give a hold and handle to affliction.

Wherefore my faults and sins,
Lord, I acknowledge; take thy plagues away:
For since confession pardon wins,
I challenge here the brightest day,
The clearest diamond: let them do their best,
They shall be thick and cloudy to my breast.

Giddiness

O, what a thing is man! how far from power,
From settled peace and rest!
He is some twenty sev'ral men at least
Each sev'ral hour.

One while he counts of heav'n, as of his treasure:
But then a thought creeps in,
And calls him coward, who for fear of sin
Will lose a pleasure.

Now he will fight it out, and to the wars;
Now eat his bread in peace,
And snudge in quiet: now he scorns increase;
Now all day spares.

He builds a house, which quickly down must go,
As if a whirlwind blew
And crushed the building: and it's partly true,
His mind is so.

O what a sight were Man, if his attires
Did alter with his mind;
And like a Dolphin's skin, his clothes combined
With his desires!

Surely if each one saw another's heart,
There would be no commerce,
No sale or bargain pass: all would disperse,
And live apart.

Lord, mend or rather make us: one creation
Will not suffice our turn:
Except thou make us daily, we shall spurn
Our own salvation.

The Bunch of Grapes

Joy, I did lock thee up: but some bad man
Hath let thee out again:
And now, methinks, I am where I began
Sev'n years ago: one vogue and vein,
One air of thoughts usurps my brain.
I did toward Canaan draw; but now I am
Brought back to the Red Sea, the sea of shame.

For as the Jews of old by God's command
Travelled, and saw no town:
So now each Christian hath his journeys spanned:

Their story pens and sets us down.
A single deed is small renown.
God's works are wide, and let in future times;
His ancient justice overflows our crimes.

Then have we too our guardian fires and clouds;
Our Scripture-dew drops fast:
We have our sands and serpents, tents and shrouds;
Alas! our murmurings come not last.
But where's the cluster? where's the taste
Of mine inheritance? Lord, if I must borrow,
Let me as well take up their joy, as sorrow.

But can he want the grape, who hath the wine?
I have their fruit and more.
Blessèd be God, who prospered *Noah's* vine,
And make it bring forth grapes good store.
But much more him I must adore,
Who of the law's sour juice sweet wine did make,
Ev'n God himself, being pressed for my sake.

Love Unknown

Dear Friend, sit down, the tale is long and sad:
And in my faintings I presume your love
Will more comply, than help. A Lord I had,
And have, of whom some grounds which may improve,
I hold for two lives, and both lives in me.
To him I brought a dish of fruit one day,
And in the middle placed my heart. But he
(I sigh to say)
Looked on a servant, who did know his eye
Better than you know me, or (which is one)
Than I myself. The servant instantly
Quitting the fruit, seized on my heart alone,
And threw it in a font, wherein did fall
A stream of blood, which issued from the side

Of a great rock: I well remember all,
And have good cause: there it was dipped and dyed,
And washed, and wrung: the very wringing yet
Enforceth tears. *Your heart was foul, I fear.*
Indeed 'tis true. I did and do commit
Many a fault more than my lease will bear;
Yet still asked pardon, and was not denied.
But you shall hear. After my heart was well,
And clean and fair, as I one even-tide
(I sigh to tell)
Walked by myself abroad, I saw a large
And spacious furnace flaming, and thereon
A boiling cauldron, round about whose verge
Was in great letters set *AFFLICTION*.
The greatness showed the owner. So I went
To fetch a sacrifice out of my fold,
Thinking with that, which I did thus present,
To warm his love, which I did fear grew cold.
But as my heart did tender it, the man
Who was to take it from me, slipped his hand,
And threw my heart into the scalding pan;
My heart, that brought it (do you understand?)
The offerer's heart. *Your heart was hard, I fear.*
Indeed 'tis true. I found a callous matter
Began to spread and to expatiate there:
But with a richer drug than scalding water,
I bathed it often, ev'n with holy blood,
Which at a board, while many drunk bare wine,
A friend did steal into my cup for good,
Ev'n taken inwardly, and most divine
To supple hardnesses. But at the length
Out of the cauldron getting, soon I fled
Unto my house, where to repair the strength
Which I had lost, I hasted to my bed.
But when I thought to sleep out all these faults
(I sigh to speak)
I found that some had stuffed the bed with thoughts,

I would say *thorns*. Dear, could my heart not break,
When with my pleasures ev'n my rest was gone?
Full well I understood, who had been there:
For I had giv'n the key to none, but one:
It must be he. *Your heart was dull, I fear.*
Indeed a slack and sleepy state of mind
Did oft possess me, so that when I prayed,
Though my lips went, my heart did stay behind.
But all my scores were by another paid,
Who took the debt upon him. *Truly, Friend,*
For ought I hear, your Master shows to you
More favour than you wot of. Mark the end.
The Font did only, what was old, renew:
The Cauldron suppled, what was grown too hard:
The Thorns did quicken, what was grown too dull:
All did but strive to mend, what you had marred.
Wherefore be cheered, and praise him to the full
Each day, each hour, each moment of the week,
Who fain would have you be, new, tender, quick.

Man's Medley

Hark, how the birds do sing,
And woods do ring.
All creatures have their joy: and man hath his.
Yet if we rightly measure,
Man's joy and pleasure
Rather hereafter, than in present, is.

To this life things of sense
Make their pretence:
In th' other Angels have a right by birth:
Man ties them both alone,
And makes them one,
With th' one hand touching heav'n, with th' other earth.

In soul he mounts and flies,
In flesh he dies.

He wears a stuff whose thread is coarse and round,
But trimmed with curious lace,
And should take place
After the trimming, not the stuff and ground.

Not, that he may not here
Taste of the cheer,
But as birds drink, and straight lift up their head,
So must he sip and think
Of better drink
He may attain to, after he is dead.

But as his joys are double;
So is his trouble.
He hath two winters, other things but one:
Both frosts and thoughts do nip,
And bite his lip;
And he of all things fears two deaths alone.

Yet ev'n the greatest griefs
May be reliefs,
Could he but take them right, and in their ways.
Happy is he, whose heart
Hath found the art
To turn his double pains to double praise.

The Storm

If as the winds and waters here below
Do fly and flow,
My sighs and tears as busy were above;
Sure they would move
And much affect thee, as tempestuous times
Amaze poor mortals, and object their crimes.

Stars have their storms, ev'n in a high degree,
As well as we.

A throbbing conscience spurred by remorse
Hath a strange force:
It quits the earth, and mounting more and more,
Dares to assault, and besiege thy door.

There it stands knocking, to thy music's wrong,
And drowns the song.
Glory and honour are set by till it
An answer get.
Poets have wronged poor storms: such days are best;
They purge the air without, within the breast.

Paradise

I bless thee, Lord, because I GROW
Among thy trees, which in a ROW
To thee both fruit and order OW.

What open force, or hidden CHARM
Can blast my fruit, or bring me HARM,
While the inclosure is thine ARM?

Inclose me still for fear I START.
Be to me rather sharp and TART,
Than let me want thy hand and ART.

When thou dost greater judgements SPARE,
And with thy knife but prune and PARE,
Ev'n fruitful trees more fruitful ARE.

Such sharpness shows the sweetest FREND:
Such cuttings rather heal than REND:
And such beginnings touch their END.

The Method

Poor heart, lament.
For since thy God refuseth still,
There is some rub, some discontent,
Which cools his will.

Thy Father *could*
Quickly effect, what thou dost move;
For he is *Power*: and sure he *would*;
For he is *Love*.

Go search this thing,
Tumble thy breast, and turn thy book.
If thou hadst lost a glove or ring,
Wouldst thou not look?

What do I see
Written above there? *Yesterday*
I did behave me carelessly,
When I did pray.

And should God's ear
To such indifferents chainèd be,
Who do not their own motions hear?
Is God less free?

But stay! what's there?
Late when I would have something done,
I had a motion to forbear,
Yet I went on.

And should God's ear,
Which needs not man, be tied to those
Who hear not him, but quickly hear
His utter foes?

Then once more pray:
Down with thy knees, up with thy voice.
Seek pardon first, and God will say,
Glad heart rejoice.

Divinity

As men, for fear the stars should sleep and nod,
    And trip at night, have spheres supplied;
As if a star were duller than a clod,
    Which knows his way without a guide:

Just so the other heav'n they also serve,
    Divinity's transcendent sky:
Which with the edge of wit they cut and carve.
    Reason triumphs, and faith lies by.

Could not that wisdom, which first broached the wine,
    Have thickened it with definitions?
And jagged his seamless coat, had that been fine,
    With curious questions and divisions?

But all the doctrine, which he taught and gave,
    Was clear as heav'n, from whence it came.
At least those beams of truth, which only save,
    Surpass in brightness any flame.

Love God, and love your neighbour. Watch and pray.
    Do as ye would be done unto.
O dark instructions; ev'n as dark as day!
    Who can these Gordian knots undo?

But he doth bid us take his blood for wine.
    Bid what he please; yet I am sure,
To take and taste what he doth there design,
    Is all that saves, and not obscure.

Then burn thy Epicycles, foolish man;
    Break all thy spheres, and save thy head.
Faith needs no staff of flesh, but stoutly can
    To heav'n alone both go, and lead.

Ephesians 4:30. Grieve not the Holy Spirit, etc.

And art thou grieved, sweet and sacred Dove,
When I am sour,
And cross thy love?
Grieved for me? the God of strength and power
Grieved for a worm, which when I tread,
I pass away and leave it dead?

Then weep mine eyes, the God of love doth grieve:
Weep foolish heart,
And weeping live:
For death is dry as dust. Yet if ye part,
End as the night, whose sable hue
Your sins express; melt into dew.

When saucy mirth shall knock or call at door,
Cry out, Get hence,
Or cry no more.
Almighty God doth grieve, he puts on sense:
I sin not to my grief alone,
But to my God's too; he doth groan.

O take thy lute, and tune it to a strain,
Which may with thee
All day complain.
There can no discord but in ceasing be.
Marbles can weep; and surely strings
More bowels have, than such hard things.

Lord, I adjudge myself to tears and grief,
Ev'n endless tears
Without relief.
If a clear spring for me no time forbears,
But runs, although I be not dry;
I am no Crystal, what shall I?

Yet if I wail not still, since still to wail
Nature denies;
And flesh would fail,
If my deserts were masters of mine eyes:
Lord, pardon, for thy son makes good
My want of tears with store of blood.

The Family

What doth this noise of thoughts within my heart
As if they had a part?
What do these loud complaints and puling fears,
As if there were no rule or ears?

But, Lord, the house and family are thine,
Though some of them repine.
Turn out these wranglers, which defile thy seat:
For where thou dwellest all is neat.

First Peace and Silence all disputes control,
Then Order plays the soul;
And giving all things their set forms and hours,
Makes of wild woods sweet walks and bowers.

Humble Obedience near the door doth stand,
Expecting a command:
Than whom in waiting nothing seems more slow,
Nothing more quick when she doth go.

Joys oft are there, and griefs as oft as joys;
But griefs without a noise:
Yet speak they louder, than distempered fears.
What is so shrill as silent tears?

This is thy house, with these it doth abound:
And where these are not found,
Perhaps thou com'st sometimes, and for a day;
But not to make a constant stay.

The Size

Content thee, greedy heart.
Modest and moderate joys to those, that have
Title to more hereafter when they part,
Are passing brave.
Let th' upper springs into the low
Descend and fall, and thou dost flow.

What though some have a fraught
Of cloves and nutmegs, and in cinnamon sail;
If thou hast wherewithal to spice a draught,
When griefs prevail;
And for the future time art heir
To th' Isle of spices? Is't not fair?

To be in both worlds full
Is more than God was, who was hungry here.
Wouldst thou his laws of fasting disannul?
Enact good cheer?
Lay out thy joy, yet hope to save it?
Wouldst thou both eat thy cake, and have it?

Great joys are all at once;
But little do reserve themselves for more:
Those have their hopes; these what they have renounce,
And live on score:
Those are at home; these journey still,
And meet the rest on Sion's hill.

Thy Saviour sentenced joy,
And in the flesh condemned it as unfit,
At least in lump: for such doth oft destroy;
Whereas a bit
Doth 'tice us on to hopes of more,
And for the present health restore.

A Christian's state and case
Is not a corpulent, but a thin and spare,
Yet active strength: whose long and bony face
Content and care
Do seem to equally divide,
Like a pretender, not a bride.

Wherefore sit down, good heart;
Grasp not at much, for fear thou losest all.
If comforts fell according to desert,
They would great frosts and snows destroy:
For we should count, since the last joy.

Then close again the seam,
Which thou hast opened: do not spread thy robe
In hope of great things. Call to mind thy dream,
An earthly globe,
On whose meridian was engraven,
These seas are tears, and heav'n the haven.

Artillery

As I one ev'ning sat before my cell,
Methoughts a star did shoot into my lap.
I rose, and shook my clothes, as knowing well,
That from small fires comes oft no small mishap.
When suddenly I heard one say,
Do as thou usest, disobey,
Expel good motions from thy breast,
Which have the face of fire, but end in rest.

I, who had heard of music in the spheres,
But not of speech in stars, began to muse:
But turning to my God, whose ministers
The stars and all things are; If I refuse,
Dread Lord, said I, so oft my good;
Then I refuse not ev'n with blood

To wash away my stubborn thought:
For I will do, or suffer what I ought.

But I have also stars and shooters too,
Born where thy servants both artilleries use.
My tears and prayers night and day do woo,
And work up to thee; yet thou dost refuse.
Not but I am (I must say still)
Much more obliged to do thy will,
Than thou to grant mine: but because
Thy promise now hath ev'n set thee thy laws.

Then we are shooters both, and thou dost deign
To enter combat with us, and contest
With thine own clay. But I would parley fain:
Shun not my arrows, and behold my breast.
Yet if thou shunnest, I am thine:
I must be so, if I am mine.
There is no articling with thee:
I am but finite, yet thine infinitely.

Church-Rents and Schisms

Brave rose, (alas!) where art thou? in the chair
Where thou didst lately so triumph and shine,
A worm doth sit, whose many feet and hair
Are the more foul, the more thou wert divine.
This, this hath done it, this did bite the root
And bottom of the leaves: which when the wind
Did once perceive, it blew them under foot,
Where rude unhallowed steps do crush and grind
Their beauteous glories. Only shreds of thee,
And those all bitten, in thy chair I see.

Why doth my Mother blush? is she the rose,
And shows it so? Indeed Christ's precious blood
Gave you a colour once; which when your foes

Thought to let out, the bleeding did you good,
And made you look much fresher than before.
But when debates and fretting jealousies
Did worm and work within you more and more,
Your colour faded, and calamities
    Turned your ruddy into pale and bleak:
    Your health and beauty both began to break.

Then did your sev'ral parts unloose and start:
Which when your neighbours saw, like a north-wind,
They rushed in, and cast them in the dirt
Where Pagans tread. O Mother dear and kind,
Where shall I get me eyes enough to weep,
As many eyes as stars? since it is night,
And much of Asia and Europe fast asleep,
And ev'n all Afric'; would at least I might
    With these two poor ones lick up all the dew,
    Which falls by night, and pour it out for you!

Justice (2)

O dreadful Justice, what a fright and terror
            Wast thou of old,
            When sin and error
        Did show and shape thy looks to me,
        And through their glass discolour thee!
He that did but look up, was proud and bold.

The dishes of thy balance seemed to gape,
            Like two great pits;
            The beam and scape
        Did like some tort'ring engine show:
        Thy hand above did burn and glow,
Daunting the stoutest hearts, the proudest wits.

But now that Christ's pure veil presents the sight,
            I see no fears:

Thy hand is white,
Thy scales like buckets, which attend
And interchangeably descend,
Lifting to heaven from this well of tears.

For where before thou still didst call on me,
Now I still touch
And harp on thee.
God's promises have made thee mine;
Why should I justice now decline?
Against me there is none, but for me much.

The Pilgrimage

I travelled on, seeing the hill, where lay
My expectation.
A long it was and weary way.
The gloomy cave of Desperation
I left on th' one, and on the other side
The rock of Pride.

And so I came to Fancy's meadow strowed
With many a flower:
Fain would I here have made abode,
But I was quickened by my hour.
So to Care's copse I came, and there got through
With much ado.

That led me to the wild of Passion, which
Some call the wold;
A wasted place, but sometimes rich.
Here I was robbed of all my gold,
Save one good Angel, which a friend had tied
Close to my side.

At length I got unto the gladsome hill,
Where lay my hope,
Where lay my heart; and climbing still,

When I had gained the brow and top,
A lake of brackish waters on the ground
Was all I found.

With that abashed and struck with many a sting
Of swarming fears,
I fell, and cried, Alas my King;
Can both the way and end be tears?
Yet taking heart I rose, and then perceived
I was deceived:

My hill was further: so I flung away,
Yet heard a cry
Just as I went, *None goes that way*
And lives: If that be all, said I,
After so foul a journey death is fair,
And but a chair.

The Holdfast

I threat'ned to observe the strict decree
Of my dear God with all my power and might.
But I was told by one, it could not be;
Yet I might trust in God to be my light.
Then will I trust, said I, in him alone.
Nay, ev'n to trust in him, was also his:
We must confess, that nothing is our own.
Then I confess that he my succour is:
But to have nought is ours, not to confess
That we have nought. I stood amazed at this,
Much troubled, till I heard a friend express,
That all things were more ours by being his.
What Adam had, and forfeited for all,
Christ keepeth now, who cannot fail or fall.

Complaining

Do not beguile my heart,
Because thou art
My power and wisdom. Put me not to shame,
Because I am
Thy clay that weeps, thy dust that calls.

Thou art the Lord of glory;
The deed and story
Are both thy due: but I a silly fly,
That live or die
According as the weather falls.

Art thou all justice, Lord?
Shows not thy word
More attributes? Am I all throat or eye,
To weep or cry?
Have I no parts but those of grief?

Let not thy wrathful power
Afflict my hour,
My inch of life: or let thy gracious power
Contract my hour,
That I may climb and find relief.

The Discharge

Busy inquiring heart, what wouldst thou know?
Why dost thou pry,
And turn, and leer, and with a licorous eye
Look high and low;
And in thy lookings stretch and grow?

Hast thou not made thy counts, and summed up all?
Did not thy heart
Give up the whole, and with the whole depart?
Let what will fall:
That which is past who can recall?

Thy life is God's, thy time to come is gone,
And is his right.
He is thy night at noon: he is at night
Thy noon alone.
The crop is his, for he hath sown.

And well it was for thee, when this befell,
That God did make
Thy business his, and in thy life partake:
For thou canst tell,
If it be his once, all is well.

Only the present is thy part and fee.
And happy thou,
If, though thou didst not beat thy future brow,
Thou couldst well see
What present things required of thee.

They ask enough; why shouldst thou further go?
Raise not the mud
Of future depths, but drink the clear and good.
Dig not for woe
In times to come; for it will grow.

Man and the present fit: if he provide,
He breaks the square.
This hour is mine: if for the next I care,
I grow too wide,
And do encroach upon death's side.

For death each hour environs and surrounds.
He that would know
And care for future chances, cannot go
Unto those grounds,
But through a churchyard which them bounds.

Things present shrink and die: but they that spend
Their thoughts and sense
On future grief, do not remove it thence,
But it extend,
And draw the bottom out an end.

God chains the dog till night; wilt loose the chain,
And wake thy sorrow?
Wilt thou forestall it, and now grieve tomorrow
And then again
Grieve over freshly all thy pain?

Either grief will not come: or if it must,
Do not forecast.
And while it cometh, it is almost past.
Away distrust:
My God hath promised, he is just.

Praise (2)

King of Glory, King of Peace,
I will love thee;
And that love may never cease,
I will move thee.

Thou hast granted my request,
Thou hast heard me:
Thou didst note my working breast,
Thou hast spared me.

Wherefore with my utmost art
I will sing thee,
And the cream of all my heart
I will bring thee.

Though my sins against me cried,
Thou didst clear me;
And alone, when they replied,
Thou didst hear me.

Sev'n whole days, not one in seven,
I will praise thee.
In my heart, though not in heaven,
I can raise thee.

Thou grew'st soft and moist with tears,
Thou relentedst:
And when Justice called for fears,
Thou dissentedst.

Small it is, in this poor sort
To enrol thee:
Ev'n eternity is too short
To extol thee.

An Offering

Come, bring thy gift. If blessings were as slow
As men's returns, what would become of fools?
What hast thou there? a heart? but is it pure?
Search well and see; for hearts have many holes.
Yet one pure heart is nothing to bestow:
In Christ two natures met to be thy cure.

O that within us hearts had propagation,
Since many gifts do challenge many hearts!
Yet one, if good, may title to a number;
And single things grow fruitful by deserts.
In public judgements one may be a nation,
And fence a plague, while others sleep and slumber.

But all I fear is lest thy heart displease,
As neither good, nor one: so oft divisions
Thy lusts have made, and not thy lusts alone;
Thy passions also have their set partitions.
These parcel out thy heart: recover these,
And thou mayst offer many gifts in one.

There is a balsam, or indeed a blood,
Dropping from heav'n, which doth both cleanse and close
All sorts of wounds; of such strange force it is.
Seek out this All-heal, and seek no repose,
Until thou find and use it to thy good:
Then bring thy gift, and let thy hymn be this;

Since my sadness
Into gladness
Lord thou dost convert,
O accept
What thou hast kept,
As thy due desert.

Had I many,
Had I any,
(For this heart is none)
All were thine
And none of mine:
Surely thine alone.

Yet thy favour
May give savour
To this poor oblation;
And it raise
To be thy praise,
And be my salvation.

Longing

With sick and famished eyes,
With doubling knees and weary bones,
To thee my cries,
To thee my groans,
To thee my sighs, my tears ascend:
No end?

My throat, my soul is hoarse;
My heart is withered like a ground

Which thou dost curse.
My thoughts turn round,
And make me giddy; Lord, I fall,
Yet call.

From thee all pity flows.
Mothers are kind, because thou art,
And dost dispose
To them a part:
Their infants, them; and they suck thee
More free.

Bowels of pity, hear!
Lord of my soul, love of my mind,
Bow down thine ear!
Let not the wind
Scatter my words, and in the same
Thy name!

Look on my sorrows round!
Mark well my furnace! O what flames,
What heats abound!
What griefs, what shames!
Consider, Lord; Lord, bow thine ear,
And hear!

Lord Jesu, thou didst bow
Thy dying head upon the tree:
O be not now
More dead to me!
Lord hear, *Shall he that made the ear*
Not hear?

Behold, thy dust doth stir,
It moves, it creeps, it aims at thee:
Wilt thou defer
To succour me,
Thy pile of dust, wherein each crumb
Says, Come?

To thee help appertains.
Hast thou left all things to their course,
And laid the reins
Upon the horse?
Is all locked? hath a sinner's plea
No key?

Indeed the world's thy book,
Where all things have their leaf assigned:
Yet a meek look
Hath interlined.
Thy board is full, yet humble guests
Find nests.

Thou tarriest, while I die,
And fall to nothing: thou dost reign,
And rule on high,
While I remain
In bitter grief: yet am I styled
Thy child.

Lord, didst thou leave thy throne,
Not to relieve? how can it be,
That thou art grown
Thus hard to me?
Were sin alive, good cause there were
To bear.

But now both sin is dead,
And all thy promises live and bide.
That wants his head;
These speak and chide,
And in thy bosom pour my tears,
As theirs.

Lord JESU, hear my heart,
Which hath been broken now so long,
That ev'ry part
Hath got a tongue!

Thy beggars grow; rid them away
To day.

My love, my sweetness, hear!
By these thy feet, at which my heart
Lies all the year,
Pluck out thy dart,
And heal my troubled breast which cries,
Which dies.

The Bag

Away despair; my gracious Lord doth hear.
Though winds and waves assault my keel,
He doth preserve it: he doth steer,
Ev'n when the boat seems most to reel.
Storms are the triumph of his art:
Well may he close his eyes, but not his heart.

Hast thou not heard, that my Lord JESUS died?
Then let me tell thee a strange story.
The God of power, as he did ride
In his majestic robes of glory,
Resolved to light; and so one day
He did descend, undressing all the way.

The stars his tire of light and rings obtained,
The cloud his bow, the fire his spear,
The sky his azure mantle gained.
And when they asked, what he would wear;
He smiled and said as he did go,
He had new clothes a-making here below.

When he was come, as travellers are wont,
He did repair unto an inn.
Both then, and after, many a brunt
He did endure to cancel sin:
And having given the rest before,
Here he gave up his life to pay our score.

But as he was returning, there came one
That ran upon him with a spear.
He, who came hither all alone,
Bringing nor man, nor arms, nor fear,
Received the blow upon his side,
And straight he turned, and to his brethren cried,

If ye have any thing to send or write,
(I have no bag, but here is room)
Unto my father's hands and sight
(Believe me) it shall safely come.
That I shall mind, what you impart;
Look, you may put it very near my heart.

Or if hereafter any of my friends
Will use me in this kind, the door
Shall still be open; what he sends
I will present, and somewhat more,
Not to his hurt. Sighs will convey
Any thing to me. Hark despair, away.

The Jews

Poor nation, whose sweet sap, and juice
Our scions have purloined, and left you dry:
Whose streams we got by the Apostles' sluice,
And use in baptism, while ye pine and die:
Who by not keeping once, became a debtor;
And now by keeping lose the letter:

O that my prayers! mine, alas!
O that some Angel might a trumpet sound;
At which the Church falling upon her face
Should cry so loud, until the trump were drowned,
And by that cry of her dear Lord obtain,
That your sweet sap might come again!

The Collar

I struck the board, and cried, No more.
I will abroad.
What? shall I ever sigh and pine?
My lines and life are free; free as the road,
Loose as the wind, as large as store.
Shall I be still in suit?
Have I no harvest but a thorn
To let me blood, and not restore
What I have lost with cordial fruit?
Sure there was wine
Before my sighs did dry it: there was corn
Before my tears did drown it.
Is the year only lost to me?
Have I no bays to crown it?
No flowers, no garlands gay? All blasted?
All wasted?
Not so, my heart: but there is fruit,
And thou hast hands.
Recover all thy sigh-blown age
On double pleasures: leave thy cold dispute
Of what is fit, and not. Forsake thy cage,
Thy rope of sands,
Which petty thoughts have made, and made to thee
Good cable, to enforce and draw,
And be thy law,
While thou didst wink and wouldst not see.
Away; take heed:
I will abroad.
Call in thy death's head there: tie up thy fears.
He that forbears
To suit and serve his need,

Deserves his load.
But as I raved and grew more fierce and wild
At every word,
Me thoughts I heard one calling, *Child:*
And I replied, *My Lord.*

The Glimpse

Whither away delight?
Thou cam'st but now; wilt thou so soon depart,
And give me up to night?
For many weeks of ling'ring pain and smart
But one half hour of comfort for my heart?

Methinks delight should have
More skill in music, and keep better time.
Wert thou a wind or wave,
They quickly go and come with lesser crime:
Flowers look about, and die not in their prime.

Thy short abode and stay
Feeds not, but adds to the desire of meat.
Lime begged of old (they say)
A neighbour spring to cool his inward heat;
Which by the spring's access grew much more great.

In hope of thee my heart
Picked here and there a crumb, and would not die;
But constant to his part
Whenas my fears foretold this, did reply,
A slender thread a gentle guest will tie.

Yet if the heart that wept
Must let thee go, return when it doth knock.
Although thy heap be kept
For future times, the droppings of the stock
May oft break forth, and never break the lock.

If I have more to spin,
The wheel shall go, so that thy stay be short.
Thou knowst how grief and sin
Disturb the work. O make me not their sport,
Who by thy coming may be made a court!

Assurance

O spiteful bitter thought!
Bitterly spiteful thought! Couldst thou invent
So high a torture? Is such poison bought?
Doubtless, but in the way of punishment,
When wit contrives to meet with thee,
No such rank poison can there be.

Thou said'st but even now,
That all was not so fair, as I conceived,
Betwixt my God and me; that I allow
And coin large hopes; but, that I was deceived:
Either the league was broke, or near it;
And, that I had great cause to fear it.

And what to this? what more
Could poison, if it had a tongue, express?
What is thy aim? wouldst thou unlock the door
To cold despairs, and gnawing pensiveness?
Wouldst thou raise devils? I see, I know,
I writ thy purpose long ago.

But I will to my Father,
Who heard thee say it. O most gracious Lord,
If all the hope and comfort that I gather,
Were from myself, I had not half a word,
Not half a letter to oppose
What is objected by my foes.

But thou art my desert:
And in this league, which now my foes invade,
Thou art not only to perform thy part,

But also mine; as when the league was made
Thou didst at once thyself indite,
And hold my hand, while I did write.

Wherefore if thou canst fail,
Then can thy truth and I: but while rocks stand,
And rivers stir, thou canst not shrink or quail:
Yea, when both rocks and all things shall disband,
Then shalt thou be my rock and tower,
And make their ruin praise thy power.

Now foolish thought go on,
Spin out thy thread, and make thereof a coat
To hide thy shame: for thou hast cast a bone
Which bounds on thee, and will not down thy throat:
What for itself love once began,
Now love and truth will end in man.

The Call

Come, my Way, my Truth, my Life:
Such a Way, as gives us breath:
Such a Truth, as ends all strife:
And such a Life, as killeth death.

Come, my Light, my Feast, my Strength:
Such a Light, as shows a feast:
Such a Feast, as mends in length:
Such a Strength, as makes his guest.

Come, my Joy, my Love, my Heart:
Such a Joy, as none can move:
Such a Love, as none can part:
Such a Heart, as joys in love.

Clasping of Hands

Lord, thou art mine, and I am thine,
If mine I am: and thine much more,

Than I or ought, or can be mine.
Yet to be thine, doth me restore;
So that again I now am mine,
And with advantage mine the more,
Since this being mine, brings with it thine,
And thou with me dost thee restore.
If I without thee would be mine,
I neither should be mine nor thine.

Lord, I am thine, and thou art mine:
So mine thou art, that something more
I may presume thee mine, than thine.
For thou didst suffer to restore
Not thee, but me, and to be mine:
And with advantage mine the more,
Since thou in death wast none of thine,
Yet then as mine didst me restore.
O be mine still! still make me thine!
Or rather make no Thine and Mine!

Praise (3)

Lord, I will mean and speak thy praise,
Thy praise alone.
My busy heart shall spin it all my days:
And when it stops for want of store,
Then will I wring it with a sigh or groan,
That thou mayst yet have more.

When thou dost favour any action,
It runs, it flies:
All things concur to give it a perfection.
That which had but two legs before,
When thou dost bless, hath twelve: one wheel doth rise
To twenty then, or more.

But when thou dost on business blow,
It hangs, it clogs:

Not all the teams of Albion in a row
Can hail or draw it out of door.
Legs are but stumps, and Pharaoh's wheels but logs,
And struggling hinders more.

Thousands of things do thee employ
In ruling all
This spacious globe: Angels must have their joy,
Devils their rod, the sea his shore,
The winds their stint: and yet when I did call,
Thou heardst my call, and more.

I have not lost one single tear:
But when mine eyes
Did weep to heav'n, they found a bottle there
(As we have boxes for the poor)
Ready to take them in; yet of a size
That would contain much more.

But after thou hadst slipped a drop
From thy right eye,
(Which there did hang like streamers near the top
Of some fair church, to show the sore
And bloody battle which thou once didst try)
The glass was full and more.

Wherefore I sing. Yet since my heart,
Though pressed, runs thin;
O that I might some other hearts convert,
And so take up at use good store:
That to thy chests there might be coming in
Both all my praise, and more!

Joseph's Coat

Wounded I sing, tormented I indite,
Thrown down I fall into a bed, and rest:
Sorrow hath changed its note: such is his will,

Who changeth all things, as him pleaseth best.
  For well he knows, if but one grief and smart
Among my many had his full career,
Sure it would carry with it ev'n my heart,
And both would run until they found a bier
  To fetch the body; both being due to grief.
But he hath spoiled the race; and giv'n to anguish
One of Joy's coats, 'ticing it with relief
To linger in me, and together languish.
  I live to show his power, who once did bring
  My *joys* to *weep*, and now my *griefs* to *sing*.

The Pulley

  When God at first made man,
Having a glass of blessings standing by,
Let us (said he) pour on him all we can:
Let the world's riches, which dispersed lie,
  Contract into a span.

  So strength first made a way;
Then beauty flowed, then wisdom, honour, pleasure:
When almost all was out, God made a stay,
Perceiving that alone of all his treasure
  Rest in the bottom lay.

  For if I should (said he)
Bestow this jewel also on my creature,
He would adore my gifts instead of me,
And rest in Nature, not the God of Nature:
  So both should losers be.

  Yet let him keep the rest,
But keep them with repining restlessness:
Let him be rich and weary, that at least,
If goodness lead him not, yet weariness
  May toss him to my breast.

The Priesthood

Blest Order, which in power dost so excel,
That with th' one hand thou liftest to the sky,
And with the other throwest down to hell
In thy just censures; fain would I draw nigh,
Fain put thee on, exchanging my lay-sword
For that of th' holy Word.

But thou art fire, sacred and hallowed fire;
And I but earth and clay: should I presume
To wear thy habit, the severe attire
My slender compositions might consume.
I am both foul and brittle; much unfit
To deal in holy Writ.

Yet have I often seen, by cunning hand
And force of fire, what curious things are made
Of wretched earth. Where once I scorned to stand,
That earth is fitted by the fire and trade
Of skilful artists, for the boards of those
Who make the bravest shows.

But since those great ones, be they ne'er so great,
Come from the earth, from whence those vessels come;
So that at once both feeder, dish, and meat
Have one beginning and one final sum:
I do not greatly wonder at the sight,
If earth in earth delight.

But th' holy men of God such vessels are,
As serve him up, who all the world commands:
When God vouchsafeth to become our fare,
Their hands convey him, who conveys their hands.
O what pure things, most pure must those things be,
Who bring my God to me!

Wherefore I dare not, I, put forth my hand
To hold the Ark, although it seem to shake
Through th' old sins and new doctrines of our land.
Only, since God doth often vessels make
Of lowly matter for high uses meet,
I throw me at his feet.

There will I lie, until my Maker seek
For some mean stuff whereon to show his skill:
Then is my time. The distance of the meek
Doth flatter power. Lest good come short of ill
In praising might, the poor do by submission
What pride by opposition.

The Search

Whither, O, whither art thou fled,
My Lord, my Love?
My searches are my daily bread;
Yet never prove.

My knees pierce th' earth, mine eyes the sky;
And yet the sphere
And centre both to me deny
That thou art there.

Yet can I mark how herbs below
Grow green and gay,
As if to meet thee they did know,
While I decay.

Yet can I mark how stars above
Simper and shine,
As having keys unto thy love,
While poor I pine.

I sent a sigh to seek thee out,
Deep drawn in pain,

Winged like an arrow: but my scout
Returns in vain.

I turned another (having store)
Into a groan;
Because the search was dumb before:
But all was one.

Lord, dost thou some new fabric mould,
Which favour wins,
And keeps thee present, leaving th' old
Unto their sins?

Where is my God? what hidden place
Conceals thee still?
What covert dare eclipse thy face?
Is it thy will?

O let not that of anything;
Let rather brass,
Or steel, or mountains be thy ring,
And I will pass.

Thy will such an entrenching is,
As passeth thought:
To it all strength, all subtilties
Are things of nought.

Thy will such a strange distance is,
As that to it
East and West touch, the poles do kiss,
And parallels meet.

Since then my grief must be as large,
As is thy space,
Thy distance from me; see my charge,
Lord, see my case.

O take these bars, these lengths away;
Turn, and restore me:

Be not Almighty, let me say,
Against, but for me.

When thou dost turn, and wilt be near;
What edge so keen,
What point so piercing can appear
To come between?

For as thy absence doth excel
All distance known:
So doth thy nearness bear the bell,
Making two one.

Grief

O who will give me tears? Come all ye springs,
Dwell in my head and eyes: come clouds, and rain:
My grief hath need of all the wat'ry things,
That nature hath produced. Let ev'ry vein
Suck up a river to supply mine eyes,
My weary weeping eyes too dry for me,
Unless they get new conduits, new supplies
To bear them out, and with my state agree.
What are two shallow fords, two little spouts
Of a less world? the greater is but small,
A narrow cupboard for my griefs and doubts,
Which want provision in the midst of all.
Verses, ye are too fine a thing, too wise
For my rough sorrows: cease, be dumb and mute,
Give up your feet and running to mine eyes,
And keep your measures for some lover's lute,
Whose grief allows him music and a rhyme:
For mine excludes both measure, tune, and time.
Alas, my God!

The Cross

What is this strange and uncouth thing?
To make me sigh, and seek, and faint, and die,

Until I had some place, where I might sing,
And serve thee; and not only I,
But all my wealth, and family might combine
To set thy honour up, as our design.

And then when after much delay,
Much wrestling, many a combat, this dear end,
So much desired, is giv'n, to take away
My power to serve thee; to unbend
All my abilities, my designs confound,
And lay my threat'nings bleeding on the ground.

One ague dwelleth in my bones,
Another in my soul (the memory
What I would do for thee, if once my groans
Could be allowed for harmony):
I am in all a weak disabled thing,
Save in the sight thereof, where strength doth sting.

Besides, things sort not to my will,
Ev'n when my will doth study thy renown:
Thou turnest th' edge of all things on me still,
Taking me up to throw me down:
So that, ev'n when my hopes seem to be sped,
I am to grief alive, to them as dead.

To have my aim, and yet to be
Farther from it than when I bent my bow;
To make my hopes my torture, and the fee
Of all my woes another woe,
Is in the midst of delicates to need,
And ev'n in Paradise to be a weed.

Ah my dear Father, ease my smart!
These contrarieties crush me: these cross actions
Do wind a rope about, and cut my heart:
And yet since these thy contradictions
Are properly a cross felt by thy Son,
With but four words, my words, *Thy will be done.*

The Flower

How fresh, O Lord, how sweet and clean
Are thy returns! ev'n as the flowers in spring;
To which, besides their own demean,
The late-past frosts tributes of pleasure bring.
Grief melts away
Like snow in May,
As if there were no such cold thing.

Who would have thought my shrivelled heart
Could have recovered greenness? It was gone
Quite underground; as flowers depart
To see their mother-root, when they have blown;
Where they together
All the hard weather,
Dead to the world, keep house unknown.

These are thy wonders, Lord of power,
Killing and quick'ning, bringing down to hell
And up to heaven in an hour;
Making a chiming of a passing-bell.
We say amiss,
This or that is:
Thy word is all, if we could spell.

O that I once past changing were,
Fast in thy Paradise, where no flower can wither!
Many a spring I shoot up fair,
Off'ring at heav'n, growing and groaning thither:
Nor doth my flower
Want a spring-shower,
My sins and I joining together:

But while I grow in a straight line,
Still upwards bent, as if heav'n were mine own,
Thy anger comes, and I decline:
What frost to that? what pole is not the zone,

Where all things burn,
When thou dost turn,
And the least frown of thine is shown?

And now in age I bud again,
After so many deaths I live and write;
I once more smell the dew and rain,
And relish versing: O my only light,
It cannot be
That I am he
On whom thy tempests fell all night.

These are thy wonders, Lord of love,
To make us see we are but flowers that glide:
Which when we once can find and prove,
Thou hast a garden for us, where to bide.
Who would be more,
Swelling through store,
Forfeit their Paradise by their pride.

Dotage

False glozing pleasures, casks of happiness,
Foolish night-fires, women's and children's wishes,
Chases in arras, gilded emptiness,
Shadows well mounted, dreams in a career,
Embroidered lies, nothing between two dishes;
These are the pleasures here.

True earnest sorrows, rooted miseries,
Anguish in grain, vexations ripe and blown,
Sure-footed griefs, solid calamities,
Plain demonstrations, evident and clear,
Fetching their proofs ev'n from the very bone;
These are the sorrows here.

But O the folly of distracted men,
Who griefs in earnest, joys in jest pursue;

Preferring, like brute beasts, a loathsome den
Before a court, ev'n that above so clear,
Where are no sorrows, but delights more true,
Than miseries are here!

The Son

Let foreign nations of their language boast,
What fine variety each tongue affords:
I like our language, as our men and coast:
Who cannot dress it well, want wit, not words.
How neatly do we give one only name
To parents' issue and the sun's bright star!
A son is light and fruit; a fruitful flame
Chasing the father's dimness, carried far
From the first man in th' East, to fresh and new
Western discov'ries of posterity.
So in one word our Lord's humility
We turn upon him in a sense most true:
For what Christ once in humbleness began,
We him in glory call, *The Son of Man.*

A True Hymn

My joy, my life, my crown!
My heart was meaning all the day,
Somewhat it fain would say:
And still it runneth mutt'ring up and down
With only this, *My joy, my life, my crown.*

Yet slight not these few words:
If truly said, they may take part
Among the best in art.
The fineness which a hymn or psalm affords,
Is, when the soul unto the lines accords.

He who craves all the mind,
And all the soul, and strength, and time,
If the words only rhyme,
Justly complains, that somewhat is behind
To make his verse, or write a hymn in kind.

Whereas if th' heart be moved,
Although the verse be somewhat scant,
God doth supply the want.
As when th' heart says (sighing to be approved)
O, *could I love!* and stops: God writeth, *Loved*.

The Answer

My comforts drop and melt away like snow:
I shake my head, and all the thoughts and ends,
Which my fierce youth did bandy, fall and flow
Like leaves about me: or like summer friends,
Flies of estates and sunshine. But to all,
Who think me eager, hot, and undertaking,
But in my prosecutions slack and small;
As a young exhalation, newly waking,
Scorns his first bed of dirt, and means the sky;
But cooling by the way, grows pursy and slow,
And settling to a cloud, doth live and die
In that dark state of tears: to all, that so
Show me, and set me, I have one reply,
Which they that know the rest, know more than I.

A Dialogue-Anthem

Christian. Death.

Christian Alas, poor Death, where is thy glory?
Where is thy famous force, thy ancient sting?

Death *Alas poor mortal, void of story,*
Go spell and read how I have killed thy King.
Christian Poor Death! and who was hurt thereby?
Thy curse being laid on him, makes thee accurst.
Death *Let losers talk: yet thou shalt die;*
These arms shall crush thee.
Christian Spare not, do thy worst.
I shall be one day better than before:
Thou so much worse, that thou shalt be no more.

The Water-Course

Thou who dost dwell and linger here below,
Since the condition of this world is frail,
Where of all plants afflictions soonest grow;
If troubles overtake thee, do not wail:
For who can look for less, that loveth { Life, / Strife.

But rather turn the pipe, and water's course
To serve thy sins, and furnish thee with store
Of sov'reign tears, springing from true remorse:
That so in pureness thou mayst him adore,
Who gives to man, as he sees fit { Salvation. / Damnation.

Self-Condemnation

Thou who condemnest Jewish hate,
For choosing Barabbas a murderer
Before the Lord of Glory;
Look back upon thine own estate,
Call home thine eye (that busy wanderer)
That choice may be thy story.

He that doth love, and love amiss
This world's delights before true Christian joy,
Hath made a Jewish choice:
The world an ancient murderer is;
Thousands of souls it hath and doth destroy
With her enchanting voice.

He that hath made a sorry wedding
Between his soul and gold, and hath preferred
False gain before the true,
Hath done what he condemns in reading:
For he hath sold for money his dear Lord,
And is a Judas-Jew.

Thus we prevent the last great day,
And judge our selves. That light, which sin and passion
Did before dim and choke,
When once those snuffs are ta'en away,
Shines bright and clear, ev'n unto condemnation,
Without excuse or cloak.

Bitter-Sweet

Ah my dear angry Lord,
Since thou dost love, yet strike;
Cast down, yet help afford;
Sure I will do the like.

I will complain, yet praise;
I will bewail, approve:
And all my sour-sweet days
I will lament, and love.

The Glance

When first thy sweet and gracious eye
Vouchsafed ev'n in the midst of youth and night

To look upon me, who before did lie
Welt'ring in sin;
I felt a sug'red strange delight,
Passing all cordials made by any art,
Bedew, embalm, and overrun my heart,
And take it in.

Since that time many a bitter storm
My soul hath felt, ev'n able to destroy,
Had the malicious and ill-meaning harm
His swing and sway:
But still thy sweet original joy
Sprung from thine eye, did work within my soul,
And surging griefs, when they grew bold, control,
And got the day.

If thy first glance so powerful be,
A mirth but opened and sealed up again;
What wonders shall we feel, when we shall see
Thy full-eyed love!
When thou shalt look us out of pain,
And one aspect of thine spend in delight
More than a thousand suns disburse in light,
In heav'n above.

The Twenty-third Psalm

The God of love my shepherd is,
And he that doth me feed:
While he is mine, and I am his,
What can I want or need?

He leads me to the tender grass,
Where I both feed and rest;
Then to the streams that gently pass:
In both I have the best.

Or if I stray, he doth convert
    And bring my mind in frame:
And all this not for my desert,
    But for his holy name.

Yea, in death's shady black abode
    Well may I walk, not fear:
For thou art with me; and thy rod
    To guide, thy staff to bear.

Nay, thou dost make me sit and dine,
    Ev'n in my enemies' sight:
My head with oil, my cup with wine
    Runs over day and night.

Surely thy sweet and wondrous love
    Shall measure all my days;
And as it never shall remove,
    So neither shall my praise.

Mary Magdalene

When blessed Mary wiped her Saviour's feet,
(Whose precepts she had trampled on before)
And wore them for a jewel on her head,
    Showing his steps should be the street,
    Wherein she thenceforth evermore
With pensive humbleness would live and tread:

She being stained herself, why did she strive
To make him clean, who could not be defiled?
Why kept she not her tears for her own faults,
    And not his feet? Though we could dive
    In tears like seas, our sins are piled
Deeper than they, in words, and works, and thoughts.

Dear soul, she knew who did vouchsafe and deign
To bear her filth; and that her sins did dash
Ev'n God himself: wherefore she was not loth,

As she had brought wherewith to stain,
So to bring in wherewith to wash:
And yet in washing one, she washed both.

Aaron

Holiness on the head,
Light and perfections on the breast,
Harmonious bells below, raising the dead
To lead them unto life and rest.
Thus are true Aarons dressed.

Profaneness in my head,
Defects and darkness in my breast,
A noise of passions ringing me for dead
Unto a place where is no rest.
Poor priest thus am I dressed.

Only another head
I have, another heart and breast,
Another music, making live not dead,
Without whom I could have no rest:
In him I am well dressed.

Christ is my only head,
My alone only heart and breast,
My only music, striking me ev'n dead;
That to the old man I may rest,
And be in him new dressed.

So holy in my head,
Perfect and light in my dear breast,
My doctrine tuned by Christ (who is not dead,
But lives in me while I do rest),
Come people; Aaron's dressed.

The Odour. 2 Corinthians 2

How sweetly doth *My Master* sound! *My Master*!
As Ambergris leaves a rich scent
Unto the taster:
So do these words a sweet content,
An oriental fragrancy, *My Master*.

With these all day I do perfume my mind,
My mind ev'n thrust into them both:
That I might find
What cordials make this curious broth,
This broth of smells, that feeds and fats my mind.

My Master, shall I speak? O that to thee
My servant were a little so,
As flesh may be;
That these two words might creep and grow
To some degree of spiciness to thee!

Then should the Pomander, which was before
A speaking sweet, mend by reflection,
And tell me more:
For pardon of my imperfection
Would warm and work it sweeter than before.

For when *My Master*, which alone is sweet,
And ev'n in my unworthiness pleasing,
Shall call and meet,
My servant, as thee not displeasing,
That call is but the breathing of the sweet.

This breathing would with gains by sweet'ning me
(As sweet things traffic when they meet)
Return to thee.
And so this new commerce and sweet
Should all my life employ, and busy me.

The Foil

If we could see below
The sphere of virtue, and each shining grace
As plainly as that above doth show;
This were the better sky, the brighter place.

God hath made stars the foil
To set off virtues; griefs to set off sinning:
Yet in this wretched world we toil,
As if grief were not foul, nor virtue winning.

The Forerunners

The harbingers are come. See, see their mark;
White is their colour, and behold my head.
But must they have my brain? must they dispark
Those sparkling notions, which therein were bred?
Must dullness turn me to a clod?
Yet have they left me, *Thou art still my God*.

Good men ye be, to leave me my best room,
Ev'n all my heart, and what is lodged there:
I pass not, I, what of the rest become,
So *Thou art still my God*, be out of fear.
He will be pleased with that ditty;
And if I please him, I write fine and witty.

Farewell sweet phrases, lovely metaphors.
But will ye leave me thus? when ye before
Of stews and brothels only knew the doors,
Then did I wash you with my tears, and more,
Brought you to Church well dressed and clad:
My God must have my best, ev'n all I had.

Lovely enchanting language, sugar-cane,
Honey of roses, whither wilt thou fly?
Hath some fond lover 'ticed thee to thy bane?
And wilt thou leave the Church, and love a sty?
Fie, thou wilt soil thy 'broidered coat,
And hurt thyself, and him that sings the note.

Let foolish lovers, if they will love dung,
With canvas, not with arras clothe their shame:
Let folly speak in her own native tongue.
True beauty dwells on high: ours is a flame
But borrowed thence to light us thither.
Beauty and beauteous words should go together.

Yet if you go, I pass not; take your way:
For, *Thou art still my God*, is all that ye
Perhaps with more embellishment can say.
Go birds of spring: let winter have his fee,
Let a bleak paleness chalk the door,
So all within be livelier than before.

The Rose

Press me not to take more pleasure
In this world of sug'red lies,
And to use a larger measure
Than my strict, yet welcome size.

First, there is no pleasure here:
Coloured griefs indeed there are,
Blushing woes, that look as clear
As if they could beauty spare.

Or if such deceits there be,
Such delights I meant to say;
There are no such things to me,
Who have passed my right away.

But I will not much oppose
Unto what you now advise:
Only take this gentle rose,
And therein my answer lies.

What is fairer than a rose?
What is sweeter? yet it purgeth.
Purgings enmity disclose,
Enmity forbearance urgeth.

If then all that worldlings prize
Be contracted to a rose;
Sweetly there indeed it lies,
But it biteth in the close.

So this flower doth judge and sentence
Worldly joys to be a scourge:
For they all produce repentance,
And repentance is a purge.

But I health, not physic choose:
Only though I you oppose,
Say that fairly I refuse,
For my answer is a rose.

Discipline

Throw away thy rod,
Throw away thy wrath:
O my God,
Take the gentle path.

For my heart's desire
Unto thine is bent:
I aspire
To a full consent.

Not a word or look
I affect to own,

But by book,
And thy book alone.

Though I fail, I weep:
Though I halt in pace,
Yet I creep
To the throne of grace.

Then let wrath remove;
Love will do the deed:
For with love
Stony hearts will bleed.

Love is swift of foot;
Love's a man of war,
And can shoot,
And can hit from far.

Who can scape his bow?
That which wrought on thee,
Brought thee low,
Needs must work on me.

Throw away thy rod;
Though man frailties hath,
Thou art God:
Throw away thy wrath.

The Invitation

Come ye hither all, whose taste
Is your waste;
Save your cost, and mend your fare.
God is here prepared and dressed,
And the feast,
God, in whom all dainties are.

Come ye hither all, whom wine
Doth define,

Naming you not to your good:
Weep what ye have drunk amiss,
And drink this,
Which before ye drink is blood.

Come ye hither all, whom pain
Doth arraign,
Bringing all your sins to sight:
Taste and fear not: God is here
In this cheer,
And on sin doth cast the fright.

Come ye hither all, whom joy
Doth destroy,
While ye graze without your bounds:
Here is joy that drowneth quite
Your delight,
As a flood the lower grounds.

Come ye hither all, whose love
Is your dove,
And exalts you to the sky:
Here is love, which having breath
Ev'n in death,
After death can never die.

Lord I have invited all,
And I shall
Still invite, still call to thee:
For it seems but just and right
In my sight,
Where is all, there all should be.

The Banquet

Welcome sweet and sacred cheer,
Welcome dear;
With me, in me, live and dwell:

For thy neatness passeth sight,
Thy dclight
Passeth tongue to taste or tell.

O what sweetness from the bowl
Fills my soul,
Such as is, and makes divine!
Is some star (fled from the sphere)
Melted there,
As we sugar melt in wine?

Or hath sweetness in the bread
Made a head
To subdue the smell of sin;
Flowers, and gums, and powders giving
All their living,
Lest the enemy should win?

Doubtless, neither star nor flower
Hath the power,
Such a sweetness to impart:
Only God, who gives perfumes,
Flesh assumes,
And with it perfumes my heart.

But as Pomanders and wood
Still are good,
Yet being bruised are better scented:
God, to show how far his love
Could improve,
Here, as broken, is presented.

When I had forgot my birth,
And on earth
In delights of earth was drowned;
God took blood, and needs would be
Spilt with me,
And so found me on the ground.

Having raised me to look up,
In a cup
Sweetly he doth meet my taste.
But I still being low and short,
Far from court,
Wine becomes a wing at last.

For with it alone I fly
To the sky:
Where I wipe mine eyes, and see
What I seek, for what I sue;
Him I view,
Who hath done so much for me.

Let the wonder of this pity
Be my ditty,
And take up my lines and life:
Harken under pain of death,
Hands and breath;
Strive in this, and love the strife.

The Posy

Let wits contest,
And with their words and posies windows fill:
Less than the least
Of all thy mercies, is my posy still.

This on my ring,
This by my picture, in my book I write:
Whether I sing,
Or say, or dictate, this is my delight.

Invention rest,
Comparisons go play, wit use thy will:
Less than the least
Of all God's mercies, is my posy still.

A Parody

Soul's joy, when thou art gone,
And I alone,
Which cannot be,
Because thou dost abide with me,
And I depend on thee;

Yet when thou dost suppress
The cheerfulness
Of thy abode,
And in my powers not stir abroad,
But leave me to my load:

O what a damp and shade
Doth me invade!
No stormy night
Can so afflict or so affright,
As thy eclipsed light.

Ah Lord! do not withdraw,
Lest want of awe
Make Sin appear;
And when thou dost but shine less clear,
Say, that thou art not here.

And then what life I have,
While Sin doth rave,
And falsely boast,
That I may seek, but thou art lost;
Thou and alone thou know'st.

O what a deadly cold
Doth me infold!
I half believe,
That Sin says true: but while I grieve,
Thou com'st and dost relieve.

The Elixir

Teach me, my God and King,
In all things thee to see,
And what I do in anything,
To do it as for thee:

Not rudely, as a beast,
To run into an action;
But still to make thee prepossessed,
And give it his perfection.

A man that looks on glass,
On it may stay his eye;
Or if he pleaseth, through it pass,
And then the heav'n espy.

All may of thee partake:
Nothing can be so mean,
Which with his tincture (for thy sake)
Will not grow bright and clean.

A servant with this clause
Makes drudgery divine:
Who sweeps a room, as for thy laws,
Makes that and th' action fine.

This is the famous stone
That turneth all to gold:
For that which God doth touch and own
Cannot for less be told.

A Wreath

A wreathed garland of deserved praise,
Of praise deserved, unto thee I give,
I give to thee, who knowest all my ways,
My crooked winding ways, wherein I live,

Wherein I die, not live: for life is straight,
Straight as a line, and ever tends to thee,
To thee, who art more far above deceit,
Than deceit seems above simplicity.
Give me simplicity, that I may live,
So live and like, that I may know thy ways,
Know them and practise them: then shall I give
For this poor wreath, give thee a crown of praise.

Death

Death, thou wast once an uncouth hideous thing,
Nothing but bones,
The sad effect of sadder groans:
Thy mouth was open, but thou couldst not sing.

For we considered thee as at some six
Or ten years hence,
After the loss of life and sense,
Flesh being turned to dust, and bones to sticks.

We looked on this side of thee, shooting short;
Where we did find
The shells of fledge souls left behind,
Dry dust, which sheds no tears, but may extort.

But since our Saviour's death did put some blood
Into thy face;
Thou art grown fair and full of grace,
Much in request, much sought for, as a good.

For we do now behold thee gay and glad,
As at doomsday;
When souls shall wear their new array,
And all thy bones with beauty shall be clad.

Therefore we can go die as sleep, and trust
Half that we have
Unto an honest faithful grave;
Making our pillows either down, or dust.

Doomsday

Come away,
Make no delay.
Summon all the dust to rise,
Till it stir, and rub the eyes;
While this member jogs the other,
Each one whisp'ring, *Live you brother?*

Come away,
Make this the day.
Dust, alas, no music feels,
But thy trumpet: then it kneels,
As peculiar notes and strains
Cure Tarantula's raging pains.

Come away,
O make no stay!
Let the graves make their confession,
Lest at length they plead possession:
Flesh's stubbornness may have
Read that lesson to the grave.

Come away,
Thy flock doth stray.
Some to winds their body lend,
And in them may drown a friend:
Some in noisome vapours grow
To a plague and public woe.

Come away,
Help our decay.
Man is out of order hurled,

Parcelled out to all the world.
Lord, thy broken consort raise,
And the music shall be praise.

Judgement

Almighty Judge, how shall poor wretches brook
Thy dreadful look,
Able a heart of iron to appal,
When thou shalt call
For ev'ry man's peculiar book?

What others mean to do, I know not well;
Yet I hear tell,
That some will turn thee to some leaves therein
So void of sin,
That they in merit shall excel.

But I resolve, when thou shalt call for mine,
That to decline,
And thrust a Testament into thy hand:
Let that be scanned.
There thou shalt find my faults are thine.

Heaven

O who will show me those delights on high?
Echo. *I.*
Thou Echo, thou art mortal, all men know.
Echo. *No.*
Wert thou not born among the trees and leaves?
Echo. *Leaves.*
And are there any leaves, that still abide?
Echo. *Bide.*
What leaves are they? impart the matter wholly.
Echo. *Holy.*

Are holy leaves the Echo then of bliss?
Echo. Yes.
Then tell me, what is that supreme delight?
Echo. Light.
Light to the mind: what shall the will enjoy?
Echo. Joy.
But are there cares and business with the pleasure?
Echo. Leisure.
Light, joy, and leisure; but shall they persever?
Echo. Ever.

Love (3)

Love bade me welcome: yet my soul drew back,
Guilty of dust and sin.
But quick-eyed Love, observing me grow slack
From my first entrance in,
Drew nearer to me, sweetly questioning,
If I lacked anything.

A guest, I answered, worthy to be here:
Love said, You shall be he.
I the unkind, ungrateful? Ah my dear,
I cannot look on thee.
Love took my hand, and smiling did reply,
Who made the eyes but I?

Truth Lord, but I have marred them: let my shame
Go where it doth deserve.
And know you not, says Love, who bore the blame?
My dear, then I will serve.
You must sit down, says Love, and taste my meat:
So I did sit and eat.

FINIS.

Glory be to God on high, and on earth peace, good will towards men.

THE CHURCH MILITANT

Almighty Lord, who from thy glorious throne
Seest and rulest all things ev'n as one:
The smallest ant or atom knows thy power,
Known also to each minute of an hour:
Much more do Commonweals acknowledge thee,
And wrap their policies in thy decree,
Complying with thy counsels, doing nought
Which doth not meet with an eternal thought.
But above all, thy Church and Spouse doth prove
Not the decrees of power, but bands of love.
Early didst thou arise to plant this vine,
Which might the more endear it to be thine.
Spices come from the East; so did thy Spouse,
Trim as the light, sweet as the laden boughs
Of Noah's shady vine, chaste as the dove;
Prepared and fitted to receive thy love.
The course was westward, that the sun might light
As well our understanding as our sight.
Where th' Ark did rest, there Abraham began
To bring the other Ark from Canaan.
Moses pursued this; but King Solomon
Finished and fixed the old religion.
When it grew loose, the Jews did hope in vain
By nailing Christ to fasten it again.
But to the Gentiles he bore cross and all,
Rending with earthquakes the partition-wall:
Only whereas the Ark in glory shone,
Now with the cross, as with a staff, alone,
Religion, like a pilgrim, westward bent,
Knocking at all doors, ever as she went.
Yet as the sun, though forward be his flight,

Listens behind him, and allows some light,
Till all depart: so went the Church her way,
Letting, while one foot stepped, the other stay
Among the eastern nations for a time,
Till both removed to the western clime.
To Egypt first she came, where they did prove
Wonders of anger once, but now of love.
The ten Commandments there did flourish more
Than the ten bitter plagues had done before.
Holy Macarius and great Anthony
Made Pharaoh Moses, changing th' history.
Goshen was darkness, Egypt full of lights,
Nilus for monsters brought forth Israelites.
Such power hath mighty Baptism to produce
For things misshapen, things of highest use.
How dear to me, O God, thy counsels are!
Who may with thee compare?
Religion thence fled into Greece, where arts
Gave her the highest place in all men's hearts.
Learning was posed, Philosophy was set,
Sophisters taken in a fisher's net.
Plato and Aristotle were at a loss,
And wheeled about again to spell *Christ-Cross*.
Prayers chased syllogisms into their den,
And *Ergo* was transformed into *Amen*.
Though Greece took horse as soon as Egypt did,
And Rome as both: yet Egypt faster rid,
And spent her period and prefixed time
Before the other. Greece being past her prime,
Religion went to Rome, subduing those,
Who, that they might subdue, made all their foes.
The Warrior his dear scars no more resounds,
But seems to yield Christ hath the greater wounds,
Wounds willingly endured to work his bliss,
Who by an ambush lost his Paradise.
The great heart stoops, and taketh from the dust
A sad repentance, not the spoils of lust:

Quitting his spear, lest it should pierce again
Him in his members, who for him was slain.
The Shepherd's hook grew to a sceptre here,
Giving new names and numbers to the year.
But th' Empire dwelt in Greece, to comfort them
Who were cut short in Alexander's stem.
In both of these Prowess and Arts did tame
And tune men's hearts against the Gospel came:
Which using, and not fearing skill in th' one,
Or strength in th' other, did erect her throne.
Many a rent and struggling th' Empire knew,
(As dying things are wont) until it flew
At length to Germany, still westward bending,
And there the Church's festival attending:
That as before Empire and Arts made way,
(For no less harbingers would serve than they)
So they might still, and point us out the place
Where first the Church should raise her downcast face.
Strength levels grounds, Art makes a garden there;
Then showers Religion, and makes all to bear.
Spain in the Empire shared with Germany,
But England in the higher victory:
Giving the Church a crown to keep her state,
And not go less than she had done of late.
Constantine's British line meant this of old,
And did this mystery wrap up and fold
Within a sheet of paper, which was rent
From time's great Chronicle, and hither sent.
Thus both the Church and Sun together ran
Unto the farthest old meridian.
How dear to me, O God, thy counsels are!
Who may with thee compare?
Much about one and the same time and place,
Both where and when the Church began her race,
Sin did set out of Eastern Babylon,
And travelled westward also: journeying on
He chid the Church away, where'er he came,

Breaking her peace, and tainting her good name.
At first he got to Egypt, and did sow
Gardens of gods, which ev'ry year did grow,
Fresh and fine deities. They were at great cost,
Who for a god clearly a sallet lost.
Ah, what a thing is man devoid of grace,
Adoring garlic with an humble face,
Begging his food of that which he may eat,
Starving the while he worshippeth his meat!
Who makes a root his god, how low is he,
If God and man be severed infinitely!
What wretchedness can give him any room,
Whose house is foul, while he adores his broom?
None will believe this now, though money be
In us the same transplanted foolery.
Thus sin in Egypt sneaked for a while;
His highest was an ox or crocodile,
And such poor game. Thence he to Greece doth pass,
And being craftier much than Goodness was,
He left behind him garrisons of sins
To make good that which ev'ry day he wins.
Here Sin took heart, and for a garden-bed
Rich shrines and oracles he purchased:
He grew a gallant, and would needs foretell
As well what should befall, as what befell.
Nay, he became a poet, and would serve
His pills of sublimate in that conserve.
The world came both with hands and purses full
To this great lottery, and all would pull.
But all was glorious cheating, brave deceit,
Where some poor truths were shuffled for a bait
To credit him, and to discredit those
Who after him should braver truths disclose.
From Greece he went to Rome: and as before
He was a God, now he's an Emperor.
Nero and others lodged him bravely there,
Put him in trust to rule the Roman sphere.

Glory was his chief instrument of old:
Pleasure succeeded straight, when that grew cold.
Which soon was blown to such a mighty flame,
That though our Saviour did destroy the game,
Disparking oracles, and all their treasure,
Setting affliction to encounter pleasure;
Yet did a rogue with hope of carnal joy
Cheat the most subtle nations. Who so coy,
So trim, as Greece and Egypt? yet their hearts
Are given over, for their curious arts,
To such Mahometan stupidities,
As the old heathen would deem prodigies.
How dear to me, O God, thy counsels are!
Who may with thee compare?
Only the West and Rome do keep them free
From this contagious infidelity.
And this is all the Rock, whereof they boast,
As Rome will one day find unto her cost.
Sin being not able to extirpate quite
The Churches here, bravely resolved one night
To be a Churchman too, and wear a Mitre:
This old debauched ruffian would turn writer.
I saw him in his study, where he sat
Busy in controversies sprung of late.
A gown and pen became him wondrous well:
His grave aspect had more of heav'n than hell:
Only there was a handsome picture by,
To which he lent a corner of his eye.
As Sin in Greece a Prophet was before,
And in old Rome a mighty Emperor;
So now being Priest he plainly did profess
To make a jest of Christ's three offices:
The rather since his scattered jugglings were
United now in one both time and sphere.
From Egypt he took petty deities,
From Greece oracular infallibilities,
And from old Rome the liberty of pleasure,

By free dispensings of the Church's treasure.
Then in memorial of his ancient throne
He did surname his palace, Babylon.
Yet that he might the better gain all nations,
And make that name good by their transmigrations;
From all these places, but at divers times,
He took fine vizards to conceal his crimes:
From Egypt anchorism and retiredness,
Learning from Greece, from old Rome stateliness:
And blending these he carried all men's eyes,
While Truth sat by, counting his victories:
Whereby he grew apace and scorned to use
Such force as once did captivate the Jews;
But did bewitch, and finely work each nation
Into a voluntary transmigration.
All post to Rome: Princes submit their necks
Either t' his public foot or private tricks.
It did not fit his gravity to stir,
Nor his long journey, nor his gout and fur.
Therefore he sent out able ministers,
Statesmen within, without doors cloisterers:
Who without spear, or sword, or other drum
Than what was in their tongue, did overcome;
And having conquered, did so strangely rule,
That the whole world did seem but the Pope's mule.
As new and old Rome did one Empire twist;
So both together are one Antichrist,
Yet with two faces, as their Janus was;
Being in this their old cracked looking-glass.
How dear to me, O God, thy counsels are!
Who may with thee compare?
Thus Sin triumphs in Western Babylon;
Yet not as Sin, but as Religion.
Of his two thrones he made the latter best,
And to defray his journey from the east.
Old and new Babylon are to hell and night,
As is the moon and sun to heav'n and light.

When th' one did set, the other did take place,
Confronting equally the law and grace.
They are hell's landmarks, Satan's double crest:
They are Sin's nipples, feeding th' east and west.
But as in vice the copy still exceeds
The pattern, but not so in virtuous deeds;
So though Sin made his latter seat the better,
The latter Church is to the first a debtor.
The second Temple could not reach the first:
And the late reformation never durst
Compare with ancient times and purer years;
But in the Jews and us deserveth tears.
Nay, it shall ev'ry year decrease and fade;
Till such a darkness do the world invade
At Christ's last coming, as his first did find:
Yet must there such proportions be assigned
To these diminishings, as is between
The spacious world and Jewry to be seen.
Religion stands on tip-toe in our land,
Ready to pass to the American strand.
When height of malice, and prodigious lusts,
Impudent sinning, witchcrafts, and distrusts
(The marks of future bane) shall fill our cup
Unto the brim, and make our measure up;
When Seine shall swallow Tiber, and the Thames
By letting in them both, pollutes her streams:
When Italy of us shall have her will,
And all her calendar of sins fulfil;
Whereby one may foretell, what sins next year
Shall both in France and England domineer:
Then shall Religion to America flee:
They have their times of Gospel, ev'n as we.
My God, thou dost prepare for them a way
By carrying first their gold from them away:
For gold and grace did never yet agree:
Religion always sides with poverty.
We think we rob them, but we think amiss:

We are more poor, and they more rich by this.
Thou wilt revenge their quarrel, making grace
To pay our debts, and leave our ancient place
To go to them, while that which now their nation
But lends to us, shall be our desolation.
Yet as the Church shall thither westward fly,
So Sin shall trace and dog her instantly:
They have their period also and set times
Both for their virtuous actions and their crimes.
And where of old the Empire and the Arts
Ushered the Gospel ever in men's hearts,
Spain hath done one; when Arts perform the other,
The Church shall come, and Sin the Church shall smother:
That when they have accomplished the round,
And met in th' east their first and ancient sound,
Judgement may meet them both and search them round.
Thus do both lights, as well in Church as Sun,
Light one another, and together run.
Thus also Sin and Darkness follow still
The Church and Sun with all their power and skill.
But as the Sun still goes both west and east;
So also did the Church by going west
Still eastward go; because it drew more near
To time and place, where judgement shall appear.
How dear to me, O God, thy counsels are!
Who may with thee compare?

L'Envoy

King of Glory, King of Peace,
With the one make war to cease;
With the other bless thy sheep,
Thee to love, in thee to sleep.
Let not Sin devour thy fold,
Bragging that thy blood is cold,
That thy death is also dead,

While his conquests daily spread;
That thy flesh hath lost his food,
And thy Cross is common wood.
Choke him, let him say no more,
But reserve his breath in store,
Till thy conquests and his fall
Make his sighs to use it all,
And then bargain with the wind
To discharge what is behind.

Blessed be God alone,
Thrice blessed Three in One.

FINIS.

ENGLISH POEMS IN THE WILLIAMS MANUSCRIPT NOT INCLUDED IN *THE TEMPLE*

The Holy Communion

O gracious Lord, how shall I know
Whether in these gifts thou be so
  As thou art ev'rywhere;
Or rather so, as thou alone
Tak'st all the lodging, leaving none
  For thy poor creature there?

First I am sure, whether bread stay
Or whether bread do fly away
  Concerneth bread not me.
But that both thou, and all thy train
Be there, to thy truth, and my gain
  Concerneth me and Thee.

And if in coming to thy foes
Thou dost come first to them, that shows
  The haste of thy good will.
Or if that thou two stations makest
In Bread and me, the way thou takest
  Is more, but for me still.

Then of this also I am sure
That thou didst all those pains endure
  To'abolish Sin, not wheat.
Creatures are good, and have their place;
Sin only, which did all deface,
  Thou drivest from his seat.

I could believe an Impanation
At the rate of an Incarnation
If thou hadst died for bread.
But which made my soul to die
My flesh, and fleshly villainy,
That also made thee dead.

That flesh is there, mine eyes deny:
And what should flesh but flesh descry,
The noblest sense of five.
If glorious bodies pass the sight
Shall they be food and strength, and might
Even there, where they deceive?

Into my soul this cannot pass;
Flesh (though exalted) keeps his grass
And cannot turn to soul.
Bodies and minds are different spheres
Nor can they change their bounds and meres,
But keep a constant pole.

This gift of all gifts is the best,
Thy flesh the least that I request.
Thou took'st that pledge from me:
Give me not that I had before,
Or give me that, so I have more;
My God, give me all Thee.

Love

Thou art too hard for me in Love:
There is no dealing with thee in that Art:
That is thy Masterpiece I see.
When I contrive and plot to prove
Something that may be conquest on my part
Thou still, O Lord, outstrippest me.

Sometimes, when as I wash, I say
And shrewdly, as I think, Lord wash my soul
More spotted than my flesh can be.
But then there comes into my way
Thy ancient baptism, which when I was foul
And knew it not, yet cleansed me.

I took a time when thou didst sleep,
Great waves of trouble combating my breast:
I thought it brave to praise thee then,
Yet then I found, that thou didst creep
Into my heart with joy, giving more rest
Than flesh did lend thee, back again.

Let me but once the conquest have
Upon the matter, 'twill thy conquest prove:
If thou subdue mortality
Thou dost no more, than doth the grave:
Whereas if I o'ercome thee and thy Love
Hell, Death and Devil come short of me.

Trinity Sunday

He that is one,
Is none.
Two reacheth thee
In some degree.
Nature and Grace
With Glory may attain thy Face.
Steel and a flint strike fire,
Wit and desire
Never to thee aspire,
Except life catch and hold those fast.
That which belief
Did not confess in the first Thief
His fall can tell,
From Heaven, through Earth, to Hell.

Let two of those alone
To them that fall,
Who God and Saints and Angels lose at last.
He that has one,
Has all.

Evensong

The Day is spent, and hath his will on me:
I and the Sun have run our races,
I went the slower, yet more paces,
For I decay, not he.

Lord make my losses up, and set me free:
That I who cannot now by day
Look on his daring brightness, may
Shine then more bright than he.

If thou defer this light, then shadow me:
Lest that the Night, earth's gloomy shade,
Fouling her nest, my earth invade,
As if shades knew not Thee.

But Thou art Light and Darkness both together:
If that be dark we cannot see:
The sun is darker than a Tree,
And thou more dark than either.

Yet Thou art not so dark, since I know this,
But that my darkness may touch thine:
And hope, that may teach it to shine,
Since Light thy Darkness is.

O let my Soul, whose keys I must deliver
Into the hands of senseless Dreams
Which know not thee, suck in thy beams
And wake with thee for ever.

The Knell

The Bell doth toll:
Lord help thy servant whose perplexed Soul
Doth wishly look
On either hand
And sometimes offers, sometimes makes a stand
Struggling on th' hook.

Now is the season,
Now the great combat of our flesh and reason!
O help, my God!
See, they break in
Disbanded humours, sorrows, troops of Sin,
Each with his rod.

Lord make thy Blood
Convert and colour all the other flood
And streams of grief
That they may be
Juleps and cordials when we call on thee
For some relief.

Perseverance

My God, the poor expressions of my Love
Which warm these lines, and serve them up to thee
Are so, as for the present I did move,
Or rather as thou movedst me.

But what shall issue, whether these my words
Shall help another, but my judgement be;
As a burst fowling-piece doth save the birds
But kill the man, is sealed with thee.

For who can tell, though thou hast died to win
And wed my soul in glorious paradise;
Whether my many crimes and use of sin
May yet forbid the banes and bliss.

Only my soul hangs on thy promises
With face and hands clinging unto thy breast,
Clinging and crying, crying without cease,
Thou art my rock, thou art my rest.

POEMS FROM IZAAK WALTON'S *THE LIFE OF MR GEORGE HERBERT*

Sonnets

1.

My God, where is that ancient heat towards thee,
Wherewith whole shoals of Martyrs once did burn,
Besides their other flames? Doth poetry
Wear Venus' livery? only serve her turn?
Why are not sonnets made of thee? and lays
Upon thine altar burnt? Cannot thy love
Heighten a spirit to sound out thy praise
As well as any she? Cannot thy dove
Outstrip their Cupid easily in flight?
Or, since thy ways are deep, and still the same,
Will not a verse run smooth that bears thy name!
Why doth that fire, which by thy power and might
Each breast does feel, no braver fuel choose
Than that, which one day worms may chance refuse?

2.

Sure Lord, there is enough in thee to dry
Oceans of ink; for, as the Deluge did
Cover the Earth, so doth thy Majesty:
Each Cloud distills thy praise, and doth forbid
Poets to turn it to another use.
Roses and lilies speak thee; and to make
A pair of cheeks of them, is thy abuse.
Why should I women's eyes for crystal take?
Such poor invention burns in their low mind,
Whose fire is wild, and doth not upward go
To praise, and on thee Lord, some ink bestow.

Open the bones, and you shall nothing find
  In the best face but filth; when Lord, in thee
  The beauty lies in the discovery.

To My Successor

If thou chance for to find
A new House to thy mind,
And built without thy Cost:
Be good to the Poor,
As God gives thee store,
And then my Labour's not lost.

ADDITIONAL ENGLISH POEMS

To the Right Hon. the L. Chancellor (Bacon)

My Lord, a diamond to me you sent
And I to you a blackamoor present.
Gifts speak their givers. For as those refractions,
Shining and sharp, point out your rare perfections;
So by the other, you may read in me
(Whom scholar's habit and obscurity
Hath ere soiled with black) the colour of my state,
Till your bright gift my darkness did abate.
Only, most noble Lord, shut not the door
Against this mean and humble blackamoor.
  Perhaps some other subject I had tried
  But that my ink was factious for this side.

To the Lady Elizabeth Queen of Bohemia

Bright soul, of whom if any country known
Had worthy been, thou had'st not lost thine own,
No earth can be thy jointure, for the sun
And stars alone unto thy pitch do run
And pace of thy sweet virtues; only they
Are thy dominions. Those that rule in clay
Stick fast therein; but thy transcendent soul
Doth for two clods of earth ten spheres control.
And though stars shot from Heaven lose their light,
Yet thy brave beams, excluded from their right,
Maintain their lustre still, and shining clear,
Turn wat'rish Holland to a crystal sphere.
Methinks in that Dutch optic I do see
Thy curious virtues much more visibly.

There is thy best throne, for afflictions are
A foil to set off worth, and make it rare.
Through that black tiffany, thy virtues shine
Fairer and richer, now we know what's thine
And what is fortune's. Thou hast singled out
Sorrows and griefs, to fight with them a bout
At their own weapons, without pomp or state
To second thee against their cunning hate.

O, what a poor thing 'tis to be a queen
When sceptres, state, attendants are the screen
Betwixt us and the people; whenas glory
Lies round about us, to help out the story;
When all things pull and hale, that they may bring
A slow behaviour to the style of king;
When sense is made by comments! But that face,
Whose native beauty needs not dress or lace
To set it forth, and being stripped of all,
Is self-sufficient to be the self-thrall
Of thousand hearts; that face doth figure thee
And show thy undivided majesty,
Which misery cannot untwist, but rather
Adds to the union, as lights, to gather
Splendours from darkness. So close sits the crown
About thy temples that the furious frown
Of opposition cannot place thee where
Thou should'st not be a queen, and conquer there.
Yet hast thou more dominions: God doth give
Children for kingdoms to thee. They shall live
To conquer new ones, and shall share the frame
Of th' universe, like as the winds, and name
The world anew. The sun shall never rise
But it shall spy some of thy victories.
Their hands shall clip the eagle's wings and chase
Those ravening harpies, which peck at their face,
At once to Hell, without a baiting-while
At Purgatory, their Enchanted Isle

And Paris Garden. Then let their perfume
And Spanish saints, wisely laid up, presume
To deal with brimstone, that untimed stench
Whose fire, like their malice, nought can quench.

But joys are stored for thee, thou shalt return
Laden with comfort thence, where now to mourn
Is thy chief government, to manage woe,
To curb some rebel tears, which fain would flow,
Making a head and spring against thy reason.
This is thy empire yet, till better season
Call thee from out of that surrounded land,
That habitable sea and brinish strand,
Thy tears not needing. For that hand divine,
Which mingles water with thy Rhenish wine,
Will pour full joys to thee, but dregs to those
(And meet their taste) who are thy bitter foes.

Envoi
To the Same. Another.

Shine on, majestic soul, abide
Like David's tree planted beside
The Flemish rivers. In the end,
Thy fruit shall with their drops contend.
Our God will surely dry those tears
Which now that moist land to thee bears.
Then shall thy glory, fresh as flowers
In water kept, maugre the powers
Of Devil, Jesuit, and Spain,
From Holland sail into the main.
Thence, wheeling on, it compass shall
This, our great sublunary ball;
And with that ring, thy fame shall wed
Eternity into one bed.

A PRIEST TO THE TEMPLE

OR,
THE COUNTRY PARSON
HIS CHARACTER,
AND RULE OF HOLY LIFE

The Author to the Reader

Being desirous (through the mercy of God) to please him, for whom I am, and live, and who giveth me my desires and performances; and considering with myself that the way to please him is to feed my flock diligently and faithfully, since our Saviour hath made that the argument of a pastor's love,[1] I have resolved to set down the form and character of a true pastor, that I may have a mark to aim at: which also I will set as high as I can, since he shoots higher that threatens the moon than he that aims at a tree. Not that I think, if a man do not all which is here expressed, he presently sins and displeases God, but that it is a good strife to go as far as we can in pleasing of him who hath done so much for us. The Lord prosper the intention to myself, and others, who may not despise my poor labours, but add to those points which I have observed, until the book grow to a complete pastoral.[2]

1632 GEO. HERBERT.

Chapter 1: Of a Pastor

A pastor is the Deputy of Christ for the reducing[1] of man to the obedience of God. This definition is evident, and contains the direct steps of pastoral duty and authority. For first, man fell from God by disobedience. Secondly, Christ is the glorious instrument of God for the revoking[2] of man. Thirdly, Christ being not to continue on earth, but after he had fulfilled the work of reconciliation, to be received up into heaven, he constituted deputies in his place, and these are priests. And therefore St Paul in the beginning of his Epistles professeth this, and in the First to the

Colossians plainly avoucheth that he 'fills up that which is behind of the afflictions of Christ in his flesh for his body's sake, which is the Church'.[3] Wherein is contained the complete definition of a minister. Out of this charter of the priesthood may be plainly gathered both the dignity thereof, and the duty: the dignity, in that a priest may do that which Christ did, and by his authority, and as his vicegerent;[4] the duty, in that a priest is to do that which Christ did, and after his manner, both for doctrine and life.

Chapter 2: Their Diversities

Of pastors (intending mine own nation only, and also therein setting aside the reverend prelates of the Church, to whom this discourse ariseth not) some live in the universities, some in noble houses, some in parishes residing on their cures.[1] Of those that live in the universities some live there in office, whose rule is that of the Apostle: Romans 12:6, 'Having gifts differing according to the grace that is given to us, whether prophecy, let us prophesy according to the proportion of faith; or ministry, let us wait on our ministering: or he that teacheth, on teaching . . . he that ruleth, let him do it with diligence', etc.; some in a preparatory way, whose aim and labour must be not only to get knowledge, but to subdue and mortify all lusts and affections, and not to think that when they have read the Fathers or Schoolmen a minister is made, and the thing done. The greatest and hardest preparation is within: for, 'unto the ungodly saith God: Why dost thou preach my laws, and takest my covenant in thy mouth?' Psalm 50:16. Those that live in noble houses are called chaplains, whose duty and obligation being the same to the houses they live in as a parson's to his parish, in describing the one (which is indeed the bent of my discourse) the other will be manifest. Let not chaplains think themselves so free *as many of them do*, and because they have different names, think their office different. Doubtless they are parsons of the families they live in, and are entertained to that end, either by an open, or implicit covenant. Before they are in orders, they may be received for companions, or discoursers; but after a man is once minister, he cannot agree to come into any house where he shall not exercise what he is, unless he forsake his plough, and look back. Wherefore they are not to be over-submissive, and base, but to keep up with the lord and lady of the house, and to preserve a boldness with them and all, even so far as reproof to their very face when occasion calls, but seasonably and discreetly. They who do not thus, while they remember their earthly lord do much forget their heavenly; they wrong the priesthood, neglect their duty and shall be so far from that which they seek with their over-submissiveness and cringings that they shall ever be despised. They who for the hope of promotion neglect any necessary admonition or reproof sell (with Judas) their Lord and Master.

Chapter 3: The Parson's Life

The country parson is exceeding exact in his life, being holy, just, prudent, temperate, bold, grave in all his ways. And because the two highest points of life, wherein a Christian is most seen, are patience[1] and mortification,[2] patience in regard of afflictions, mortification in regard of lusts and affections and the stupefying and deadening of all the clamorous powers of the soul, therefore he hath thoroughly studied these that he may be an absolute master and commander of himself for all the purposes which God hath ordained him. Yet in these points he labours most in those things which are most apt to scandalise[3] his parish. And first, because country people live hardly and therefore as feeling their own sweat and consequently knowing the price of money are offended much with any who by hard usage increase their travail, the country parson is very circumspect in avoiding all covetousness, neither being greedy to get, nor niggardly to keep, nor troubled to lose any worldly wealth; but in all his words and actions slighting and disesteeming it, even to a wondering that the world should so much value wealth, which in the day of wrath hath not one dram of comfort for us. Secondly, because luxury is a very visible sin, the parson is very careful to avoid all the kinds thereof, but especially that of drinking, because it is the most popular vice into which if he come *he prostitutes himself* both to shame and sin, and by having *fellowship with the unfruitful works of darkness* he disableth himself of authority *to reprove them*; for sins make all equal whom they find together; and then they are worst who ought to be best. Neither is it for the servant of Christ to haunt inns and taverns or alehouses *to the dishonour of his person and office*. The parson does not so, but orders his life in such a fashion that when death takes him, as the Jews and Judas did Christ, he may say as he did, 'I sat daily with you teaching in the Temple.'[4] Thirdly, because country people (as indeed all honest men) do much esteem their word, it being the life of buying and selling and dealing in the world, therefore the parson is very strict in keeping his word, though it be to his own hindrance, as knowing that if he be not so, he will quickly be discovered and disregarded; neither will they believe him in the pulpit whom they cannot trust in his conversation. As for oaths and apparel, the disorders thereof are also very manifest. The parson's yea is yea, and nay, nay; and his apparel plain, but reverend, and clean, without spots, or dust, or smell, the purity of his mind breaking out and dilating itself[5] even to his body, clothes, and habitation.

Chapter 4: The Parson's Knowledge

The country parson is full of all knowledge. They say it is an ill mason that refuseth any stone: and there is no knowledge but in a skilful hand serves either positively as it is, or else to illustrate some other knowledge. He condescends even to the knowledge of tillage, and pastorage, and makes great use of them in teaching, because people by what they understand are best led to what they understand not. But the chief and top of his knowledge consists in the book of books, the storehouse and magazine of life and comfort, the holy Scriptures. There he sucks[1] and lives. In the Scriptures he finds four things: precepts for life, doctrines for knowledge, examples for illustration, and promises for comfort; these he hath digested severally. But for the understanding of these, the means he uses are first, a holy life, remembering what his Master sayeth, that 'if any do God's will, he shall know of the doctrine', John 7,[2] and assuring himself that wicked men, however learned, do not know the Scriptures because they feel them not, and because they are not understood but with[3] the same Spirit that writ them. The second means is prayer, which if it be necessary even in temporal things, how much more in things of another world, where the well is deep, and we have nothing of ourselves to draw with? Wherefore he ever begins the reading of the Scripture with some short inward ejaculation, as, 'Lord, open mine eyes, that I may see the wondrous thing of thy Law . . .' The third means is a diligent collation[4] of Scripture with Scripture. For all Truth being consonant to itself, and all being penned by one hand and the selfsame Spirit, it cannot be but that an industrious and judicious comparing of place with place must be a singular help for the right understanding of the Scriptures. To this may be added the consideration of any text with the coherence thereof, touching what goes before and what follows after, as also the scope of the Holy Ghost. When the Apostles would have called down fire from heaven, they were reproved as ignorant of what spirit they were. For the Law required one thing and the Gospel another; yet as diverse, not as repugnant: therefore the spirit of both is to be considered and weighed. The fourth means are commenters and Fathers, who have handled the places controverted,[5] which the parson by no means refuseth. As he doth not so study others as to neglect the grace of God in himself and what the Holy Spirit teacheth him, so doth he assure himself that God in all ages hath had his servants to whom he hath revealed his Truth, as well as to him; and that as one country doth not bear[6] all things that there may be a commerce, so neither hath God opened or will open all to one, that there may be a traffic in knowledge between the servants of God for the planting both of love and humility. Wherefore he hath one comment at least upon every book of Scripture, and ploughing with this, and his own meditations, he enters into the secrets of God treasured in the holy Scripture.

Chapter 5: The Parson's Accessory Knowledge

The country parson hath read the Fathers also, and the Schoolmen,[1] and the later writers, or a good proportion of all, out of all which he hath compiled a book and body of Divinity, which is the storehouse of his sermons and which he preacheth all his life, but diversely clothed, illustrated, and enlarged. For though the world is full of such composures, yet every man's own is fittest, readiest, and most savoury to him. Besides, this being to be done in his younger and preparatory times, it is an honest joy ever after to look upon his well spent hours. This body he made by way of expounding the Church catechism, to which all divinity may easily be reduced. For it being indifferent in itself to choose any method, that is best to be chosen, of which there is likeliest to be most use. Now catechising being a work of singular and admirable benefit to the Church of God, and a thing required under canonical obedience, the expounding of our catechism must needs be the most useful form. Yet has the Parson, besides this laborious work, a slighter form of catechising fitter for country people; according as his audience is, so he useth one, or other; or sometimes both, if his audience be intermixed. He greatly esteems also of cases of conscience, wherein he is much versed. And indeed, herein is the greatest ability of a parson to lead his people exactly in the ways of Truth, so that they neither decline to the right hand, nor to the left. Neither let any think this is a slight thing. For everyone hath not digested when it is a sin to take something for money lent, or when not; when it is a fault to discover another's fault, or when not; when the affections of the soul in desiring and procuring most increase of means, or honour, be a sin of covetousness or ambition, and when not; when the appetites of the body in eating, drinking, sleep, and the pleasure that comes with sleep, be sins of gluttony, drunkenness, sloth, lust, and when not, and so in many circumstances and actions. Now if a shepherd know not which grass will bane,[2] or which not, how is he fit to be a shepherd? Wherefore the parson hath thoroughly canvassed all the particulars of human actions, at least all those which he observeth are most incident to his parish.

Chapter 6: The Parson Praying

The country parson, when he is to read divine services, composeth himself to all possible reverence, lifting up his heart and hands and eyes, and using all other gestures which may express a hearty and unfeigned devotion. This he doth, first, as being truly touched and amazed with the Majesty of God, before whom he then presents himself; yet not as himself alone, but as presenting with himself the whole congregation, whose sins he then bears and brings with his own to the heavenly altar to be bathed and washed in the sacred laver[1] of Christ's blood. Secondly, as this is the true reason of his inward fear, so he is content to express this outwardly to the utmost of his power; that being first affected himself, he may affect also his people, knowing that no sermon moves them so much to a reverence, which they forget again when they come to pray, as a devout behaviour in the very act of praying. Accordingly his voice is humble, his words treatable[2] and slow; yet not so slow neither as to let the fervency of the supplicant hang and die between speaking, but with a grave liveliness between fear and zeal, pausing yet pressing, he performs his duty. Besides his example, he having often instructed his people how to carry themselves in divine service, exacts of them all possible reverence, by no means enduring either talking, or sleeping, or gazing, or leaning, or half-kneeling, or any undutiful behaviour in them, but causing them, when they sit, or stand, or kneel, to do all in a straight and steady posture, as attending to what is done in the church, and everyone, man and child, answering aloud both Amen and all other answers, which are on the clerk's and people's part to answer; which answers are not to be done in a huddling or slubbering[3] fashion, gaping, or scratching the head, or spitting even in the midst of their answer, but gently and pauseably, thinking what they say; so that while they answer, 'As it was in the beginning . . .' they meditate as they speak that God hath ever had his people that have glorified him as well as now, and that he shall have so forever. And the like in other answers. This is that which the Apostle calls a reasonable service, Romans 12,[4] when we speak not as parrots without reason, or offer up such sacrifices as they did of old, which was of beasts devoid of reason; but when we use our reason and apply our powers to the service of him that gives them. If there be any of the gentry or nobility of the parish who sometimes make it a piece of state not to come at the beginning of service with their poor neighbours but at mid-prayers, both to their own loss and of theirs also who gaze upon them when they come in and neglect the present service of God, he by no means suffers it, but after divers gentle admonitions, if they persevere, he causes them to be presented;[5] or if the poor churchwardens be affrighted with their greatness, notwithstanding his instruction that they ought not to be so, but even to let the world sink, so they do their duty; he presents them himself, only protesting to them that not any ill will draws him to it, but the debt and obligation of his calling, being to obey God rather than men.

Chapter 7: The Parson Preaching

The country parson preacheth constantly; the pulpit is his joy and his throne: if he at any time intermit, it is either for want of health, or against some great festival, that he may the better celebrate it, or for the variety of the hearers, that he may be heard at his return more attentively. When he intermits, he is ever very well supplied by some able man who treads in his steps and will not throw down what he hath built, whom also he entreats to press some point that he himself hath often urged with no great success, that so in the mouth of two or three witnesses the truth may be more established. When he preacheth, he procures attention by all possible art, both by earnestness of speech, it being natural to men to think that where is much earnestness there is somewhat worth hearing; and by a diligent and busy cast of his eye on his auditors, with letting them know that he observes who marks and who not; and with particularising of his speech now to the younger sort, then to the elder, now to the poor, and now to the rich. This is for you, and this is for you; for particulars ever touch and awake more than generals. Herein also he serves himself of the judgements of God, as of those of ancient times, so especially of the late ones; and those most which are nearest to his parish; for people are very attentive at such discourses and think it behoves them to be so when God is so near them, and even over their heads. Sometimes he tells them stories and sayings of others, according as his text invites him; for them also men heed and remember better than exhortations, which, though earnest, yet often die with the sermon, especially with country people which are thick and heavy, and hard to raise to a point of zeal and fervency, and need a mountain of fire to kindle them; but stories and sayings they will well remember. He often tells them that sermons are dangerous things, that none goes out of church as he came in, but either better or worse, that none is careless before his judge, and that the word of God shall judge us. By these and other means the parson procures attention, but the character[1] of his sermon is holiness; he is not witty, or learned, or eloquent, but holy. A character that Hermogenes[2] never dreamed of, and therefore he could give no precepts thereof. But it is gained, first, by choosing texts of devotion, not controversy, moving and ravishing[3] texts whereof the Scriptures are full. Secondly, by dipping and seasoning all our words and sentences in our hearts before they come into our mouths, truly affecting and cordially expressing all that we say, so that the auditors may plainly perceive that every word is heart-deep. Thirdly, by turning often and making many apostrophes[4] to God, as, Oh Lord, bless my people, and teach them this point; or, Oh my Master, on whose errand I come, let me hold my peace, and do thou speak thyself; for thou art Love, and when thou teachest, all are scholars. Some such irradiations scatteringly[5] in the sermon carry great holiness in them. The Prophets are admirable in this. So Isaiah 64, 'Oh that thou wouldst rent the Heavens, that thou wouldst come down . . .' And Jeremy, Chapter 10,[6] after he had complained of the desolation of Israel, turns to God suddenly, 'Oh Lord, I know that the way of man is not in himself . . .' Fourthly, by frequent wishes of the people's good, and joying therein, though he himself were with Saint Paul even sacrificed upon the service of their faith. For there is no greater sign of holiness than the procuring, and rejoicing in, another's good. And herein St Paul excelled in all his Epistles. How did he put the Romans in all his prayers! Romans 1:9. And ceased not to give thanks for the Ephesians, Ephesians 1:16. And for the Corinthians, Chapter 1:4.[7] And for the Philippians made request with joy, Chapter 1:4. And is in contention for them whether to live or die, be with them or Christ, verse 23, which, setting aside his care of his flock, were a madness to doubt of. What an admirable Epistle is the second to the Corinthians! how full of affections! he joys, and he is sorry, he grieves, and he glories; never was there such care of a flock expressed, save in the great shepherd of the fold who first shed tears over Jerusalem, and afterwards blood. Therefore this care may be learned there and then woven into sermons, which will make them appear exceeding reverend and holy. Lastly, by an often urging of the presence and majesty of God, by these, or such like speeches: Oh let us all take heed what we do, God sees us, he sees whether I speak as I ought, or you hear as you ought, he sees hearts, as we see faces: he is among us; for if we be here, he must be here, since we are here by him, and without him could not be here. Then turning the discourse to his Majesty: And he is a great God, and terrible, as great in mercy, so great in judgement: there are but two devouring elements, fire and water, he hath both in him; 'His voice is as the sound of many waters,' Revelations 1.[8] And he himself 'is a consuming fire,' Hebrews 12. Such discourses show very holy. The parson's method in handling of a text consists of two parts: first, a plain and evident declaration of the meaning of the text; and secondly, some choice observations drawn out of the whole text as it lies entire and unbroken in the Scripture itself. This he thinks natural, and sweet, and grave. Whereas the other way of crumbling a text into small parts, as, the person speaking or spoken to, the subject and object, and the like, has neither in it sweetness, nor gravity, nor variety, since the words apart arc not Scripture[9] but a dictionary, and may be considered alike in all the Scripture. The parson exceeds not an hour in preaching, because all ages have thought that a competency, and he that profits not in that time will less afterwards, the same affection which made him not profit before making him then weary, and so he grows from not relishing to loathing.

Chapter 8: The Parson on Sundays

The country parson, as soon as he awakes on Sunday morning, presently falls to work and seems to himself so as a market-man is, when the market day comes, or a shopkeeper, when customers use to come in. His thoughts are full of making the best of the day, and contriving it to his best gains. To this end, besides his ordinary prayers he makes a peculiar one for a blessing on the exercises of the day, that nothing befall him unworthy of that Majesty before which he is to present himself, but that all may be done with reverence to his glory and with edification to his flock, humbly beseeching his Master that how or whenever he punish him, it be not in his ministry; then he turns to request for his people that the Lord would be pleased to sanctify them all, that they may come with holy hearts, awful minds into the congregation, and that the good God would pardon all those who come with less prepared hearts than they ought. This done he sets himself to the consideration of the duties of the day, and if there be any extraordinary addition to the customary exercises, either from the time of the year, or from the State, or from God by a child born or dead, or any other accident, he contrives how and in what manner to induce it to the best advantage. Afterwards when the hour calls, with his family attending him, he goes to church, at his first entrance *humbly adoring and worshipping the invisible majesty and presence of Almighty God*, and blessing the people either openly, or to himself. Then having read divine service twice fully, and preached in the morning, and catechised in the afternoon, he thinks he hath in some measure, according to poor and frail man, discharged the public duties of the congregation. The rest of the day he spends either in reconciling neighbours that are at variance or in visiting the sick, or in exhortations to some of his flock by themselves whom his sermons cannot or do not reach. And every one is more awaked, when we come, and say, 'Thou art the man.'[1] This way he finds exceeding useful and winning, and these exhortations he calls his privy purse, even as princes have theirs, besides their public disbursements. At night he thinks it a very fit time, both suitable to the joy of the day and without hindrance to public duties, either to entertain some of his neighbours, or to be entertained of them, where he takes occasion to discourse *of such things as are both profitable and pleasant, and to raise up their minds to apprehend God's good blessing to our Church and State; that order is kept in the one, and peace in the other, without disturbance or interruption of public divine offices*. As he opened the day with prayer, so he closeth it, humbly beseeching the Almighty to pardon and accept our poor services, and to improve them, that we may grow therein and that our feet may be like hinds'[2] feet ever climbing up higher and higher unto him.

Chapter 9: The Parson's State of Life

The country parson considering that virginity is a higher state than matrimony and that the ministry requires the best and highest things is rather unmarried than married. But yet as the temper of his body may be, or as the temper of his parish may be, where he may have occasion to converse with women, and that among suspicious men, *and other like circumstances considered*, he is rather married than unmarried. Let him communicate the thing often by prayer unto God and as his grace shall direct him, so let him proceed. If he be unmarried and keep house, he hath not a woman in his house, but finds opportunities of having his meat dressed and other services done by men-servants at home and his linen washed abroad. If he be unmarried and sojourn, he never talks with any woman alone, but in the audience of others, and that seldom, and then also in a serious manner, never jestingly or sportfully. *He is very circumspect in all companies, both in his behaviour, speech and very looks, knowing himself to be both suspected and envied. If he stands steadfast in his heart, having no necessity, but hath power over his own will, and hath so decreed in his heart that he will keep himself a virgin, he spends his days in fasting and prayer and blesseth God for the gift of continency, knowing that it can no way be preserved but only by those means by which at first it was obtained. He therefore thinks it not enough for him to observe the fasting days of the Church and the daily prayers enjoined him by authority, which he observeth out of humble conformity and obedience; but adds to them, out of choice and devotion, some other days for fasting and hours for prayers; and by these he keeps his body tame, serviceable, and healthful; and his soul fervent, active, young, and lusty as an eagle. He often readeth the Lives of the Primitive Monks, Hermits and Virgins, and wondereth not so much at their patient suffering and cheerful dying under persecuting emperors (though that indeed be very admirable) as at their daily temperance, abstinence, watchings, and constant prayers and mortifications in the times of peace and prosperity. To put on the profound humility and the exact temperance of our Lord Jesus, with other exemplary virtues of that sort, and keep them on in the sunshine and noon of prosperity, he findeth to be as necessary and as difficult at least as to be clothed with perfect patience and Christian fortitude in the cold midnight storms of persecution and adversity. He keepeth his watch and ward night and day against the proper and peculiar temptations of his state of life, which are principally these two, spiritual pride and impurity of heart: against these ghostly enemies he girdeth up his loins, keeps the imagination from roving, puts on the whole armour of God,*[1] *and by the virtue of the shield of faith, he is not afraid of the pestilence that walketh in darkness (carnal impurity), nor of the sickness that destroyeth at noonday (ghostly pride and self-conceit). Other temptations he hath, which, like mortal enemies, may sometimes disquiet him likewise; for the human soul*[2] *being bounded and kept in in her sensitive faculty, will run out more or less in her intellectual. Original concupiscence is such an active thing, by reason of continual inward or outward temptations, that it is ever attempting, or doing, one mischief or other. Ambition, or untimely desire of promotion to an higher state or place, under colour of accommodation or necessary provision, is a common temptation to men of any eminency, especially being single men. Curiosity in prying into high speculative and unprofitable questions is another great stumbling block to the holiness of scholars. These and many other spiritual wickednesses in high places doth the parson fear, or experiment,*[3] or both; and that *much more being single than if he were married; for then commonly the stream of temptations is turned another way, into covetousness, love of pleasure, or ease, or the like. If the parson be unmarried, and means to continue so, he doth at least as much as hath been said*. If he be married, the choice of his wife was made rather by his ear than by his eye; his judgement not his affection found out a fit wife for him, whose humble and liberal disposition he preferred before beauty, riches, or honour. *He knew that (the good instrument of God to bring women to heaven) a wise and loving husband*[4] *could out of humility produce any special grace of faith, patience, meekness, love, obedience, etc., and out of liberality make her fruitful in all good works*. As he is just in all things, so is he to his wife also, counting nothing so much his own as that he may be unjust unto it. Therefore he gives her respect both afore her servants and others, and half at least of the government of the house, reserving so much of the affairs as serve for a diversion for him; yet never so giving over the reins, but that he sometimes looks how things go, demanding an account, but not by the way of an account. And this must be done the oftener or the seldomer, according as he is satisfied of his wife's discretion.

Chapter 10: The Parson in his House

The parson is very exact in the governing of his house, making it a copy and model for his parish. He knows the temper and pulse of every person in his house, and accordingly either meets with their vices, or advanceth their virtues. His wife is either religious, or night and day he is winning her to it.[1] Instead of the qualities of the world, he requires only three of her; first, a training up of her children and maids in the fear of God, with prayers, and catechising, and all religious duties. Secondly, a curing and healing of all wounds and sores with her own hands; which skill either she brought with her, or he takes care she shall learn it of some religious neighbour. Thirdly, a providing for her family in such sort, as that neither they want a competent sustentation, nor her husband be brought in debt. His children he first makes Christians, and then commonwealth-men;[2] the one he owes to his heavenly country, the other to his earthly, having no title to either except he do good to both. Therefore having seasoned them with all piety, not only of words in praying and reading, but in actions, in visiting other sick children, and tending their wounds, and sending his charity by them to the poor, and sometimes giving them a little money to do it of themselves, that they get a delight in it and enter favour with God, who weighs even children's actions, 1 Kings 14:12, 13. He afterwards turns his care to fit all their dispositions with some calling, not sparing the eldest, but giving him the prerogative of his father's profession, which haply for his other children he is not able to do. Yet in binding them prentices (in case he think fit to do so) he takes care not to put them into vain trades, and unbefitting the reverence of their father's calling, such as are taverns for men and lace-making for women; because those trades, for the most part, serve but the vices and vanities of the world, which he is to deny, and not augment. However, he resolves with himself never to omit any present good deed of charity in consideration of providing a stock for his children; but assures himself that money thus lent to God is placed surer for his children's advantage, than if it were given to the Chamber of

London.[3] Good deeds and good breeding are his two great stocks for his children; if God give anything above those, and not spent in them, he blesseth God, and lays it out as he sees cause. His servants are all religious, and were it not his duty to have them so, it were his profit, for none are so well served, as by religious servants, both because they do best and because what they do is blessed, and prospers. After religion, he teacheth them that three things make a complete servant, truth and diligence and neatness or cleanliness. Those that can read are allowed times for it, and those that cannot are taught; for all in his house are either teachers or learners or both, so that his family is a school of religion, and they all account that to teach the ignorant is the greatest alms. Even the walls are not idle, but something is written or painted there, which may excite the reader to a thought of piety; especially the 101 Psalm,[4] which is expressed in a fair table,[5] as being the rule of a family. And when they go abroad, his wife among her neighbours is the beginner of good discourses, his children among children, his servants among other servants; so that as in the house of those that are skilled in music, all are musicians, so in the house of a preacher, all are preachers. He suffers not a lie or equivocation by any means in his house, but counts it the art and secret of governing to preserve a directness and open plainness in all things, so that all his house know that there is no help for a fault done but confession. He himself, or his wife, takes account of sermons and how everyone profits, comparing this year with the last: and besides the common prayers of the family, he straitly[6] requires of all to pray by themselves before they sleep at night and stir out in the morning, and knows what prayers they say, and till they have learned them, makes them kneel by him, esteeming that this private praying is a more voluntary act in them than when they are called to others' prayers, and that which when they leave the family they carry with them. He keeps his servants between love and fear, according as he finds them; but generally he distributes it thus: to his children he shows more love than terror, to his servants more terror than love; but an old good servant boards a child.[7] The furniture of his house is very plain, but clean, whole and sweet, as sweet as his garden can make; for he hath no money for such things, charity being his only perfume, which deserves cost when he can spare it. His fare is plain and common, but wholesome, what he hath is little, but very good; it consisteth most of mutton, beef and veal; if he adds anything for a great day, or a stranger, his garden or orchard supplies it, or his barn and back-side:[8] he goes no further for any entertainment lest he go into the world, esteeming it absurd that he should exceed, who teacheth others temperance. But those which his home produceth he refuseth not, as coming cheap and easy, and arising from the improvement of things which otherwise would be lost. Wherein he admires and imitates the wonderful providence and thrift of the great householder of the world: for there being two things, which as they are are unuseful to man, the one for smallness, as crumbs and scattered corn and the like; the other for the foulness, as wash and dirt and things thereinto fallen; God hath provided creatures for both; for the first, poultry; for the second, swine. These save man the labour, and doing that which either he could not do or was not fit for him to do, by taking both sorts of food into them, do as it were dress and prepare both for man in themselves, by growing themselves fit for his table. The parson in his house observes fasting days; and particularly, as Sunday is his day of joy so Friday his day of humiliation, which he celebrates not only with abstinence of diet, but also of company, recreation and all outward contentments; and besides, with confession of sins and all acts of mortification. Now fasting days contain a treble obligation; first, of eating less that day than on other days; secondly, of eating no pleasing or over-nourishing things, as the Israelites did eat sour herbs; thirdly, of eating no flesh, which is but the determination of the second rule by authority to this particular. The two former obligations are much more essential to a true fast than the third and last; and fasting days were fully performed by keeping of the two former, had not authority interposed: so that to eat little, and that unpleasant, is the natural rule of fasting, although it be flesh. For since fasting in Scripture language is an afflicting of our souls, if a piece of dry flesh at my table be more unpleasant to me than some fish there, certainly to eat the flesh, and not the fish, is to keep the fasting day naturally.

And it is observable that the prohibiting of flesh came from hot countries where both flesh alone, and much more with wine, is apt to nourish more than in cold regions, and where flesh may be much better spared, and with more safety than elsewhere, where both the people and the drink being cold and phlegmatic, the eating of flesh is an antidote to both. For it is certain that a weak stomach being prepossessed with flesh shall much better brook and bear[9] a draught of beer than if it had taken before either fish, or roots, or such things, which will discover itself by spitting and rheum, or phlegm. To conclude, the parson, if he be in full health, keeps the three obligations, eating fish, or roots, and that for quantity little, for quality unpleasant. If his body be weak and obstructed, as most students are, he cannot keep the last obligation, nor suffer others in his house that are so, to keep it; but only the two former, which also in diseases of exinanition[10] (as consumptions) must be broken: for meat was made for man, not man for meat.[11] To all this may be added, not for emboldening the unruly, but for the comfort of the weak, that not only sickness breaks these obligations of fasting, but sickliness also. For it is as unnatural to do anything that leads me to a sickness, to which I am inclined, as not to get out of that sickness, when I am in it, by any diet. One thing is evident, that an English body, and a student's body, are two great obstructed vessels, and there is nothing that is food, and not physic, which doth less obstruct, than flesh moderately taken; as being immoderately taken, it is exceeding obstructive. And obstructions are the cause of most diseases.

Chapter 11: The Parson's Courtesy

The country parson owing a debt of charity to the poor, and of courtesy to his other parishioners, he so distinguisheth that he keeps his money for the poor and his table for those that are above alms. Not but that the poor are welcome also to his table, whom he sometimes purposely takes home with him, setting them close by him and carving for them, both for his own humility and their comfort, who are much cheered with such friendliness. But since both is to be done, the better sort invited and meaner relieved, he chooseth rather to give the poor money, which they can better employ to their own advantage and suitably to their needs than so much given in meat at dinner. Having then invited some of his parish, he taketh his times to do the like to the rest; so that in the compass of the year he hath them all with him, because country people are very observant of such things and will not be persuaded but, being not invited, they are hated.[1] With persuasion the parson by all means avoids, knowing that where there are such conceits,[2] there is no room for his doctrine to enter. Yet doth he oftenest invite those whom he sees take best courses, that so both they may be encouraged to persevere and others spurred to do well that they may enjoy the like courtesy. For though he desire that all should live well and virtuously, not for any reward of his but for virtue's sake, yet that will not be so: and therefore as God, although we should love him only for his own sake yet out of his infinite pity hath set forth heaven for a reward to draw men to piety, and is content, if at least so, they will become good, so the country parson, who is a diligent observer and tracker of God's ways, sets up as many encouragements to goodness as he can, both in honour and profit and fame; that he may, if not the best way, yet any way, make his parish good.

Chapter 12: The Parson's Charity

The country parson is full of charity; it is his predominant element. For many and wonderful things are spoken of thee, thou great Virtue. To charity is given the covering of sins, 1 Peter 4:8, and the forgiveness of sins, Matthew 6:14, Luke 7:47.The fulfilling of the Law, Romans 13:10. The life of faith, James 2:26. The blessings of this life, Proverbs 22:9, Psalm 41:2. And the reward of the next,

Matthew 25:35.[1] In brief, it is the body of religion, John 13:35. And the top of Christian virtues, 1 Corinthians 13. Wherefore all his works relish of charity. When he riseth in the morning, he bethinketh himself what good deeds he can do that day, and presently does them, counting that day lost wherein he hath not exercised his charity. He first considers his own parish, and takes care that there be not a beggar or idle person in his parish, but that all be in a competent way of getting their living. This he effects either by bounty, or persuasion, or by authority, making use of that excellent statute[2] which binds all parishes to maintain their own. If his parish be rich, he exacts this of them; if poor, and he able, he easeth them therein. But he gives no set pension to any; for this in time will lose the name and effect of charity with the poor people, though not with God; for then they will reckon upon it, as on a debt; and if it be taken away, though justly, they will murmur and repine as much as he that is disseised[3] of his own inheritance. But the parson having a double aim, and making a hook of his charity, causeth them still to depend on him; and so by continual and fresh bounties, unexpected to them but resolved to himself, he wins them to praise God more, to live more religiously and to take more pains in their vocation, as not knowing when they shall be relieved; which otherwise they would reckon upon, and turn to idleness. Besides this general provision, he hath other times of opening his hand, as at great festivals and communions, not suffering any that day that he receives to want a good meal suiting to the joy of the occasion. But specially, at hard times and dearths, he even parts his living and life among them, giving some corn outright and selling other at under rates; and when his own stock serves not, working those that are able to the same charity, still pressing it in the pulpit, and out of the pulpit, and never leaving them till he obtain his desire. Yet in all his charity, he distinguisheth, giving them most who live best and take most pains and are most charged: so is his charity in effect a sermon. After the consideration of his own parish, he enlargeth himself, if he be able, to the neighbourhood; for that also is some kind of obligation; so doth he also to those at his door, whom God puts in his way and makes his neighbours, but these he helps not without some testimony,[4] except the evidence of the misery bring testimony with it. For though these testimonics also may be falsified, yet considering that the law allows these in case they be true but allows by no means to give without testimony, as he obeys authority in the one, so, that being once satisfied, he allows his charity some blindness in the other; especially since of the two commands we are more enjoined to be charitable than wise. But evident miseries have a natural privilege and exemption from all law. Whenever he gives anything, and sees them labour in thanking of him, he exacts of them to let him alone and say rather God be praised, God be glorified; that so the thanks may go the right way, and thither only where they are only due. So doth he also before giving make them say their prayers first, or the Creed and ten Commandments, and as he finds them perfect, rewards them the more. For other givings are lay and secular, but this is to give like a priest.

Chapter 13: The Parson's Church

The country parson has a special care of his church, that all things there be decent and befitting his Name by which it is called. Therefore first he takes order that all things be in good repair; as walls plastered, windows glazed, floor paved, seats whole, firm and uniform, especially that the pulpit and desk and Communion table and font be as they ought for those great duties that are performed in them. Secondly, that the church be swept and kept clean without dust or cobwebs, and at great festivals strawed[1] and stuck with boughs and perfumed with incense. Thirdly, that there be fit and proper texts of Scripture everywhere painted, and that all the painting be grave and reverend, not with light colours or foolish antics. Fourthly, that all the books appointed by authority be there, and those not torn or fouled, but whole and clean and well bound; and that there be a fitting and sightly Communion cloth of fine linen, with an handsome and seemly carpet of good and costly stuff or cloth, and all kept sweet and clean in a strong and decent chest, with a chalice and cover, and a stoup or flagon; and a basin for alms and offerings; besides which, he hath a poor-man's box conveniently seated to receive the charity of well-minded people and to lay up treasure for the sick and needy. And all this he doth not out of necessity or as putting a holiness in the things, but as desiring to keep the middle way between superstition and slovenliness, and as following the Apostle's two great and admirable rules in things of this nature: the first whereof is, 'Let all things be done decently, and in order;' the second, 'Let all things be done to edification,' 1 Corinthians 14.[2] For these two rules comprise and include the double object of our duty, God and our neighbour; the first being for the honour of God, the second for the benefit of our neighbour. So that they excellently score out the way, and fully and exactly contain, even in external and indifferent things, what course is to be taken, and put them to great shame who deny the Scripture to be perfect.

Chapter 14: The Parson in Circuit

The country parson upon the afternoons in the weekdays takes occasion sometimes to visit in person now one quarter of his parish, now another. For there he shall find his flock most naturally as they are, wallowing in the midst of their affairs, whereas on Sundays it is easy for them to compose themselves to order, which they put on as their holy-day clothes and come to church in frame, but commonly the next day put off both. When he comes to any house, first he blesseth it and then as he finds the persons of the house employed so he forms his discourse. Those that he finds religiously employed he both commends them much, and furthers them when he is gone, in their employment; as if he finds them reading, he furnisheth them with good books; if curing poor people, he supplies them with receipts[1] and instructs them further in that skill, showing them how acceptable such works are to God and wishing them ever to do the cures with their own hands and not to put them over to servants. Those that he finds busy in the works of their calling, he commendeth them also: for it is a good and just thing for everyone to do their own business. But then he admonisheth them of two things: first, that they dive not too deep into worldly affairs, plunging themselves over head and ears into carking[2] and caring, but that they so labour as neither to labour anxiously nor distrustfully nor profanely. Then they labour anxiously when they overdo it, to the loss of their quiet and health: then distrustfully when they doubt God's providence, thinking that their own labour is the cause of their thriving, as if it were in their own hands to thrive or not to thrive. Then they labour profanely when they set themselves to work like brute beasts, never raising their thoughts to God nor sanctifying their labour with daily prayer; when on the Lord's day they do unnecessary servile work or in time of divine service on other holy days, except in the cases of extreme poverty and in the seasons of seed-time and harvest. Secondly, he adviseth them so to labour for wealth and maintenance as that they make not that the end of their labour but that they may have wherewithal to serve God the better and to do good deeds. After these discourses, if they be poor and needy whom he thus finds labouring, he gives them somewhat; and opens not only his mouth but his purse to their relief, that so they go on more cheerfully in their vocation, and himself be ever the more welcome to them. Those that the parson finds idle or ill-employed he chides not at first, for that were neither civil nor profitable; but always in the close, before he departs from them; yet in this he distinguisheth, for if he[3] be a plain countryman he reproves him plainly, for they are not sensible of fineness; if they be of higher quality, they commonly are quick and sensible and very tender of reproof, and therefore he lays his discourse so that he comes to the point very leisurely, and oftentimes, as Nathan did,[4] in the person of another, making them to reprove themselves. However, one way or other he ever reproves them, that he may keep himself pure and not be entangled in others' sins. Neither in this doth he forbear, though there be company by: for as when the offence is particular and against me, I am to follow our Saviour's rule and to take my brother aside and reprove him; so when the offence is public and against God, I am then to follow the Apostle's rule, 1 Timothy 5:20, and to *rebuke openly* that which is done openly. Besides these occasional discourses, the Parson questions what order is kept in the house, as about prayers morning and evening on their knees, reading of Scripture, catechising, singing of Psalms at their work and on holy days; who can read, who not; and sometimes he hears the children read himself and blesseth them, encouraging also the servants to learn to read and offering to have them taught on holy-days by his servants. If the parson were ashamed of particularising in these things, he were not fit to be a parson, but he holds the rule, that nothing is little in God's service: if it once have the honour of that Name it grows great instantly. Wherefore neither disdaineth he to enter into the poorest cottage, though he even creep into it and though it smell never so loathsomely. For both God is there also and those for whom God died: and so much the rather doth he so, as his access to the poor is more comfortable than to the rich; and in regard of himself, it is more humiliation. These are the parson's general aims in his circuit, but with these he mingles other discourses for conversation sake and to make his higher purposes slip the more easily.

Chapter 15: The Parson Comforting

The country parson, when any of his cure is sick, or afflicted with loss of friend or estate, or any ways distressed, fails not to afford his best comforts, and rather goes to them than sends for the afflicted, though they can and otherwise ought to come to him. To this end he hath thoroughly digested all the points of consolation, as having continual use of them, such as are from God's general providence extended even to lilies,[1] from his particular to his Church; from his promises, from the examples of all Saints that ever were; from Christ himself, perfecting our Redemption no other way than by sorrow; from the benefit of affliction, which softens and works the stubborn heart of man; from the certainty both of deliverance and reward if we faint not; from the miserable comparison of the moment of griefs here with the weight of joys hereafter. Besides this, in his visiting the sick or otherwise afflicted, he followeth the Church's counsel, namely, in persuading them to particular confession, labouring to make them understand the great good use of this ancient and pious ordinance and how necessary it is in some cases; he also urgeth them to do some pious charitable works, as a necessary evidence and fruit of their faith at that time especially; the participation of the holy Sacrament, how comfortable and sovereign a medicine it is to all sin-sick souls; what strength and joy and peace it administers against all temptations, even to death itself, he plainly and generally intimateth to the disaffected or sick person, that so the hunger and thirst after it may come rather from themselves than from his persuasion.

Chapter 16: The Parson a Father

The country parson is not only a father to his flock, but also professeth himself thoroughly of the opinion,[1] carrying it about with him as fully as if he had begot his whole parish. And of this he makes great use. For by this means, when any sins, he hateth him not[2] as an officer, but pities him as a father; and even in those wrongs which either in tithing or otherwise are done to his own person, he considers the offender as a child and forgives so he may have any sign of amendment; so also when after many admonitions any continue to be refractory, yet he gives him not over, but is long before he proceed to disinheriting, or perhaps never goes so far; knowing that some are called at the eleventh hour, and therefore he still expects and waits, lest he should determine God's hour of coming; which as he cannot, touching the last day, so neither touching the intermediate days of conversion.

Chapter 17: The Parson in Journey

The country parson, when a just occasion calleth him out of his parish (which he diligently and strictly weigheth, his parish being all his joy and thought) leaveth not his ministry behind him; but is himself wherever he is. Therefore those he meets on the way he blesseth audibly and with those he overtakes or that overtake him, he begins good discourses such as may edify, interposing sometimes some short and honest refreshments which may make his other discourses more welcome and less tedious. And when he comes to his inn he refuseth not to join, that he may enlarge the glory of God to the company he is in by a due blessing of God for their safe arrival, and saying grace at meat, and at going to bed by giving the host notice that he will have prayers in the hall, wishing him to inform his guests thereof, that if any be willing to partake they may resort thither. The like he doth in the morning, using pleasantly the outlandish[1] proverb that 'Prayers and Provender never hinder journey.' When he comes to any other house where his kindred or other relations give him any authority over the family, if he be to stay for a time he considers diligently the state thereof to Godward, and that in two points: first, what disorders there are either in apparel, or diet, or too open a buttery,[2] or reading vain books, or swearing, or breeding up children to no calling but in idleness or the like. Secondly, what means of piety, whether daily prayers be used, grace, reading of Scriptures and other good books, how Sundays, holy-days and feasting days are kept. And accordingly as he finds any defect in these, he first considers with himself what kind of remedy fits the temper of the house best, and then he faithfully and boldly applieth it; yet seasonably and discreetly, by taking aside the lord or lady, or master and mistress, of the house and showing them clearly that they respect them most who wish them best, and that not a desire to meddle with others' affairs, but the earnestness to do all the good he can moves him to say thus and thus.

Chapter 18: The Parson in Sentinel

The country parson, wherever he is, keeps God's watch; that is, there is nothing spoken or done in the company where he is but comes under his test and censure. If it be well spoken or done he takes occasion to commend and enlarge it; if ill, he presently lays hold of it, lest the poison steal into some young and unwary spirits and possess them even before they themselves heed it. But this he does discreetly, with mollifying and suppling[1] words: this was not so well said as it might have been forborne; we cannot allow this; or else, if the thing will admit interpretation, your meaning is not thus, but thus; or, so far indeed what you say is true and well said, but this will not stand. This is called keeping God's watch, when the baits which the enemy lays in company are discovered and avoided: this is to be on God's side, and be true to his party. Besides, if he perceive in company any discourse tending to ill, either by the wickedness or quarrelsomeness thereof, he either prevents it judiciously or breaks it off seasonably by some diversion. Wherein a pleasantness of disposition is of great use, men being willing to sell the interest and engagement of their discourses for no price sooner than that of mirth; whither the nature of man, loving refreshment, gladly betakes itself even to the loss of honour.

Chapter 19: The Parson in Reference

The country parson is sincere and upright in all his relations. And first, he is just to his country; as when he is set at an armour[1] or horse he borrows them not to serve the turn, nor provides slight and unuseful, but such as are every way fitting to do his country true and laudable service when occasion requires. To do otherwise is deceit and therefore not for him, who is hearty and true in all his ways, as being the servant of him in whom there was no guile. Likewise in any other country-duty, he considers what is the end of any command and then he suits things faithfully according to that end. Secondly, he carries himself very respectively[2] as to all the Fathers of the Church, so especially to his Diocesan,[3] honouring him both in word and behaviour, and resorting unto him in any difficulty either in his studies or in his parish. He observes visitations,[4] and being there makes due use of them, as of clergy councils, for the benefit of the diocese. And therefore before he comes, having observed some defects in the ministry, he then either in sermon, if he preach, or at some other time of the day, propounds among his brethren what were fitting to be done. Thirdly, he keeps good correspondence with all the neighbouring pastors round about him, performing for them any ministerial office which is not to the prejudice of his own parish. Likewise he welcomes to his house any minister, how poor or mean soever, with as joyful a countenance as if he were to entertain some great lord. Fourthly, he fulfils the duty and debt of neighbourhood to all the parishes which are near him. For the Apostle's rule, Philippians 4,[5] being admirable and large, that 'we should do whatsoever things are honest, or just, or pure, or lovely, or of good report, if there be any virtue, or any praise;' and neighbourhood being ever reputed, even among the heathen, as an obligation to do good, rather than to those that are further, where things are otherwise equal, therefore he satisfies this duty also. Especially, if God have sent any calamity either by fire, or famine, to any neighbouring parish, then he expects no brief, but taking his parish together the next Sunday, or holy-day, and exposing to them the uncertainty of human affairs, none knowing whose turn may be next, and then when he hath affrighted them with this, exposing the obligation of charity and neighbourhood, he first gives himself liberally, and then incites them to give; making together a sum either to be sent, or, which were more comfortable, all together choosing some fit day to carry it themselves and cheer the afflicted. So, if any neighbouring village be overburdened with poor, and his own less charged, he finds some way of relieving it and reducing the manna and bread of charity to some equality, representing to his people that the blessing of God to them ought to make them the more charitable, and not the less, lest he cast their neighbours' poverty on them also.

Chapter 20: The Parson in God's Stead

The country parson is in God's stead to his parish, and dischargeth God what he can of his promises. Wherefore there is nothing done, either well or ill, whereof he is not the rewarder or punisher. If he chance to find any reading in another's Bible, he provides him one of his own. If he find another giving a poor man a penny, he gives him a tester[1] for it, if the giver be fit to receive it; or if he be of a condition above such gifts, he sends him a good book, or easeth him in his tithes, telling him when he hath forgotten it, This I do, because at such and such a time you were charitable. This is in some sort a discharging of God as concerning this life, who hath promised that godliness shall be gainful;[2] but in the other God is his own immediate paymaster, rewarding all good deeds to their full proportion. The Parson's punishing of sin and vice is rather by withdrawing his bounty and courtesy from the parties offending, or by private or public reproof as the case requires, than by causing them to be presented or otherwise complained of. And yet as the malice of the person or heinousness of the crime may be, he is careful to see condign punishment inflicted, and with truly godly zeal, without hatred to the person, hungereth and thirsteth after righteous punishment of unrighteousness. Thus both in rewarding virtue and in punishing vice the parson endeavoureth to be in God's stead, knowing that country people are drawn or led by sense more than by faith, by present rewards or punishments more than by future.

Chapter 21: The Parson Catechising

The country parson values catechising highly: for there being three points of his duty, the one, to infuse a competent knowledge of salvation in every one of his flock; the other, to multiply and build up this knowledge to a spiritual Temple; the third, to inflame this knowledge, to press and drive it to practice, turning it to reformation of life by pithy and lively exhortations; catechising is the first point and but by catechising the other cannot be attained. Besides, whereas in sermons there is a kind of state, in catechising there is an humbleness very suitable to Christian regeneration,[1] which exceedingly delights him as by way of exercise upon himself and by way of preaching to himself for the advancing of his own mortification; for in preaching to others he forgets not himself, but is first a sermon to himself and then to others, growing with the growth of his parish. He useth and preferreth the ordinary Church-catechism, partly for obedience to authority, partly for uniformity sake, that the same common truths may be everywhere professed, especially since many remove from parish to parish, who like Christian soldiers are to give the word[2] and to satisfy the congregation by their catholic[3] answers. He exacts of all the doctrine of the catechism; of the younger sort, the very words; of the elder, the substance. Those he catechiseth publicly, these privately, giving age honour according to the Apostle's rule, 1 Timothy 5:1.[4] He requires all to be present at catechising: first, for the authority of the work; secondly, that parents and masters, as they hear the answers prove, may when they come home either commend or reprove, either reward or punish. Thirdly, that those of the elder sort who are not well grounded may then by an honourable way take occasion to be better instructed. Fourthly, that those who are well grown in the knowledge of religion may examine their grounds, renew their vows, and by occasion of both enlarge their meditations. When once all have learned the words of the catechism, he thinks it the most useful way that a pastor can take, to go over the same, but in other words: for many say the catechism by rote, as parrots, without ever piercing into the sense of it. In this course the order of the catechism would be kept, but the rest varied: as thus, in the Creed: how came this world to be as it is? Was it made, or came it by chance? Who made it? Did you see God make it? Then are there some things to be believed that are not seen? Is this the nature of belief? Is not Christianity full of such things, as are not to be seen, but believed? You said, God made the world; who is God? And so forward, requiring answers to all these, and helping and cherishing the answerer by making the question very plain with comparisons, and making much even of a word of truth from him. This order being used to one, would be a little varied to another. And this is an admirable way of teaching, wherein the catechised will at length find delight, and by which the catechizer, if he once get the skill of it, will draw out of ignorant and silly[5] souls, even the dark and deep points of religion. Socrates did thus in philosophy, who held that the seeds of all truths lay in everybody, and accordingly by questions well ordered he found philosophy in silly tradesmen. That position will not hold in Christianity because it contains things above nature; but after that the catechism is once learned, that which nature is towards philosophy the catechism is towards divinity. To this purpose some dialogues in Plato were worth the reading, where the singular dexterity of Socrates in this kind may be observed and imitated. Yet the skill consists but in these three points: first, an aim and mark of the whole discourse, whither to drive the answerer, which the questionist must have in his mind before any question be propounded, upon which and to which the questions are to be chained. Secondly, a most plain and easy framing the question, even containing in virtue the answer also, especially to the more ignorant. Thirdly, when the answerer sticks, an illustrating the thing by something else which he knows, making what he knows to serve him in that which he knows not: as, when the parson once demanded after other questions about man's misery, since man is so miserable, what is to be done? And the answerer could not tell; he asked him again, what he would do if he were in a ditch? This familiar illustration made the answer so plain that he was even ashamed of his ignorance; for he could not but say he would haste out of it as fast as he could. Then he proceeded to ask whether he could get out of the ditch alone or whether he needed a helper, and who was that helper. This is the skill, and doubtless the Holy Scripture intends thus much when it condescends to the naming of a plough, a hatchet,[6] a bushel of leaven, boys piping and dancing; showing that things of ordinary use are not only to serve in the way of drudgery, but to be washed and cleansed, and serve for lights even of heavenly truths. This is the practice which the parson so much commends to all his fellow-labourers, the secret of whose good consists in this, that at sermons, and prayers, men may sleep or wander; but when one is asked a question, he must discover[7] what he is. This practice exceeds even sermons in teaching: but there being two things in sermons, the one informing, the other inflaming; as sermons come short of questions in the one, so they far exceed them in the other. For questions cannot inflame or ravish; that must be done by a set and laboured and continued speech.

Chapter 22: The Parson in Sacraments

The country parson, being to administer the Sacraments, is at a stand with himself how or what behaviour to assume for so holy things. Especially at Communion times he is in a great confusion, as being not only to receive God, but to break and administer him. Neither finds he any issue in this but to throw himself down at the throne of grace, saying, Lord, thou knowest what thou didst, when thou appointedst it to be done thus; therefore do thou fulfil what thou didst appoint; for thou art not only the feast but the way to it. At Baptism, being himself in white, he requires the presence of all and baptiseth not willingly but on Sundays or great days. He admits no vain or idle names, but such as are usual and accustomed. He says that prayer with great devotion where God is thanked for calling us to the knowledge of his grace, Baptism being a blessing that the world hath not the like. He willingly and cheerfully crosseth the child, and thinketh the ceremony not only innocent but reverend. He instructeth the godfathers and godmothers that it is no complimental or light thing to sustain that place, but a great honour and no less burden, as being done both in the presence of God and his saints, and by way of undertaking for a Christian soul. He adviseth all to call to mind their Baptism often; for if wise men have thought it the best way of preserving a state to reduce it to its principles by which it grew great, certainly it is the safest course for Christians also to meditate on their Baptism often (being the first step into their great and glorious calling) and upon what terms and with what vows they were baptised. At the times of the Holy Communion, he first takes order with the churchwardens that the elements be of the best, not cheap or coarse, much less ill-tasted or unwholesome. Secondly, he considers and looks into the ignorance or carelessness of his flock and accordingly applies himself with catechisings and lively exhortations, not on the Sunday of the Communion only (for then it is too late) but the Sunday or Sundays before the Communion, or on the eves of all those days. If there be any, who having not received yet, are to enter into this great work, he takes the more pains with them, that he may lay the foundation of future blessings. The time of everyone's first receiving is not so much by years as by understanding; particularly, the rule may be this; when any one can distinguish the sacramental from common bread, knowing the institution and the difference, he ought to receive, of what age soever. Children and youths are usually deferred too long under pretence of devotion to the Sacrament, but it is for want of instruction; their understandings being ripe enough for ill things, and why not then for better? But parents and masters should make haste in this, as to a great purchase for their children and servants; which while they defer, both sides suffer; the one, in wanting many excitings of grace; the other, in being worse served and obeyed. The saying of the catechism is necessary but not enough; because to answer in form may still admit ignorance: but the questions must be propounded loosely and wildly,[1] and then the answerer will discover what he is. Thirdly, for the manner of receiving, as the parson useth all reverence himself so he administers to none but to the reverent. The feast indeed requires sitting, because it is a feast; but man's unpreparedness asks kneeling. He that comes to the

Sacrament hath the confidence of a guest, and he that kneels confesseth himself an unworthy one, and therefore differs from other feasters; but he that sits or lies puts up to an Apostle: contentiousness in a feast of charity is more scandal than any posture. Fourthly, touching the frequency of the Communion, the parson celebrates it if not duly once a month, yet at least five or six times in the year; as at Easter, Christmas, Whitsuntide,[2] afore and after harvest, and the beginning of Lent. And this he doth not only for the benefit of the work, but also for the discharge of the churchwardens, who being to present all that receive not thrice a year, if there be but three Communions, neither can all the people so order their affairs as to receive just at those times, nor the churchwardens so well take notice who receive thrice, and who not.

Chapter 23: The Parson's Completeness

The country parson desires to be all to his parish, and not only a pastor, but a lawyer also and a physician. Therefore he endures not that any of his flock should go to law; but in any controversy that they should resort to him as their judge. To this end, he hath gotten to himself some insight in things ordinarily incident and controverted, by experience and by reading some initiatory treatises in the law, with Dalton's *Justice of Peace*[1] and the *Abridgements of the Statutes*, as also by discourse with men of that profession whom he hath ever some cases to ask when he meets with them; holding that rule that to put men to discourse of that wherein they are most eminent is the most gainful way of conversation. Yet whenever any controversy is brought to him he never decides it alone, but sends for three or four of the ablest of the parish to hear the cause with him, whom he makes to deliver their opinion first; out of which he gathers, in case he be ignorant himself, what to hold; and so the thing passeth with more authority and less envy. In judging, he follows that which is altogether right; so that if the poorest man of the parish detain but a pin unjustly from the richest, he absolutely restores it as a judge; but when he hath so done, then he assumes the parson and exhorts to charity. Nevertheless, there may happen sometimes some cases wherein he chooseth to permit his parishioners rather to make use of the law than himself: as in cases of an obscure and dark nature, not easily determinable by lawyers themselves; or in cases of high consequence, as establishing of inheritances: or lastly, when the persons in difference are of a contentious disposition, and cannot be gained, but that they still fall from all compromises that have been made. But then he shows them how to go to law even as brethren and not as enemies, neither avoiding therefore one another's company, much less defaming one another. Now as the parson is in law, so is he in sickness also: if there be any of his flock sick he is their physician, or at least his wife, of whom instead of the qualities of the world he asks no other but to have the skill of healing a wound or helping the sick. But if neither himself nor his wife have the skill, and his means serve, he keeps some young practitioner in his house for the benefit of his parish, whom yet he ever exhorts not to exceed his bounds, but in tickle[2] cases to call in help. If all fail, then he keeps good correspondence with some neighbour physician, and entertains him for the cure of his parish. Yet is it easy for any scholar to attain to such a measure of physic[3] as may be of much use to him both for himself and others. This is done by seeing one anatomy,[4] reading one book of physic, having one herbal by him. And let Fernelius[5] be the physic author, for he writes briefly, neatly and judiciously; especially let his method of physic be diligently perused as being the practical part and of most use. Now both the reading of him and the knowing of herbs may be done at such times as they may be an help and a recreation to more divine studies, Nature serving Grace both in comfort of diversion and the benefit of application when need requires; as also by way of illustration, even as our Saviour made plants and seeds to teach the people: for he was the true householder, who bringeth out of his treasure things new and old, the old things of philosophy and the new of Grace, and maketh the one serve the other. And I conceive our Saviour did this for three reasons: first, that by familiar things he might make his doctrine slip the more easily into the hearts even of the meanest. Secondly, that labouring people (whom he chiefly considered) might have everywhere monuments of his doctrine, remembering in gardens his mustard-seed and lilies, in the field his seed-corn and tares;[6] and so not be drowned altogether in the works of their vocation, but sometimes lift up their minds to better things, even in the midst of their pains. Thirdly, that he might set a copy for parsons. In the knowledge of simples,[7] wherein the manifold wisdom of God is wonderfully to be seen, one thing would be carefully observed; which is, to know what herbs may be used instead of drugs of the same nature, and to make the garden the shop: for home-bred medicines are both more easy for the parson's purse, and more familiar for all men's bodies. So, where the apothecary useth either for loosing, rhubarb, or for binding, bolearmena,[8] the parson useth damask or white roses for the one, and plaintain,[9] shepherd's purse, knot-grass for the other, and that with better success. As for spices, he doth not only prefer home-bred things before them but condemns them for vanities, and so shuts them out of his family, esteeming that there is no spice comparable for herbs to rosemary, thyme, savoury, mints; and for seeds, to fennel and caraway seeds. Accordingly, for salves his wife seeks not the city, but prefers her garden and fields before all outlandish gums. And surely hyssop, valerian, mercury, adder's tongue, yerrow, melilot, and Saint John's wort made into a salve; and elder, camomile, mallows, comfrey and smallage made into a poultice have done great and rare cures.[10] In curing of any the parson and his family use to premise prayers, for this is to cure like a parson, and this raiseth the action from the shop to the church. But though the parson sets forward all charitable deeds, yet he looks not in this point of curing beyond his own parish, except the person be so poor that he is not able to reward the physician: for as he is charitable, so he is just also. Now it is a justice and debt to the commonwealth he lives in not to encroach on others' professions, but to live on his own. And justice is the ground of charity.

Chapter 24: The Parson Arguing

The country parson, if there be any of his parish that hold strange doctrines, useth all possible diligence to reduce them to the common faith. The first means he useth is prayer, beseeching the Father of lights to open their eyes, and to give him power so to fit his discourse to them that it may effectually pierce their hearts and convert them. The second means is a very loving and sweet usage of them, both in going to and sending for them often, and in finding out courtesies to place on them, as in their tithes, or otherwise. The third means is the observation what is the main foundation and pillar of their cause, whereon they rely; as if he be a Papist, the Church is the hinge he turns on; if a schismatic,[1] scandal.[2] Wherefore the parson hath diligently examined these two with himself, as what the Church is, how it began, how it proceeded, whether it be a rule to itself, whether it hath a rule, whether having a rule, it ought not to be guided by it; whether any rule in the world be obscure, and how then should the best be so, at least in fundamental things, the obscurity in some points being the exercise of the Church, the light in the foundations being the guide, the Church needing both an evidence and an exercise.[3] So for scandal: what scandal is, when given or taken; whether, there being two precepts, one of obeying authority, the other of not giving scandal, that ought not to be preferred, especially since in disobeying there is scandal also; whether things once indifferent being made by the precept of authority more than indifferent it be in our power to omit or refuse them. These and the like points he hath accurately digested, having ever besides two great helps and powerful persuaders on his side; the one, a strict religious life; the other an humble and ingenuous search of truth, being unmoved in arguing and void of all contentiousness: which are two great lights able to dazzle the eyes of the misled, while they consider that God cannot be wanting to them in doctrine to whom he is so gracious in life.

Chapter 25: The Parson Punishing

Whensoever the country parson proceeds so far as to call in authority, and to do such things of legal opposition either in the presenting or punishing of any, as the vulgar ever consters[1] for signs of ill will, he forbears not in any wise to use the delinquent as before in his behaviour and carriage towards him, not avoiding his company or doing anything of averseness save in the very act of punishment: neither doth he esteem him for an enemy, but as a brother still, except some small and temporary estranging may corroborate the punishment to a better subduing and humbling of the delinquent; which if it happily take effect, he then comes on the faster and makes so much the more of him as before he alienated himself, doubling his regards, and showing by all means that the delinquent's return is to his advantage.

Chapter 26: The Parson's Eye

The country parson at spare times from action, standing on a hill and considering his flock, discovers two sorts of vices and two sorts of vicious persons. There are some vices whose natures are always clear and evident, as adultery, murder, hatred, lying, etc. There are other vices whose natures, at least in the beginning, are dark and obscure, as covetousness and gluttony. So likewise there are some persons who abstain not even from known sins; there are others, who when they know a sin evidently, they commit it not. It is true, indeed, they are long a-knowing it, being partial to themselves, and witty to others who shall reprove them from it. A man may be both covetous and intemperate, and yet hear sermons against both, and himself condemn both in good earnest: and the reason hereof is, because the natures of these vices being not evidently discussed, or known commonly, the beginnings of them are not easily observable; and the beginnings of them are not observed, because of the sudden passing from that which was just now lawful, to that which is presently unlawful, even in one continued action. So a man dining eats at first lawfully; but proceeding on, comes to do unlawfully, even before he is aware, not knowing the bounds of the action, nor when his eating begins to be unlawful. So a man storing up money for his necessary provisions, both in present for his family and in future for his children, hardly perceives when his storing becomes unlawful; yet is there a period for his storing and a point, or centre, when his storing, which was even now good, passeth from good to bad. Wherefore the parson being true to his business hath exactly sifted the definitions of all virtues and vices, especially canvassing those whose natures are most stealing and beginnings uncertain. Particularly concerning these two vices, not because they are all that are of this dark and creeping disposition, but for example sake, and because they are most common, he thus thinks: first, for covetousness he lays this ground: whosoever when a just occasion calls, either spends not at all, or not in some proportion to God's blessing upon him, is covetous. The reason of the ground is manifest, because wealth is given to that end to supply our occasions. Now, if I do not give everything its end, I abuse the creature, I am false to my reason which should guide me, I offend the supreme judge in perverting that order which he hath set both to things and to reason. The application of the ground would be infinite; but in brief, a poor man is an occasion, my country is an occasion, my friend is an occasion, my table is an occasion, my apparel is an occasion: if in all these and those more which concern me, I either do nothing, or pinch and scrape, and squeeze blood undecently to the station wherein God hath placed me, I am covetous. More particularly, and to give one instance for all, if God have given me servants and I either provide too little for them or that which is unwholesome, being sometimes baned[1] meat, sometimes too salt, and so not competent nourishment, I am covetous. I bring this example because men usually think that servants for their money are as other things that they buy, even as a piece of wood which they may cut, or hack, or throw into the fire, and so they pay them their wages, all is well. Nay, to descend yet more particularly, if a man hath wherewithal to buy a spade and yet he chooseth rather to use his neighbour's, and wear out that, he is covetous. Nevertheless, few bring covetousness thus low or consider it so narrowly, which yet ought to be done since there is a justice in the least things and for the least there shall be a judgement. Country people are full of these petty injustices, being cunning to make use of another and spare themselves, and scholars ought to be diligent in the observation of these and driving of their general school rules ever to the smallest actions of life, which while they dwell in their books they will never find, but being seated in the country and doing their duty faithfully, they will soon discover, especially if they carry their eyes ever open, and fix them on their charge and not on their preferment. Secondly, for gluttony the parson lays this ground: he that either for quantity eats more than his health or employments will bear, or for quality is likerous after dainties, is a glutton; as he that eats more than his estate will bear is a prodigal;[2] and he that eats offensively to the company, either in his order or length of eating, is scandalous and uncharitable. These three rules generally comprehend the faults of eating, and the truth of them needs no proof: so that men must eat neither to the disturbance of their health, or of their affairs (which being overburdened, or studying dainties too much, they cannot well dispatch) nor of their estate, nor of their brethren. One act in these things is bad, but it is the custom and habit that names a glutton. Many think they are at more liberty than they are, as if they were masters of their health, and so they will stand to the pain all is well. But to eat to one's hurt comprehends besides the hurt an act against reason, because it is unnatural to hurt one's self; and this they are not masters of. Yet of hurtful things I am more bound to abstain from those which by mine own experience I have found hurtful than from those which by a common tradition and vulgar knowledge are reputed to be so. That which is said of hurtful meats extends to hurtful drinks also. As for the quantity, touching our employments none must eat so as to disable themselves from a fit discharging either of divine duties, or duties of their calling. So that if after dinner they are not fit (or unwieldy) either to pray or work, they are gluttons. Not that all must presently work after dinner (for they rather must not work, especially students and those that are weakly); but that they must rise so as that it is not meat or drink that hinders them from working. To guide them in this there are three rules: first, the custom and knowledge of their own body, and what it can well digest; the second, the feeling of themselves in time of eating, which because it is deceitful (for one thinks in eating that he can eat more than afterwards he finds true); the third is the observation with what appetite they sit down. This last rule, joined with the first, never fails. For knowing what one usually can well digest, and feeling when I go to meat in what disposition I am, either hungry or not according as I feel myself, either I take my wonted proportion or diminish of it. Yet physicians bid those that would live in health not keep an uniform diet but to feed variously, now more, now less: and Gerson,[3] a spiritual man, wishes all to incline rather to too much than to too little; his reason is because diseases of exinanition are more dangerous than diseases of repletion. But the parson distinguisheth according to his double aim, either of abstinence, a moral virtue, or mortification, a divine. When he deals with any that is heavy and carnal, he gives him those freer rules: but when he meets with a refined and heavenly disposition he carries them higher, even sometimes to a forgetting of themselves, knowing that there is one who when they forget, remembers for them, as when the people hungered and thirsted after our Saviour's doctrine and tarried so long at it that they would have fainted had they returned empty, he suffered it not; but rather made food miraculously, than suffered so good desires to miscarry.

Chapter 27: The Parson in Mirth

The country parson is generally sad,[1] because he knows nothing but the Cross of Christ, his mind being defixed on it with those nails wherewith his Master was: or if he have any leisure to look off from thence he meets continually with two most sad spectacles, sin and misery; God dishonoured every day and man afflicted. Nevertheless, he sometimes refresheth himself, as knowing that nature will not bear everlasting droopings and that pleasantness of disposition is a great key to do good, not only because all men shun the company of perpetual severity, but also for that when they are in company, instructions seasoned with pleasantness both enter sooner and root deeper. Wherefore he condescends to human frailties both in himself and others; and intermingles some mirth in his discourses occasionally, according to the pulse of the hearer.

Chapter 28: The Parson in Contempt

The country parson knows well that both for the general ignominy which is cast upon the profession, and much more for those rules which out of his choicest judgement he hath resolved to observe and which are described in this book, he must be despised, because this hath been the portion of God his Master, and of God's Saints his brethren, and this is foretold that it shall be so still, until things be no more. Nevertheless, according to the Apostle's rule,[1] he endeavours that none shall despise him; especially in his own parish he suffers it not to his utmost power; for that, where contempt is there is no room for instruction. This he procures first, by his holy and unblameable life, which carries a reverence with it even above contempt. Secondly, by a courteous carriage and winning behaviour: he that will be respected must respect, doing kindnesses but receiving none, at least of those who are apt to despise: for this argues a height and eminency of mind which is not easily despised, except it degenerate to pride. Thirdly, by a bold and impartial reproof even of the best in the parish when occasion requires, for this may produce hatred in those that are reproved, but never contempt either in them or others. Lastly, if the contempt shall proceed so far as to do anything punishable by law, as contempt is apt to do if it be not thwarted, the parson having a due respect both to the person and to the cause referreth the whole matter to the examination and punishment of those which are in authority; that so the sentence lighting upon one, the example may reach to all. But if the contempt be not punishable by law, or being so, the parson think it in his discretion either unfit or bootless[2] to contend, then when any despises him he takes it either in an humble way, saying nothing at all; or else in a slighting way, showing that reproaches touch him no more than a stone thrown against heaven, where he is and lives; or in a sad way, grieved at his own and others' sins, which continually break God's laws and dishonour him with those mouths which he continually fills and feeds; or else in a doctrinal way, saying to the contemner, Alas, why do you thus? you hurt yourself, not me; he that throws a stone at another hits himself; and so between gentle reasoning and pitying, he overcomes the evil; or lastly, in a triumphant way, being glad and joyful that he is made conformable to his Master; and being in the world as he was, hath this undoubted pledge of his salvation. These are the five shields wherewith the godly receive the darts of the wicked; leaving anger and retorting and revenge to the children of the world, whom another's ill mastereth, and leadeth captive without any resistance, even in resistance, to the same destruction. For while they resist the person that reviles they resist not the evil which takes hold of them and is far the worse enemy.

Chapter 29: The Parson with his Churchwardens

The country parson doth often both publicly and privately instruct his churchwardens what a great charge lies upon them, and that indeed the whole order and discipline of the parish is put into their hands. If himself reform anything, it is out of the overflowing of his conscience, whereas they are to do it by command, and by oath. Neither hath the place its dignity from the ecclesiastical laws only, since even by the common statute-law they are taken for a kind of corporation, as being persons enabled by that name to take moveable goods or chattels, and to sue and to be sued at the law concerning such goods for the use and profit of their parish: and by the same law they are to levy penalties for negligence in resorting to church or for disorderly carriage in time of divine service. Wherefore the parson suffers not the place to be vilified or debased by being cast on the lower rank of people, but invites and urges the best unto it, showing that they do not lose or go less, but gain by it, it being the greatest honour of this world to do God and his chosen service, or as David says,[1] to be even a door-keeper in the house of God. Now the Canons[2] being the churchwardens' rule, the parson adviseth them to read or hear them read often, as also the visitation articles which are grounded upon the Canons, that so they may know their duty and keep their oath the better; in which regard, considering the great consequence of their place, and more of their oath, he wisheth them by no means to spare any, though never so great; but if after gentle and neighbourly admonitions they still persist in ill, to present them; yea though they be tenants or otherwise engaged to the delinquent: for their obligation to God and their own soul is above any temporal tie. Do well and right, and let the world sink.

Chapter 30: The Parson's Consideration of Providence

The country parson, considering the great aptness country people have to think that all things come by a kind of natural course, and that if they sow and soil[1] their grounds they must have corn;[2] if they keep and fodder well their cattle they must have milk and calves, labours to reduce them to see God's hand in all things and to believe that things are not set in such an inevitable order, but that God often changeth it according as he sees fit, either for reward or punishment. To this end he represents to his flock that God hath and exerciseth a threefold power in everything which concerns man. The first is a sustaining power, the second a governing power, the third a spiritual power. By his sustaining power he preserves and actuates everything in his being, so that corn doth not grow by any other virtue[3] than by that which he continually supplies as the corn needs it, without which supply the corn would instantly dry up as a river would if the fountain were stopped. And it is observable that if anything could presume of an inevitable course and constancy in its operations, certainly it should be either the sun in heaven or the fire on earth by reason of their fierce, strong, and violent natures; yet when God pleased, the sun stood still, the fire burned not.[4] By God's governing power he preserves and orders the references of things one to the other, so that though the corn do grow, and be preserved in that act by his sustaining power, yet if he suit not other things to the growth, as seasons, and weather, and other accidents by his governing power, the fairest harvests come to nothing. And it is observable that God delights to have men feel, and acknowledge, and reverence his power, and therefore he often overturns things, when they are thought past danger; that is his time of interposing, as when a merchant has a ship come home after many a storm which it hath escaped, he destroys it sometimes in the very haven; or if the goods be housed, a fire hath broken forth and suddenly consumed them. Now this he doth that men should perpetuate and not break off their acts of dependence, how fair soever the opportunities present themselves. So that if a farmer should depend upon God all the year, and being ready to put hand to sickle shall then secure himself and think all cock-sure, then God sends such weather as lays the corn, and destroys it: or if he depend on God further, even till he imbarn his corn, and then think all sure, God sends a fire, and consumes all that he hath: for that he ought not to break off, but to continue his dependence on God, not only before the corn is inned, but after also; and indeed to depend and fear continually. The third power is spiritual, by which God turns all outward blessings to inward advantages. So that if a farmer hath both a fair harvest, and that also well inned, and imbarned, and continuing safe there, yet if God give him not the grace to use and utter[5] this well, all his advantages are to his loss. Better were his corn burnt than not spiritually improved. And it is observable in this how God's goodness strives with man's refractoriness; man would sit down at this world, God bids him sell it, and purchase a better: just as a father, who hath in his hand an apple, and a piece of gold under it; the child comes, and with pulling, gets the apple out of his father's hand: his father bids him throw it away, and he will give him the gold for it, which the child utterly refusing, eats it, and is troubled with worms: so is the carnal and wilful man with the worm of the grave in this world, and the worm of conscience in the next.

Chapter 31: The Parson in Liberty

The country parson observing the manifold wiles of Satan (who plays his part sometimes in drawing God's servants from him, sometimes in perplexing them in the service of God) stands fast in the liberty wherewith Christ hath made us free. This liberty he compasseth by one distinction, and that is of what is necessary and what is additionary. As for example: it is necessary that all Christians should pray twice a day every day of the week, and four times on Sunday, if they be well. This is so necessary and essential to a Christian that he cannot without this maintain himself in a Christian state. Besides this, the godly have ever added some hours of prayer, as at nine, or at three, or at midnight, or as they think fit and see cause, or rather as God's spirit leads them. But these prayers are not necessary, but additionary. Now it so happens, that the godly petitioner upon some emergent[1] interruption in the day, or by oversleeping himself at night, omits his additionary prayer. Upon this his mind begins to be perplexed and troubled, and Satan, who knows the exigent,[2] blows the fire, endeavouring to disorder the Christian and put him out of his station, and to enlarge the perplexity until it spread and taint his other duties of piety, which none can perform so well in trouble as in calmness. Here the parson interposeth with his distinction, and shows the perplexed Christian that this prayer being additionary not necessary, taken in not commanded, the omission thereof upon just occasion ought by no means to trouble him. God knows the occasion as well as he, and he is as a gracious father, who more accepts a common course of devotion than dislikes an occasional interruption. And of this he is so to assure himself as to admit no scruple, but to go on as cheerfully as if he had not been interrupted. By this it is evident that the distinction is of singular use and comfort, especially to pious minds which are ever tender and delicate. But here there are two cautions to be added. First, that this interruption proceed not out of slackness or coldness, which will appear if the pious soul foresee and prevent such interruptions what he may,[3] before they come, and when for all that they do come he be a little affected therewith, but not afflicted or troubled; if he resent it to a mislike but not a grief.[4] Secondly, that this interruption proceed not out of shame. As for example: a godly man, not out of superstition but of reverence to God's house, resolves whenever he enters into a church to kneel down and pray, either blessing God that he will be pleased to dwell among man; or beseeching him that whenever he repairs to his house, he may behave himself so as befits so great a presence; and this briefly. But it happens that near the place where he is to pray, he spies some scoffing ruffian, who is likely to deride him for his pains: if he now shall either for fear or shame break his custom, he shall do passing ill: so much the rather ought he to proceed, as that by this he may take into his prayer humiliation also. On the other side, if I am to visit the sick in haste, and my nearest way lie through the church, I will not doubt to go without staying to pray there (but only, as I pass, in my heart) because this kind of prayer is additionary, not necessary, and the other duty overweighs it: so that if any scruple arise, I will throw it away, and be most confident that God is not displeased. This distinction may run through all Christian duties, and it is a great stay and settling to religious souls.

Chapter 32: The Parson's Surveys

The country parson hath not only taken a particular survey of the faults of his own parish, but a general also of the diseases of the time, that so, when his occasions carry him abroad or bring strangers to him, he may be the better armed to encounter them. The great and national sin of this land he esteems to be idleness; great in itself, and great in consequence: for when men have nothing to do, then they fall to drink, to steal, to whore, to scoff, to revile, to all sorts of gamings. Come, say they, we have nothing to do, let's go to the tavern, or to the stews, or what not. Wherefore the parson strongly opposeth this sin wheresoever he goes. And because idleness is twofold, the one in having no calling, the other in walking carelessly in our calling, he first represents to everybody the necessity of a vocation.[1] The reason of this assertion is taken from the nature of man, wherein God hath placed two great instruments, reason in the soul and a hand in the body, as engagements of working: so that even in Paradise man had a calling, and how much more out of Paradise, when the evils which he is now subject unto may be prevented or diverted by reasonable employment. Besides, every gift or ability is a talent to be accounted for, and to be improved to our Master's advantage. Yet it is also a debt to our country to have a calling, and it concerns the commonwealth that none should be idle, but all busied. Lastly, riches are the blessing of God, and the great instrument of doing admirable good; therefore all are to procure them honestly and seasonably, when they are not better employed. Now this reason crosseth not our Saviour's precept of selling what we have, because when we have sold all and given it to the poor, we must not be idle, but labour to get more, that we may give more, according to St Paul's rule, Ephesians 4:28, 1 Thessalonians 4:11–12. So that our Saviour's selling is so far from crossing Saint Paul's working that it rather establisheth it, since they that have nothing are fittest to work. Now because the only opposer of this doctrine is the gallant who is witty enough to abuse both others and himself, and who is ready to ask if he shall mend shoes, or what he shall do? Therefore the parson, unmoved, showeth that *ingenuous*[2] *and fit* employment is never wanting to those that seek it. But if it should be, the assertion stands thus: all are either to have a calling or prepare for it: he that hath or can have yet no employment, if he truly and seriously prepare for it, he is safe and within bounds. Wherefore all are either presently to enter into a calling, if they be fit for it and it for them; or else to examine with care and advice what they are fittest for, and to prepare for that with all diligence. But it will not be amiss in this exceeding useful point to descend to particulars, for exactness lies in particulars. Men are either single or married:[3] the married and housekeeper hath his hands full if he do what he ought to do. For there are two branches of his affairs; first, the improvement of his family by bringing them up in the fear and nurture of the Lord, and secondly, the improvement of his grounds, by drowning, or draining, or stocking, or fencing, and ordering his land to the best advantage both of himself and his neighbours. The Italian[4] says, none fouls his hands in his own business: and it is an honest and just care, so it exceed not bounds, for everyone to employ himself to the advancement of his affairs that he may have wherewithal to do good. But his family is his best care, to labour Christian souls and raise them to their height, even to heaven; to dress and prune them and take as much joy in a straight-growing child or servant as a gardener doth in a choice tree. Could men find out this delight, they would seldom be from home, whereas now, of any place they are least there. But if after all this care well dispatched, the housekeeper's family be so small and his dexterity so great that he have leisure to look out, the village or parish which either he lives in, or is near unto it, is his employment. He considers everyone there and either helps them in particular, or hath both general propositions to the whole town or hamlet of advancing the public stock, and managing commons or woods according as the place suggests. But if he may be of the Commission of Peace, there is nothing to that: no commonwealth in the world hath a braver institution than that of Justices of the Peace, for it is both a security to the King, who hath so many dispersed officers at his beck throughout the kingdom accountable for the public good, and also an honourable employment of a gentle- or noble-man in the country he lives in, enabling him with power to do good and to restrain all those who else might trouble him and the whole state. Wherefore it behoves all who are come to the gravity and ripeness of judgement for so excellent a place not to refuse, but rather to procure it. And whereas there are usually three objections made against the place, the one, the abuse of it by taking petty country bribes, the other, the casting of it on mean persons, especially in some shires, and lastly, the trouble of it, these are so far from deterring any good man from the place that they kindle them rather to redeem the dignity either from true faults, or unjust aspersions. Now, for single men, they are either heirs or younger brothers: the heirs are to prepare in all the fore-mentioned points against the time of their practice. Therefore they are to mark their father's discretion in ordering his house and affairs, and also elsewhere when they see any remarkable point of education or good husbandry, and to transplant it in time to his own home with the same care as others, when they meet with good fruit, get a graft of the tree, enriching their orchard and neglecting their house. Besides, they are to read books of law and justice, especially the Statutes at large. As for better books of divinity, they are not in this consideration, because we are about a calling and a preparation thereunto. But chiefly, and above all things, they are to frequent sessions and sizes,[5] for it is both an honour which they owe to the reverend judges and magistrates to attend them, at least in their shire, and it is a great advantage to know the practice of the land, for our law is practice. Sometimes he may go to court, as the eminent place both of good and ill. At other times he is to travel over the King's dominions, cutting out the kingdom into portions which every year he surveys piecemeal. When there is a parliament, he is to endeavour by all means to be a knight or burgess there, for there is no school to a parliament. And when he is there, he must not only be a morning man, but at committees also; for there the particulars are exactly discussed which are brought from thence to the House but in general. When none of these occasions call him abroad, every morning that he is at home he must either ride the great horse[6] or exercise some of his military gestures. For all gentlemen that are not weakened and disarmed with sedentary lives are to know the use of their arms: and as the husbandman labours for them, so must they fight for and defend them when occasion calls. This is the duty of each to other which they ought to fulfil: and the parson is a lover of and exciter to justice in all things, even as John the Baptist squared out[7] to everyone (even to soldiers[8]) what to do. As for younger brothers, those whom the parson finds loose, and not engaged into some profession by their parents, whose neglect in this point is intolerable and a shameful wrong both to the commonwealth and their own house; to them, after he hath showed the unlawfulness of spending the day in dressing, complimenting, visiting and sporting, he first commends the study of the civil law as a brave and wise knowledge, the professors whereof were much employed by Queen Elizabeth because it is the key of commerce and discovers the rules of foreign nations. Secondly, he commends the mathematics, as the only wonder-working knowledge, and therefore requiring the best spirits. After the several knowledge of these, he adviseth to insist and dwell chiefly on the two noble branches thereof, of fortification and navigation; the one being useful to all countries, and the other especially to islands. But if the young gallant think these courses dull and phlegmatic, where can he busy himself better than in those new plantations and discoveries, which are not only a noble, but also as they may be handled, a religious employment? Or let him travel into Germany and France, and observing the artifices and manufactures there, transplant them hither, as divers have done lately to our country's advantage.

Chapter 33: The Parson's Library

The country parson's library is a holy life, for besides the blessing that that brings upon it, there being a promise that if the Kingdom of God be first sought,[1] all other things shall be added, even itself is a sermon. For the temptations with which a good man is beset, and the ways which he used to overcome them, being told to another, whether in private conference, or in the church, are a sermon. He that hath considered how to carry himself at table about his appetite, if he tell this to another, preacheth; and much more feelingly, and judiciously, than he writes his rules of temperance out of books. So that the parson having studied, and mastered all his lusts and affections within and the whole army of temptations without, hath ever so many sermons ready penned, as he has victories. And it fares in this as it doth in physic: he that hath been sick of a consumption and knows what recovered him is a physician so far as he meets with the same disease and temper, and can much better and particularly do it, than he that is generally learned, and was never sick. And if the same person had been sick of all diseases, and were recovered of all by things that he knew, there were no such physician as he, both for skill and tenderness. Just so it is in divinity, and that not without manifest reason: for the temptations may be diverse in divers Christians, yet the victory is alike in all, being by the self-same Spirit. Neither is this true only in the military state of a Christian life, but even in the peaceable also; when the servant of God, freed for awhile from temptation, in a quiet sweetness seeks how to please his God. Thus the parson considering that repentance is the great virtue of the Gospel and one of the first steps of pleasing God, having for his own use examined the nature of it, is able to explain it after to others. And particularly, having doubted sometimes whether his repentance were true, or at least in that degree it ought to be, since he found himself sometimes to weep more for the loss of some temporal things than for offending God, he came at length to this resolution that repentance is an act of the mind, not of the body, even as the original signifies; and that the chief thing which God in Scriptures requires is the heart and the spirit, and to worship him in truth and spirit. Wherefore in case a Christian endeavour to weep, and cannot since we are not masters of our bodies, this sufficeth. And consequently he found that the essence of repentance, that it may be alike in all God's children (which as concerning weeping it cannot be, some being of a more melting temper than others) consisteth in a true detestation of the soul, abhorring, renouncing sin, and turning unto God in truth of heart and newness of life: which acts of repentance are and must be found in all God's servants; not that weeping is not useful where it can be, that so the body may join in the grief as it did in the sin; but that, so the other acts be, that is not necessary: so that he as truly repents who performs the other acts of repentance when he cannot more, as he that weeps a flood of tears. This instruction and comfort the parson getting for himself, when he tells it to others, becomes a sermon. The like he doth in other Christian virtues, as of faith and love and the cases of conscience belonging thereto, wherein (as Saint Paul implies that he ought, Romans 2[2]) he first preacheth to himself and then to others.

Chapter 34: The Parson's Dexterity in Applying of Remedies

The country parson knows that there is a double state of a Christian even in this life, the one military, the other peaceable. The military is, when we are assaulted with temptations either from within or from without. The peaceable is, when the Devil for a time leaves us, as he did our Saviour,[1] and the angels minister to us their own food, even joy and peace and comfort in the Holy Ghost. These two states were in our Saviour, not only in the beginning of his preaching, but afterwards also, as Matthew 22:35, he was tempted: and Luke 10:21, he rejoiced in spirit; and they must be likewise in all that are his. Now the parson having a spiritual judgement, according as he discovers any of his flock to be in one or the other state, so he applies himself to them. Those that he finds in the peaceable state, he adviseth to be very vigilant, and not to let go the reins as soon as the horse goes easy. Particularly he counselleth them to two things: first, to take heed, lest their quiet betray them (as it is apt to do) to a coldness and carelessness to their devotions, but to labour still to be as fervent in Christian duties, as they remember themselves were, when affliction did blow the coals. Secondly, not to take the full compass and liberty of their peace: not to eat of all those dishes at table which even their present health otherwise admits, nor to store their house with all those furnitures which even their present plenty of wealth otherwise admits, nor when they are among them that are merry to extend themselves to all the mirth which the present occasion of wit and company otherwise admits, but to put bounds and hoops to their joys: so will they last the longer, and when they depart, return the sooner. If we would judge ourselves, we should not be judged; and if we would bound ourselves, we should not be bounded. But if they shall fear that at such or such a time their peace and mirth have carried them further than this moderation, then to take Job's admirable course,[2] who sacrificed lest his children should have transgressed in their mirth: so let them go and find some poor afflicted soul, and there be bountiful and liberal, for with such sacrifices God is well pleased. Those that the parson finds in the military state, he fortifies and strengthens with utmost skill. Now in those that are tempted, whatsoever is unruly falls upon two heads; either they think that there is none that can or will look after things, but all goes by chance or wit: or else, though there be a great Governor of all things, yet to them he is lost, as if they said God doth forsake and persecute them and there is none to deliver them. If the Parson suspect the first, and find sparks of such thoughts now and then to break forth, then without opposing directly (for disputation is no cure for atheism) he scatters in his discourse three sorts of arguments; the first taken from Nature, the second from the Law, and the third from Grace.

For Nature, he sees not how a house could be either built without a builder, or kept in repair without a housekeeper. He conceives not possibly how the winds should blow so much as they can and the sea rage so much as it can, and all things do what they can, and all not only without dissolution of the whole but also of any part, by taking away so much as the usual seasons of summer and winter, earing[3] and harvest. Let the weather be what it will, still we have bread, though sometimes more, sometimes less; wherewith also a careful Joseph[4] might meet. He conceives not possible how he that would believe a divinity, if he had been at the creation of all things, should less believe it, seeing the preservation of all things, for preservation is a creation, and more, it is a continued creation, and a creation every moment.

Secondly, for the Law, there may be so evident though unused a proof of divinity taken from thence, and the atheist or Epicurean[5] can have nothing to contradict. The Jews yet live, and are known:

they have their law and language bearing witness to them, and they to it; they are circumcised to this day, and expect the promises of the Scripture; their country also is known, the places and rivers travelled unto, and frequented by others, but to them an unpenetrable rock, unaccessible desert. Wherefore if the Jews live, all the great wonders of the old live in them, and then who can deny the stretched out arm of a mighty God? Especially since it may be a just doubt whether, considering the stubbornness of the nation, their living then in their country under so many miracles were a stranger thing than their present exile and disability to live in their country. And it is observable that this very thing was intended by God, and the Jews should be his proof and witnesses, as he calls them, Isaiah 43:12.[6] And their very dispersion in all lands was intended not only for a punishment to them, but for an exciting of others by their sight, to the acknowledging of God and his power, Psalm 59:11.[7] And therefore this kind of punishment was chosen rather than any other.

Thirdly, for Grace. Besides the continual succession (since the Gospel) of holy men who have born witness to the truth (there being no reason why any should distrust Saint Luke, or Tertullian, or Chrysostom, more than Tully, Virgil or Livy[8]), there are two prophecies in the Gospel which evidently argue Christ's divinity by their success: the one concerning the woman that spent the ointment on our Saviour, for which he told that it should never be forgotten but with the Gospel itself be preached to all ages, Matthew 26:13. The other concerning the destruction of Jerusalem, of which our Saviour said that that generation should not pass till all were fulfilled, Luke 21:32. Which Josephus's *History*[9] confirms, and the continuance of which verdict is yet evident. To these might be added the preaching of the Gospel in all nations, Matthew 24:14, which we see even miraculously effected in these new discoveries, God turning men's covetousness and ambitions to the effecting of his word. Now a prophecy is a wonder sent to posterity, lest they complain of want of wonders. It is a letter sealed and sent which to the bearer is but paper, but to the receiver and opener is full of power. He that saw Christ open a blind man's eyes saw not more divinity than he that reads the woman's ointment in the Gospel, or sees Jerusalem destroyed. With some of these heads enlarged, and woven in his discourse at several times and occasions, the parson settleth wavering minds. But if he sees them nearer desperation than atheism, not so much doubting a God, as that he is theirs, then he dives unto the boundless ocean of God's love and the unspeakable riches of his loving kindness. He hath one argument unanswerable. If God hate them, either he doth it as they are creatures, dust and ashes, or as they are sinful. As creatures, he must needs love them; for no perfect artist ever yet hated his own work. As sinful, he must much more love them, because notwithstanding his infinite hate of sin, his love overcame that hate, and with an exceeding great victory which in the Creation needed not, gave them love for love, even the son of his love out of his bosom of love. So that man, which way soever he turns, hath two pledges of God's love that in the mouth of two or three witnesses every word may be established; the one in his being, the other in his sinful being: and this as the more faulty in him, so the more glorious in God. And all may certainly conclude that God loves them, till either they despise that love, or despair of his mercy: not any sin else but is within his love; but the despising of love must needs be without it. The thrusting away of his arm makes us only not embraced.[10]

Chapter 35: The Parson's Condescending[1]

The country parson is a lover of old customs if they be good, and harmless, and the rather, because country people are much addicted to them, so that to favour them therein is to win their hearts, and to oppose them therein is to deject them. If there be any ill in the custom that may be severed from the good, he pares the apple and gives them the clean to feed on. Particularly, he loves procession,[2] and maintains it because there are contained therein four manifest advantages. First, a blessing of God for the fruits of the field; secondly, justice in the preservation of bounds; thirdly, charity in loving walking, and neighbourly accompanying one another, with reconciling of differences at that time, if there be any; fourthly, mercy in relieving the poor by a liberal distribution and largesse which at that time is or ought to be used. Wherefore he exacts of all to be present at the perambulation, and those that withdraw and sever themselves from it, he mislikes and reproves as uncharitable and unneighbourly, and if they will not reform, presents them. Nay, he is so far from condemning such assemblies that he rather procures them to be often, as knowing that absence breeds strangeness, but presence love. Now love is his business and aim; wherefore he likes well that his parish at good times invite one another to their houses, and he urgeth them to it: and sometimes, where he knows there has been or is a little difference, he takes one of the parties and goes with him to the other, and all dine or sup together. There is much preaching in this friendliness. Another old custom there is of saying, when light is brought in, God send us the light of heaven, and the parson likes this very well, neither is he afraid of praising or praying to God at all times, but is rather glad of catching opportunities to do them. Light is a great blessing and as great a food, for which we give thanks: and those that think this superstitious neither know superstition nor themselves. As for those that are ashamed to use this form, as being old and obsolete and not the fashion, he reforms and teaches them that at Baptism they professed not to be ashamed of Christ's Cross, or for any shame to leave that which is good. He that is ashamed in small things will extend his pusillanimity to greater. Rather should a Christian soldier take such occasions to harden himself, and to further his exercises of mortification.

Chapter 36: The Parson Blessing

The country parson wonders that blessing the people is in so little use with his brethren, whereas he thinks it not only a grave and reverend thing, but a beneficial also. Those who use it not, do so either out of niceness, because they like the salutations and compliments and forms of worldly language better, which conformity and fashionableness is so exceeding unbefitting a minister that it deserves reproof not refutation; or else because they think it empty and superfluous. But that which the Apostles used so diligently in their writings, nay, which our Saviour himself used, Mark 10:16,[1] cannot be vain and superfluous. But this was not proper to Christ or the Apostles only, no more than to be a spiritual father was appropriated to them. And if temporal fathers bless their children, how much more may, and ought spiritual fathers? Besides, the priests of the Old Testament were commanded to bless the people, and the form thereof is prescribed, Numbers 6.[2] Now as the Apostle[3] argues in another case: if the ministration of condemnation[4] did bless, how shall not the ministration of the spirit exceed in blessing? The fruit of this blessing good Hannah found, and received with great joy, 1 Samuel 1:18, though it came from a man disallowed by God, for it was not the person but the priesthood that blessed, so that even ill priests may bless. Neither have the ministers power of blessing only, but also of cursing. So in the Old Testament Elisha cursed the children, 2 Kings 2:24, which though our Saviour reproved as unfitting for his particular, who was to show all humility before his Passion, yet he allows in his Apostles. And therefore St Peter used that fearful imprecation to Simon Magus, Acts 8,[5] 'Thy money perish with thee:' and the event confirmed it. So did St Paul, 2 Timothy 4:14, and 1 Timothy 1:20. Speaking of Alexander the coppersmith,[6] who had withstood his preaching, 'The Lord,' saith he, 'reward him according to his works.' And again, of Hymeneus and Alexander, he saith, he had 'delivered them to Satan, that they might learn not to blaspheme'.[7] The forms both of blessing and cursing are expounded in the Common Prayer-book: the one in The Grace of our Lord Jesus Christ, etc. and The Peace of God, etc. The other in general in the Commination.[8] Now blessing differs from prayer, in assurance, because it is not performed by way of request, but of confidence and power, effectually applying God's favour to the blessed by the interesting of that dignity wherewith God hath invested the priest, and engaging of God's own power and institution for a blessing. The neglect of this duty in ministers themselves hath made the people also neglect it; so that they are so far from craving this benefit from their ghostly father that they oftentimes go out of church, before he hath blessed them. In the time of Popery the priest's 'Benedicite'[9] and his holy water were over-highly valued, and now we are fallen to the clean contrary, even from superstition to coldness and atheism. But the parson first values the gift in himself and teacheth his parish to value it. And it is observable that if a minister talk with a great man in the ordinary course of complimenting language, he shall be esteemed as ordinary complimentors, but if he often interpose a blessing when the other gives him just opportunity by speaking any good, this unusual form begets a reverence and makes him esteemed according to his profession. The same is to be observed in writing letters also. To conclude, if all men are to bless upon occasion, as appears Romans 12:14,[10] how much more those who are spiritual fathers?

Chapter 37: Concerning Detraction

The country parson perceiving that most when they are at leisure make others' faults their entertainment and discourse, and that even some good men think so they speak truth they may disclose another's fault, finds it somewhat difficult how to proceed in this point. For if he absolutely shut up men's mouths, and forbid all disclosing of faults, many an evil may not only be, but also spread in his parish, without any remedy (which cannot be applied without notice) to the dishonour of God and the infection of his flock, and the discomfort, discredit and hindrance of the pastor. On the other side, if it be unlawful to open faults, no benefit or advantage can make it lawful: for we must not do evil that good may come of it. Now the parson taking this point to task, which is so exceeding useful and hath taken so deep root that it seems the very life and substance of conversation, hath proceeded thus far in the discussing of it. Faults are either notorious or private. Again notorious faults are either such as are made known by common fame (and of these, those that know them may talk, so they do it not with sport but commiseration) or else such as have passed judgement and been corrected either by whipping, or imprisoning, or the like. Of these also men may talk, and more, they may discover them to those that know them not: because infamy is a part of the sentence against malefactors which the law intends, as is evident by those which are branded for rogues that they may be known; or put into the stocks that they may be looked upon. But some may say, though the law allow this the Gospel doth not, which hath so much advanced charity and ranked backbiters among the generation of the wicked, Romans 1:30.[1] But this is easily answered: as the executioner is not uncharitable that takes away the life of the condemned, except besides his office he add a tincture of private malice in the joy, and haste of acting his part; so neither is he that defames him whom the law would have defamed except he also do it out of rancour. For in infamy, all are executioners, and the law gives a malefactor to all to be defamed. And as malefactors may lose and forfeit their goods or life, so may they their good name, and the possession thereof, which before their offence and judgement they had in all men's breasts: for all are honest till the contrary be proved. Besides, it concerns the commonwealth that rogues should be known, and charity to the public hath the precedence of private charity. So that it is so far from being a fault to discover such offenders that it is a duty rather which may do much good and save much harm. Nevertheless, if the punished delinquent shall be much troubled for his sins, and turn quite another man, doubtless then also men's affections and words must turn and forbear to speak of that which even God himself hath forgotten.

The Author's Prayer before Sermon

O Almighty and ever-living Lord God! Majesty, and Power, and Brightness, and Glory! How shall we dare to appear before thy face, who are contrary to thee in all we call thee? for we are darkness, and weakness, and filthiness, and shame. Misery and sin fill our days: yet art thou our Creator and we thy work. Thy hands both made us, and also made us lords of all thy creatures; giving us one world in ourselves, and another to serve us; then didst thou place us in Paradise, and wert proceeding still on in thy favours, until we interrupted thy counsels, disappointed thy purposes, and sold our God, our glorious, our gracious God for an apple. O write it! O brand it in our foreheads for ever: for an apple once we lost our God, and still lose him for no more; for money, for meat, for diet; but thou, Lord, art patience, and pity, and sweetness, and love; therefore we sons of men are not consumed. Thou hast exalted thy mercy above all things and hast made our salvation, not our punishment, thy glory: so that then where sin abounded, not death, but grace superabounded; accordingly, when we had sinned beyond any help in heaven or earth, then thou said, Lo, I come! then did the Lord of life, unable himself to die, contrive to do it. He took flesh, he wept, he died; for his enemies he died; even for those that derided him then, and still despise him. Blessed Saviour! many waters could not quench thy love! nor no pit overwhelm it. But though the streams of thy blood were current through darkness, grave, and hell; yet by these thy conflicts, and seemingly hazards, didst thou arise triumphant, and therein mad'st us victorious.

Neither doth thy love yet stay here! for this word of thy rich peace and reconciliation thou hast committed not to thunder, or angels, but to silly and sinful men: even to me, pardoning my sins and bidding me go feed the people of thy love.

Blessed be the God of Heaven and Earth! who only doth wondrous things. Awake therefore, my lute, and my viol! Awake all my powers to glorify thee! We praise thee! We bless thee! We magnify thee for ever! And now, O Lord! in the power of thy victories, and in the ways of thy ordinances, and in the truth of thy love, lo, we stand here, beseeching thee to bless thy word, wherever spoken this day throughout the universal Church. O make it a word of power and peace, to convert those who are not yet thine, and to confirm those that are: particularly, bless it in this thy own kingdom, which thou hast made a land of light, a store-house of thy treasures and mercies: O let not our foolish and unworthy hearts rob us of the continuance of this thy sweet love: but pardon our sins and perfect what thou hast begun. Ride on Lord, because of the word of truth and meekness and righteousness; and thy right hand shall teach thee terrible things. Especially, bless this portion here assembled together, with thy unworthy servant speaking unto them: Lord Jesu! teach thou me, that I may teach them: sanctify, enable all my powers, that in their full strength they may deliver thy message reverently, readily, faithfully and fruitfully. O make thy word a swift word, passing from the ear to the heart, from the heart to the life and conversation: that as the rain returns not empty, so neither may thy word, but accomplish that for which it is given. O Lord hear, O Lord forgive! O Lord, harken, and do so for thy blessed Son's sake, in whose sweet and pleasing words, we say, 'Our Father', etc.

A Prayer after Sermon

Blessed be God! and the Father of all mercy! who continueth to pour his benefits upon us. Thou hast elected us, thou hast called us, thou hast justified us, sanctified and glorified us. Thou wast born for us, and thou livedst and diedst for us. Thou hast given us the blessings of this life and of a better. O Lord! thy blessings hang in clusters,[1] they come trooping upon us! they break forth like mighty waters on every side. And now Lord, thou hast fed us with the bread of life: so man did eat angels' food: O Lord, bless it: O Lord, make it health and strength unto us; still striving and prospering so long within us until our obedience reach the measure of thy love, who hast done for us as much as may be. Grant this dear Father, for thy Son's sake, our only Saviour: to whom with thee, and the Holy Ghost, three Persons, but one most glorious, incomprehensible God, be ascribed all Honour, and Glory, and Praise, ever. Amen.

IZAAK WALTON'S *THE LIFE OF MR GEORGE HERBERT*

The Introduction

In a late retreat from the business of this world, and those many little cares with which I have too often cumbered myself, I fell into a contemplation of some of those historical passages that are recorded in Sacred Story; and, more particularly, of what had passed betwixt our Blessed Saviour and that wonder of women, and sinners, and mourners, Saint Mary Magdalene.[1] I call her Saint, because I did not then, nor do now consider her, as when she was possessed with seven devils; not as when her wanton eyes, and dishevelled hair, were designed and managed, to charm and ensnare amorous beholders. But I did then, and do now consider her, as after she had expressed a visible and sacred sorrow for her sensualities; as after those eyes had wept such a flood of penitential tears as did wash, and that hair had wiped, and she most passionately kissed the feet of hers, and our blessed Jesus. And I do now consider, that because she loved much, not only much was forgiven her, but that, beside that blessed blessing of having her sins pardoned, and the joy of knowing her happy condition, she also had from him a testimony, that her alabaster box of precious ointment poured on his head and feet, and that spikenard,[2] and those spices that were by her dedicated to embalm and preserve his sacred body from putrefaction, should so far preserve her own memory, that these demonstrations of her sanctified love, and of her officious and generous gratitude, should be recorded and mentioned wheresoever his Gospel should be read: intending thereby, that as his so her name should also live to succeeding generations, even till time itself shall be no more.

Upon occasion of which fair example, I did lately look back, and not without some content (at least to myself) that I have endeavoured to deserve the love and preserve the memory of my two deceased friends, Dr Donne,[3] and Sir Henry Wotton,[4] by declaring the several employments and various accidents of their lives. And though Mr George Herbert (whose life I now intend to write) were to me a stranger as to his person, for I have only seen him; yet since he was, and was worthy to be, their friend, and very many of his have been mine, I judge it may not be unacceptable to those that knew any of them in their lives, or do now know them by mine or their own writings, to see this conjunction of them after their deaths; without which many things that concerned the age in which they lived would be less perfect and lost to posterity.

For these reasons I have undertaken it, and if I have prevented any abler person, I beg pardon of him and my reader.

The Life

George Herbert was born the third day of April, in the year of our Redemption 1593. The place of his birth was near to the town of Montgomery, and in that castle that did then bear the name of that town and county; that castle was then a place of state and strength, and had been successively happy in the family of the Herberts, who had long possessed it; and, with it, a plentiful estate and hearts as liberal to their poor neighbours. A family that hath been blest with men of remarkable wisdom, and a willingness to serve their country, and indeed, to do good to all mankind; for which they are eminent; but alas! this family did in the late rebellion suffer extremely in their estates; and the heirs of that castle saw it laid level with that earth that was too good to bury those wretches that were the cause of it.[5]

The father of our George, was Richard Herbert, the son of Edward Herbert, knight, the son of Richard Herbert, knight, the son of the famous Sir Richard Herbert of Colebrook in the County of Monmouth, banneret, who was the youngest brother of that memorable William Herbert, Earl of Pembroke, that lived in the reign of our King Edward the Fourth.

His mother was Magdalen Newport, the youngest daughter of Sir Richard, and sister to Sir Francis Newport of High Ercall in the county of Salop,[6] knight, and grandfather of Francis, Lord

Newport, now Comptroller of His Majesty's Household. A family that for their loyalty have suffered much in their estates, and seen the ruin of that excellent structure where their ancestors have long lived and been memorable for their hospitality.

This mother of George Herbert (of whose person and wisdom, and virtue, I intend to give a true account in a seasonable place) was the happy mother of seven sons and three daughters, which, she would often say, was Job's number, and Job's distribution; and as often bless God, that they were neither defective in their shapes or in their reason; and very often reproved them that did not praise God for so great a blessing. I shall give the reader a short account of their names, and not say much of their fortunes.

Edward the eldest was first made Knight of the Bath, at that glorious time of our late Prince Henry's[7] being installed Knight of the Garter; and after many years' useful travel, and the attainment of many languages, he was by King James sent Ambassador Resident to the then French King, Lewis[8] the Thirteenth. There he continued about two years; but he could not subject himself to a compliance with the humours of the Duke de Luines,[9] who was then the great and powerful favourite at Court; so that upon a complaint to our King, he was called back into England in some displeasure; but at his return he gave such an honourable account of his employment, and so justified his comportment to the Duke and all the Court, that he was suddenly sent back upon the same embassy, from which he returned in the beginning of the reign of our good King Charles the First, who made him first Baron of Castle-Island;[10] and not long after of Cherbery in the county of Salop. He was a man of great learning and reason, as appears by his printed book *De Veritate*; and by his *History of the Reign of King Henry the Eighth*, and by several other tracts.

The second and third brothers were Richard and William, who ventured their lives to purchase honour in the wars of the Low Countries, and died officers in that employment. Charles was the fourth, and died Fellow of New College in Oxford. Henry was the sixth, who became a menial servant to the Crown in the days of King James, and hath continued to be so for fifty years, during all which time he hath been Master of the Revels; a place that requires diligent wisdom, with which God hath blest him. The seventh son was Thomas, who being made captain of a ship in that fleet with which Sir Robert Mansel was sent against Algiers, did there show a fortunate and true English valour. Of the three sisters, I need not say more, than that they were all married to persons of worth and plentiful fortunes, and lived to be examples of virtue, and to do good in their generations.

I now come to give my intended account of George, who was the fifth of those seven brothers.

George Herbert spent much of his childhood in a sweet content under the eye and care of his prudent mother, and the tuition of a chaplain or tutor to him, and two of his brothers, in her own family (for she was then a widow), where he continued, till about the age of twelve years; and being at that time well instructed in the rules of grammar, he was not long after commended to the care of Dr Neale,[11] who was then Dean of Westminster, and by him to the care of Mr Ireland, who was then chief Master of that school, where the beauties of his pretty behaviour and wit shined and became so eminent and lovely in this his innocent age, that he seemed to be marked out for piety, and to become the care of Heaven, and of a particular good Angel to guard and guide him. And thus he continued in that school, till he came to be perfect in the learned languages,[12] and especially in the Greek tongue, in which he after proved an excellent critic.

About the age of fifteen, he, being then a King's Scholar, was elected out of that school for Trinity College in Cambridge, to which place he was transplanted about the year 1608. And his prudent mother, well knowing that he might easily lose, or lessen, that virtue and innocence which her advice and example had planted in his mind, did therefore procure the generous and liberal Dr Nevil,[13] who was then Dean of Canterbury, and Master of that College, to take him into his particular care and provide him a tutor; which he did most gladly undertake, for he knew the excellencies of his mother, and how to value such a friendship.

This was the method of his education, till he was settled in Cambridge, where we will leave him in his study, till I have paid my promised account of his excellent mother, and I will endeavour to make it short.

I have told her birth, her marriage, and the number of her children, and have given some short account of them; I shall next tell the reader that her husband died when our George was about the age of four years; I am next to tell that she continued twelve years a widow, that she then married happily to a noble gentleman, the brother and heir of the Lord Danvers, Earl of Danby, who did highly value both her person and the most excellent endowments of her mind.

In this time of her widowhood, she being desirous to give Edward her eldest son[14] such advantages of learning and other education as might suit his birth and fortune, and thereby make him the more fit for the service of his country, did at his being of a fit age remove from Montgomery Castle with him and some of her younger sons to Oxford; and, having entered Edward into Queen's College and provided him a fit tutor, she commended him to his care; yet she continued there with him, and still kept him in a moderate awe of herself, and so much under her own eye as to see and converse with him daily; but she managed this power over him without any such rigid sourness as might make her company a torment to her child, but with such a sweetness and compliance with the recreations and pleasures of youth, as did incline him willingly to spend much of his time in the company of his dear and careful mother, which was to her great content. For she would often say, 'that as our bodies take a nourishment suitable to the meat on which we feed: so, our souls do as insensibly take in vice by the example or conversation with wicked Company'; and would therefore as often say, 'that ignorance of Vice was the best preservation of Virtue: and, that the very knowledge of wickedness was as tinder to inflame and kindle sin, and to keep it burning'. For these reasons she endeared him to her own company; and continued with him in Oxford four years, in which time her great and harmless wit, her cheerful gravity and her obliging behaviour gained her an acquaintance and friendship with most of any eminent worth or learning that were at that time in or near that University; and particularly with Mr John Donne, who then came accidentally to that place in this time of her being there. It was that John Donne who was after Dr Donne, and Dean of St Paul's,

London; and he at his leaving Oxford writ and left there in verse a character of the beauties of her body and mind; and of the first he says,

> No Spring nor Summer-Beauty, has such grace
> As I have seen in an Autumnal face.

Of the latter he says,

> In all her words to every hearer fit
> You may at Revels, or at Council sit.

The rest of her character may be read in his printed *Poems*, in that Elegy which bears the name of the 'Autumnal Beauty'. For both he and she were then past the meridian of man's life.

This amity, begun at this time and place, was not an amity that polluted their souls; but an amity made up of a chain of suitable inclinations and virtues; an amity like that of St Chrysostom's to his dear and virtuous Olympias, whom, in his Letters, he calls his Saint; or an amity indeed more like that of St Jerome to his Paula,[15] whose affection to her was such that he turned poet in his old age and then made her epitaph, wishing all his body was turned into tongues that he might declare her just praises to posterity. – And this amity betwixt her and Mr Donne was begun in a happy time for him, he being then near to the fortieth year of his age (which was some years before he entered into Sacred Orders), a time when his necessities needed a daily supply for the support of his wife, seven children, and a family; and in this time she proved one of his most bountiful benefactors, and he as grateful an acknowledger of it. You may take one testimony for what I have said of these two worthy persons from this following letter and sonnet.

MADAM,

Your favours to me are everywhere; I use them, and have them. I enjoy them at London, and leave them there; and yet find them at Micham:[16] such riddles as these become things inexpressible; and such is your goodness. I was almost sorry to find your servant here this day, because I was loath to have any witness of my not coming home last night, and indeed of my coming this morning; but my not coming was excusable, because earnest business detained me; and my coming this day is by the example of your St Mary Magdalen, who rose early upon Sunday to seek that which she loved most; and so did I. And from her and myself, I return such thanks as are due to one to whom we owe all the good opinion, that they whom we need most, have of us – by this messenger, and on this good day, I commit the enclosed Holy Hymns and Sonnets (which for the matter, not the workmanship, have yet escaped the fire) to your judgement, and to your protection too, if you think them worthy of it; and I have appointed this enclosed sonnet to usher them to your happy hand.

Your unworthiest servant,

Micham
July 11
1607

unless your accepting him to be so,
have mended him.

JO. DONNE

TO THE LADY MAGDALEN HERBERT, OF ST MARY MAGDALEN

Her of your name, whose fair inheritance
  Bethina[17] was, and jointure Magdalo:[18]
An active faith so highly did advance,
  That she once knew, more than the Church did know,
The Resurrection; so much good there is
  Delivered of her, that some Fathers be
Loath to believe one woman could do this;
  But think these Magdalens were two or three.
Increase their number, Lady, and their fame:
  To their devotion, add your innocence:
Take so much of th' example, as of the name;
  The latter half; and in some recompense
That they did harbour Christ himself, a guest,
  Harbour these hymns, to his dear name addressed.

J. D.

These hymns are now lost to us; but doubtless they were such, as they two now sing in Heaven.

There might be more demonstrations of the friendship and the many sacred endearments betwixt these two excellent persons (for I have many of their letters in my hand), and much more might be said of her great prudence and piety; but my design was not to write hers but the life of her son; and therefore I shall only tell my reader that about that very day twenty years that this letter was dated and sent her, I saw and heard this Mr John Donne (who was then Dean of St Paul's) weep and preach her funeral sermon in the parish church of Chelsea near London, where she now rests in her quiet grave; and where we must now leave her and return to her son George, whom we left in his study in Cambridge.

And in Cambridge we may find our George Herbert's behaviour to be such that we may conclude he consecrated the first fruits of his early age to virtue and a serious study of learning. And that he did so, this following letter and sonnets, which were in the first year of his going to Cambridge sent his dear mother for a New Year's gift, may appear to be some testimony.

> But I fear the heat of my late ague hath dried up those springs,[19] by which scholars say, the Muses use to take up their habitations. However, I need not their help to reprove the vanity of those many love-poems that are daily writ and consecrated to Venus; nor to bewail that so few are writ that look towards God and Heaven. For my own part my meaning (dear Mother) is in these sonnets,[20] to declare my resolution to be, that my poor abilities in poetry shall be all, and ever consecrated to God's glory. And I beg you to receive this as one testimony.

My God, where is that ancient heat[21] towards thee,
  Wherewith whole shoals of Martyrs once did burn,
  Besides their other flames? Doth poetry
Wear Venus' livery? only serve her turn?
Why are not sonnets made of thee? and lays
  Upon thine altar burnt? Cannot thy love
  Heighten a spirit to sound out thy praise
As well as any she? Cannot thy dove[22]
Outstrip their Cupid easily in flight?
  Or, since thy ways are deep, and still the same,

Will not a verse run smooth that bears thy name!
Why doth that fire, which by thy power and might
Each breast does feel, no braver fuel choose
Than that, which one day, worms may chance refuse.

Sure Lord, there is enough in thee to dry
Oceans of ink; for, as the Deluge did
Cover the earth, so doth thy Majesty:
Each cloud distils thy praise, and doth forbid
Poets to turn it to another use.
Roses and lilies speak thee; and to make
A pair of cheeks of them, is thy abuse.
Why should I women's eyes for crystal take?
Such poor invention burns in their low mind,
Whose fire is wild, and doth not upward go
To praise, and on thee Lord, some ink bestow.
Open the bones, and you shall nothing find
In the best face but filth; when Lord, in thee
The beauty lies in the discovery.

G. H.

This was his resolution at the sending this letter to his dear mother; about which time he was in the seventeenth year of his age; and, as he grew older, so he grew in learning, and more and more in favour both with God and man;[23] insomuch that in this morning of that short day of his life, he seemed to be marked out for virtue and to become the care of Heaven; for God still kept his soul in so holy a frame, that he may and ought to be a pattern of virtue to all posterity; and especially to his brethren of the clergy, of which the reader may expect a more exact account in what will follow.

I need not declare that he was a strict student, because that he was so there will be many testimonies in the future part of his life. I shall therefore only tell that he was made Bachelor of Art in the year 1611. Major Fellow of the College, March 15, 1615.[24] And that in that year, he was also made Master of Arts, he being then in the twenty-second year of his age; during all which time, all, or the greatest diversion from his study, was the practice of music, in which he became a great master; and of which he would say, 'That it did relieve his drooping spirits, compose his distracted thoughts, and raised his weary soul so far above earth, that it gave him an earnest[25] of the joys of Heaven, before he possessed them.' And it may be noted that from his first entrance into the College, the generous Dr Nevil was a cherisher of his studies, and such a lover of his person, his behaviour and the excellent endowments of his mind that he took him often into his own company; by which he confirmed his native gentleness;[26] and, if during this time he expressed any error, it was that he kept himself too much retired and at too great a distance with all his inferiors; and his clothes seemed to prove that he put too great a value on his parts and parentage.

This may be some account of his disposition and of the employment of his time, till he was Master of Arts, which was *Anno* 1615. And in the year 1619 he was chosen Orator for the University. His two precedent Orators were Sir Robert Nanton, and Sir Francis Nethersoll.[27] The first was not long after made Secretary of State; and Sir Francis, not very long after his being Orator, was made Secretary to the Lady Elizabeth, Queen of Bohemia.[28] In this place of Orator, our George Herbert continued eight years; and managed it with as becoming and grave a gaiety, as any had ever before or since his time. For he had acquired great learning and was blest with a high fancy, a civil and sharp wit, and with a natural elegance, both in his behaviour, his tongue and his pen. Of all which there might be very many particular evidences, but I will limit myself to the mention of but three.

And the first notable occasion of showing his fitness for this employment of Orator was manifested in a letter to King James, upon the occasion of his sending that University his book, called *Basilicon Doron*;[29] and their Orator was to acknowledge this great honour and return their gratitude to His Majesty for such a condescension; at the close of which letter he writ,

Quid Vaticanam Bodleianamque objicis hospes!
Unicus est nobis Bibliotheca Liber.[30]

This letter was writ in such excellent Latin, was so full of conceits, and all the expressions so suited to the genius of the King, that he inquired the Orator's name, and then asked William, Earl of Pembroke, if he knew him? whose answer was, 'that he knew him very well; and that he was his kinsman, but he loved him more for his learning and virtue than for that he was of his name and family'. At which answer the King smiled, and asked the Earl leave, 'that he might love him too; for he took him to be the Jewel of that University'.

The next occasion he had and took to show his great abilities was, with them, to show also his great affection to that Church in which he received his baptism, and of which he professed himself a member; and the occasion was this: there was one Andrew Melvin,[31] a Minister of the Scotch Church, and Rector of St Andrews; who, by a long and constant converse with a discontented part of that clergy which opposed Episcopacy, became at last to be a chief leader of that faction; and had proudly appeared to be so to King James, when he was but king of that nation, who, the second year after his coronation in England, convened a part of the bishops and other learned divines of his Church to attend him at Hampton Court, in order to a friendly conference with some Dissenting Brethren, both of this and the Church of Scotland; of which Scotch party, Andrew Melvin was one; and, he being a man of learning, and inclined to satirical poetry, had scattered many malicious bitter verses against our liturgy, our ceremonies and our Church government; which were by some of that party so magnified for the wit, that they were therefore brought into Westminster School, where Mr George Herbert then and often after made such answers to them, and such reflection on him and his kirk, as might unbeguile any man that was not too deepy pre-engaged in such a quarrel. – But to return to Mr Melvin at Hampton Court Conference, he there appeared to be a man of an unruly wit, of a strange confidence, of so furious a zeal, and of so ungoverned passions, that his insolence to the King and others at this Conference lost him both his Rectorship of St Andrews and his liberty too: for his former verses and his present reproaches there used against the Church and State caused him to be committed prisoner to the Tower of London, where he remained very angry for three years. At which time of his commitment he found the Lady Arabella an innocent prisoner there; and he pleased himself much in sending the next day after his commitment these two verses to the good Lady, which I will under-write, because they may give the reader a taste of his others, which were like these.

Causa tibi mecum est communis, Carceris, Ara-
Bella; tibi causa est, Araque sacra mihi.[32]

I shall not trouble my reader with an account of his enlargement from that prison or his death; but tell him Mr Herbert's verses were thought so worthy to be preserved that Dr Duport,[33] the learned Dean of Peterborough, hath lately collected and caused many of them to be printed as an honourable memorial of his friend Mr George Herbert and the cause he undertook.

And, in order to my third and last observation of his great abilities, it will be needful to declare, that about this time King James came very often to hunt at New Market and Royston; and was almost as often invited to Cambridge, where his entertainment was comedies suited to his pleasant humour; and where Mr George Herbert was to welcome him with gratulations and the applauses of an Orator; which he always performed so well that he still grew more into the King's favour, insomuch that he had a particular appointment to attend his Majesty at Royston, where after a discourse with him, His Majesty declared to his kinsman, the Earl of Pembroke, 'that he found the Orator's learning and wisdom much above his age or wit'. The year following, the King appointed to end his progress at Cambridge, and to stay there certain days; at which time he was attended by the great Secretary of Nature and all Learning, Sir Francis Bacon[34] (Lord Verulam), and by the ever memorable and learned Dr Andrewes,[35] Bishop of Winchester, both which did at that time begin a desired friendship with our Orator. Upon whom the first put such a value on his judgement that he usually desired his approbation before he would expose any of his books to be printed, and thought him so worthy of his friendship that, having translated many of the prophet David's psalms into English verse, he made George Herbert his patron by a public dedication of them to him as the best judge of divine poetry. And for the learned Bishop, it is observable that at that time there fell to be a modest debate betwixt them two about Predestination and sanctity of life; of both which the Orator did not long after send the Bishop some safe and useful aphorisms in a long letter written in Greek; which letter was so remarkable for the language and reason of it that after the reading it, the Bishop put it into his bosom and did often show it to many scholars, both of this and foreign nations; but did always return it back to the place where he first lodged it and continued it so near his heart till the last day of his life.

To these I might add the long and entire friendship betwixt him and Sir Henry Wotton, and Dr Donne, but I have promised to contract myself and shall therefore only add one testimony to what is also mentioned in the *Life* of Dr Donne; namely, that a little before his death he caused many seals to be made, and in them to be engraven the figure of Christ crucified on an anchor (the emblem of hope) and of which Dr Donne would often say, *Crux mihi Anchora.*[36] – These seals he gave or sent to most of those friends on which he put a value; and, at Mr Herbert's death these verses were found wrapt up with that seal which was by the Doctor given to him.

When my dear Friend could write no more,
He gave this Seal, and so gave o'er.

When winds and waves rise highest, I am sure,
This Anchor keeps my faith, that me secure.

At this time of being Orator he had learnt to understand the Italian, Spanish and French tongues very perfectly; hoping, that as his predecessors, so he might in time attain the place of a Secretary of State, he being at that time very high in the King's favour; and not meanly valued and loved by the most eminent and most powerful of the Court nobility. This, and the love of a Court conversation mixed with a laudable ambition to be something more than he then was, drew him often from Cambridge to attend the King wheresoever the Court was, who then gave him a Sine

Cure,[37] which fell into his Majesty's disposal, I think, by the death of the Bishop of St Asaph. It was the same that Queen Elizabeth had formerly given to her favourite Sir Philip Sidney;[38] and valued to be worth an hundred and twenty pounds per annum. With this, and his annuity, and the advantage of his College, and his Oratorship, he enjoyed his gentle humour for clothes and Court-like company, and seldom looked towards Cambridge, unless the King were there, but then he never failed; and at other times left the manage of his Orator's place to his learned friend Mr Herbert Thorndike, who is now prebend[39] of Westminster.

I may not omit to tell that he had often designed to leave the University and decline all study, which he thought did impair his health; for he had a body apt to a consumption, and to fevers, and other infirmities which he judged were increased by his studies; for he would often say, 'He had too thoughtful a wit: a wit, like a pen-knife in too narrow a sheath, too sharp for his body.' But his mother would by no means allow him to leave the University or to travel; and, though he inclined very much to both, yet he would by no means satisfy his own desires at so dear a rate, as to prove an undutiful son to so affectionate a mother; but did always submit to her wisdom. And what I have now said may partly appear in a copy of verses in his printed poems; 'tis one of those that bears the title of 'Affliction';[40] and it appears to be a pious reflection on God's Providence, and some passages of his life, in which he says,

> Whereas my birth and spirit rather took
>   The way that takes the town:
> Thou didst betray me to a ling'ring book,
>   And wrap me in a gown;
> I was entangled in a world of strife,
> Before I had the power to change my life.
>
> Yet, for I threat'ned oft the siege to raise,
>   Not simp'ring all mine age:
> Thou often didst with academic praise,
>   Melt and dissolve my rage:
> I took the sweet'ned pill, till I came where
> I could not go away, nor persevere.

Yet lest perchance I should too happy be
    In my unhappiness,
Turning my purge to food, thou throwest me
    Into more sicknesses.
Thus doth thy power cross-bias me, not making
Thine own gift good; yet me from my ways taking.

Now I am here, what thou wilt do with me
    None of my books will show:
I read, and sigh, and wish I were a tree,
    For then sure I should grow
To fruit or shade: at least some bird would trust
Her household with me, and I would be just.

Yet, though thou troublest me, I must be meek;
    In weakness must be stout:
Well, I will change my service, and go seek
    Some other master out:
Ah my dear God! though I am clean forgot,
Let me not love thee, if I love thee not.

G.H.

In this time of Mr Herbert's attendance and expectation of some good occasion to remove from Cambridge to Court, God, in whom there is an unseen chain of causes, did in a short time put an end to the lives of two of his most obliging and most powerful friends, Lodowick, Duke of Richmond,[41] and James, Marquess of Hamilton; and not long after him King James died also, and with them all Mr Herbert's Court hopes. So that he presently betook himself to a retreat from London, to a friend in Kent, where he lived very privately and was such a lover of solitariness as was judged to impair his health more than his study had done. In this time of retirement he had many conflicts with himself, whether he should return to the painted pleasures of a Court life or betake himself to a study of Divinity and enter into Sacred Orders? (to which his dear mother had often persuaded him). These were such conflicts, as they only can know that have endured them; for ambitious desires and the outward glory of this world are not easily laid aside; but, at last, God inclined him to put on a resolution to serve at his Altar.

He did at his return to London acquaint a Court friend with his resolution to enter into Sacred Orders, who persuaded him to alter it, as too mean an employment, and too much below his birth, and the excellent abilities and endowments of his mind. To whom he replied, 'It hath been formerly judged that the domestic servants of the King of Heaven should be of the noblest families on earth; and, though the iniquity of the late times have made clergymen meanly valued and the sacred name of Priest contemptible, yet I will labour to make it honourable by consecrating all my learning and all my poor abilities to advance the glory of that God that gave them; knowing that I can never do too much for him that hath done so much for me, as to make me a Christian. And I will labour to be like my Saviour, by making humility lovely in the eyes of all men and by following the merciful and meek example of my dear Jesus.'

This was then his resolution, and the God of constancy, who intended him for a great example of virtue, continued him in it; for within that year he was made deacon, but the day when, or by whom, I cannot learn; but that he was about that time made deacon is most certain; for I find by the records of Lincoln that he was made prebend of Leighton Ecclesia,[42] in the Diocese of Lincoln, July 15, 1626. And that this prebend was given him by John, then Lord Bishop of that see.[43] And now he had a fit occasion to show that piety and bounty that was derived from his generous mother and his other memorable ancestors, and the occasion was this.

This Leighton Ecclesia is a village near to Spalden in the county of Huntingdon, and the greatest part of the parish church was fallen down, and that of it which stood was so decayed, so little and so useless that the parishioners could not meet to perform their duty to God in public prayer and praises; and thus it had been for almost twenty years, in which time there had been some faint endeavours for a public collection to enable the parishioners to rebuild it, but with no success, till Mr Herbert undertook it; and he, by his own and the contribution of many of his kindred and other noble friends, undertook the re-edification of it; and made it so much his whole business that he became restless, till he saw it finished as it now stands; being, for the workmanship, a costly mosaic; for the form, an exact cross; and for the decency and beauty, I am assured it is the most remarkable parish church that this nation affords. He lived to see it so wainscoted as to be exceeded by none; and, by his order, the reading pew and pulpit were a little distant from each other and both of an equal height; for he would often say, 'They should neither have a precedency or priority of the other, but that prayer and preaching being equally useful, might agree like brethren and have an equal honour and estimation.'

Before I proceed farther, I must look back to the time of Mr Herbert's being made prebend, and tell the reader that not long after, his mother being informed of his intentions to rebuild that church and apprehending the great trouble and charge that he was like to draw upon himself, his relations, and friends, before it could be finished, sent for him from London to Chelsea (where she then dwelt) and at his coming, said, 'George, I sent for you, to persuade you to commit simony, by giving your patron as good a gift as he has given to you; namely, that you give him back his prebend; for, George, it is not for your weak body and empty purse to undertake to build churches.' Of which he desired he might have a day's time to consider, and then make her an answer. And at his return to her the next day, when he had first desired her blessing, and she given it him, his next request was, 'That she would at the age of thirty-three years allow him to become an undutiful son; for he had made a vow to God that if he were able, he would rebuild that church'; and then showed her such reasons for his resolution that she presently subscribed to be one of his benefactors, and undertook to solicit William, Earl of Pembroke, to become another, who subscribed for fifty pounds; and not long after, by a witty and persuasive letter from Mr Herbert, made it fifty pounds more. And in this nomination of some of his benefactors, James, Duke of Lennox, and his brother Sir Henry Herbert, ought to be remembered; as also the bounty of Mr Nicholas Ferrar,[44] and Mr Arthur Woodnoth; the one, a gentleman in the neighbourhood of Leighton, and the other, a goldsmith[45] in Foster Lane, London, ought not to be forgotten, for the memory of such men ought to outlive their lives. Of Master Ferrar I shall hereafter give an account in a more seasonable place; but before I proceed farther, I will give this short account of Master Arthur Woodnoth.

He was a man that had considered overgrown estates do often require more care and watchfulness to preserve than get them, and considered that there be many discontents that riches cure not; and did therefore set limits to himself as to desire of wealth. And having attained so much as to be able to show some mercy to the poor and preserve a competence for himself, he dedicated the remaining part of his life to the service of God; and to be useful for his friends; and he proved to be so to Mr Herbert; for, beside his own bounty, he collected and returned most of the money that was paid for the rebuilding of that church; he kept all the account of the charges and would often go down to state them and see all the workmen paid. When I have said that this good man was a useful friend to Mr Herbert's father and to his mother, and continued to be so to him, till he closed his eyes on his death-bed, I will forbear to say more, till I have the next fair occasion to mention the holy friendship that was betwixt him and Mr Herbert. – From whom Mr Woodnoth carried to his mother this following letter and delivered it to her in a sickness which was not long before that which proved to be her last.

A LETTER OF MR GEORGE HERBERT TO HIS MOTHER, IN HER SICKNESS

MADAM,

At my last parting from you I was the better content because I was in hope I should myself carry all sickness out of your family, but since I know I did not, and that your share continues, or rather increaseth, I wish earnestly that I were again with you and would quickly make good my wish, but that my employment does fix me here, it being now but a month to our commencement: wherein, my absence by how much it naturally augmenteth suspicion, by so much shall it make my prayers the more constant and the more earnest for you to the God of all consolation. – In the meantime I beseech you to be cheerful and comfort yourself in the God of all comfort, who is not willing to behold any sorrow but for sin. – What hath affliction grievous in it more than for a moment? or why should our afflictions here have so much power or boldness as to oppose the hope of our joys hereafter? – Madam! As the earth is but a point in respect of the heavens, so are earthly troubles compared to heavenly joys; therefore, if either age or sickness lead you to those joys, consider what advantage you have over youth and health, who are now so near those true comforts. – Your last letter gave me earthly preferment, and I hope kept heavenly for yourself; but would you divide and choose too? Our College customs allow not that, and I should account myself most happy if I might change with you; for I have always observed the thread of life to be like other threads or skeins of silk, full of snarls and encumbrances: Happy is he, whose bottom[46] is wound up and laid ready for work in the New Jerusalem. – For myself, dear Mother, I always feared sickness more than death, because sickness hath made me unable to perform those offices for which I came into the world and must yet be kept in it; but you are freed from that fear who have already abundantly discharged that part, having both ordered your family and so brought up your children that they have attained to the years of discretion and competent maintenance. – So that now if they do not well, the fault cannot be charged on you, whose example and care of them will justify you both to the world and your own conscience: insomuch that whether you turn your thoughts on the life past or on the joys that are to come, you have strong preservatives against all disquiet. – And for temporal afflictions: I beseech you consider all that can happen to you are either afflictions of estate, or body, or mind. – For those of estate, of what poor regard ought they to be, since if we had riches, we are commanded to give them away, so that the best use of them is, having, not to have them. – But perhaps, being above the common people, our credit and estimation calls on us to live in a more splendid fashion? – but, O God! how easily is that answered, when we consider that the blessings in the holy Scripture are never given to the rich but to the poor. I never find Blessed be the rich; or Blessed be the noble; but Blessed be the meek, and Blessed be the poor, and Blessed be the mourners, for they shall be comforted. – And yet, O God! most carry themselves so, as if they not only not desired but even feared to be blessed. – And for afflictions of the body, dear Madam, remember the holy Martyrs of God, how they have been burnt by thousands, and have endured such other tortures, as the very mention of them might beget amazement; but their fiery trials have had an end, and yours (which praised be God are less) are not like to continue long. – I beseech you, let such thoughts as these moderate your present fear and sorrow; and know that if any of yours should prove a Goliath-like trouble,[47] yet you may say with David, – That God who hath delivered me out of the paws of the lion and bear will also deliver me out of the hands of this uncircumcised Philistine. – Lastly, for those afflictions of the soul: consider that God intends that to be as a sacred Temple for himself to dwell in and will not allow any room there for such an inmate as grief; or allow that any sadness shall be his competitor. – And above all, if any care of future things molest you, remember those admirable words of the Psalmist (Psalm 55):[48] 'Cast thy Care on the Lord and he shall nourish thee.' To which join that of St Peter (I Peter 5:7): 'Casting all your Care on the Lord, for he careth for you.' – What an admirable thing is this, that God puts his shoulder to our burden! and entertains our care for us that we may the more quietly intend his service. – To conclude, let me commend only one place more to you (Philippians 4:4). St Paul saith there: 'Rejoice in the Lord always, and again I say rejoice.' He doubles it to take away the scruple of those that might say, 'What shall we rejoice in afflictions?' Yes, I say again rejoice; so that it is not left to us to rejoice or not rejoice: but whatsoever befalls us, we must always, at all times, rejoice in the Lord, who taketh care for us: and it follows in the next verse: 'Let your moderation appear to all men, the Lord is at hand: be careful for nothing.' What can be said more comfortably? Trouble not yourselves, God is at hand to deliver us from all or in all. – Dear Madam, pardon my boldness and accept the good meaning of,

Trinity College
May 25
1622[49]

Your most obedient son,
George Herbert

About the year 1629[50] and the thirty-fourth of his age, Mr Herbert was seized with a sharp quotidian ague[51] and thought to remove it by the change of air; to which end he went to Woodford in Essex, but thither more chiefly to enjoy the company of his beloved brother Sir Henry Herbert[52] and other friends then of that family. In his house he remained about twelve months, and there became his own physician, and cured himself of his ague by forbearing drink and not eating any meat, no not mutton, nor hen, or pigeon, unless they were salted; and by such a constant diet he removed his ague but with inconveniences that were worse; for he brought upon himself a disposition to rheums, and other weaknesses, and a supposed consumption. And it is to be noted that in the sharpest of his extreme fits he would often say, 'Lord, abate my great affliction or increase my patience; but, Lord, I repine not, I am dumb, Lord, before thee, because thou doest it.' By which, and a sanctified submission to the will of God, he showed he was inclinable to bear the sweet yoke of Christian discipline, both then and in the latter part of his life, of which there will be many true testimonies.

And now his care was to recover from his consumption by a change from Woodford into such an air as was most proper to that end. And his remove was to Dantsey[53] in Wiltshire, a noble house which stands in a choice air; the owner of it then was the Lord Danvers, Earl of Danby, who loved Mr Herbert so very much that he allowed him such an apartment in it as might best suit with his accommodation and liking. And in this place, by a spare diet, declining all perplexing studies, moderate exercise and a cheerful conversation, his health was apparently improved to a good degree of strength and cheerfulness; and then he declared his resolution both to marry and to enter into the sacred orders of priesthood. These had long been the desires of his mother and his other relations; but she lived not to see either, for she died in the year 1627. And though he was disobedient to her about Leighton Church, yet in conformity to her will he kept his Orator's place till after her death; and then presently declined it; and, the more willingly, that he might be succeeded by his friend Robert Creighton, who now is Dr Creighton and the worthy Bishop of Wells.

I shall now proceed to his marriage; in order to which, it will be convenient, that I first give the reader a short view of his person, and then an account of his wife, and of some circumstances concerning both. – He was for his person of a stature inclining towards tallness;[54] his body was very straight, and so far from being cumbered with too much flesh that he was lean to an extremity. His aspect was cheerful, and his speech and motion did both declare him a gentleman; for they were all so meek and obliging that they purchased love and respect from all that knew him.

These and his other visible virtues begot him much love from a gentleman of a noble fortune and a near kinsman to his friend the Earl of Danby; namely, from Mr Charles Danvers of Bainton,[55] in the county of Wiltshire, Esq.; this Mr Danvers, having known him long and familiarly, did so much affect him that he often and publicly declared a desire that Mr Herbert would marry any of his nine daughters (for he had so many), but rather his daughter Jane than any other, because Jane was his beloved daughter: and he had often said the same to Mr Herbert himself; and that if he could like her for a wife, and she him for a husband, Jane should have a double blessing; and Mr Danvers had so often said the like to Jane, and so much commended Mr Herbert to her, that Jane became so much a Platonic as to fall in love with Mr Herbert unseen.

This was a fair preparation for a marriage; but alas, her father died before Mr Herbert's retirement to Dantsey; yet some friends to both parties procured their meeting; at which time a mutual affection entered into both their hearts, as a conqueror enters into a surprised city, and Love, having got such possession, governed, and made there such laws and resolutions as neither party was able to resist; insomuch that she changed her name into Herbert the third day after this first interview.

This haste might in others be thought a love-frenzy, or worse; but it was not; for they had wooed so like princes as to have select proxies; such as were true friends to both parties; such as well understood Mr Herbert's and her temper of mind; and also their estates so well before this interview that the suddenness was justifiable by the strictest rules of prudence; and the more, because it proved so happy to both parties; for the eternal Lover of mankind made them happy in each other's mutual and equal affections and compliance; indeed, so happy that there never was any opposition betwixt them, unless it were a contest which should most incline to a compliance with the other's desires. And though this begot and continued in them such a mutual love, and joy, and content, as was no way defective; yet this mutual content, and love, and joy, did receive a daily augmentation by such daily obligingness to each other as still added such new affluences to the former fullness of these divine souls as was only improvable in Heaven, where they now enjoy it.

About three months after his marriage, Dr Curle, who was then rector of Bemerton in Wiltshire, was made Bishop of Bath and Wells (and not long after translated to Winchester), and by that means the presentation[56] of a clerk to Bemerton did not fall to the Earl of Pembroke (who was the undoubted patron of it) but to the King, by reason of Dr Curle's advancement; but Philip, then Earl of Pembroke (for William was lately dead), requested the King to bestow it upon his kinsman George Herbert; and the King said, 'Most willingly' to Mr Herbert, 'if it be worth his acceptance'; and the Earl as willingly and suddenly sent it him without seeking; but though Mr Herbert had formerly put on a resolution for the clergy, yet, at receiving this presentation, the apprehension of the last great account that he was to make for the cure of so many souls made him fast and pray often, and consider, for not less than a month, in which time he had some resolutions to decline both the priesthood and that living. And in this time of considering he endured (as he would often say) such spiritual conflicts as none can think, but only those that have endured them.[57]

In the midst of these conflicts his old and dear friend Mr Arthur Woodnoth took a journey to salute him at Bainton (where he then was with his wife's friends and relations) and was joyful to be an eyewitness of his health and happy marriage. And after they had rejoiced together some few days, they took a journey to Wilton, the famous seat of the Earls of Pembroke; at which time the King, the Earl and the whole Court were there, or at Salisbury, which is near to it. And at this time Mr Herbert presented his thanks to the Earl for his presentation to Bemerton, but had not yet resolved to accept it, and told him the reason why; but that night the Earl acquainted Dr Laud, then Bishop of London, and after Archbishop of Canterbury, with his kinsman's irresolution. And the Bishop did the next day so convince Mr Herbert that the refusal of it was a sin, that a tailor was sent for to come speedily from Salisbury to Wilton to take measure and make him canonical clothes against next day; which the tailor did; and Mr Herbert, being so habited, went with his presentation to the learned Dr Davenant, who was then Bishop of Salisbury, and he gave him institution immediately (for Mr Herbert had been made deacon[58] some years before), and he was also the same day (which was April 26, 1630) inducted into the good, and more pleasant than healthful, parsonage of Bemerton, which is a mile from Salisbury.

I have now brought him to the parsonage of Bemerton and to the thirty-sixth[59] year of his age, and must stop here, and bespeak the reader to prepare for an almost incredible story of the great sanctity of the short remainder of his holy life; a life so full of Charity, Humility and all Christian virtues that it deserves the eloquence of St Chrysostom[60] to commend and declare it! A life that if it were related by a pen like his, there would then be no need for this age to look back into times past for the examples of primitive piety, for they might be all found in the life of George Herbert. But now, alas! who is fit to undertake it! I confess I am not: and am not pleased with myself that I must; and profess myself amazed when I consider how few of the clergy lived like him then, and how many live so unlike him now; but it becomes not me to censure: my design is rather to assure the reader that I have used very great diligence to inform myself, that I might inform him of the truth of what follows; and though I cannot adorn it with eloquence, yet I will do it with sincerity.

When at his induction he was shut into Bemerton Church, being left there alone to toll the bell (as the law requires him), he stayed so much longer than an ordinary time, before he returned to those friends that stayed expecting him at the church door, that his friend Mr Woodnoth looked in at the church window and saw him lie prostrate on the ground before the altar; at which time and place (as he after told Mr Woodnoth) he set some rules to himself for the future manage of his life; and then and there made a vow to labour to keep them.

And the same night that he had his induction, he said to Mr Woodnoth, 'I now look back upon my aspiring thoughts and think myself more happy than if I had attained what then I so ambitiously thirsted for; and I can now behold the Court with an impartial eye and see plainly that it is made up of fraud, and titles, and flattery, and many other such empty, imaginary painted pleasures, pleasures that are so empty as not to satisfy when they are enjoyed; but in God and his service is a fullness of all joy and pleasure, and no satiety; and I will now use all my endeavours to bring my relations and dependants to a love and reliance on him who never fails those that trust him. But above all I will be sure to live well, because the virtuous life of a clergyman is the most powerful eloquence to persuade all that see it to reverence and love and, at least, to desire to live like him. And this I will do, because I know we live in an age that hath more need of good examples than precepts. And I beseech that God who hath honoured me so much as to call me to serve him at his altar, that as by his special Grace he hath put into my heart these good desires and resolutions, so he will by his assisting Grace give me ghostly strength to bring the same to good effect; and I beseech him that my humble and charitable life may so win upon others as to bring glory to my JESUS, whom I have this day taken to be my Master and Governor; and I am so proud of his service that I will always observe, and obey, and do his will; and always call him Jesus my Master, and I will always contemn my birth, or any title or dignity that can be conferred upon me, when I shall compare them with my title of being a priest and serving at the altar of Jesus my Master.'

And that he did so may appear in many parts of this book of *Sacred Poems*; especially, in that which he calls 'The Odour'.[61] In which he seems to rejoice in the thoughts of that word 'Jesus', and say that the adding these words 'my Master' to it, and the often repetition of them, seemed to perfume his mind and leave an oriental fragrancy in his very breath. And for his unforced choice to serve at God's altar, he seems in another place of his poems ('The Pearl, Matthew 13'[62]) to rejoice and say – He knew the ways of learning; knew what nature does willingly; and what, when 'tis forced by fire; knew the ways of honour, and when glory inclines the soul to noble expressions; knew the Court; knew the ways of pleasure, of love, of wit, of music, and upon what terms he declined all these for the service of his Master JESUS, and then concludes, saying,

> That, through these labyrinths, not my grovelling wit,
> But thy silk-twist, let down from Heaven to me,
> Did both conduct, and teach me, how by it
> To climb to thee.

The third day after he was made rector of Bemerton and had changed his sword and silk clothes into a canonical coat, he returned so habited with his friend Mr Woodnoth to Bainton; and immediately after he had seen and saluted his wife, he said to her, 'You are now a minister's wife, and must now so far forget your father's house as not to claim a precedence of any of your parishioners; for you are to know that a priest's wife can challenge no precedence or place but that which she purchases by her obliging humility; and, I am sure, places so purchased, do best become them. And let me tell you that I am so good a herald as to assure you that this is truth.' And she was so meek a wife as to assure him it was no vexing news to her, and that he should see her observe it with a cheerful willingness. And indeed her unforced humility, that was in her so original as to be born with her, made her so happy as to do so; and her doing so begot her an unfeigned love and a serviceable respect from all that conversed with her; and this love followed her in all places as inseparably as shadows follow substances in sunshine.

It was not many days before he returned back to Bemerton, to view the church and repair the chancel;[63] and, indeed, to rebuild almost three parts of his house which was fallen down or decayed by reason of his predecessors living at a better parsonage house; namely, at Minal, sixteen or twenty miles from this place. At which time of Mr Herbert's coming alone to Bemerton, there came to him a poor old woman with an intent to acquaint him with her necessitous condition, as also with some troubles of her mind; but after she had spoke some words to him, she was surprised with a fear, and that begot a shortness of breath, so that her spirits and speech failed her; which he perceiving, did so compassionate her, and was so humble, that he took her by the hand, and said, 'Speak good mother, be not afraid to speak to me; for I am a man that will hear you with patience; and will relieve your necessities too, if I be able; and this I will do willingly, and therefore, mother, be not afraid to acquaint me with what you desire.' After which comfortable speech he again took her by the hand, made her sit down by him, and, understanding she was of his parish, he told her he would be acquainted with her and take her into his care: and, having with patience heard and understood her wants (and it is some relief for a poor body to be but heard with patience), he like a Christian clergyman comforted her by his meek behaviour and counsel; but because that cost him nothing, he relieved her with money too, and so sent her home with a cheerful heart, praising God and praying for him. Thus worthy and (like David's blessed man[64]) thus lowly was Mr George Herbert in his own eyes; and thus lovely in the eyes of others.

At his return that night to his wife at Bainton, he gave her an account of the passages 'twixt him and the poor woman, with which she was so affected that she went next day to Salisbury, and there bought a pair of blankets and sent them as a token of her love to the poor woman; and with them a message that she would see and be acquainted with her when her house was built at Bemerton.

There be many such passages both of him and his wife, of which some few will be related; but I shall first tell that he hasted to get the parish church repaired; then to beautify the chapel (which stands near his house) and that at his own great charge. He then proceeded to rebuild the greatest part of the parsonage house, which he did also very completely and at his own charge; and, having done this good work, he caused these verses to be writ upon or engraven in the mantle of the chimney in his hall.

To my successor.
If thou chance for to find
A new House to thy mind,
And built without thy Cost:

Be good to the Poor,
As God gives thee store,
And then my Labour's not lost.

We will now by the reader's favour suppose him fixed at Bemerton, and grant him to have seen the church repaired and the chapel belonging to it very decently adorned at his own great charge (which is a real truth) and, having now fixed him there, I shall proceed to give an account of the rest of his behaviour both to his parishioners and those many others that knew and conversed with him.

Doubtless Mr Herbert had considered and given rules to himself for his Christian carriage both to God and man before he entered into holy orders. And 'tis not unlike but that he renewed those resolutions at his prostration before the holy altar, at his induction into the church of Bemerton; but as yet he was but a deacon and therefore longed for the next Ember week[65] that he might be ordained priest and made capable of administering both the sacraments. At which time the Reverend Dr Humphrey Hinchman, now Lord Bishop of London (who does not mention him but with some veneration for his life and excellent learning), tell me he laid his hand on Mr Herbert's head, and (alas!) within less than three years lent his shoulder to carry his dear friend to his grave.

And that Mr Herbert might the better preserve those holy rules which such a priest as he intended to be, ought to observe; and that time might not insensibly blot them out of his memory, but that the next year might show him his variations from this year's resolutions; he therefore did set down his rules, then resolved upon, in that order, as the world now sees them printed in a little book, called, *The Country Parson*,[66] in which some of his rules are:

The Parson's Knowledge
The Parson on Sundays
The Parson Praying
The Parson Preaching
The Parson's Charity
The Parson Comforting the Sick

The Parson Arguing
The Parson Condescending
The Parson in his Journey
The Parson in his Mirth
The Parson with his Churchwardens
The Parson Blessing the People

And his behaviour toward God and man may be said to be a practical comment on these and the other holy rules set down in that useful book. A book so full of plain, prudent and useful rules that that country parson that can spare 12 pence and yet wants it is scarce excusable; because it will both direct him what he ought to do and convince him for not having done it.

At the death of Mr Herbert this book fell into the hands of his friend Mr Woodnoth; and he commended it into the trusty hands of Mr Barnabas Oley,[67] who published it with a most conscientious and excellent preface; from which I have had some of those truths that are related in this life of Mr Herbert.

The text for his first sermon[68] was taken out of Solomon's proverbs, and the words were, 'Keep thy heart with all diligence.' In which first sermon he gave his parishioners many necessary, holy, safe rules for the discharge of a good conscience, both to God and man. And delivered his sermon after a most florid manner, both with great learning and eloquence. But at the close of this sermon told them that should not be his constant way of preaching, for, since Almighty God does not intend to lead men to Heaven by hard questions, he would not therefore fill their heads with unnecessary notions; but that for their sakes his language and his expressions should be more plain and practical in his future sermons. And he then made it his humble request that they would be constant to the afternoon's service and catechising. And showed them convincing reasons why he desired it; and his obliging example and persuasions brought them to a willing conformity to his desires.

The texts for all his future sermons (which God knows were not many) were constantly taken out of the Gospel for the day; and he did as constantly declare why the Church did appoint that portion of Scripture to be that day read; and in what manner the collect for every Sunday does refer to the Gospel, or to the Epistle[69] then read to them; and that they might pray with understanding, he did usually take occasion to explain, not only the collect[70] for every particular Sunday, but the reasons of all the other collects and responses in our Church service; and made it appear to them that the whole service of the Church was a reasonable and therefore an acceptable sacrifice to God; as namely, that we begin with confession of ourselves to be vile, miserable sinners, and that we begin so, because till we have confessed ourselves to be such, we are not capable of that mercy which we acknowledge we need and pray for; but having in the Prayer of our Lord begged pardon for those sins which we have confessed, and hoping that as the priest hath declared our absolution, so by our public confession and real repentance we have obtained that pardon, then we dare and do proceed to beg of the Lord to open our lips, that our mouths may show forth his praise, for, till then, we are neither able nor worthy to praise him. But this being supposed, we are then fit to say, 'Glory be to the Father, and to the Son, and to the Holy Ghost'; and fit to proceed to a further service of our God, in the collects, and psalms, and lauds[71] that follow in the service.

And as to these psalms and lauds, he proceeded to inform them, why they were so often and some of them daily repeated in our Church service: namely, the psalms every month, because they be an historical and thankful repetition of mercies past; and such a composition of prayers and praises as ought to be repeated often and publicly; for which such sacrifices God is honoured and well-pleased. This for the psalms.

And for the hymns and lauds, appointed to be daily repeated or sung after the first and second lessons are read to the congregation, he proceeded to inform them that it was most reasonable, after they have heard the will and goodness of God declared or preached by the priest in his reading the two chapters, that it was then a seasonable duty to rise up and express their gratitude to Almighty God for those his mercies to them and to all mankind; and then say with the blessed Virgin that their souls do magnify the Lord, and that their spirits do also rejoice in God their Saviour;[72] and that it was their duty also to rejoice with Simeon[73] in this song and say with him, 'That their eyes have also seen their salvation'; for they have seen that salvation which was but prophesied till his time: and he then broke out into those expressions of joy that he did see it; but they live to see it daily, in the history of it, and therefore ought daily to rejoice and daily to offer up their sacrifices of praise to their God for that particular mercy. A service which is now the constant employment of that Blessed Virgin, and Simeon, and all those blessed saints that are possessed of Heaven: and where they are at this time interchangeably and constantly singing, 'Holy, Holy, Holy Lord God, Glory be to God on High, and on Earth peace.' – And he taught them that to do this was an acceptable service to God, because the Prophet David says in his psalms, 'He that praiseth the Lord, honoureth him.'

He made them to understand how happy they be that are freed from the encumbrances of that Law which our forefathers groaned under: namely, from the legal sacrifices; and from the many ceremonies of the Levitical law: freed from circumcision, and from the strict observation of the Jewish Sabbath, and the like; and he made them know that having received so many and so great blessings by being born since the days of our Saviour, it must be an acceptable sacrifice to Almighty God for them to acknowledge those blessings daily, and stand up and worship, and say as Zacharias did, 'Blessed be the Lord God of Israel, for he hath (in our days) visited and redeemed his people; and (he hath in our days) remembered and showed that mercy which by the mouth of the Prophets he promised to our forefathers: and this he hath done, according to his holy Covenant made with them';[74] and he made them to understand that we live to see and enjoy the benefit of it in his Birth, in his Life, his Passion, his Resurrection and Ascension into Heaven, where he now sits sensible of all our temptations and infirmities; and where he is at this present time making intercession for us to his and our Father; and therefore they ought daily to express their public gratulations and say daily with Zacharias, 'Blessed be that Lord God of Israel that hath thus visited and thus redeemed his people.' – These were some of the reasons by which Mr Herbert instructed his congregation for the use of the psalms, and the hymns appointed to be daily sung or said in the Church service.

He informed them also when the priest did pray only for the congregation and not for himself; and when they did only pray for him, as namely, after the repetition of the Creed, before he proceeds to pray the Lord's Prayer or any of the appointed collects, the priest is directed to kneel down and pray for them, saying, 'The Lord be with you.' – And when they pray for him, saying, 'And with thy spirit'; and then they join together in the following collects, and he assured them that when there is such mutual love and such joint prayers offered for each other, then the holy Angels look down from Heaven, and are ready to carry such charitable desires to God Almighty; and he as ready to receive them; and that a Christian congregation calling thus upon God, with one heart, and one voice, and in one reverend and humble posture, look as beautifully as Jerusalem, that is at peace with itself.

He instructed them also why the prayer of our Lord was prayed often in every full service of the Church: namely, at the conclusion of the several parts of that service; and prayed then, not only because it was composed and commanded by our Jesus that made it, but as a perfect pattern for our less perfect forms of prayer, and therefore fittest to sum up and conclude all our imperfect petitions.

He instructed them also that as by the second commandment we are required not to bow down, or worship an idol, or false god; so, by the contrary rule, we are to bow down and kneel, or stand up and worship the true God. And he instructed them why the Church required the congregation to stand up at the repetition of the Creeds; namely, because they did thereby declare both their obedience to the Church and an assent to that faith into which they had been baptised. And he taught them that in that shorter Creed, or Doxology,[75] so often repeated daily, they also stood up to testify their belief to be that the God that they trusted in was one God and three persons: the Father, the Son and the Holy Ghost, to whom they and the priest gave glory; and because there had been heretics that had denied some of these three persons to be God, therefore the congregation stood up and honoured him by confessing and saying, 'It was so in the beginning, is now so, and shall ever be so World without end.' And all gave their assent to this belief by standing up and saying, 'Amen.'

He instructed them also what benefit they had by the Church's appointing the celebration of Holy days and the excellent use of them; namely, that they were set apart for particular commemorations of particular mercies received from Almighty God; and (as Reverend Mr Hooker[76] says) to be the landmarks to distinguish times; for by them we are taught to take notice how time passes by us; and that we ought not to let the years pass without a celebration of praise for those mercies which those days give us occasion to remember; and therefore they were to note that the year is appointed to begin the twenty-fifth day of March,[77] a day in which we commemorate the Angel's appearing to the Blessed Virgin, with the joyful tidings that she should conceive and bear a Son, that should be the redeemer of mankind; and she did so forty weeks after this joyful salutation; namely, at our Christmas, a day in which we commemorate his birth with joy and praise; and that eight days after this happy birth we celebrate his Circumcision; namely, in that which we call New Year's day. And that upon that day which we call Twelfth Day[78] we commemorate the manifestation of the unsearchable riches of Jesus to the Gentiles; and that that day we also celebrate the memory of his goodness in sending a star to guide the three wise men from the East to Bethlehem, that they might there worship and present him with their oblations of gold, frankincense and myrrh. And he (Mr Herbert) instructed them that Jesus was forty days after his birth presented by his Blessed Mother in the Temple; namely, on that day which we call the Purification of the Blessed Virgin, St Mary. And he instructed them that by the Lent fast, we imitate and commemorate our Saviour's humiliation in fasting forty days; and that we ought to endeavour to be like him in purity. And that on Good Friday we commemorate and condole his Crucifixion. And at Easter commemorate his glorious Resurrection. And he taught them that after Jesus had manifested himself to his Disciples, to be that Christ that was crucified, dead and buried; and by his appearing and conversing with his Disciples for the space of forty days after his Resurrection, he then, and not till then, ascended into Heaven in the sight of those Disciples; namely, on that day which we call the Ascension, or Holy Thursday. And that we then celebrate the performance of the promise which he made to his Disciples, at or before his Ascension: namely, that though he left them, yet he would send them the Holy Ghost to be their Comforter; and that he did so on that day which the Church calls Whitsunday. – Thus the Church keeps an historical and circular commemoration[79] of times, as they pass by us; of such times as ought to incline us to occasional praises for the particular blessing which we do or might receive by those holy commemorations.

He made them know also why the Church hath appointed Ember weeks; and to know the reason why the commandments, and the Epistles and Gospels, were to be read at the altar or communion table; why the priest was to pray the litany[80] kneeling; and why to pray some collects standing; and he gave them many other observations fit for his plain congregation but not fit for me now to mention; for I must set limits to my pen and not make that a treatise, which I intended to be a much shorter account than I have made it; – but I have done when I have told the reader that he was constant in catechising every Sunday in the afternoon, and that his catechising was after his second lesson, and in the pulpit, and that he never exceeded his half hour, and was always so happy as to have an obedient and a full congregation.

And to this I must add that if he were at any time too zealous in his sermons, it was in reproving the indecencies of the people's behaviour in the time of divine service; and of those ministers that huddled up the Church prayers without a visible reverence and affection; namely, such as seemed to say the Lord's Prayer or a collect in a breath; but for himself his custom was to stop betwixt every collect and give the people time to consider what they had prayed and to force their desires affectionately to God, before he engaged them into new petitions.

And by this account of his diligence to make his parishioners understand what they prayed, and why they praised and adored their Creator, I hope I shall the more easily obtain the reader's belief to the following account of Mr Herbert's own practice, which was to appear constantly with his wife, and three nieces (the daughters of a deceased sister), and his whole family, twice every day at the Church prayers in the chapel which does almost join to his parsonage house. And for the time of his appearing it was strictly at the canonical hours of ten and four; and then and there he lifted up pure and charitable hands to God in the midst of the congregation. And he would joy to have spent that time in that place where the honour of his Master Jesus dwelleth; and there, by that inward devotion which he testified constantly by an humble behaviour and visible adoration, he, like Joshua,[81] brought not only his own household thus to serve the Lord; but brought most of his parishioners and many gentlemen in the neighbourhood constantly to make a part of his congregation twice a day; and some of the meaner sort of his parish did so love and reverence Mr Herbert that they would let their plough rest when Mr Herbert's Saints Bell[82] rung to prayers that they might also offer their devotions to God with him; and would then return back to their plough. And his most holy life was such that it begot such reverence to God and to him, that they thought themselves the happier when they carried Mr Herbert's blessing back with them to their labour. –Thus powerful was his reason and example to persuade others to a practical piety and devotion.

And his constant public prayers did never make him to neglect his own private devotions, nor those prayers that he thought himself bound to perform with his family, which always were a set-form and not long; and he did always conclude them with that collect which the Church hath appointed for the day or week. – Thus he made every day's sanctity a step towards that kingdom where impurity cannot enter.

His chiefest recreation was music, in which heavenly art he was a most excellent master and did himself compose many divine hymns and anthems, which he set and sung to his lute or viol; and though he was a lover of retiredness, yet his love to music was such that he went usually twice every week on certain appointed days to the cathedral church in Salisbury; and at his return would say, 'that his time spent in prayer and cathedral music elevated his soul, and was his Heaven upon earth'; but before his return thence to Bemerton, he would usually sing and play his part at an appointed private music meeting; and, to justify this practice, he would often say, 'Religion does not banish mirth, but only moderates and sets rules to it.'

And as his desire to enjoy his Heaven upon earth drew him twice every week to Salisbury, so his walks thither were the occasion of many happy accidents to others, of which I will mention some few.

In one of his walks to Salisbury he overtook a gentleman that is still living in that city, and in their walk together Mr Herbert took a fair occasion to talk with him and humbly begged to be excused, if he asked him some account of his faith, and said, 'I do this the rather, because though you are not of my parish, yet I receive tithe from you by the hand of your tenant; and, Sir, I am the bolder to do it, because I know there be some sermon-hearers that be like those fishes that always live in salt water and yet are always fresh.'

After which expression, Mr Herbert asked him some needful questions, and, having received his answer, gave him such rules for the trial of his sincerity and for a practical piety, and in so loving and meek a manner, that the gentleman did so fall in love with him and his discourse that he would often contrive to meet him in his walk to Salisbury or to attend him back to Bemerton; and still mentions the name of Mr George Herbert with veneration and still praiseth God for the occasion of knowing him.

In another of his Salisbury walks he met with a neighbour minister, and, after some friendly discourse betwixt them and some condolement for the decay of piety and too general contempt of the clergy, Mr Herbert took occasion to say, 'One cure for these distempers would be for the clergy themselves to keep the

Ember weeks strictly, and beg of their parishioners to join with them in fasting and prayers, for a more religious clergy.'

And another cure would be, 'for themselves to restore the great and neglected duty of catechising, on which the salvation of so many of the poor and ignorant lay-people does depend; but principally that the clergy themselves would be sure to live unblameably; and that the dignified clergy especially, which preach temperance, would avoid surfeiting and take all occasions to express a visible humility and charity in their lives; for this would force a love and an imitation, and an unfeigned reverence, from all that knew them to be such. (And for proof of this we need no other testimony than the life and death of Dr Lake,[83] late Lord Bishop of Bath and Wells.) 'This' (said Mr Herbert) 'would be a cure for the wickedness and growing atheism of our Age. And, my dear Brother, till this be done by us, and done in earnest, let no man expect a reformation of the manners of the laity: for 'tis not learning, but this, this only, that must do it; and till then the fault must lie at our doors.'

In another walk to Salisbury he saw a poor man with a poorer horse that was fallen under his load; they were both in distress and needed present help; which, Mr Herbert perceiving, put off his canonical coat and helped the poor man to unload, and after to load his horse. The poor man blest him for it, and he blest the poor man; and was so like the good Samaritan[84] that he gave him money to refresh both himself and his horse; and told him, 'That if he loved himself, he should be merciful to his beast.' – Thus he left the poor man, and at his coming to his musical friends at Salisbury, they began to wonder that Mr George Herbert which used to be so trim and clean came into that company so soiled and discomposed; but he told them the occasion; and when one of the company told him he had disparaged himself by so dirty an employment, his answer was, 'That the thought of what he had done would prove music to him at midnight; and that the omission of it would have upbraided and made discord in his conscience, whensoever he should pass by that place; for, if I be bound to pray for all that be in distress, I am sure that I am bound so far as it is in my power to practise what I pray for. And though I do not wish for the like occasion every day, yet let me tell you, I would not willingly pass one day of my life without comforting a sad soul or showing mercy; and I praise God for this occasion: and now let's tune our instruments.'

Thus, as our blessed Saviour after his Resurrection did take occasion to interpret the Scripture to Cleopas, and that other Disciple which he met with and accompanied in their journey to Emmaus,[85] so Mr Herbert, in his path toward Heaven, did daily take any fair occasion to instruct the ignorant or comfort any that were in affliction; and did always confirm his precepts by showing humility and mercy, and ministering grace to the hearers.

And he was most happy in his wife's unforced compliance with his acts of charity, whom he made his almoner,[86] and paid constantly into her hand a tenth penny of what money he received for tithe,[87] and gave her power to dispose that to the poor of his parish, and with it a power to dispose a tenth part of the corn that came yearly into his barn; which trust she did most faithfully perform, and would often offer to him an account of her stewardship, and as often beg an enlargement of his bounty, for she rejoiced in the employment; and this was usually laid out by her in blankets and shoes for some such poor people as she knew to stand in most need of them. This, as to her charity. – And for his own, he set no limits to it; nor did ever turn his face from any that he saw in want but would relieve them, especially his poor neighbours; to the meanest of whose houses he would go and inform himself of their wants and relieve them cheerfully if they were in distress; and would always praise God as much for being willing as for being able to do it. – And when he was advised by a friend to be more frugal, because he might have children, his answer was, he 'would not see the danger of want so far off; but, being the Scripture does so commend charity, as to tell us, that charity is the top of Christian virtues, the covering of sins, the fulfilling of the Law, the life of faith: and that charity hath a promise of the blessings of this life, and of a reward in that life which is to come, being these, and more excellent things are in Scripture spoken of thee, O Charity, and that, being all my tithes, and Church dues, are a deodate[88] from thee, O my God! make me, O my God, so far to trust thy promise as to return them back to thee; and, by thy Grace, I will do so, in distributing them to any of thy poor members that are in distress, or do but bear the image of Jesus my Master. Sir (said he to his friend), my wife hath a competent maintenance secured after my death, and therefore as this is my prayer, so this my resolution shall by God's grace be unalterable.'

This may be some account of the excellencies of the active part of his life; and thus he continued, till a consumption so weakened him as to confine him to his house, or to the chapel, which does almost join it; in which he continued to read prayers constantly twice every day, though he were very weak; in one of which times of his reading his wife observed him to read in pain and told him so, and that it wasted his spirits, and weakened him; and he confessed it did, but said, 'his life could not be better spent than in the service of his Master Jesus, who had done and suffered so much for him; but, said he, I will not be wilful: for though my spirit be willing, yet I find my flesh is weak; and therefore Mr Bostock[89] shall be appointed to read prayers for me tomorrow, and I will now be only a hearer of them, till this mortal shall put on immortality.' And Mr Bostock did the next day undertake and continue this happy employment, till Mr Herbert's death. – This Mr Bostock was a learned and virtuous man, an old friend of Mr Herbert's, and then his curate to the church of Fuggleston,[90] which is a mile from Bemerton, to which church, Bemerton is but a chapel of ease.[91] – And, this Mr Bostock did also constantly supply the Church service for Mr Herbert in that chapel, when the music meeting at Salisbury caused his absence from it.

About one month before his death, his friend Mr Ferrar (for an account of whom I am by promise indebted to the reader, and intend to make him sudden payment), hearing of Mr Herbert's sickness, sent Edmund Duncon (who is now rector of Fryer Barnet[92] in the county of Middlesex) from his house of Gidden Hall, which is near to Huntingdon, to see Mr Herbert and to assure him he wanted not his daily prayers for his recovery; and Mr

Duncon was to return back to Gidden,[93] with an account of Mr Herbert's condition. Mr Duncon found him weak and at that time lying on his bed, or on a pallet; but at his seeing Mr Duncon, he raised himself vigorously, saluted him, and with some earnestness inquired the health of his brother Ferrar; of which Mr Duncon satisfied him; and after some discourse of Mr Ferrar's holy life and the manner of his constant serving God, he said to Mr Duncon, 'Sir, I see by your habit that you are a priest, and I desire you to pray with me'; which being granted, Mr Duncon asked him, 'What prayers?' to which Mr Herbert's answer was, 'O Sir, the prayers of my mother, the Church of England, no other prayers are equal to them! but, at this time, I beg of you to pray only the Litany, for I am weak and faint'; and Mr Duncon did so. After which and some other discourse of Mr Ferrar, Mrs Herbert provided Mr Duncon a plain supper and a clean lodging, and he betook himself to rest. – This Mr Duncon tells me; and tells me that at his first view of Mr Herbert, he saw majesty and humility so reconciled in his looks and behaviour, as begot in him an awful reverence for his person: and says his discourse was so pious, and his motion so gentle and meek, that after almost forty years yet they remain still fresh in his memory.

The next morning Mr Duncon left him and betook himself to a journey to Bath, but with a promise to return back to him within five days, and he did so; but before I shall say anything of what discourse then fell betwixt them two, I will pay my promised account of Mr Ferrar.

Mr Nicholas Ferrar (who got the reputation of being called St Nicholas, at the age of six years) was born in London; and doubtless had good education in his youth; but certainly was at an early age made Fellow of Clare Hall in Cambridge, where he continued to be eminent for his piety, temperance and learning. – About the twenty-sixth year of his age, he betook himself to travel; in which he added to his Latin and Greek a perfect knowledge of all the languages spoken in the western parts of our Christian world; and understood well the principles of their religion, and of their manner, and the reasons of their worship. – In this his travel met with many persuasions to come into a communion with that

Church which calls itself Catholic: but he returned from his travels as he went, eminent for his obedience to his mother, the Church of England. In his absence from England, Mr Ferrar's father (who was a merchant) allowed him a liberal maintenance; and, not long after his return into England, Mr Ferrar had by the death of his father, or an elder brother, or both, an estate left to him that enabled him to purchase land to the value of four or five hundred pounds a year; the greatest part of which land was at Little Gidding, four or six miles from Huntingdon, and about eighteen from Cambridge; which place he chose for the privacy of it and for the hall, which had the parish church, or chapel, belonging, and adjoining near to it; for Mr Ferrar, having seen the manners and vanities of the world, and found them to be, as Mr Herbert says, 'A nothing between two dishes', did so contemn it, that he resolved to spend the remainder of his life in mortifications, and in devotion, and charity, and to be always prepared for death; – and his life was spent thus.

He and his family, which were like a little college, and about thirty in number, did most of them keep Lent and all Ember weeks strictly, both in fasting and using all those mortifications and prayers that the Church hath appointed to be then used; and he and they did the like constantly on Fridays and on the Vigils, or Eves, appointed to be fasted before the Saints' days; and this frugality and abstinence turned to the relief of the poor; but this was but a part of his charity, none but God and he knew the rest.

This family, which I have said to be in number about thirty, were a part of them his kindred, and the rest chosen to be of a temper fit to be moulded into a devout life; and all of them were for their dispositions serviceable and quiet, and humble and free from scandal. Having thus fitted himself for his family, he did about the year 1630 betake himself to a constant and methodical service of God, and it was in this manner. – He being accompanied with most of his family, did himself use to read the common prayers (for he was a deacon) every day, at the appointed hours of ten and four, in the parish church which was very near his house, and which he had both repaired and adorned; for it was fallen into a great ruin, by reason of a depopulation of the village before Mr Ferrar bought the manor; and he did also constantly read the matins every morning at the hour of six, either in the church or in an oratory, which was within his own house; and many of the family did there continue with him after the prayers were ended, and there they spent some hours in singing hymns, or anthems, sometimes in the church, and often to an organ in the oratory. And there they sometimes betook themselves to meditate, or to pray privately, or to read a part of the New Testament to themselves, or to continue their praying or reading the psalms: and, in case the psalms were not all always read in the day, then Mr Ferrar, and others of the congregation, did at night, at the ring of a watch-bell, repair to the church or oratory, and there betake themselves to prayers, and lauding God, and reading the psalms that had not been read in the day; and when these or any part of the congregation grew weary or faint, the watch-bell was rung, sometimes before and sometimes after midnight: and then another part of the family rose and maintained the watch, sometimes by praying, or singing lauds to God, or reading the psalms; and when after some hours they also grew weary or faint, then they rung the watch-bell, and were also relieved by some of the former, or by a new part of the society, which continued their devotions (as hath been mentioned) until morning. – And it is to be noted that in this continued serving of God, the Psalter, or whole Book of Psalms, was in every four and twenty hours sung or read over, from the first to the last verse; and this was done as constantly as the sun runs his circle every day about the world, and then begins again the same instant that it ended.

Thus did Mr Ferrar and his happy family serve God day and night; thus did they always behave themselves, as in his presence. And they did always eat and drink by the strictest rules of temperance; eat and drink, so as to be ready to rise at midnight or at the call of a watch-bell and perform their devotions to God. – And 'tis fit to tell the reader that many of the clergy that were more inclined to practical piety and devotion than to doubtful and needless disputations did often come to Gidden Hall and make themselves a part of that happy society and stay a week or more, and then join with Mr Ferrar and the family in these devotions and assist and ease him or them in their watch by night; and these various devotions had never less than two of the domestic family in the night; and the watch was always kept in the church or oratory, unless in extreme cold winter nights, and then it was maintained in a parlour which had a fire in it; and the parlour was fitted for that purpose; and this course of piety and great liberality to his poor neighbours Mr Ferrar maintained till his death, which was in the year 1639.

Mr Ferrar's and Mr Herbert's devout lives were both so noted that the general report of their sanctity gave them occasion to renew that slight acquaintance which was begun at their being contemporaries in Cambridge; and this new holy friendship was long maintained without any interview but only by loving and endearing letters. And one testimony of their friendship and pious designs may appear by Mr Ferrar's commending the considerations of John Valdesso (a book which he had met with in his travels, and translated out of Spanish into English)[94] to be examined and censured by Mr Herbert before it was made public; which excellent book Mr Herbert did read and return back with many marginal notes, as they be now printed with it, and with them, Mr Herbert's affectionate letter to Mr Ferrar.

This John Valdesso was a Spaniard and was for his learning and virtue much valued and loved by the great Emperor Charles the Fifth,[95] whom Valdesso had followed as a cavalier all the time of his long and dangerous wars; and when Valdesso grew old, and grew weary both of war and the world, he took his fair opportunity to declare to the Emperor that his resolution was to decline His Majesty's service and betake himself to a quiet and contemplative life, because there ought to be a vacancy of time betwixt fighting and dying. – The Emperor had himself, for the same, or other like reasons, put on the same resolution, but God and himself did till then only know them; and he did therefore desire Valdesso to consider well of what he had said and to keep his purpose within his own breast, till they two might have a second opportunity of a friendly discourse: which Valdesso promised to do.

In the meantime the Emperor appoints privately a day for him and Valdesso to meet again, and, after a pious and free discourse, they both agreed on a certain day to receive the blessed Sacrament publicly: and appointed an eloquent and devout friar to preach a sermon of contempt of the world, and of the happiness and benefit of a quiet and contemplative life; which the friar did most affectionately. – After which sermon the Emperor took occasion to declare openly that the preacher had begot in him a resolution to lay down his dignities, and to forsake the world, and betake himself to a monastical life. And he pretended he had persuaded John Valdesso to do the like; but this is most certain, that after the Emperor had called his son Philip out of England and resigned to him all his kingdoms, that then the Emperor and John Valdesso did perform their resolutions.

This account of John Valdesso I received from a friend that had it from the mouth of Mr Ferrar; and the reader may note that in this retirement John Valdesso writ his *Hundred and Ten Considerations* and many other treatises of worth, which want a second Mr Ferrar to procure and translate them.

After this account of Mr Ferrar and John Valdesso, I proceed to my account of Mr Herbert and Mr Duncon, who, according to his promise, returned from Bath the fifth day, and then found Mr Herbert much weaker than he left him; and therefore their discourse could not be long; but at Mr Duncon's parting with him, Mr Herbert spoke to this purpose: 'Sir, I pray give my brother Ferrar an account of the decaying condition of my body, and tell him, I beg him to continue his daily prayers for me; and let him know that I have considered that God only is what he would be; and that I am by his Grace become now so like him as to be pleased with what pleaseth him; and tell him that I do not repine but am pleased with my want of health; and tell him my heart is fixed on that place where true joy is only to be found; and that I long to be there, and do wait for my appointed change with hope and patience.' Having said this, he did with so sweet a humility as seemed to exalt him, bow down to Mr Duncon, and with a thoughtful and contented look, say to him, 'Sir, I pray deliver this little book to my dear brother Ferrar, and tell him he shall find in it a picture of the many spiritual conflicts that have passed betwixt God and my soul, before I could subject mine to the will of Jesus my Master, in whose service I have now found perfect freedom; desire him to read it: and then, if he can think it may turn to the advantage of any dejected poor soul, let it be made public; if not, let him burn it; for I and it are less than the least of God's mercies.'[96] – Thus meanly did this humble man think of this excellent book, which now bears the name of *The Temple: Or, Sacred Poems and Private Ejaculations*; of which, Mr Ferrar would say, 'There was in it the picture of a divine soul in every page; and that the whole book was such a harmony of holy passions, as would enrich the world with pleasure and piety.' And it appears to have done so; for there have been more than twenty thousand of them sold since the first impression.

And this ought to be noted, that when Mr Ferrar sent this book to Cambridge to be licensed for the press, the Vice-Chancellor would by no means allow the two so much noted verses,

> Religion stands a Tip-toe[97] in our Land,
> Ready to pass to the American Strand.

to be printed; and Mr Ferrar would by no means allow the book to be printed and want them: but after some time and some arguments for and against their being made public, the Vice-Chancellor said, 'I knew Mr Herbert well and know that he had many heavenly speculations and was a divine poet; but I hope the world will not take him to be an inspired prophet, and therefore I license the whole book'; so that it came to be printed without the diminution or addition of a syllable, since it was delivered into the hands of Mr Duncon, save only that Mr Ferrar hath added that excellent preface that is printed before it.

At the time of Mr Duncon's leaving Mr Herbert (which was about three weeks before his death), his old and dear friend Mr Woodnoth came from London to Bemerton and never left him till he had seen him draw his last breath and closed his eyes on his death-bed. In this time of his decay he was often visited and prayed for by all the clergy that lived near to him, especially by his friends the Bishop and prebends of the cathedral church in Salisbury; but by none more devoutly than his wife, his three nieces (then a part of his family) and Mr Woodnoth, who were the sad witnesses of his daily decay; to whom he would often speak to this purpose. – 'I now look back upon the pleasures of my life past, and see the content I have taken in beauty, in wit, in music, and pleasant conversation, are now all passed by me, like a dream, or as a shadow that returns not, and are now all become dead to me, or I to them; and I see that as my father and generation hath done before me, so I also shall now suddenly (with Job) make my bed also in the dark; and I praise God I am prepared for it; and I praise him, that I am not to learn patience, now I stand in such need of it; and that I have practised mortification, and endeavoured to die daily, that I might not die eternally; and my hope is that I shall shortly leave this valley of tears, and be free from all fevers and pain: and which will be a more happy condition, I shall be free from sin, and all the temptations and anxieties that attend it; and this being past, I shall dwell in the new Jerusalem, dwell there with men made perfect; dwell, where these eyes shall see my Master and Saviour Jesus; and with him see my dear mother, and all my relations and friends; – but I must die, or not come to that happy place; and this is my content, that I am going daily towards it; and that every day which I have lived, hath taken a part of my appointed time from me; and that I shall live the less time, for having lived this, and the day past.' – These, and the like expressions, which he uttered often, may be said to be his enjoyment of Heaven, before he enjoyed it. – The Sunday before his death he rose suddenly from his bed or couch, called for one of his instruments, took it into hand, and said,

My God, My God,
My music shall find thee,
And every string
Shall have his attribute to sing.

And having tuned it, he played and sung:

> The Sundays of man's life,
> Threaded together on time's string,
> Make bracelets, to adorn the wife
> Of the eternal glorious King:
> On Sundays, Heaven's door[98] stands ope;
> Blessings are plentiful and rife,
> More plentiful than hope.

Thus he sung on earth such hymns and anthems as the angels and he, and Mr Ferrar, now sing in Heaven.

Thus he continued meditating, and praying, and rejoicing, till the day of his death; and on that day, said to Mr Woodnoth, 'My dear Friend, I am sorry I have nothing to present to my merciful God but sin and misery; but the first is pardoned; and a few hours will now put a period to the latter; for I shall suddenly go hence and be no more seen.' Upon which expression Mr Woodnoth took occasion to remember him of the re-edifying Leighton Church and his many acts of mercy; to which he made answer, saying, 'They be good works, if they be sprinkled with the blood of Christ, and not otherwise.' After this discourse he became more restless, and his soul seemed to be weary of her earthly tabernacle; and this uneasiness became so visible that his wife, his three nieces and Mr Woodnoth stood constantly about his bed, beholding him with sorrow, and an unwillingness to lose the sight of him whom they could not hope to see much longer. – As they stood thus beholding him, his wife observed him to breath faintly and with much trouble; and observed him to fall into a sudden agony; which so surprised her that she fell into a sudden passion and required of him to know, how he did? to which his answer was, that he had 'passed a conflict with his last Enemy,[99] and had overcome him, by the merits of his Master Jesus'. After which answer he looked up and saw his wife and nieces weeping to an extremity, and charged them, 'If they loved him, to withdraw into the next room, and there pray every one alone for him, for nothing but their lamentations could make his death uncomfortable.' To which request their sighs and tears would not suffer them to make any reply, but they yielded him a sad obedience, leaving only with him Mr Woodnoth and Mr Bostock. Immediately after they had left him, he said to Mr Bostock, 'Pray, Sir, open that door, then look into that cabinet, in which you may easily find my last will, and give it into my hand;' which being done Mr Herbert delivered it into the hand of Mr Woodnoth and said, 'My old Friend, I here deliver you my last will, in which you will find that I have made you my sole executor for the good of my wife and nieces; and I desire you to show kindness to them, as they shall need it; I do not desire you to be just; for I know you will be so for your own sake; but I charge you by the religion[100] of our friendship to be careful of them.' And having obtained Mr Woodnoth's promise to be so, he said, 'I am now ready to die'; after which word he said, 'Lord, forsake me not now my strength faileth me; but grant me mercy for the merits of my Jesus; and now Lord, Lord now receive my soul.' And with those words he breathed forth his divine soul, without any apparent disturbance,[101] Mr Woodnoth and Mr Bostock attending his last breath and closing his eyes.

Thus he lived, and thus he died like a saint, unspotted of the world, full of alms-deeds, full of humility, and all the examples of a virtuous life; which I cannot conclude better, than with this borrowed observation:

> – All must to their cold graves;
> But the religious actions of the just,
> Smell sweet in death, and blossom in the dust.[102]

Mr George Herbert's have done so to this, and will doubtless do so to succeeding generations. – I have but this to say more of him: that if Andrew Melvin died before him, then George Herbert died without an enemy. – I wish (if God shall be so pleased) that I may be so happy as to die like him.

JZ. Wa.

APPENDIX: A SELECTION OF HERBERT'S LATIN VERSE

The classically educated Herbert had as a boy learned to compose verse in Greek and Latin. Herbert's Latin poetry ranges from the satiric to the panegyric to the elegiac. The following examples show something of his skill, his instinct for the paradoxical and his personal association with both Bacon and Donne. The translations are prose versions which reveal what he is saying if not the pointed elegance with which he is saying it.

From Passio Discerpta
IX In Flagellum

Christe, flagellati spes & victoria mundi,
   Crimina cum turgent, & mea poena prope est,
Suaviter admoveas notum tibi carne flagellum,
   Sufficiat virgae saepius umbra tuae.
Mitis agas: tenerae duplicant sibi verbera mentes,
   Ipsaque sunt ferulae mollia corda suae.

On the Scourge

O Christ, the hope and conquest of the scourged world, when indictments swell and my punishment is close, sweetly inflict the scourge on the flesh felt by you, let the mere shadow of your rod more often be adequate. Be merciful: sensitive consciences themselves double the strokes, and gentle hearts are their very own lashes.

X In Vestes Divisas

Si, Christe, dum suffigeris, tuae vestes
Sunt hostium legata, non amicorum,
Ut postulat mos, quid tuis dabis? Teipsum.

On the Parted Garments

If, O Christ, while you are crucified, your garments are legacies of your enemies, not of your friends, as custom demands, what will you bequeath to your friends? Yourself.

XVIII Terrae-motus

Te fixo vel Terra movet: nam, cum Cruce, totam
Circumferre potes; Sampson ut ante fores.
Heu stolidi, primum fugientem figite Terram,
Tunc Dominus clavis aggrediendus erit.

Earthquake

As you are nailed, yet the Earth moves: because, together with the Cross, you carry the entire world round; so Samson previously carried the doors. Alas, stupid people, first of all nail the fast-moving earth, then the Lord can be attached with spikes.

From Lucus
XXII In Improbum Disertum

Sericus es dictis, factis pannusia Baucis:
Os & lingua tibi dives, egena manus:
Ni facias, ut opes linguae per brachia serpant,
Aurea pro naulo lingua Charontis erit.

On the Rhetoric of the Unprincipled

Silken in words, in acts like the rags of Baucis, your mouth and tongue are precious, needy is your hand: unless you see to it that the influence of your tongue glides through your arm, your gilded, ready tongue will be for Charon's boat fare.

XXV Roma Anagr. { *Oram, Maro* / *Ramo, Armo* / *Mora, Amor* }

Roma, tuum nomen quam non pertransiit ORAM,
  Cum Latium ferrent secula prisca iugum?
Non deerat vel fama tibi, vel carmina famae,
  Unde MARO laudes duxit ad astra tuas.
At nunc exucco similis tua gloria RAMO
  A veteri trunco & nobilitate cadit.
Laus antiqua & honor periit: quasi scilicet ARMO
  Te deiecissent tempora longa suo.
Quin tibi tam desperatae MORA nulla medetur,
  Qua Fabio quondam sub duce nata salus.
Hinc te olim gentes miratae odere vicissim;
  Et cum sublata laude recedit AMOR.

Roma. An Anagram { *Border, Maro* / *Branch, Shoulder* / *Delay, Love* }

O Rome, what *border* did your name not pass right through, when ancient generations bore the Latin yoke? Neither was glory missing, nor the song of glory, on the basis of which *Maro* led your virtues to the stars. But now your honour is like a dried up *branch* from a long standing tree trunk and from nobility is fallen former renown and respect has vanished: as if, if you please, remote times had thrown you from their *shoulder* to the ground. In fact, for you all the same the *lapse of time* does not cure hopelessness. As under Fabian direction once in former times salvation did grow from it. Following on this, mankind, once awe-struck, conversely hates you, seeing that *Love* withdraws from lost glory.

XXIX Λογικὴ Θυσία

Ararumque Hominumque ortum si mente pererres,
  Cespes vivus, Homo; mortuus, Ara fuit:
Quae divisa nocent, Christi per foedus, in unum
  Conveniunt; & Homo viva fit Ara Dei.

XXIX A Reasonable Sacrifice

If you go over in your mind the origin of altars and of human beings, a living sod was man, dead turf was an altar: these elements divided cause harm, they come together in one by means of Christ's partnerships, and man becomes God's living altar.

From Alia Poemata Latina
In Honorem Illustr. D.D. Verulamii, Sti. Albani, Mag. Sigilli Custodis post editam ab eo Instaurationem Magnam

Quis iste tandem? non enim vultu ambulat
Quotidiano! Nescis, ignare? Audies!
Dux Notionum; veritatis Pontifex;
Inductionis Dominus, & Verulamii;
Rerum magister unicus, at non Artium;
Profunditatis pinus, atque Elegantiae;
Naturae Aruspex intimus; Philosophiae
Aerarium; sequester experientiae,
Speculationisque; Aequitatis signifer;
Scientiarum, sub pupillari statu
Degentium olim, Emancipator; Luminis
Promus; Fugator Idolum, atque nubium;
Collega Solis; Quadra Certitudinis;
Sophismato mastix; Brutus Literarius,
Authoritatis exuens tyrannidem;
Rationis & sensus stupendus Arbiter;
Repumicator mentis; Atlas Physicus,
Alcide succumbente Stagiritico;
Columba Noae, quae in vetustis artibus
Nullum locum requieme cernens perstitit
Ad se suaeque matris Arcam regredi:
Subtilitatis Terebra; Temporis Nepos
Ex Veritate matre; Mellis alveus;
Mundique & Animarum sacerdos unicus;
Securis errorum; inque Naturalibus
Granum Sinapis, acre Aliis, crescens sibi:
O me probe lassum! Iuvate, Posteri!

G. Herbert Orat. Pub. in *Acad. Cantab.*

To the Honour of the Most Illustrious Baron Verulam, Viscount St Albans, Keeper of the Great Seal, on the publication of his Instauratio Magna

Who is this man, I ask you? For he doesn't walk about with a countenance that is unremarkable. Don't you know, stupid fellow? Pay attention. This man is the commander of ideas, high priest of truth, sovereign of logical argumentation, and Verulam; sole lord of physical phenomena, but not of things magical, pine tree of loftiness and gracefulness; most profound interpreter of nature; treasury of philosophical thought. Trustee of demonstration and speculation; the standard-bearer of justice, liberator of knowledge, which formerly was passing the time as a ward; steward of light, attacker of the idols, as well as of cloudy thoughts; associate of the sun, the squire of certainty; the scourge of sophistry; the Brutus of erudition, throwing off the tyranny of authority; wonderful judge of reason and perception; polisher of the mind; scientific Atlas (submitted to by Herculean Aristotle); Dove of Noah, which, discerning no place of rest in old, established techniques, determined to return itself to its own original Ark; piercer of subtlety; grandson of Time by the agency of foster-mother Truth; bee-hive of honey; The world's and its souls' sole priest; the executioner's axe of mistakes; that is to say the mustard seed of the physical sciences, pungent to others, growing to itself. O I am absolutely exhausted. Future generations, pitch in.

Aethiopissa Ambit Cestum Diversi Coloris Virum

Quid mihi si facies nigra est? hoc, Ceste, colore
   Sunt etiam tenebrae, quas tamen optat amor.
Cernis ut exusta semper sit fronte viator;
   Ah longum, quae te deperit, errat iter.
Si nigro sit terra solo, quis despicit arvum?
   Claude oculos, & erunt omnia nigra tibi:
Aut aperi, & cernes corpus quas proiicit umbras;
   Hoc saltem officio fungar amore tui.
Cum mihi sit facies fumus, quas pectore flammas
      Iamdudum tacite delitisse putes?
Dure, negas? O fata mihi praesaga doloris,
   Quae mihi lugubres contribuere genas!

A Black Girl Embraces Cestus, a Man of the Opposite Colour

What is it to me if my outward appearance is black, for, Cestus, darkness is of this complexion, which nevertheless love desires. You perceive clearly that the traveller always sports a tanned brow; ah this trip has carried on a long time in an uncertain direction for the girl who loves you to distraction. If the earth be black in its topsoil, does anybody disdain the furrow? Close your eyes and everything is black to you. Now open them up and you will see clearly the shadows which your body makes. Anyhow I will perform this friendly act out of my love for you. Since my appearance is smoke, what flames do you think have hidden themselves in my soul some while ago now without being noticed? O pitiless man, do you refuse me? O fates portending my anguish what gloomy cheeks you have allotted me.

In Sacram Anchoram Piscatoris G. Herbert

Quod Crux nequibat fixa, Clavique additi,
(Tenere Christum scilicet, ne ascenderet)
Tuive Christum devocans facundia
Ultra loquendi tempus; addit Anchora:
Nec hoc abunde est tibi, nisi certae Anchorae
Addas sigillum: nempe Symbolum suae
Tibi debet Unda & Terra certitudinis.

Munde, fluas fugiasque licet, nos nostraque fixi:
Deridet motus sancta catena tuos.
Quondam fessus Amor loquens Amato,
Tot & tanta loquens amica, scripsit:
Tandem & fessa manus, dedit sigillum.

Suavis erat, qui scripta dolens lacerando recludi,
Sanctius in Regno Magni credebat Amoris
(In quo fas nihil est rumpi) donare sigillum.

Although the Cross could not Christ here detain,
Though nailed unto't, but he ascends again,
Nor yet thy eloquence here keep him still,
But only while thou speak'st; This Anchor will.
Nor canst thou be content, unless thou to
This certain Anchor add a Seal, and so
The Water, and the Earth both unto thee
Do owe the symbol of their certainty.
Let the world reel, we and all ours stand sure,
This holy Cable's of all storms secure.

When Love being weary made an end
Of kind Expressions to his friend,
He writ; when's hand could write no more,
He gave the Seal, and so left o'er.

How sweet a friend was he, who being grieved
His letters were broke rudely up, believed
'Twas more secure in great Love's Common-weal
(Where nothing should be broke) to add a Seal.

NOTES

Abbreviations Used in the Notes

AV	The Authorised Version of the Bible, the King James Bible
BCP	The Book of Common Prayer
Bloch	Chana Bloch, *Spelling the Word: George Herbert and the Bible*
Donne	John Donne, *The Complete English Poems*
EIC	*Essays in Criticism*
ELN	*English Language Notes*
Empson	William Empson, *Seven Types of Ambiguity*
GHJ	*George Herbert Journal*
HLQ	*Huntington Library Quarterly*
Hutchinson	*The Works of George Herbert*, ed. F. E. Hutchinson
MSB	Bodleian MS Tanner 307
MSW	MS Jones B 62 in Dr Williams's Library, Gordon Square, London
N&Q	*Notes and Queries*
OED	*Oxford English Dictionary*
ODCC	*The Oxford Dictionary of the Christian Church*, second edition, F. L. Cross and E. A. Livingstone
Patrides	*The English Poems of George Herbert*, ed. C. A. Patrides
PQ	*Philological Quarterly*
RES	*Review of English Studies*
RQ	*Renaissance Quarterly*
SEL	*Studies in English Literature*
Tuve	Rosemond Tuve, *A Reading of George Herbert*

Full bibliographical information on sources may be found in the section on Further Reading, pp. xxiii–xxviii.

THE TEMPLE

The Printers to the Reader

This preface is the work of Nicholas Ferrar, the spiritual leader of Little Gidding, and the recipient of the manuscript of *The Temple* (see pp. 310–11) from the dying George Herbert.

Helicon the Spring of the Muses and the symbol of pagan poetry.
his Word Holy Scripture
less than the least see Walton, p. 311.

The Dedication

first fruits Cf. Deuteronomy 26:10, 'And now, behold, I have brought the first fruits of the land, which thou, O Lord, hast given me . . .'

THE CHURCH-PORCH

The advice this didactic section of *The Temple* offers is as much ethical as religious, aphoristic in form and necessary for the moral education of the young believer being prepared to enter the Church proper. The lines have the same palpable design upon us as the verses in Proverbs or in Polonius's words to Laertes, *sans* parody. Louis L. Martz notes the three-part division of *The Church-Porch* into faults of individual conduct (stanzas 1–34), of social conduct (stanzas 35–62), and of religious obligation (stanzas 63–77) in *The Poetry of Meditation* (1954), p. 291.

Perirrhanterium

Title an instrument for sprinkling holy water, especially upon the newly baptised. It is the sub-title of *The Church-Porch*, though placed above the stanzas of 'Superliminare' (MSW). The shift suggests that the *The Church-Porch* offers instruction to catechumens who will be thus prepared for entry into the Church proper. See, especially, Stanley Fish, *The Living Temple: George Herbert and Catechising* (1978), Chapter 1, and Stanley Stewart, *George Herbert* (1986), pp. 84–9.

3 *a Verser* both a maker of verses and a trickster. See, especially, Robert B. Hinman, 'The "Verser" at *The Temple* Door: Herbert's *The Church-Porch*' in '*Too Rich to Clothe the Sunne': Essays on George Herbert*, ed. Claude J. Summers and Ted-Larry Pebworth (1980), pp. 55–75.

7 *lust* sexual desire, not merely desire in general.

13 *Abstain wholly* The second edition of 1633, which has a considerable number of minor alterations in typography, provides one substantive change of doubtful improvement: 'Wholly abstain'.

18 *rottenness* Proverbs 12:4, 'A virtuous woman is a crown to her husband: but she that maketh ashamed, is as rottenness in his bones.'

20 *incloser* one who appropriates common land to himself.

21 *impaled* fenced in, but with the suggestion of another sense of impaled, i.e., pierced with a stake, man has impaled God.

24 *cross* perverse.

25 *the third glass* the point of intoxication, as in 'one glass of wine is gold, two silver, three lead'.

30 *keep the round* drink equally with the others.

35 *Man* the dignity of a rational creature.

devest lay aside, abandon, with a play on unclothe, i.e., make naked like a beast.

39 *can* drinking vessel.

42 *modest* shy, bashful.

43 *gallants* men of fashion and pleasure.

58 *sluice* drain with reference to the opening of a tap in a wine or beer barrel.

60 *Epicure* 'one who recognises no religious motives for conduct' (*OED*).

bate give up; take the edge off.

66 *stake* that which is placed as a hazard, a valuable commodity.

80 *mistressing* paying court to, dallying with a girl. Herbert is echoing Donne's poem, 'To Mr Tilman after he had taken orders' (1618/19):

Why do they think unfit
That gentry should join families with it?
As if their day were only to be spent
In dressing, mistressing and compliment. (lines 27–30)

87 *his* time's; Time is often represented as a devourer, as in Ovid, 'Tempus edax rerum' ('time, the devourer of all things'), *Metamorphoses* XV, line 234.

91 *sloth* idleness, laziness, one of the Seven Deadly Sins. Each of the European countries was varyingly associated with one of the Deadly Sins, for example, Spain with Pride, Italy with Wrath.

92 *phlegm* that humour or fluid the excess of which causes idleness or laziness.

96 *gone to grass* idle, unemployed.

100 *ship them over* send them packing, get rid of them.

117 *stour* strong, sturdy.

118 *thrall* servitude, bondage.

120 *shelf* submerged ledge of rock and thus a danger to a ship.

123 *Simp'ring* smiling in a foolishly affected manner, as in *King Lear* IV, vi, lines 118–19, 'Behold yond simp'ring dame/Whose face between her forks presages snow.'

124 *clue undoes* ball of thread unwinds.

128 *sconces* small forts; safeguards.

130 *carves* the phrase is 'to carve to (someone)', hence the following 'two'.

131 *eat a bit* Job 28:5, 'As for the earth, out of it cometh bread . . .'

132 *Earth to earth I commit* from BCP Burial Office, in which the priest says,

> Forasmuch as it hath pleased Almighty God of his great mercy to take unto himself the soul of our dear brother here departed, we therefore commit his body to the ground; earth to earth, ashes to ashes, dust to dust; in sure and certain hope of the Resurrection to eternal life, through our Lord Jesus Christ . . .

133 *sickly healths* 'unhealthy toasts', the phrase itself combining pun and oxymoron.

137 *Ecliptic line* the great circle of the celestial sphere that is the apparent orbit of the sun.

142 *underwrites* subscribes to.
143 *humours* passions.
149 *good fellows* comrades, with the pejorative connotation of low companions.
153 *scraper* skinflint.
163 *misdoubt* suspect the existence of.
168 *to the quick* to the tender flesh beneath the skin.
169 *What skills it* what does it matter.
171 *Take . . . stars* Luke 12:33, 'Sell what ye have, and give alms: provide yourselves bags which wax not old, a treasure in the heavens that faileth not, where no thief approacheth, neither moth corrupteth.'
179 *curious* fastidious.
187 *bear the bell* win first prize.
190 *brave* splendid.
198 *cracked name* damaged reputation.
209 *gallant* in a smart fashion.
212 *allay* alloy, in the sense of an inferior metal mixed with one of greater value, for the purpose of strengthening the greater one.
213 *sharp* shrill.
lour scowl.
218 *home* heart of the matter.
223 *toy* trifle.
posed nonplussed, at a disadvantage.
227 *plays* deals with.
232 *Thy person share, and the conceit advance* 'The hearers, by seeing "Thy person" in the jest, may add a point to it, which the speaker did not intend and would prefer not to be made' (Hutchinson).
239–40 *nothing . . . vein* almost perfectly describes Herbert's special quality as a poet.
241 *engine* military apparatus, for example, a piece of ordnance.
244 *want* lack.
247 *sad* steadfast, firm.
249 *giggler* one who laughs foolishly.
252 *cock* winner.
253 *respective* courteous.

256 *rateably* proportionately.
258 *parcel-devil* in part a devil and therefore to some degree responsible.
264 *the beasts* animal passions.
265 *bate* subtract from.
268 *And not the beast* Aesop tells of the mistakenly proud ass that arrogated to itself the attention directed to the image it was carrying, and Emblem writers, for example Alciati, continued the lesson, particularising the image as that of the goddess Isis.
270 *arras* tapestry fabric of high quality.
271 *Thy friend* Proverbs 27:10, 'Thine own friend and thy father's friend forsake not . . .'
276 *David had his Jonathan* the archetypal image of friendship equated with the classical Damon and Pythias.

John the disciple 'whom Jesus loved', author of the Fourth Gospel, often shown reclining on the bosom of Christ at the Last Supper.
277 *surety* a person who guarantees the performance of a second person primarily liable, for example the co-signer of a loan.
288 *score* twenty, as labour combined with love.
293 *draw the card* begin to play the game of social conversation.
297 *rest* the stakes kept in reserve in the card game Primero. The loss of those stakes means the end of the game.
301 *Master-gunner* the person having the floor in the exchange of verbal volleys.
305 *As if thou mad'st thy will* as if you were giving everything away and therefore did not care that others were deprived of a chance to speak.
314 *him . . . his* himself . . . the chafer's.
315 *frets* vexations.
317 *bow* rainbow.
318 *sphere* the outer limit of space.
322 *dram* small amount, usually of spirits.
324 *troth* covenant, bond.
327 *great places* high social positions.
328 *compass* attain.

329 *go less* are not equal to.

334 *means* aims at.

342 *Write on the others* as an epitaph.

348 *quit* repay.

352 *a little sling* the weapon used by David to slay Goliath: cf. 1 Samuel 17:50, 'So David prevailed over the Philistine with a sling and with a stone, and smote the Philistine, and slew him; but there was no sword in the hand of David.'

360 *Strike off all scores* cancel all debts.

365 *fit* mood, humour.

368 *board* approach.

369 *noisomeness* offensiveness.

385 *in tithe and time* in giving one tenth of one's money and all of one's effort.

391 *on the day* Sunday, with both Morning and Evening Prayers.

399 *a weight* burden, as in Francis Quarles's *Emblems* of 1635 (i, 13), translating St Augustine, 'All things are divine by their weight, and tend to their own centre; "my weight is love; by that I am driven wheresoever I am driven"' (Hutchinson). Francis Quarles was cupbearer to Elizabeth of Bohemia when she married Frederick. See also 'To the Lady Elizabeth Queen of Bohemia', pp. 196–8

401 *six and seven* indifference to the consequence of your action (originally from dicing).

403 *bare* with uncovered head.

415 *seal up* close up; 'to seel' is to sew the eyelids of a hawk.

422 *plots* purposes, plans, not necessarily sinister in nature.

423 *Christ purged his temple* Mark 11:15, 'And they came to Jerusalem and Jesus went into the Temple, and began to cast out them that sold and bought in the Temple, and overthrew the tables of the moneychangers, and the seats of them that sold doves.'

425 *cozen* cheat.

429 *God calleth preaching folly* 1 Corinthians 1:21, 'For after that in the wisdom of God the world by wisdom knew not God, it pleased God by the foolishness of preaching to save them that believe.'

430 *To pick out treasures from an earthen pot* 2 Corinthians 4:7, 'But we have this treasure in earthen vessels, that the excellency of the power may be of God, and not of us.'
449 *The Jews refused thunder* in that they fell away from the Ten Commandments which had been delivered to Moses with thunder and lightning on Mount Sinai: 'And it came to pass on the third day in the morning, that there were thunders and lightnings, and a thick cloud upon the mount, and the voice of the trumpet exceeding loud, so that all the people that was in the camp trembled' (Exodus 19:16) and 'For the preaching of the Cross is to them that perish foolishness; but unto us which are saved it is the power of God' (1 Corinthians 1:18).
454 *watch* a small time-piece.
460 *an ell* a length of 45 inches, i.e., reducing a modest amount to one trivial.

Superliminare

The title signifies something that is preliminary or introductory. It is symbolically recalling the stone above the threshold that separates the church from the church-porch. The two stanzas are independent of one another; the first is addressed to the by now prepared reader of *The Church-Porch*, while the second speaks to the immoral or heathen reader.
2 *Sprinkled* with a kind of figurative holy water.
5 *profaneness* that which is unholy; literally, that which occurs outside the *fanum* or temple.
6 *pure* Revelation 21:27, 'And there shall in no wise enter into it anything that defileth, neither whatsoever worketh abomination, or maketh a lie: but they who are written in the Lamb's book of life.'

THE CHURCH

The Altar

One of the two clearest pattern poems (the other is 'Easter-Wings') in *The Temple*. It derives from a venerable tradition of iconographic verse from as far back as the *Greek Anthology* in pagan literature. 'The Altar' has the shape of a classical altar (although it must be noted that Old Testament altars were often portrayed in classical form, as in the illustrations to the Geneva Bible) and it presents the argument of Christian doctrine that a loving, broken and contrite heart is the only fit sacrificial offering. As is the case throughout *The Temple*, Herbert here juxtaposes allusions to passages from Scripture, usually New Testament against Old Testament, the better to indicate the movement from legal bondage to Christian liberty.

1 *A broken* ALTAR Herbert has chosen to call the communion table by this term in order to contrast the Israelite experience of sacrifice with that of the Christian, but he may also be showing his own inclination in the vexed matters of liturgy and terminology that bedevilled the sixteenth and seventeenth centuries and that were finessed in part by such Anglican statements as that of Lancelot Andrewes, 'The Holy Eucharist . . . is fitly called an *Altar*; which is as fitly called a *Table*, the Eucharist being considered as a *Sacrament*, which is nothing else but a distinction and an application of the Sacrifice to the several receivers . . .' (cited by Patrides).

Bloch notes the rich transformation in sacrificial requirements with the use of Old Testament passages, Deuteronomy 27:5–6 and Psalm 51:16–17, 'And there shalt thou build an Altar unto thy Lord thy God, an altar of stones; thou shalt not lift up any iron tool upon them. Thou shalt build the Altar of the Lord thy God of whole stones: and thou shalt offer burnt offerings thereon unto the Lord thy God:' and 'For thou desirest no sacrifice, else would I give it thee: but thou delightest not in burnt offerings. The sacrifice of God is a troubled spirit: a broken and contrite heart, O God, shalt thou not despise.'

2 *cemented* Sometimes thought to echo Donne, 'The Ecstasy', 'Our hands were firmly cemented' (line 5), but note the use of the word in Puttenham's chapter explaining and justifying pattern poems, 'Your last proportion is that of a figure, so called for that it yields an ocular representation, your metres being by good symmetry reduced into certain geometrical figures, whereby the maker is restrained to keep him within his bounds, and showeth not only more art, but serveth also much better for briefness and subtlety of device' ('The Arte of English Posie', Chapter XII, *Elizabethan Critical Essays*, ed. G. G. Smith (Oxford, 1904), II, p. 95). Some poets of China and Tartary have the verses engraved 'sometime with letters of Amethyst, ruby, emerald, or topaz curiously cemented and pieced together . . .' (p. 96). Puttenham goes on to discuss the various shapes of these pattern poems, including that of 'The Pillar, Pilaster, or Cylinder . . . by this figure is signified stay, support, rest, state, and magnificence. Your ditty then being reduced into the form of the Pillar, his base will require to bear the breadth of a metre of six or seven or eight syllables; the chapter equal with the base' (pp. 100–101). Puttenham then illustrates the figure with two examples, the second of which is an elongated version of the figure used by Herbert as an altar.

4 *tool* Cf. Exodus 20:25, 'And if thou wilt make me an altar of stone, thou shalt not build it of hewn stone: for if thou lift up thy tool upon it, thou hast polluted it.'

5 *A Heart alone* The image derives from St Paul on the transformation of the old law into the new by Christ in 2 Corinthians 3:3. This in contrast to Exodus 31:18, 'And he gave unto Moses, when he had made an end of communing with him upon Mount Sinai, two tables of testimony, tables of stone, written with the finger of God.'

6 *stone* Cf. Deuteronomy 27:2–7, where, as the AV summarises, Moses commanded the people as they passed over into Jordan 'to write the Law upon stones, and to build an Altar of whole stones' and 'thou shalt offer burnt offerings thereon unto the Lord thy

God' (27:6). These verses are to be contrasted with the words of St Paul in 2 Corinthians 3:3, as cited in the note to line 3, 'Forasmuch as ye are manifestly declared to be the Epistle of Christ ministered by us, written not with ink, but with the spirit of the living God; not in tables of stone, but in fleshy tables of the heart.'

13 *hold my peace* Luke 19:40, where Christ rebukes the Pharisees, 'I tell you that, if these [referring to the disciples] should hold their peace, the stones would immediately cry out.'

15 *SACRIFICE* In the BCP the post-communion prayer includes the words, 'O Lord and heavenly Father, we thy humble servants entirely desire thy fatherly goodness mercifully to accept this our sacrifice of praise and thanksgiving . . . And here we offer and present unto thee, O Lord, ourselves, our souls and bodies, to be a reasonable, holy, and living sacrifice unto Thee . . .'

The Sacrifice

This extended lamentation over mankind's ingratitude spoken by Christ in a dramatic monologue, unique in *The Church*, owes much to the tradition of reproaches, or *Improperia*, complaints by Christ in his Passion to the people on Good Friday, and just as much to the ironically juxtaposed biblical verses, often suggested to the attentive reader by a single word, all leading to the theme 'that the royalty of Christ, attributed to him by his persecutors in mockery, is authentic' (Hutchinson). Others had been as bold as Herbert in having Christ speak in his own person, for example Thomas Nashe in *Christ's Tears Over Jerusalem* (1593), but none has created so haunting a work or one that has produced so much fruitfully opposed criticism. See especially Empson, pp. 286–95, Tuve, and Bloch, especially pp. 65–79.

1 *O, all ye, who pass by* In Lamentations 1:12 Jerusalem beratingly cries out, 'Is it nothing to you, all ye that pass by? behold, and see, if there be any sorrow like unto my sorrow, which is done unto me, wherewith the Lord hath afflicted me in the day of his fierce anger.'

4 *Was ever grief like mine?* With the phrasing borrowed from Lamentations, this rhetorical question is based on the excruciating physical pain of Christ's sacrifice and the psychological pain created by the rejection of God's greatest gift of his Son.

5 *make a head* to resist, more particularly, to raise a body of troops.

9 *brave* defy.

13 *Mine own Apostle* Judas.

The bag purse. Cf. John 12:6, 'This he [Judas] said, not that he cared for the poor; but because he was a thief, and had the bag, and bare what was put therein.'

18 *three hundred* In Bethany, Judas objected to the waste of precious ointment by Mary Magdalene when she anointed Christ's feet, John 12:5, 'Why was not this ointment sold for three hundred pence, and given to the poor?'

26 *Balsam* 'An aromatic oily or resinous medicinal preparation, usually for external application, for healing wounds or soothing pain' (*OED*).

both the Hemispheres OED cites this phrase as one of the examples for the definition 'one of the halves of the terrestrial globe, especially as divided by the equator (Northern and Southern hemispheres). Also the halves containing Europe, Asia, and Africa (Eastern hemisphere), and America (Western hemisphere), respectively.' Given that *The Temple* ultimately speaks of religion moving westward and to America, it is East and West, rather than North and South, that are intended. Also the association of Sun and Son requires East and West.

33 *Arise, arise* An imperative echoing in form Donne's Holy Sonnets, 'Divine Meditation 7',

> At the round earth's imagined corners, blow
> Your trumpets, Angels, and arise, arise
> From death, you numberless infinities . . . (lines 1–3)

but alluding to Matthew 26:46, 'Rise, let us be going: behold, he is at hand that doth betray me.'

38 *way of truth* John 14:6, 'I am the way, the truth, and the life.'

47 *who have loosed their bands* This is a conflation of Ezekiel

34:27, '. . . they . . . shall know that I am the Lord, when I have broken the bands of their yoke,' and Psalm 116:16 (AV), 'O Lord, truly I am thy servant; I am thy servant, and the son of thine handmaid: thou hast loosed my bonds.' Herbert's original audience doubtless recalled that the verses on either side of 116:16 are 'Precious in the sight of the Lord is the death of his saints' and 'I will offer to thee the sacrifice of thanksgiving.'

57 *The Priest* 'Caiaphas the high Priest', (Matthew 26:57).

59 *Paschal* Passover; cf. 1 Corinthians 5:7, 'For even Christ our Passover is sacrificed for us,' and John 1:29, 'Behold the Lamb of God, which taketh away the sin of the world.'

61 *blasphemy* When Jesus walked in the temple in Solomon's porch, he was nearly stoned, John 10:33, 'The Jews answered him, saying, For a good work we stone thee not, but for blasphemy, and because that thou, being a man, makest thyself God.'

63 *robbery* as St Paul explains of Christ, Philippians 2:6, 'Who, being in the form of God, thought it not robbery to be equal with God.'

65 *Temple* not the building in Jerusalem but Christ's reference to his body, the temple of the Spirit.

73 *Herod* Herod Antipas (4 BC–AD 39), tetrarch of Galilee.

74 *Pilate* Procurator (i.e., governor) of Judea, AD 26–36, who gave up Christ to be crucified knowing him to be guiltless: '. . . he took water, and washed his hands before the multitude, saying, I am innocent of the blood of this just person . . .' (Matthew 27:24).

77 *set me light* value or hold me of little importance.

85 *despitefulness* contemptuousness, malicious feeling or action, cruelty.

86 *vying* 'to match (one thing) with another by way of return, rivalry, or comparison' (*OED*).

89 *prove* test, try.

109 *cankers* infects.

111 *gall* the essence of bitterness.

117 *murderer* Barabbas, the well-known criminal who was released by Pilate instead of Jesus upon the request of the crowd at the Passover just before Christ's crucifixion. Cf. Matthew 27:15–23.

119 *glass* reflect, but suggesting St Paul, 'For now we see through a glass, darkly, but then face to face' (1 Corinthians 13:12).
134 *Who by my spittle gave the blind man eyes* Mark 8:23–4.
139 *double-dark* extremely wicked, and perhaps more particularly, guilty of both Original and actual sin.
141 *abjects* outcasts; degraded persons.
142 *prophesy* Luke 23:64.
150 *blood* on the Mount of Olives, 'And being in an agony he prayed more earnestly: and his sweat was as it were great drops of blood falling down to the ground' (Luke 22:44).
155 *twelve* military support available to Christ, as 'Thinkest thou that I cannot now pray to my Father, and he shall presently give me more than twelve legions of angels? But how then shall the scriptures be fulfilled, that thus it must be?' (Matthew 26:53–4).
162 *Sion* Jerusalem's holy hill.
167 *thrall* misery flowing from the state of transferred bondage to sin and death.
170 *rock* Cf. 1 Corinthians 10:4, 'And did all drink the same spiritual drink: for they drank of that spiritual Rock that followed them: and that Rock was Christ.'
193 *engross* collect.
198 *Simon* Cf. Matthew 27:32, 'And as they came out, they found a man of Cyrene, Simon by name: him they compelled to bear his cross.'
205 *charged* laden with, bearing (but with a secondary and ironic image of an heraldic escutcheon).
207 *By words* i.e., by God's fiat 'Let there be'.

The Thanksgiving

4 *preventest* both (1) anticipates and (2) excels.
5 *store* abundance.
6 *door* Cf. John 10:9, 'I am the door: by me if any man enter in, he shall be saved, and shall go in and out, and find pasture.' There is another possibility, suggested by Hutchinson, of 'an outlet for blood' as in the description by Mark Antony of 'the most unkindest cut of all', *Julius Caesar* III, ii, lines 177–80:

And as he pluck'd his cursed steel away,
Mark how the blood of Caesar followed it,
As rushing out of doors to be resolved
If Brutus so unkindly knock'd or no.

9 *My God, my God* Cf. Matthew 27:46, 'And about the ninth hour Jesus cried with a loud voice, saying, "Eli, Eli, Lama sabachthani?" that is to say, My God, my God, why hast thou forsaken me?' This line looks back to line 213 of 'The Sacrifice'.
11 *skipping thy doleful* The fifth edition, the last corrected by Thomas Buck, deletes a comma after 'skipping', a correction which allows the phrase to parallel the 'neglecting thy sad' of MSW.
20 *poor* Cf. Proverbs 19:17, 'He that hath pity upon the poor, lendeth unto the Lord; and that which he hath given will he pay him again.'
33 *spittle* charity ward for the indigent and diseased.
common ways public roads.
38 *here* in *The Temple*, in the poems themselves.
43 *wit* a word of multiple meanings: here creative brilliance.
47 *art of love* playing on the title of Ovid's witty treatise *Ars Amatoria*, the better to suggest the superiority of divine love.

The Reprisal

Title 'The most familiar sense of "reprisal", of course, is the military one – that of retaliation in warfare. Atonement, then, is the retaliation most pleasing to Christ. But "reprisal" is also a musical term meaning a return to the original theme or subject and thus this implication both reminds us of the theme of "The Thanksgiving" and lends poignance to the poet's plea for a return to innocence through confession' (M. E. Rickey (1966), pp. 96–7).
12 *overthrow* Note the echo from another poem, asking to be made forcibly innocent, Donne's 'Holy Sonnet 14', 'That I may rise, and stand, o'erthrow me . . .' (line 3).
16 *The man* Cf. Colossians 3:9–10, 'Seeing that ye have put off the old man with his deeds; and have put on the new man, which is renewed in knowledge after the image of him that created him.'

The Agony

3 *staff* a measuring rod, but with reference to Jacob in Herbert's favourite passage, 'I am not worthy of the least of all the mercies, and of all the truth, which thou hast showed unto thy servant; for with my staff I passed over this Jordan . . .' (Genesis 32:10).

8 *Mount Olivet* site of the agony (cf. 'The Sacrifice', line 150, 'blood' and note) and the request, 'Father, if thou be willing, remove this cup from me: nevertheless not my will, but thine be done' (Luke 22:42).

11 *press* (1) instrument of torture; (2) wine-press. Hutchinson cites an extract from the *Sermons* of Lancelot Andrewes, 'This was the pain of the Press (so the Prophet calleth it, "Torcular") wherewith as if He had been in the wine-press, all his garments were stained and gored with blood.'

vice torturing device, with play on 'wickedness'.

14 *pike* spear-like weapon with a sharp iron tip. Cf. John 19:34, 'But one of the soldiers with a spear pierced his side, and forthwith came there out blood and water.'

15 *abroach* pierced and letting the liquid flow out, as in *Romeo and Juliet* I, i, line 95, where it is used figuratively by Montague, 'Who set this ancient quarrel new abroach'.

The Sinner

1 *ague* quaking; shivering or shaking.

5 *piled* heaped.

8 *circumference* So much of the circle of life is taken up by sin, with goodness but the small point at the centre. There may be an ironic allusion here to the Renaissance commonplace that God himself is a circle whose circumference is nowhere and whose centre is everywhere. The power of the centre is indicated by Donne, 'Of the Progress of the Soul: The Second Anniversary' (1611/12),

> Know that all lines which circles do contain,
> For once that they the centre touch, do touch
> Twice the circumference; and be thou such. (lines 436–8)

9 *quintessence* the purest part, a technical term in alchemy.
12 *restore thine image* echoing here, just before 'Good Friday', Donne's 'Good Friday, 1613. Riding Westward',

O think me worth thine anger, punish me,
Burn off my rusts, and my deformity,
Restore thine image, so much, by thy grace,
That thou mayst know me, and I'll turn my face. (lines 39–42)

14 *in stone* Cf. Exodus 31:18, 'And he gave unto Moses, when he had made an end of communing with him upon mount Sinai, two tables of testimony, tables of stone, written with the finger of God,' as well as, centrally and pervasively in Herbert beginning with 'The Altar', line 6 (and note), 2 Corinthians 3:3, 'Forasmuch as ye are manifestly declared to be the Epistle of Christ ministered by us, written not with ink, but with the spirit of the living God, not in tables of stone, but in fleshy tables of the heart.'

Good Friday

10 *score* keep a record of.
15–16 This image of speed anticipates Marvell, 'To His Coy Mistress', 'Rather at once our Time devour . . ./Thus, though we cannot make our sun/Stand still, yet we will make him run' (lines 39, 45–6).
21–32 MSW titles lines 21–32 as 'The Passion'.

Redemption

Title The redemption and sale metaphor for the Atonement is revealed in the etymology of redemption itself: literally, a buying, purchasing and, by extension, ransoming.
4 *cancel th' old* the Covenant of Works, to be replaced by that of grace. Cf. Hebrews 9:15–16, 'And for this cause he is the mediator of the new testament, that by means of death, for the redemption of the transgressions that were under the first testament, they which are called might receive the promise of eternal

inheritance. For where a testament is, there must also of necessity be the death of the testator.'

12 *ragged* harsh.

14 *granted* 'awarded' and 'already awarded', as the response anticipates the request.

died Bloch points out that the poem expands upon the adverbs in Paul's statement in Romans 5:8, 'But God commendeth his love towards us, in that, while we were yet sinners, Christ died for us.'

Sepulchre

5 *good store* in abundance.

7 *toys* trifles.

10 *pure rock* (1) the sepulchre itself and (2) Christ, as in 1 Corinthians 10:4, 'And did all drink the same spiritual drink: for they drank of that spiritual Rock that followed them: and that Rock was Christ.' Cf. 'The Sacrifice', line 170.

13 *took up stones* Cf. John 10:31, 'Then the Jews took up stones again to stone him.'

15 *entertain* receive as a guest.

18 *in stone* Cf. line 14 of 'The Sinner' and note.

19 *no fit heart* as St Paul had described it, 2 Corinthians 3:3, see note to line 10.

24 *Withhold* keep from, restrain, prevent.

Easter

Lines 19–30 comprise the 'song' referred to in line 13; in MSW a version of these final twelve lines is itself entitled *Easter*, leading some editors to divide the poem into 'Easter (1)' and 'Easter (2)'.

1 *Sing his praise* Cf. Psalms 57:8–10, 'My heart is fixed, O God, my heart is fixed: I will sing, and give praise. Awake up, my glory: awake, lute and harp: I myself will awake right early. I will give thanks unto thee, O Lord, among the people: and I will sing unto thee among the nations.'

5 *calcined* burned to ashes, with the suggestion of the alchemical process of purification necessary in the transformation of lead into gold.

11 *what key* In addition to the image of Christ on the cross as God's instrument playing the ultimate love song in the Passion, there is in the stretching of the sinews an example for composers of religious music, '"because the doctrine of affections coordinated certain keys with certain affections" and that the pitch of church music was "practically a minor third higher than it now is"' well above secular song. (J. H. Summers, *George Herbert*, p. 160, quoting Manfred F. Bukofzer, *Music in the Baroque Era: From Monteverdi to Bach* (New York, 1947), p. 365 and E. H. Fellowes, *English Cathedral Music from Edward VI to Edward VII* (London, 1941), p. 92.) T. A. Joscelyne notes an analogue from St Victorinus (d. *c.* AD 304), 'It is a new thing that the Son of God should become man. It is a new thing to ascend into the heavens with a body. It is a new thing to give remission of sins to men. It is a new thing for men to be sealed with the Holy Spirit. It is a new thing to receive the priesthood of sacred observance, and to look for a kingdom of unbounded promise. The harp and the chord stretched on its wooden frame signifies the flesh of Christ linked with the wood of the Passion' (trans. R. E. Wallis in 'George Herbert's "Easter" and St Victorinus's *Commentary on the Apocalypse of the Blessed John*', *N&Q*, 26 October 1979), p. 410.

13 *Consort* Noel J. Kinnamon ('A Note on Herbert's "Easter" and the Sidneian Psalms', *GHJ* 1, 1978 pp. 46–7) cites as a source for this line verses 34–6 from the Countess of Pembroke's paraphrase of Psalm 57:

> Wake my tongue, my lute awake,
> Thou my harp the console make
> My self will bear a part.

twist interweaves, as strands in a c(h)ord.

15 *vied* 'increased in number by addition or repetition' (*OED*).

19 *straw* Cf. Matthew 21:8, describing Christ's entry into Jerusalem, 'And a very great multitude spread their garments in the

way, others cut down branches from the trees, and strawed them in the way.'

29 *three hundred* that is, roughly 365, the lesser suns of each ordinary day of the year as opposed to the one Sun of Easter.

Easter-Wings

The poem is a prelude to the falling/rising movement so important in the central body of *The Temple*. Along with 'The Altar', this is the most obvious pattern poem in *The Temple*, although J. Max Patrick ('Critical Problems in Editing George Herbert's *The Temple*' in *The Editor as Critic and the Critic as Editor*, by J. Max Patrick and Alan Roper (William Andrews Clark Memorial Library, University of California, Los Angeles, 1973), pp. 1–40) has seen subtler visual patterns in several other poems, in addition to those of recognisably odd form, such as 'An Anagram', 'Heaven', 'Hope', 'Jesu', 'Love-Joy', 'Colossians 3:3' and 'A Wreath', including a cruciform shape in 'Good Friday'. Both MSB and MSW present the lines horizontally, thereby making them easier to read, but less emblematic of both the rise of the lark's flight and fall and the resurrection of man in Christ. Mario Di Cesare argues that the manuscript patterning is not only easier to read but has the 'effect of birds in flight *across* the sky, birds following each other' (*The Bodleian Manuscript of George Herbert's Poems*, p. xxxi).

7 *rise* Cf. Isaiah 40:31, 'But they that wait upon the Lord shall renew their strength; they shall mount up with wings as eagles.' See C. C. Brown and W. P. Ingoldsby, 'George Herbert's "Easter-Wings"', *HLQ*, 35 (1972), pp. 131–42.

10 *the fall* of man, which paradoxically leads to a higher flight towards heaven because it necessitated the Atonement – it is a fortunate fall, a *felix culpa*.

19 *imp* 'To engraft feathers in the wing of a bird, so as to make good losses or deficiencies, and thus restore or improve the powers of flight; hence, allusively, with reference to "taking higher flights", enlarging one's powers, and the like' (*OED*). Here the weaker the

speaker's wing the more force required by Christ's wing and paradoxically the greater flight of the 'I'.

Holy Baptism (1)

11 *plaster* medication, but the word revives the association of altar–Jordan–contrition–redemption begun in Deuteronomy 27:2, 'And it shall be on the day when ye shall pass over Jordan unto the land which the Lord thy God giveth thee, that thou shalt set thee up great stones, and plaister them with plaister.'

crime sin, violation of moral nature.

12 *Book of Life* the record of the names of those who shall inherit eternal life (cf. Philippians 4:3 and Revelation 20:12).

Holy Baptism (2)

2 *narrow way* Matthew 7:13–14, 'Enter ye in at the strait gate: for wide is the gate, and broad is the way, that leadeth to destruction, and many there be which go in thereat: Because strait is the gate, and narrow is the way, which leadeth unto life, and few there be that find it.'

4–5 *antedate/My faith* That is, according to doctrine, Baptism makes a child a Christian even before he is mature enough to accept the doctrine of the Faith, a vexed issue for sixteenth- and seventeenth-century reformers (and non-reformers).

10 *Behither* short of, barring, save (in the sense of except).

Nature

2 *travel* for the possible autobiographical element in this rebellion, see Walton's *Life*, p. 280.

6 *strong holds* 2 Corinthians 10:3–4, 'For though we walk in the flesh, we do not war after the flesh: (For the weapons of our warfare are not carnal, but mighty through God to the pulling down of strong holds.)'

10 *kind* nature.

Sin (1)

5 *sorrow* remorse.
6 *sorted* varied.
7 *fine* with a fine mesh: therefore able to catch the subtlest of sins.
14 *bosom-sin* cherished, especially favoured, that is, most frequently troubling.

Affliction (1)

Title Bloch notes Genesis 31:34–42, the story of Jacob's frustration in his dealing with the deceitful master Laban, as a source which allows for the vehemence of the speaker's complaint.
2 *brave* splendid.
7 *furniture* the natural creation; also, used not only as domestic gear but in the Lord's house, the vessels of his tabernacle, Exodus 31:7–9, '. . . and all the furniture of the Tabernacle, And the table, and his furniture, and the pure candlestick with all his furniture, and the altar of incense, And the altar of burnt offering with all his furniture . . .'
10 *'tice* entice, i.e., induce, attract (with the offer of pleasure or advantage).
13 *want* lack.
21 *strawed* covered with loosely scattered elements (i.e., flowers and happiness).
35 *fence* bulwark, protection.
40 *gown* academic robe, a university career.
47 *where* MSW reads 'where' and MSB has 'where' written above and correcting 'neere'. The *1633* reading is 'neare', which does not quite fit the context. The fifth edition also reads 'where'.
53 *cross-bias* running athwart the path of another, as in bowls, but here a reminder of Christ's suffering, with the ironic force of recalling the crucifixion of God's greatest 'gift'.
65–6 *forgot,/Let me not love thee, if I love thee not* 1 Corinthians 16:22, 'If any man love not the Lord Jesus Christ, let him be Anathema Maran-atha.' Empson, Bloch and others have pointed

out the added force given the second clause of the line by the suspended curse. The paradoxical and unexpected conclusion insists in the midst of the double negatives that the speaker maintain his love of God however unrewarded and neglected he may feel.

Repentance

7–12 *Man's age . . . fall* The life of man is of brief duration as the evidence of each day shows. Analogously, our delights are in proportion to our sorrows: that is, when reckoned ('told'), one to twelve ('two hours') or one to eight ('or three'), as is our experience because of the effects of Adam's Original Sin (borne by us).

21 *wormwood* an emblem or type of what is bitter and grievous to the soul. Cf. Jeremiah 9:15, 'Therefore thus saith the Lord of hosts, the God of Israel; Behold, I will feed them, even this people, with wormwood, and give them water of gall to drink.' Hamlet comments on the bitter implication contained in the Player Queen's 'None wed the second but who killed the first' with 'That's wormwood!', III, ii, 180–81.

25 *rebukest man* Cf. Psalms 39:12, 'When thou with rebukes dost chasten man for sin, thou makest his beauty to consume away, like as it were a moth fretting a garment; every man therefore is but vanity.'

26 *wan* pale (and sad).

27 *bowels* hearts, bosoms.

32 *bones* a pun on (1) skeletal elements and (2) crude sixteenth-century musical sticks. For the former, compare Psalm 51:8, 'Thou shalt make me hear of joy and gladness: that the bones which thou hast broken may rejoice.' For the latter, note Bottom in *A Midsummer Night's Dream* IV, 1, lines 28–9, 'I have a reasonable good ear in music. Let's have the tongs and the bones.'

36 *Fractures well cur'd make us more strong* common orthopaedic lore, reflected in Archbishop. Scroop's observation in *2 Henry IV* IV, i, lines 219–21:

If we do now make our atonement well,
Our peace will, like a broken limb united,
Grow stronger for the breaking.

Faith

6 *conceit* imagine, fancy.
9 *outlandish* foreign.
root medicinal plant.
22 *manger* a trough from which horses and cattle eat; with a reference to the humble cradle of Christ.
30 *clerk* scholar, man of learning.
32 *grace fills up uneven nature* Patrides illuminatingly cites St Thomas as the source of this axiom, 'Grace does not destroy nature but perfects it.'
35 *Impute* impart.
37 *clean* totally, quite.
42 *grain* Hutchinson compares Henry King's 'The Exequy', 'For thou must audit on thy trust/Each grain and atom of this dust.'
44 *flesh again* that is, the resurrection of the body on the Day of Judgement.

Prayer (I)

1 *Angels' age* eternity; cf. Luke 20:36, 'Neither can they die any more; for they are equal unto the Angels; and are the children of God, being the children of the resurrection.'
3 *paraphrase* expansion, fullness.
4 *plummet sounding* measuring the depth (and here, paradoxically, the height) by a piece of lead or other metal attached to a line; cf. Prospero, 'I'll break my staff . . . /And deeper than did ever plummet sound/I'll drown my book' (*The Tempest* V, i, lines 54, 56–7).
5 *Engine against th' Almighty* For prayer as condoned aggression, see *The Sermons of John Donne*, ed. George R. Potter and Evelyn M. Simpson (Berkeley and Los Angles, University of California Press, 1953–62), V, 18, p. 364, noted by Patrides: 'Earnest Prayer

hath the nature of Importunity: We press, we importune God . . . Prayer hath the nature of Impudency: We threaten God in Prayer . . . And God suffers this impudency and more. Prayer hath the nature of Violence; In the public prayers of the Congregation, we besiege God, says Tertullian, and we take God Prisoner, and bring God to our Conditions; and God is glad to be straitened by us in that siege.'

Sinners' tower a benign inversion of the tower of Babel.

7 *transposing* changing, transforming (with the suggestion of the shift in key; cf. 'tune' in the following line).

8 *kind of* sort of, included in the class of music, but not possessing all its characteristics.

10 *Manna* spiritual nourishment, food divinely supplied: cf. Exodus 16:15.

12 *bird of Paradise* a particularly gorgeous peacock-like creature, legless and perpetually hovering. See Jeremy Taylor's analogy (cited by E. B. Greenwood in 'George Herbert's Sonnet "Prayer": A Stylistic Study', *EIC* 15 (1965), pp. 27–43), 'Mankind now taking in his whole constitution, and design is like the birds of Paradise which travellers tell us of in the Molucco Islands; born without legs; but by a celestial power they have recompense made to them for that defect; and they always hover in the air, and feed on the dew of heaven; so are we birds of Paradise; but cast out from thence, and born without legs, without strength to walk in the laws of God, or go to heaven; but by a power from above, we are adopted in our new birth to a celestial conservation, we feed on the dew of heaven.'

13 *soul's blood* its vital principle of action. See Burton, 'Spirit is the most subtle vapour, which is expressed from the blood, and the instrument of the soul to perform all his actions' (cited by Greenwood in the article mentioned in the previous note).

The Holy Communion

2 *wedge of gold* In the distinction Herbert is drawing between the simple Anglican communion and the all-too-rich Roman Catholic rite, he recalls Achan's reply to Joshua, Joshua 7:21, 'When I

saw among the spoils a goodly Babylonish garment, and two hundred shekels of silver, and a wedge of gold of fifty shekels weight, then I coveted them, and took them . . .'

3 *from me* MSB offers the attractive 'for mee', a reading that might claim support from 'Dialogue', line 15, 'Who for man was sold' and 'Antiphon (2)', line 12, 'For us was sold.' Nevertheless, 'from' in opposition to 'To me' (line 4) makes complete sense in a sharp antithesis.

15 *fleshly* MSB has 'fleshy', which is in keeping with Herbert's practice of quoting Scripture exactly, as in 'the fleshy tables of the heart' (2 Corinthians 3:3), but the additional liquid consonant may have been added not merely for euphony but for the suggestion of sexual weakness as in the many words in English denoting the sensual which actually begin with *l*: *lewd*, *lascivious*, *lecherous*, *likerish*, *lustful*, etc.

16 *outworks* advanced fortifications beyond a castle or town, an image common to warfaring and wayfaring Christians, as in Donne, 'All our moralities are but our outworks, our Christianity is our Citadel' (Letter to Sir H. Goodyer, 4 October 1622).

23 *those* referring to the 'elements' (line 19), i.e., the bread and wine, the 'elements' of the Holy Communion waiting for divine grace to complete their nature.

refined purified. 'Refined' together with 'subtle' of the previous line suggests that Herbert was recalling both 'A Valediction: Forbidding Mourning' and 'The Ecstasy', poems which are contiguous in most manuscripts of Donne's *Songs and Sonnets*: 'But we by a love, so much *refined*' (line 17) and 'That *subtle* knot, which makes us man' (line 64). All three poems are concerned with 'elements', 'souls' and the separation and union of spirit and matter.

Antiphon (1)

Title 'a composition, in prose or verse, consisting of verses or passages sung alternately by two choirs in worship' (*OED*).

9 *shout* suggestive of both the 'joyful noise' the Psalmist made to the Lord and the communal response made by the congregation.

Love (1)

1 *frame* the universe, considered as a structure, as in *Hamlet* II, ii, line 298, 'this goodly frame, the earth'.
6 *invention* faculty of inventiveness, creativity.
9 *wit* human intelligence.
13–14 *Who sings . . . love* that is, mere erotic love tokens inspire secular poetry, while, it is implied, no one, even with ever so much greater material, inspires us to sacred verse.

Love (2)

6 *hearts pant* long for, as in Psalm 42:1, 'As the hart panteth after the water brooks, so panteth my soul after thee, O God' (AV).
10 *blown* (1) inflated (2) scattered.
12 *disseised* dispossessed wrongfully and, usually, by force.

The Temper (1)

Title the proper condition of mind or spirit.
5 *forty heav'ns* Hutchinson points out that St Paul speaks of 'The third Heaven' (2 Corinthians 12:2) and that the Jewish Apocalypses have 'a series of Heavens'.
9 *rack* torture by means of stretching.
15 *measure* (1) compare himself and (2) measure the length of weapons as in a duel. Cf. *Hamlet* V, ii, line 265, 'These foils have all a length?'
16 *spell* consider, contemplate, scan intently.
22 *Stretch or contract* frequently thought to refer to the tuning of a lute, but more probably to the psalmist's harp, as in the gloss of the Easter psalm by Cassiodorus, 'The harp means the glorious Passion which with stretched sinews and counted bones . . . sounded forth his bitter suffering as in a spiritual song', cited by Oliver Steele, 'Crucifixion and the Imitation of Christ in Herbert's *The Temper (1)*', *GHJ* 5 (1981–2), p. 72.
28 *Make one place ev'ry where* echoing the all-sufficiency in

Donne's 'The Sun Rising', 'Shine here to us, and thou art every where' (line 29).

The Temper (2)

4 *that* the 'mighty joy' of line 1.
5 *stands* is opposed to.
9 *fix* station; make stable in position.
chair seat, perhaps throne (note also the possibility of a macaronic pun on French '*chair*' = 'flesh').

Jordan (1)

The poem argues for sacred love poetry as against secular in a simple style that is uncomplicated by syntactical and allegorical difficulties. The Jordan is the river over which the Israelites passed to the Promised Land and in which Christ was baptised by John. Critics draw attention to the BCP rite of baptism for those 'of riper years' for its articulation of the significances of Jordan: 'Almighty and everlasting God, who of thy great mercy didst save Noah and his family in the ark from perishing by water; and also didst safely lead the children of Israel thy people through the Red Sea, figuring thereby thy holy Baptism; and by the Baptism of thy well-beloved Son Jesus Christ, in the river Jordan, didst sanctify the element of water to the mystical washing away of sin . . .' Hutchinson cites Elisha's advice to Naaman, who had been stricken with leprosy, 2 Kings 5:10, 'And Elisha sent a messenger unto him saying, Go and wash in Jordan seven times, and thy flesh shall come again to thee, and thou shalt be clean', and Thomas Lodge's Preface to his *Prosopopeia* (1596), 'Now at last after I have wounded the world with too much surfeit of vanity I may be by the true Helicon, cleansed from the leprosy of my lewd lines, and being washed in the Jordan of Grace, employ my labour to the comfort of the faithful.'
3 *winding stair* suggesting artificial complexity. The idea of deception is contained still more clearly in the essay 'Of Great Place' by Herbert's friend, Francis Bacon, 'All rising to Great Place

is by a winding stair.' See, especially, D. M. Hill, 'Allusion and Meaning in Herbert's "Jordan (1)"', *Neophilologus* 56 (1972), pp. 344–52.

5 *chair* Plato's example of the distance of art from truth is a bed, but Herbert is clearly alluding to the discussion of art at two removes from the truth in *The Republic*, Book X. The possibility of a pun on *chair* = 'flesh' (French) is heightened by Plato's imagery of cosmetics, as in 'Strip what the poet has to say of its poetical covering, and I think you must see what it comes to in plain prose. It is like a face which was never really handsome, when it has lost the fresh bloom of youth' (Cornford, trans.).

8 *purling* rippling, undulating; murmuring.

12 *Riddle* to speak (or write) enigmatically.

pull for Prime take a chance on drawing a winning card in the game Primero.

Employment (1)

12 *stuff* essential substance.

19 *husbandry* good management.

21ff. *I am no link* . . . This heartfelt plea from one in isolated unemployment rivals Donne's secular expression of a similar mood in the letter to Sir Henry Goodyer (September 1608), 'Therefore I would fain do something; but that I cannot tell what, is no wonder. For to choose is to do: but to be no part of any body, is to be nothing.' Hutchinson cites a phrase in Donne's sermon at Paul's Cross in 1616/17, 'If thou wilt be no link of God's Chain' (*The Sermons of John Donne*, ed. George R. Potter and Evelyn M. Simpson, I, 3, 208). The chain is the 'Great Chain of Being', the metaphor so frequent in the Renaissance which illustrates the hierarchical interconnectedness of all creation.

22 *weed* an unprofitable, troublesome or noxious growth (applied to persons); cf. 'the fat weed/That roots itself in ease on Lethe wharf', *Hamlet* I, v, lines 32–3.

23 *consort* a company or set of musicians, vocal or instrumental, making music together.

The Holy Scriptures (1)

2 *honey gain* Cf. Psalm 119:103, 'O how sweet are thy words unto my throat: yea, sweeter than honey unto my mouth.'

4 *mollify* soften.

8 *thankful glass* mirror deserving gratitude.

11 *lidger*, ledger, a pun involving the two meanings of 'resident ambassador' and 'register' (book). See Helen Wilcox, '"Heaven's Lidger Here": Herbert's *Temple* and Seventeenth-century Devotion' in David Jasper (ed.), *Images of Belief in Literature* (New York: St Martin Press, 1984), pp. 153–68.

13 *handsel* a first instalment, an auspicious omen of what is to follow.

heav'n lies flat in thee that is, displayed as in a map.

14 *mounter's bended knee* as in the genuflection of a self-abasing and self-advancing courtier.

The Holy Scriptures (2)

5 *This verse marks that* Critics note Herbert's discussion of the knowledge proper to the country parson in *A Priest to the Temple* Chapter 4, 'The third means is a diligent collation of Scripture with Scripture. For all Truth being consonant to itself, and all being penned by one and the selfsame Spirit, it cannot be but that an industrious and judicious comparing of place with place must be a singular help for the right understanding of the Scriptures' (p. 205). Herbert then adds that the parson, without neglecting his own interpretative powers, should make use of the Commentators and the Church Fathers.

6 *leaves* pages. Herbert repeated this idea of the disparate interconnectedness of Scripture in *The Country Parson*, Chapter 4: see note to line 5.

7 *do watch a potion* await to be combined into a potion; a much discussed expression, puzzling almost to the point of emendation. 'Watch' must by context mean 'combine', although the closest seventeenth-century sense of the word seems to be 'contrive'. Three seemingly scattered passages 'make up some Christian's destiny',

in that the stories of the Bible often presented the struggles belonging to the individual Christian who by study of the text could 'parallels bring' (line 11) to his own condition and see himself in a biblical figure, 'And in another make me understood' (line 12).

Whitsunday

Title seventh Sunday after Easter, a feast day to commemorate the descent of the Holy Spirit on the day of Pentecost.
1–2 *Dove unto my song,/And spread thy golden wings* Cf. the morning prayer on Whitsunday, Psalm 68, especially verse 13, 'Though ye have lien among the pots, yet shall ye be as the wings of a dove: that is covered with silver wings, and her feathers like gold.'
12 *mend* improve.
17 *pipes of gold* the Apostles as channels of grace, on the analogy with Zechariah 4:12–14, 'What be these two olive branches which through the two golden pipes empty the golden oil out of themselves? . . . Then said he, These are the two anointed ones, that stand by the Lord of the whole earth.'
18 *cordial* restorative, heart-reviving.
23 *braves* challenges, boasts.

Grace

Grace is the divine influence which operates in men to regenerate and sanctify, to inspire virtuous impulses, and to impart strength to endure trial and resist temptation. There is, also, a play on 'grace' and 'grass' involving the idea of manna, which fell upon the dew-covered grass during the Exodus, and that of the transitoriness and frailty of man as in 'all flesh is grass'.
1 *stock* tree-trunk deprived of branches (cf. Job 14:7–9).
19 *suppling* softening; the 'hardness' of line 18 is made supple.

Praise (1)

4 *Thou shalt have more* The concluding line of each stanza in a poem asking God's special aid recalls Donne's refrain in 'A Hymn to God the Father' (1623), 'For I have more'.

11 *sling* see note to line 352 of 'Perirrhanterium' (p. 329).
13–15 *dwell next . . . soul* Depending upon one's belief in the location of the soul, either in the heart or in the head, then the distilled herb finds its way to the stomach next to the heart or rises to the brain 'on the same floor' as the soul.

Affliction (2)

4 *in broken pay* in instalments.
5 *Methusalem's* common corruption of Methuselah; Methusaleh lived to be 969 (Genesis 5:27), hence extreme longevity.
10 *discolour* remove the colour from.
15 *imprest* pre-payment, payment in advance.

Matins

Title Morning Prayer. The order for public prayer in the Church of England since the Reformation and the Prayer Book of 1549.
4 *make a match* an appointment (or an agreement).
9–10 *what is a heart . . . and woo* echoing Psalm 8:4 in its amazement that the deity should trouble himself with man, 'What is man, that thou art mindful of him? and the son of man, that thou visitest him?'
17–19 *Teach me . . . show* in its imperative echoing Donne's 'Holy Sonnet 7': 'Teach me how to repent, for that's as good' (line 13); 'this new light' is the morning sunlight, consideration of which will lead to praise of the author of that light.

Sin (2)

3 *some good* he is an angel, however fallen.
5 *It wants the good of virtue, and of being* lacks goodness and, therefore, existence. Evil is a defect, a privation. It is the absence of goodness according to St Thomas Aquinas.
10 *perspective* not a magnifying glass, which would only frighten us more, but 'a picture or figure constructed so as to appear distorted except from one particular point of view', according to

C. T. Onions, as cited by Hutchinson. That is, we see our sins obliquely, not face to face.

Evensong

Title Vespers, but after the Reformation the term is applied to the 'Evening Prayer' of the Church of England, which is an abridgement of the offices of Evensong and Compline as used before the Reformation.

1 *God of love* a kind of Christian Cupid who blinds himself.

7 *For when he sees my ways, I die* Psalm 130:3, 'If thou, Lord, wilt be extreme to mark what is done amiss: O Lord, who may abide it?'

8 *son* sun/son.

21 *Ebony box* the night, with an added suggestion that ebony wood had the power to render poisonous fluids non-toxic (J. Unrau, 'Three Notes on George Herbert', *N&Q*, 15 (March 1968), pp. 94–5).

Church-Monuments

9 *lines* of descent; also lines in an old epitaph on a tomb.

10 *Which dissolution . . . discern* bodily disintegration divides and distinguishes most clearly our humanity.

12 *these* dust and earth.
Jet black marble.

14 *them* the monuments themselves.

20 *glass* hourglass but with a surprise to the reader, who is expecting the familiar expression 'flesh is but grass'.

24 *fit . . . fall* i.e., prepare for death, the result of Original Sin which is derived from the fall of the first man and is the inheritance of every man.

Church-Music

5 *without a body move* transported by the music into a kind of ecstasy.

8 *God help poor kings* Patrides sees an allusion to Shakespeare's *Richard II* III, ii, lines 144ff., '. . . of comfort no man speak . . . For God's sake let us sit upon the ground/And tell sad stories of the death of kings' and 'Sonnet 29', 'thy sweet love remember'd such wealth brings/That then I scorn to change my state with kings' (lines 13–14).
9 *Comfort* personification of the principle of consolation.
post ride with speed.

Church-Lock and Key

5 *angry with* both 'reddened by' and 'an unreasonable man's laying blame for his cold hands on a sulky fire' (Hutchinson).
11–12 *stones they make/His blood's sweet current* i.e., just as stones over which a stream must run increase the roar of the water, so sins increase the volume of Christ's sanguinary petition to God.

The Church-Floor

Title By the end of the poem the reader perceives the identity between the apparent subject of the poem and the heart. Summers sees this as a pattern poem: each stone (Patience, Humility, etc.) laid down separately, with lines 13–20 being the solid floor after laying.
10 *one sure band* charity (or love); at the time of the writing of this poem there was a controversy as to whether 'love' or 'charity' is the better version of *agape*. Herbert deftly transcends the issue by using both (lines 10 and 11). The scriptural verse to which Herbert refers is Colossians 3:14, 'And above all these things put on charity, which is the bond of perfectness.'
14 *curious* intricate.
15 *marble weeps* Herbert is recalling Virgil, *Georgics* I, line 480, '*Et maestum illacrimat templis ebur, aeraque sudant*', i.e., 'The melancholy ivory of the temple weeps, and the bronzes sweat.'
18 *sweeps* This domestic irony is a frequent sign of Herbert's

distinct nature as opposed to that of Donne, whose sermon preached at Whitehall, 8 March 1621/2, without the benign irony, provides a vivid image on the same theme, 'and when a whirle-winde hath blown the dust of the Church-yard into the Church, and the man sweeps out the dust of the Church into the Church-yard, who will undertake to sift those dusts again, and to pronounce, This is the Patrician, this is the noble flour, and this the yeomanly, this the Plebian bran' (*Sermons*, ed. Potter and Simpson, IV, 1, 53).

The Windows

2 *crazy* cracked.
6 *anneal* burn in colours upon glass.

Trinity Sunday

Title Trinity Sunday is the Sunday after Whitsunday, observed as a festival in honour of the Trinity, that is, the three persons of God: the Father, the Son and the Holy Ghost.
5 *score* reckoning, account.

Content

15 *let loose to* shoot at, as an arrow to a target.
16 *Take up* with 'residence' understood; an allusion to the abdication of the Emperor Charles V, who took up a monastic life, an episode said to have been much discussed at Little Gidding.
25 *Chronicle* a detailed historical record.
28 *rent* rend, tear, pull in pieces.
29–32 *When . . . strong* not quite Falstaffian in its dismissal of reputation, but clearly arguing for the idea that frail report is contingent on the merit of the reporter.
33 *discoursing* busily thinking.

The Quiddity

Title the real nature or essence of a thing; also, a subtlety in argument, a quibble: as in *Hamlet* V, i, lines 98–100, 'Why may not that be the skull of a lawyer? Where be his quiddities now, his quillities, his cases, his tenures and his tricks?'

8 *a great* MSB, MSW and the fifth edition, the last for which the printer Thomas Buck was responsible, have 'my great', which Hutchinson prefers for its vividness; nevertheless, the series of non-personalised items requires the indefinite article.

demesne estate, property.

12 *Most take all* Editors have difficulty with this phrase, which looks suspiciously like an expression used in card playing. Clearly, the union of Herbert's verse and God as subject matter or inspiration makes his poetry superior to objects listed in stanza one. F. P. Wilson suggests that 'most take all' is a proverbial expression in which '"most" is used in the sense of "the most powerful" . . . God the all-powerful takes complete possession of him' ('A Note on George Herbert's "The Quidditie"', *RES*, 19 (1943), pp. 398–9). The poem remains the most cryptic in *The Temple* for, as Michael Piret points out, 'Wilson's reading would seem to require "most" to function as the subject of a co-ordinate clause (i.e., "Most takes all" or "Let most take all"). But "most" also works neatly as an adverb, if we understand the act of "taking all" as a verbal construction standing in parallel relation to the act of being with God, indicative of something the speaker does while using poetry (i.e., "When I am with thee, then I most take all") . . . What does it mean to "use" poetry? Does such use refer to the writing or the reading of it, and how does this use evoke God's presence? And in what sense does God – or the man using poetry – "take" all? . . . [Wilson] has freed us to grapple with the real quiddity that "The Quiddity" presents: What is poetry?', 'Herbert and Proverbs', *The Cambridge Quarterly*, 17 (1988), p. 228.

Humility

This little beast fable is derived in part, according to G. H. Palmer, from Sir Philip Sidney's poem, 'As I My Little Flock on Ister Bank', sung by Philisides in *The Countess of Pembroke's Arcadia* (ed. Maurice Evans, The Penguin English Library, 1977), lines 704–9.

10 *Mansuetude* gentleness, meekness.

29 *bandying* not arguing but banding together.

31 *amerced* fined.

32 *Session-day* trial day.

Frailty

6 *Dear* costly.

fine grass, or hay Cf. the use of this emblem of human transience by Donne in a verse letter 'To Sir Henry Wotton' (1597/8), lines 5–6, 'But I should wither in one day, and pass/To a bottle of hay, that am a lock of grass.'

9 *Regiments* kingdoms, domains.

11 *sad* grave, serious.

14 *Brave* splendid, with the suggestion of boastful.

15 *quickly* as alive.

16 *And prick* and sting, a more precise and vivid term than the 'Troubling' of MSW.

19 *Affront* confront.

22 *Babel* symbol of the confusion that results from pride (cf. Genesis 11:9).

23 *commodious* convenient.

Constancy

22 *tentations* temptations.

32 *bias* obliquely.

33 *writhe* use 'body-English'; contort his body in a sympathetic attempt to keep the bowl in its curving trajectory, an involvement avoided by the constant man who is bent on straightening out elliptical ways: as noted by Hutchinson, cf. Webster, *The White Devil*, I, ii, lines 62–5,

> The duke your master visits me I thank him,
> And I perceive how like an earnest bowler
> He very passionately leans that way
> He should have his bowl run.

34 *Mark-man* that is, marksman.
35 *still . . . still* always, and, secondarily, quietly.

Affliction (3)

8 *tallies* reckonings, accounts.
11 *The sigh* Compare Donne in 'A Valediction: Of Weeping' for the idea that a sign shortens life, 'Since thou and I sigh one another's breath,/Whoe'er sighs most, is cruellest, and hastes the other's death' (lines 26–7).
18 *praise thee to thy loss* praise thee insufficiently by thinking only of the crucifixion of Good Friday, and not the involvement in the sufferings of all 'thy members' (line 16).

The Star

14 *quickness* vitality.

Sunday

5 *bay* refuge, as in a harbour, but earlier editors note also a possible reference to the protective power of the bay-tree, a belief discussed by Sir Thomas Browne, 'That Bayes will protect from the mischief of Lightning and Thunder, is a quality ascribed thereto . . .' (*Pseudodoxia Epidemica*, II, vi, 6).
11 *worky-days* working days, regular (non-Sunday) days of the week.
26 *They* Sundays.
27 *bare* without vegetation, the brown area (regular week days) between the rows of flowers (Sundays).
31 *wife* The Sabbath is imaged as the spouse of God in the Judaeo-Christian tradition.
42 *want* need.
46 *move* Cf. Matthew 27:51, 'And behold, the veil of the Temple

was rent in twain from the top to the bottom; and the earth did quake, and the rocks rent.'

47 *Samson* One of the elements in the career of Samson which contributed to his being viewed as a type of Christ was his carrying the gates of Gaza on his shoulders, as in Judges 16:3, 'And Samson lay till midnight, and arose at midnight, and took the doors of the gate of the city, and the two posts, and went away with them, bar and all, and put them upon his shoulders, and carried them to the top of an hill that is before Hebron.'

49 *unhinge* 'unsettle an established order of things . . . [for] the rest-day of the Creation, the seventh day of the week was *unhinged* by the substitution of the first day commemorating the Resurrection' (Hutchinson). Herbert had made this link between Christ and Samson in *Passio Discerpta*, XVIII, part of his poems on the Passion of Christ, unpublished in his lifetime. See Appendix, p. 315.

that day Good Friday, the day of the Crucifixion.

53 *a new* Sunday.

Avarice

Title extreme greediness, specifically for money or wealth: one of the Seven Deadly Sins.

8 *grot* grotto, den.

Ana-{Mary / Army}gram

1 *well* appropriately.

2 *pitch his tent* This is the literal meaning of the Greek word *eskenosen*, usually translated as 'dwell' in John 1:14, 'And the Word was made flesh and dwelt among us,' as Robert E. Reiter notes in 'George Herbert's *Anagram*: A Reply to Professor Leiter', *College English* 28 (1966), pp. 59–60. Lee Passarella adds the idea that 'tent' is a synonym for 'tabernacle', that if we equate Moses' tabernacle with the tent of the anagram, then Mary, the tabernacle, contains the ark, Christ, and as the Ark of the Covenant contained the Law, so Christ 'contains' the New Covenant of grace, *ELN* 21 (1986), pp. 10–13.

To All Angels and Saints

1 *bands* the bands or ranks of angels, but if in reference to the saints, 'bonds' or 'fetters'.
7 *forbear* The speaker is reluctant to involve himself with the intercession of the saints.
12 *restorative* The belief in gold's medicinal properties, usually in liquid form (*aurum potabile*), was of considerable antiquity (cf. Chaucer's Physician, 'For gold in phisik is a cordial,/Therefore he lovede gold in special', General Prologue to *The Canterbury Tales*, lines 443–4).
18 *Bids no* The speaker is just as reluctant to involve the aid of Mary. Contrast this attitude with that expressed by Donne, *The Litany*, V, 'The Virgin Mary': 'As her deeds were/Our helps, so are her prayers; nor can she sue/In vain, who hath such titles unto you.' (lines 43–5)
19 *injunction* order, directive.
21 *prerogative* limited to him, God, 'our King' (line 16), a gentle but clear exclusion of the Virgin Mary.
29 *disburse* pay out.

Employment (2)

4 *fur* a lined and therefore warm garment; with secondary sense of academic robe.
5 *complexions* spiritual as well as physical constitutions.
6 *no star* that is, not an eternal fire.
quick live.
10 *ashes choke his soul* Although the method of too little non-nourishing activity is different, the result is the same as that in Shakespeare's 'Sonnet 73':

> In me thou seest the glowing of such fire
> That on the ashes of his youth doth lie,
> As the deathbed whereon it must expire,
> Consumed with that which it was nourish'd by. (lines 9–12)

11 *elements* the four simple substances of which all material bodies were believed to be compounded: earth, water, air and fire.
16 *business* with a pun on 'busyness'.
22 *busy* because, with fragrance and fertility, it blossoms and bears fruit at the same time.
26 *young or old* that is, we rationalise that the time is not right, and thereby lose the chance to act.

Denial

The final line of the final stanza does rhyme, giving proof by that formal harmony that the speaker's request has been granted even as he is requesting.
5 *disorder* lacking rhyme; all the final lines of the stanzas except the last are unrhymed.

Christmas

1 *after* in pursuit of.
rid rode.
14 *rack* an instance of not 'either/or' but 'both/and': the manger and the cross, as a rack is both a frame of wood or metal to hold fodder for horses and cattle as well as an instrument of torture.
25 *Lord* with a pun on 'laud'.

Ungratefulness

5 *brave* splendid, glorious.
6 *we shall be better gods than he* Matthew 13:43, 'Then shall the righteous shine forth as the Sun in the Kingdom of their father.'
18 *that powder* 'A common treatment of a horse or dog with bad eyes was to blow a powder into them to clear the film' (Hutchinson).
19 *sweets* scents, perfumes.
23 *this box* that is, the second of the 'two rare cabinets' (line 8), the Incarnation.
27 *cavils* unfairly objects.

29 *box* i.e., a cabinet within the body.
30 *two for one* the Trinity and the Incarnation for the human heart.

Sighs and Groans

2 *After my sins* Cf. Psalm 103:10, 'He hath not dealt with us after our sins: nor rewarded us according to our wickedness.'
5 *silly* insignificant.
10 *magazines* storehouses.
14 *an Egyptian night* Cf. Exodus 10:22, the plague of darkness, 'And Moses stretched forth his hand toward heaven; and there was a thick darkness in all the land of Egypt three days.'
16 *fig-leaves* particularly broad leaves, but designed to recall the guilt of Adam and Eve who used such leaves to cover their nakedness, 'And the eyes of them both were opened, and they knew that they were naked; and they sewed fig leaves together, and made themselves aprons' (Genesis 3:7).
20 *the turned vial* Cf. Revelation 15:7, 'And one of the four beasts gave unto the seven Angels, seven golden vials full of the wrath of God, who liveth for ever and ever.'
28 *Corrosive* a caustic, burning substance.

The World

11 *Sycamore* the large-leaved fig tree (*Ficus Sycomorus*) that protected Adam and Eve (cf. 'Sighs and Groans' line 16).
14 *Sommers* supporting beams.
15 *shored* propped up.
that the sycamore.
20 *a braver Palace* the world after the Incarnation is more glorious than it was before the fall of man.

Colossians 3:3

'Our life is hid with Christ in God.'

Title Herbert accepts St Paul's statement, changing the 'your' to 'our', 'For ye are dead, and your life is hid with Christ in God.' This is from the Epistle for Easter according to the BCP. Critics note the answering shift of St Paul's 'your' to Herbert's 'Our' and 'My' in the epigraph and first line. The Epistle begins:

> If ye then be risen with Christ, seek those things which are above, where Christ sitteth on the right hand of God. Set your affection on things above, not on things on the earth: For ye are dead, and your life is hid with Christ in God. When Christ, who is our life, shall appear, then shall ye also appear with him in glory.

3 *diurnal* daily.
4 *obliquely* diagonally, as runs the verse of the subtitle through the poem, with an echo of Donne's 'A Valediction: forbidding Mourning', 'Such wilt thou be to me, who must/Like th' other foot, obliquely run' (lines 33–4).

Vanity (1)

5 *dances* Stars were thought to move harmoniously in a dance, a symbol of heavenly concord that did not rule our individual spontaneity, as Beatrice reminds us in *Much Ado About Nothing*, II, i, lines 334–5, 'but then there was a star danc'd, and under that was I born'.
7 *aspects* the relative positions of the heavenly bodies as they appear to an observer on the earth's surface at a given time.
11 *vent'rous* venturous, i.e., daring, risk-taking.
15 *Chymick* chemist but clearly suggestive of alchemist.
17 *callow* featherless, naked (with a recollection of Plato's definition of man as a featherless biped).
24 *mellowing* making 'soft, loamy, rich'; cf. John Blackie, 'Herbert's "Vanitie"', *Critical Quarterly*, 4(1962), p. 80.

Lent

Title Lent is the period of forty weekdays extending from Ash Wednesday to Easter eve, observed as a time of fasting and penitence, in commemoration of Christ's fasting in the wilderness. For Herbert's counsel to his congregation as to the significance of Lent, see Walton, *Life*, p. 299.

10 *use* custom.

11 *scandal* an obstacle to belief, perhaps, perplexity of conscience occasioned by the conduct of one who is looked up to as an example.

24 *Revenging* exacting punishment for.

25 *pendant* hanging in the balance, remaining undecided or unsettled, pending.

32 *Christ's forti'th day* that is, equal to the extraordinary test of Christ in the wilderness; cf. Luke 4:1–2 and Matthew 4:1–2, 'Then was Jesus led up of the Spirit into the wilderness to be tempted of the devil. And when he had fasted forty days and forty nights, he was afterward an hungred.'

35 *Be holy* This is a concise version of Leviticus 19:1–2, 'And the Lord spake unto Moses, saying, Speak unto all the congregation of the children of Israel, and say unto them, Ye shall be holy: for I the Lord your God am holy' and cf. Matthew 5:48, 'Be ye therefore perfect, even as your Father which is in heaven is perfect.'

Virtue

7 *its* MSB has 'his', the older form of the neuter possessive.

10 *box* a box for scents, and (?) a music box according to M. F. Moloney, 'A Suggested Gloss for Herbert's "Box where sweets . . .", *N&Q*, 199 (1954), p. 50.

sweets scents, perfumes.

11 *closes* conclusions of musical phrases, themes or movements.

14 *seasoned timber* properly prepared. K. M. Swaim, 'The "Season'd Timber" of Herbert's "Virtue"', *GHJ*, 6 (1982), pp. 21–5, suggests the latent image of charcoal, a powerful combustible which glows with greater intensity as less pure carbons are consumed.

gives yields to pressure.

15 *coal* ashes, cinders. Cf. 2 Peter 3:10, 'But the day of the Lord

will come as a thief in the night; in the which the heavens shall pass away with a great noise, and the elements shall melt with fervent heat, the earth also and the works that are therein shall be burned up.'

The Pearl. Matthew 13:45

Title Matthew 13:45–6, 'Again, the kingdom of heaven is like unto a merchant man, seeking goodly pearls: Who, when he had found one pearl of great price, went and sold all that he had, and bought it.'

2 *press* Cf. note to 'Whitsunday', line 17, and observe that *press* is both olive press and printing press.

huswife housewife.

13 *vies* contests.

whether which one of two.

16 *true-love-knot* 'A kind of knot, of a complicated and ornamental form (usually either a double-looped bow, or a knot formed of two loops intertwined), used as a symbol of true love' (*OED*).

17 *bundle* collection, package.

22 *relishes* musical embellishments.

23 *propositions* themes.

32 *sealed* with a play on seeled, i.e., blinded, as a hawk is by having its eyelids sewn shut.

34 *main sale, and the commodities* profits, advantages, but consider the possibility of a complex reference to the practice of usury in which a commodity is a parcel of goods sold on credit by a usurer to a needy person, who immediately raises some cash by reselling them at a lower price, generally to the usurer himself. All of this to show Christ as the benign usurer bringing back to himself his own loan, the reborn soul of the believer.

38 *twist* Just what this silk twist is remains uncertain. Critics suggest that it is a symbol of faith analogous to the Golden Chain of Zeus in Book 8 of the *Iliad* or the new Jacob's Ladder, the Cross itself or grace, but silk suggests colours, and a coloured twist suggests the rainbow 'let down from heaven', a symbol of the reciprocal commitment of God and man.

Affliction (4)

3 *A thing forgot* Cf. Psalm 31:14, 'I am clean forgotten, as a dead man out of mind: I am become like a broken vessel.'
4 *wonder* Psalm 71:7 (AV), 'I am as a wonder unto many; but thou art my strong refuge.' BCP translates the Vulgate *prodigium* as 'monster'.
7 *case of knives* Cf. Walton, 'He had a wit, like a pen-knife in a narrow sheath, too sharp for his body', *Life*, p. 280. The word 'case' recalls the phrase 'case of conscience', the practical question of moral conduct, the difficulty in the resolution of which, because of doubt, scandal, selfishness, is often the subject of Herbert's verse.
12 *prick* 'pink' in MSB and MSW: pierce, stab.
13 *attendants* servants, that is, mental and physical faculties.
15 *Unto my face* All the blood has rushed to his face in embarrassment, leaving nothing to perform the task of life.
28 *Labour* work for.

Man

Title Cf. Psalm 8, especially 4–9:

> What is man, that thou art mindful of him: and the son of man, that thou visitest him? Thou madest him lower than the angels: to crown him with glory and worship. Thou makest him to have dominion of the works of thy hands: and thou hast put all things in subjection under his feet; All sheep and oxen; yea, and the beasts of the field; The fowls of the air, and the fishes of the sea: and whatsoever walketh through the paths of the seas. O Lord our Governor: how excellent is thy Name in all the world!

5–6 *to whose creation . . . decay* That is, in comparison to whose origin the rest of the world is inferior.
8 *And more* Cf. Donne, cited by Hutchinson, in his sermon preached at the Spital Cross on Easter Monday, 1622, 'The properties, the qualities of every Creature are in man, the Essence, the Existence of every Creature is for man, so man is every Creature.

And therefore the Philosopher draws man into too narrow a table, when he says he is Microcosmos, an Abridgement of the world in little: Nazianzen gives him but his due, when he calls him Mundum Magnum, a world in which all the rest of the world is but subordinate' (*Sermons*, ed. Potter and Simpson, IV, 3, 104).

no fruit The 'more fruit' of MSW has been changed, itself perhaps only an anticipation of the final word in the next line. 'There is no greater textual difficulty in *The Temple*' (Hutchinson).

12 *go upon the score* (cf. 'Size', line 22) are in our debt (for having provided them with the words they mimic).

21 *dismount* lower, bring down from its height (presumably by means of the telescope).

39 *Distinguished* separated (the habitable land from the waters), as in Genesis 1:9–10, 'And God said, Let the waters under the heaven be gathered together unto one place, and let the dry land appear: and it was so. And God called the dry land, Earth, and the gathering together of the waters called he Seas; and God saw that it was good.'

40 *meat* food, as provided by nourishing rain.

Antiphon (2)

13 *pieces brake* Cf. Psalm 2:9, 'Thou shalt bruise them with a rod of iron: and break them in pieces like a potter's vessel.'

15 *take* in Communion.

18 *crouch* bow low in reverence.

23 *two folds one* Both angels and men unite in the praise of God, 'The greatest shepherd of the fold' (line 10). This final line is linked to 'both' in the final line of 'Man'.

Unkindness

Title both lack of sympathy and unnaturalness, cf. *Hamlet* I, ii, line 65, 'A little more than kin, and less than kind'.

1 *coy* reserved, backward.

16 *pretendeth to* aspires to, is a suitor for.

Life

1 *posy* a bouquet of flowers, but also a poem.
15 *And after death for cures* Some flowers, especially roses, were used as medicines. Patrides cites Donne, 'Since herbs, and roots by dying, lose not all,/But they, yea ashes too, are medicinal' (The First Anniversary' [1610/11], lines 403–4).

Submission

1 *But* If it were not.
10 *resume my sight* take back (by theft, 'pilf'ring') my independent selfhood.
12 *Disseise* deprive wrongfully, rob.
17 *unto my gift I stand* does not take back his selfhood, but abides by his gesture of line 2, 'both mine eyes are thine'.

Justice (1)

1 *skill* understand. The whole poem is concerned with the puzzles the understanding has with (1) the ways of God to man and (2) the ways of man to God.
10 *hand* upper hand.

Charms and Knots

Herbert was greatly influenced here (and elsewhere) by the Book of Proverbs, but the rhythm and didacticism recall the Fool in *King Lear*.
3 *a poor man's rod* i.e., a walking stick that when carried by a rider is both a weapon and an instrument with which to direct the horse left or right.
9–10 *throws a stone . . . own* Cf. *A Priest to the Temple*, 'he that throws a stone at another, hits himself' (Chapter 28, p. 244).
15 *one from ten* the practice of tithing, by which the congregation gave 10 per cent of their harvest to the priest, who in turn devoted his time and energies to their care.

Affliction (5)

2 *Paradise* the Garden of Eden, as in Genesis 2:8, 'And the Lord God planted a garden eastward in Eden; and there he put the man whom he had formed.'

3 *Ark* the large covered floating vessel in which Noah was saved in the Deluge (*OED*); hence a place of refuge, particularly a symbol of the Church.

4 *anchor* symbol of hope, so considered because of its literal nautical meaning.

11 *board* eat at God's table of pleasures and joys. 'Board' is a term for the communion table.

17 *baits* enticements, allurements.

18 *to thy mind* according to your desire.

22 *curious knots* intricately designed flower beds; Hutchinson cites the phrase, 'thy curious-knotted garden' of Don Armado's letter in *Love's Labour's Lost* I, i, line 246, and Milton's 'curious knots' of *Paradise Lost*, IV, line 242.

24 *bow* the rainbow, the sign of the covenant (Genesis 9:12–17) and the bow of a punitive archer.

Mortification

That is, the subjection of one's appetites and passions by the practice of austere living, through a kind of holy dying.

2 *sweets* sweet smelling herbs.

4 *Scarce knows the way* echoing, as Palmer notes, the opening line of Donne's 'Elegy on the Lord Chamberlain', 'Sorrow, who to this house scarce knew this way.'

5 *clouts* swaddling clothes.

17 *knell* the tolling of the bell rung as a person lay dying.

20 *house* MSW has the clearly ill-fitting 'houre'.

23 *maketh love* Cf. Hamlet of Rosencrantz and Guildenstern, V, ii, line 57, 'Why, man, they did make love to this employment'.

33 *hearse* bier.

Decay

Title The decline from Old Testament intimacy described in this poem is unqualified by the promise of a redeeming future, the only such instance in *The Temple*.

1 *Lot* the hospitable man of Sodom who entertained two angels, '. . . Behold now, my lords, turn in, I pray you, into your servant's house, and tarry all night . . .' (Genesis 19:2).

2 *Jacob* younger son of Isaac and grandson of Abraham. 'Jacob wrestled with a man who blest him with the name "Israel"' (Genesis 32:24ff., especially 30), 'And Jacob called the name of the place Peniel: for I have seen God face to face, and my life is preserved.'

Gideon Israelite champion against the Midianites; 'And the angel of the Lord appeared unto him, and said unto him, The Lord is with thee, thou mighty man of valour' (Judges 6:12).

3 *Abraham* the Hebrew patriarch who spoke several times with God, as in, 'And Abram fell on his face: and God talked with him . . .' (Genesis 17:3).

5 *Let me alone* After Aaron and others had built an altar to the Golden Calf, God told Moses that he had found the Israelites to be a stiff-necked people, 'Now therefore let me alone, that my wrath may wax hot against them, and that I may consume them: and I will make of thee a great nation' (Exodus 32:10). Yet even in the midst of his wrath God could be talked with; and even in this instance talked out of his vengeance. This readiness of communication is lost today, according to the speaker.

7 *At some fair . . . well* Cf. Judges 6:11, 'And there came an Angel of the Lord, and sat under an oak which was in Ophrah, that pertained unto Joash the Abi-Ezrite: And his son Gideon threshed wheat by the winepress, to hide it from the Midianites'; Exodus 3:1ff., 'Now Moses kept the flock of Jethro his father in law . . . and the Angel of the Lord appeared unto him in a flame of fire out of the midst of a bush: and he looked, and, behold, the bush burned with fire, and the bush was not consumed.' 1 Kings 19:7, 9, 'And the Angel of the Lord came again . . . And he came thither unto a cave, and lodged there; and, behold, the word of

the Lord came to him, and he said unto him, What doest thou here, Elijah?' and John 4:6–7, 'Now Jacob's well was there. Jesus therefore, being wearied with his journey, sat thus on the well: and it was about the sixth hour. There cometh a woman of Samaria to draw water: Jesus saith unto her, Give me to drink.'

10 *Aaron's bell* Part of the symbolic dress of the high priest, 'A golden bell and a pomegranate, a golden bell and a pomegranate, upon the hem of the robe round about. And it shall be upon Aaron to minister: and his sound shall be heard when he goeth in unto the holy place before the Lord, and when he cometh out, that he die not' (Exodus 28:34–5).

11 *immure* wall in, enclose.

14 *straiten* bind tightly.

15 *thirds* the third of the personal property of a deceased husband allowed to his widow.

16 *the world grows old* It was commonly held that the world would last 6,000 years, from about 4000 BC, the date of the creation, to AD 2000. Herbert in the seventeenth century was living in a world clearly grown old. Sir Thomas Browne, twenty-five years later in *Hydriotaphia*, memorably expressed this opinion, 'But in this latter scene of time we cannot expect such mummies unto our memories, when ambition may fear the prophecy of Elias, and Charles the fifth can never hope to live within two Methusela's of Hector', *The Works of Sir Thomas Browne*, ed. Geoffrey Keynes (1928), I, 166.

Misery

5 *Man is but grass* Cf. Isaiah 40:6 'all flesh is grass'.

16 *within his curtains* Psalm 139:2, 'Thou art . . . about my bed: and spiest out all my ways.'

20 *pin* anything very small and insignificant.

25 *quarrel* find fault with, to reprove angrily.

39 *crouch* bend low in reverence, cf. 'Antiphon (2)', line 18.

41 *this* that is, 'clay hearts' (line 39) are all we have to offer.

51 *pull'st the rug* pull the blanket over your head.

62 *winks* turns a blind eye.

69 *posy* inscription, motto.
77 *shelf* sandbank, submerged ledge of rock.

Jordan (2)

3 *invention* topics to be treated: the discovery of ideas and subject matter, the first step in literary composition. 'Invention' was the title of this poem in MSW.
4 *burnish* grow plump, increase in breadth, spread out.
5 *Curling* The more extreme rhetorical flourishes were frequently likened to the artifices of hairdressing. See, for example, Gabriel Harvey's admission of former excess (1577), 'I am compelled by a sense of shame to omit mention of those curls and curling irons with which my whole style was elegantly frizzed in every part', *Gabriel Harvey's 'Ciceronianus'*, with an introduction by Harold S. Wilson and an English translation by Clarence A. Forbes, University of Nebraska Studies in the Humanities No. 4, 1945.
10 *quick* lively, energetic.
15 *bustled* was fussily active. Cf. Richard of Gloucester in regard to another George, *Richard III* I, i, lines 150–52:

> Clarence hath not another day to live;
> Which done, God take King Edward to his mercy,
> And leave the world for me to bustle in!

friend Critics have noted Christ's self-identification as man's friend in John 15:12–15:

> This is my Commandment, That ye love one another, as I have loved you. Greater love hath no man than this, that a man lay down his life for his friends. Ye are my friends, if ye do whatsoever I command you. Henceforth I call you not servants; for the servant knoweth not what his lord doeth, but I have called you friends; for all things that I have heard of my Father I have made known unto you.

16–18 *How . . . expense* Herbert could have found the inward turn of resolution at the frustration of barren, not, as here, mistakenly overactive invention in Sidney's *Astrophil and Stella*, 1, lines 9–14:

But words came halting forth, wanting Invention's stay,
Invention, Nature's child, fled step-dame Study's blows,
And others' feet still seem'd but strangers in my way.
Thus great with child to speak, and helpless in my throes,
Biting my truant pen, beating my self for spite,
'Fool,' said my Muse to me, 'look in thy heart and write.'

16 *wide* mistaken, i.e., wide of the mark.

18 *Copy* The verb with its univocal directness is chosen for the subtle play with and against rhetorical 'copia', the technique of artificial heightening, of expansion and embellished variation, a technique of which Herbert as Public Orator at Cambridge was a master.

expense cost, but with a possible pun on pens/pence, word play more likely still when *ex* = *x*, that is, the Roman numeral for 10, such that *expense* equals *ten pence*.

Prayer (2)

9 *sphere* 'the apparent outward limit of space, conceived as a hollow globe enclosing (and at all points equidistant from) the earth' (*OED*).

15 *fain* glad, content.

curse Galatians 3:13, 'Christ hath redeemed us from the curse of the law, being made a curse for us: for it is written, Cursed is every one that hangeth on a tree.'

21 *one* that is, prayer.

24 *ell* a measure of length equal to forty-five inches; and note its origin in the distance from the shoulder to the fingertips and the 'arm' in line 8.

Obedience

2 *Convey* transfer or make over by deed or legal process.

8 *pass* transfer.

10 *present . . . deed* Cf. the legal expression 'I deliver this as my act and deed.'

12 *Cavil* object, find fault without good reason.

13 *reservation* keeping back something for one's own use; legally, a clause in a contract retaining an interest.
15 *wrangler* quarreller, angry disputant (cf. 'The Family', line 7). There is an academic suggestion here, not to a first-class mathematician at Cambridge (a sense of the word recorded first in 1750), but one of the controversialists described by Edward Herbert in his *Autobiography*, 'Teaching them the subtilities of Logic, which as it is usually practised, enables them for little more than to be excellent wranglers' (1824 edn), p. 42, cited in *OED*.
35 *purchase* buying, and thus an indication of commitment on the part of the receiver as well as the giver, a reminder that Christ purchased man's spiritual freedom with his own life. No less of a totality of commitment is required by the purchaser in the poem.
43 *Court of Rolls* registry of legal documents; office of registry and deeds.

Conscience

Herbert understands conscience here not as the voice of God or of the Holy Spirit, but as a troubling agent reminding the speaker of his failings, such failings being, the speaker argues, as nothing, given the grace that comes to him from the eucharist and that for which the eucharist is a symbol, the sacrifice of Christ. Sidney Gottlieb goes further, 'Certainly no one can miss the fact that the "conscience" in the poem is puritanical . . . but we need to take more seriously the extent to which Herbert personifies conscience as a non-conforming, radical Protestant, a danger not only to one's peace of mind but also to one's Church and society' ('Herbert's Case of "Conscience": Public or Private Poem', *SEL* 25 (1985), pp. 113–14).
1 *lour* frown, scowl.
12 *physic* medicine.
13 *receipt* the formula of the medicinal prescription.
14 *board* Communion table.
21 *bill* spear, halberd.
22 *For those that trouble me* Cf. Psalm 23:4–5, '. . . thy rod and thy staff comfort me. Thou shalt prepare a table before me against them that trouble me.'

Sion

The contrast between Solomon's external temple and the inner temple of the human heart, which runs throughout the poems of *The Temple*, here derives from the verses in Acts 7:47–8, 'But Solomon built him an house. Howbeit the most High dwelleth not in temples made with hands' and 1 Corinthians 3:16, 'Know ye not that ye are the temple of God, and that the Spirit of God dwelleth in you?'

1ff. *glory* 1 Kings has details of the splendour of Solomon's Temple, including 'pure gold', 'flowers . . . carved', 'brass', all that St Matthew (6:29) suggests in writing of the lilies of the field: 'And yet I say unto you, That even Solomon in all his glory was not arrayed like one of these.'

2 *Solomon's temple* 'And, behold, I purpose to build an house unto the name of the Lord, my God, as the Lord spake unto David my father, saying, Thy son, whom I will set upon thy throne in thy room, he shall build an house unto my name' (1 Kings 5:5).

flourished with a pun on 'flourish' as a non-structural addition, although most critics see the pun 'flourish' in the sense of 'fanfare'.

4 *embellished* ornamented unnecessarily, perhaps with a secondary reference to musical ornamentation.

11 *Architecture meets with sin* because this temple is made of the human and therefore sinful heart.

17 *All Solomon's sea of brass and world of stone* glorious materials of the external temple.

Home

2 *stay* here and usually elsewhere – lines 7, 31 and 76 – means 'delay in coming', 'stay away', but at line 31 the second 'stay' has the meaning of 'remain' as in line 67.

13–15 *When man was lost . . . was none* Cf. Isaiah 59:16, 'And he saw that there was no man, and wondered that there was no intercessor' and Isaiah 63:5, 'And I looked, and there was none to help; and I wondered that there was none to uphold . . .'

21 *Thraldom* captivity, servitude, bondage.
22 *apple* '... and sold our God, our glorious, our gracious God for an apple. O write it! O brand it in our foreheads for ever: for an apple once we lost our God, and still lose him for no more' (*A Priest to the Temple*, 'The Author's Prayer before Sermon', cited by Hutchinson: see above p. 262).
49 *brake* a clump of briers, a thicket.
56 *corn* wheat.
61 *O loose this frame, this knot of man untie* 'That subtle knot, which makes us man', Donne, 'The Ecstasy', line 64, the mysterious link which joins soul and body, with a pun on 'nought', man's ultimate worthlessness.
64 *hampered* fettered, encumbered, impeded: another of Herbert's box-like mazes.
76 *The word is, Stay* for the purposes of rhyme, but the speaker prefers the unrhyming 'Come', which is also the first word of the poem.

The British Church

Notice the use of 'British' in the title, stressing by implication the union of England and Scotland.
5 *And dates her letters from thy face* '... The Church of England officially still reckoned the beginning of the year from Lady Day, which was also Herbert's practice in dating his letters' (Hutchinson). Lady Day is the Feast of the Annunciation of the Blessed Virgin Mary, celebrated 25 March.
10 *Outlandish* foreign.
13 *She on the hills* the Roman Catholic Church (cf. the seven hills of Rome). Hutchinson notes Donne's sermon preached to the Earl of Carlisle and his company at Sion (?1622), 'Trouble not thyself to know the forms and fashions of foreign particular churches; neither of a Church in the lake, nor a Church upon seven hills; but since God hath planted thee in a Church, where all things necessary for salvation are administered to thee, and where no erroneous doctrine (even in the confession of our Adversaries) is affirmed and held, that is the Hill, and

that is the Catholic Church' (*Sermons*, ed. Potter and Simpson, V, 13, 251).
19 *She in the valley* Calvinism of Geneva.
26 *The mean* the middle way between extremes, the *via media*.
29 *double-moat* Britain is already surrounded by a moat of water; God has added a second protective moat of grace. Compare John of Gaunt's lines (*Richard II* II, i, lines 46–9):

> This precious stone set in the silver sea,
> Which serves it in the office of a wall,
> Or as a moat defensive to a house,
> Against the envy of less happier lands.

The Quip

Title a sharp retort.
2 *train-bands* companies of citizen soldiers.
8ff. *But thou shalt answer* Cf. Psalm 38:15, 'For in thee, O Lord, have I put my trust: thou shalt answer for me, O Lord my God.'
14 *silks* Cf. Walton's description of Herbert as at one time excessively concerned with appearance (p. 276).
23 *'I am thine'* The force of the quip is greater in direct quotation, although critics and editors preserve the ambiguity of pronouns by the use of indirect discourse.
24 *answer home* final answer (one which strikes to the heart of the matter).

Vanity (2)

1 *silly* simple.
9 *for repenting* at the expense of repentance.

The Dawning

Title the special dawning of Easter morning.
13 *Arise, arise* Herbert here echoes Donne's 'Holy Sonnet 7', about the resurrection of all bodies for the Day of Judgement:

At the round earth's imagined corners, blow
Your trumpets, angels, and arise, arise
From death, you numberless infinities
Of souls . . . (lines 1–4)

14 *burial-linen* the grave clothes which become the healing instrument of the handkerchief in a conceit created by Herbert.
16 *handkerchief* Summers notes the constellation of related scriptural passages, including Isaiah 25:8, 'He will swallow up death in victory; and the Lord God will wipe away tears from off all faces', Revelation 7:10–17 and 21:4, and Acts 19:11–12, 'And God wrought special miracles by the hands of Paul: So that from his body were brought unto the sick handkerchiefs or aprons, and the diseases departed from them, and the evil spirits went out of them.'

Jesu

The early seventeenth century did not always differentiate *i* and *j* in script or print. Here the reader is expected to understand that the letter at the end of line 5 is a vowel, but elsewhere, as in lines 1 and 10, a consonant.

Business

3–11 *Rivers run . . . hast thou not?* built on the macrocosm/microcosm pattern – 'Rivers' equal tears; 'winds' equal sighs.
22 *two deaths* the physical death of the body and here the subsequent damnation of the soul at the Day of Judgement. See Revelation 20:6, 'Blessed and holy is he that hath part in the first resurrection: on such the second death hath no power, but they shall be priests of God and of Christ, and shall reign with him a thousand years.'
fee reward.
34 *a silver vein* Job 28:1, illustrating that 'there is knowledge of natural things . . . But wisdom is an excellent gift of God', argues,

'Surely there is a vein for the silver, and a place for gold where they fine it.'

Dialogue

Title The dialogue is between the 'I' and Christ.
4 *waiving* declining an offer, with the secondary meaning 'wavering'.
6 *give . . . gains* make one something worth having.
9–10 *What . . . measure?* that is, is it your place to decide?
20 *savour* but not beyond my Saviour; perception, understanding.

Dullness

2 *earth* that is, the lowest and the most material of the four elements.
8 *Curl o'er again* See note on 'Jordan (2)', line 5.
12 *Pure red and white* applying conventional colours to the complexion of a loved object in lyrical poetry, e.g., 'No white nor red was ever seen/So am'rous as this lovely green', Marvell, 'The Garden', lines 17–18, to the Lord; perhaps, according to Patrides, influenced by the Song of Solomon 5:10, 'My beloved is white and ruddy', but certainly suggesting the two species of the eucharist, bread and wine.
18 *window-songs* serenades.
19 *pretending* wooing.
25 *clear* discharge the implied promise of the 'quickness' asked for in line 3.

Love-Joy

Title Galatians 5:22, 'But the fruit of the spirit is love, joy, peace, longsuffering, gentleness, goodness, faith' and 1 Peter 1:7–8, '. . . at the appearing of Jesus Christ: Whom having not seen, ye love; in whom, though now ye see him not, yet believing, ye rejoice with joy unspeakable and full of glory'.

2 *vine* See John 15:1, 'I am the true vine.'
3 *Annealed* stained, having colours burnt in, with the possible pun on 'aneled' 'oiled' as in the rite of Baptism. See J. L. Kirkwood and G. W. Williams, 'Anneal'd as Baptism in Herbert's "Love-Joy"', *American Notes and Queries*, 4 (September 1965), pp. 3–5.
One standing by Christ himself, as Helen Vendler suggests, *The Poetry of George Herbert*, p. 70.
5 *spend* utter, express.

Providence

Title Cf. Psalm 104 which begins, 'Praise the Lord, O my soul: O Lord my god, Thou art become exceeding glorious; thou art clothed with majesty and honour.'
9 *ditty* add lyrics.
14 *they below* that is, in the Great Chain of Being: 'beasts' (line 21), 'trees' (line 23).
51 *net* their mouths.
53 *prevent* come before, i.e., the food necessary for sustenance exists before the arrival of the new creature.
58 *twist* a cord made of two or more fibres or filaments.
60 *bowls* balls used in lawn bowling, built with a bias (creating the 'turning all the way').
63 *callow* featherless.
64 *fledge* ready for flight, having the feathers fully developed.
73 *express* articulate as well as squeeze out.
74 *curious* excellent.
virtues healing properties.
75 *herb for that* that is, a herb that would make articulation or 'expression' possible.
76 *expressions* poetic articulations; secondarily, drinks, liquors squeezed out of fruit or berries.
78 *cure* Roses were believed to have medicinal powers. In *A Priest to the Temple* Herbert argues for having a garden of such aids, 'In the knowledge of simples, wherein the manifold wisdom of God is wonderfully to be seen, one thing would be carefully

observed; which is, to know what herbs may be used instead of drugs of the same nature, and to make the garden the shop: for home-bred medicines are both more easy for the parson's purse, and more familiar for all men's bodies. So, where the apothecary uses either for loosing, rhubarb, or for binding, bolearmena, the parson uses damask or white roses . . .' (Chapter 23, p. 237).

93 *house is full* according to the Neo-Platonic doctrine of 'plenitude'; see note to line 133.

112 *fuel in desire* that is, fuel whenever he wants it.

116 *grew* grew into or became.

121 *to* compared to.

126 *The Indian nut* the coconut.

127 *trencher* wooden plate, platter.

132 *whey* the serum or watery part of milk.

133 *Thy creatures leap not* '*Natura non facit saltus*', the then standard belief in the linked plenitude of creation with no missing links in the chain of being. Patrides notes that Herbert turns the image into one of Communion.

135 *marry* unite, join, i.e., form a link between fish and animals.

140 *Elephant leans or stands* because 'nature hath given him no knees to bend', Donne, 'The Progress of the Soul', stanza 39, line 5, or so the Renaissance in general thought.

144 *owes* owns.

146 *advice* opinion, judgement.

148 *twice* 'In this poem only, the poet offers praise both in his own person and as the spokesman or priest of all creation: cf. lines 13–14, 25–6' (Hutchinson).

152 *Extolleth* raises high in praise, magnifies.

Hope

Title St Paul in illustrating that God is 'most sure in his promise' writes of 'hope we have as an anchor of the soul, both sure and stedfast' (Hebrews 6:19). Hutchinson and others point out that Walton writes of seals which Donne had made 'ingraven [with] the figure of Christ crucified on an Anchor, which is the emblem of hope'. Herbert received one of these seals as a gift from Donne and wrote a Latin poem on the symbolism of the design, 'In Sacram Anchoram Piscatoris'. See Appendix, p. 322.

1 *watch* as a suggestion that the time had come for his 'hope' to be realised.

4 *optic* telescope, magnifying glass.

5 *vial full of tears* Psalm 56:8, 'Thou tellest my flittings; put my tears into thy bottle: are not these things noted in thy book?'

6 *green ears* Leviticus 2:14, 'And if thou offer a meat offering of thy firstfruits unto the Lord, thou shalt offer for the meat offering of thy firstfruits green ears of corn dried by the fire, even corn beaten out of full ears.'

8 *ring* wedding ring, symbolic of union between Christ and the believer, also a symbol of 'completion'.

Sin's Round

Title A round is a country dance in which the dancers join hands. Note that line 3 ('thoughts'), line 7 ('words') and line 13 ('hands') echo the BCP in Confession, 'We have erred in thought, word, and deed against thy divine majesty by provoking most justly thy wrath and indignation against us.'

4 *cockatrice* a serpent, identified with the basilisk, fabulously said to kill by its mere glance or breath (cf. Isaiah 59:5).

8 *Sicilian hill* Mount Etna, Europe's largest active volcano, beneath which the Cyclops were said to have forged their weapons of destruction. Cf. M. E. Rickey, *Utmost Art*, p. 51.

9 *vent* discharge, pour out. Some have seen a play on vent/vend, to sell; vent was a common spelling for vend in the seventeenth century.

14 *stories* that is, storeys.

15 *Babel* Cf. Genesis 11:9, the lofty tower of high ambition (destroyed).

Time

23 *wants* lacks.

Gratefulness

24 *take* take the fancy of, delight, charm.

Peace

9 *lace* ornamental braid used as trimming for a man's coat.
15 *Crown Imperial* botanically, a handsome, large flower, *Fritillaria imperialis*.
22 *Prince of old* Melchizedek, priest of Salem (who brought bread and wine to Abraham), a type of Christ in his offices of king and priest.
24 *flock and fold* sheep and the sheep-pen.
28 *twelve stalks of wheat* symbolising the twelve Apostles.

Confession

5 *till* a closed compartment within a larger box, chest or cabinet, used for keeping valuables more safely.
7 *piercer* an auger or awl, a tool used to make a hole.
12 *rheums* drops of pernicious moisture.
15 *foot* seize or clutch with talons.
19 *breast* heart.
30 *to* compared to.

Giddiness

3 *sev'ral* individual.
11 *snudge* remain snug and quiet, nestle.
19 *a Dolphin's skin* Hutchinson suggests that this is not the aquatic mammal, but the dorado, a fish celebrated for its beautiful colours, which, when it is taken from the water, undergoes rapid changes of hue.

The Bunch of Grapes

This is the clearest of George Herbert's uses of typology, both in its image and in its direct statement of the prefiguring function of the Old Testament events for the Christian and his Church (lines 11–14). Both the cluster of grapes found by and offered to the Israelites on their journey into the wilderness and Noah's vine were traditionally interpreted as signs of God's grace and as a type of Christ who said, John 15:1, 'I am the true vine, and my Father is the husbandman.' The AV glosses this passage as an illustration of 'The consolation and mutual love between Christ and his members, under the parable of the vine', reminding us thereby that the prefigurings of the grapes at Eshcol and those of Noah's vine are improved upon by the New Testament in that the Israelites on the way to their promised land misinterpreted the joy represented by the 'cluster of grapes' (Numbers 13:23), and that while Noah's vine prospered, it was subject to abuse by Noah himself (Genesis 9:20ff.). J. H. Summers (*George Herbert*, pp. 126–8) is especially helpful. Bloch points out that St Paul had been at pains to warn Christians against making the same mistake the Israelites had made in misunderstanding God's signs and succumbing to temptation, 'Now all these things happened unto them for ensamples: and they are written for our admonition' (1 Corinthians 10:11).

4 *vogue* general course or tendency.

10 *spanned* measured out, having a limit or bound set.

11 *pens* writes down, i.e., forecasts.

15 *guardian fires and clouds* Exodus 13:21, 'And the Lord went before them by day in a pillar of a cloud, to lead them the way; and by night in a pillar of fire, to give them light; to go by day and night.'

16 *Scripture-dew* Manna, as in Numbers 11:9, 'And when the dew fell upon the camp in the night, the manna fell upon it.' Christ contrasts himself with manna in John 6:31ff:

> Our fathers did eat manna in the desert; as it is written, He gave them bread from heaven to eat. Then Jesus said unto them, Verily, verily I say unto you, Moses gave you not that bread from heaven;

> but my Father giveth you the true bread from heaven. For the bread of God is he which cometh down from heaven, and giveth life unto the world. Then said they unto him, Lord, evermore give us this bread. And Jesus said unto them, I am the bread of life: he that cometh to me shall never hunger; and he that believeth on me shall never thirst.

17 *shrouds* sheds, temporary shelters.

19 *taste* There is a pun here on (1) taste as sample, evidence (2) relish or pleasure and (3) ironically, 'test' or 'trial' as in *King Lear*, Edmund's 'I hope, for my brother's justification, he wrote this but as an essay, or taste of my virtue' (I, ii, lines 44–5), or, itself punningly, *Paradise Lost*, I, line 1–3, 'The fruit/Of that forbidden tree, whose mortal taste/Brought Death into the world, and all our woe.' Behind the complaint lie the words of the Psalmist, 'O taste, and see, how gracious the Lord is' (Psalm 34:8), and 'The Lord himself is the portion of my inheritance, and of my cup' (Psalm 16:6).

24 *Noah's vine* Genesis 9:20, referred to above: 'And Noah began to be an husbandman, and he planted a vineyard.' Accordingly, Noah is credited with being the founder of viticulture.

Love Unknown

15 *Of a great rock* St Paul, 1 Corinthians 10:4: 'And did all drink the same spiritual drink: for they drank of that spiritual Rock that followed them: and that Rock was Christ.'

28 *AFFLICTION* Isaiah 48:10, 'Behold, I have refined thee, but not with silver; I have chosen thee in the furnace of affliction.'

30 *sacrifice* For one of the many expressions of Old Testament dismissals of animal sacrifice made by sinful man, cf. Isaiah 1:11: 'To what purpose is the multitude of your sacrifices unto me? saith the Lord: I am full of the burnt offerings of rams, and the fat of fed beasts; and I delight not in the blood of bullocks, or of lambs, or of he goats.' Herbert contrasts the speaker's misplaced confidence in his sacrifice by the implicit allusion to Psalm 51,

especially verses 2, 10, 16: 'Wash me throughly from my wickedness: and cleanse me from my sin . . . Make me a clean heart, O God: and renew a right spirit within me . . . For thou desirest no sacrifice, else would I give it thee: but thou delightest not in burnt-offerings. The sacrifice of God is a troubled spirit: a broken and contrite heart, O God, shalt thou not despise.'

37 *Your heart was hard* Cf. 'Grace', lines 17–20, and Milton, *Paradise Lost*, XI, lines 3–5, 'Prevenient grace descending had removed/The stony from their hearts, and made new flesh/Regenerate grow instead . . .'

38 *callous* hardened.

39 *expatiate* expand.

45 *supple* soften.

63 *wot of* know of.

Man's Medley

Medley is 'a cloth woven with different colours or shades', as well as 'a musical composition consisting of parts or subjects of a diversified or incongruous character' (*OED*).

10–12 *Man . . . earth* Man above, in the Great Chain of Being, enjoys both sense and reason.

15 *round* thick.

16 *curious* exquisite.

18 *after* according to.

ground that portion of the cloth surface which is not decorated.

30 *two deaths* as in 'Business,' the death of the natural body and the damnation of the soul.

The Storm

6 *object* express disapproval of, bring forward a reason against.

Paradise

The form of the poem imitates its subject, pruning the words at the end of lines into fruitful meanings. The poem is an emblem of the ordered life under God's pruning.

1 *Lord* God is the gardener.

11 *prune* Cf. John 15:1–2 and 5, 'I am the true vine, and my Father is the husbandman. Every branch in me that beareth not fruit he taketh away: and every branch that beareth fruit, he purgeth it, that it may bring forth more fruit . . . I am the vine, ye are the branches: He that abideth in me, and I in him, the same bringeth forth much fruit: for without me ye can do nothing.'

15 *END* purpose, goal.

The Method

3 *rub* obstacle, hindrance.

10 *turn thy book* examine your accounts or reckoning.

18 *indifferents* those careless and apathetic.

Divinity

2 *spheres* globes illustrating the place and motions of the celestial bodies.

8 *lies by* remains unused.

9 *broached* tapped, set running.

11 *jagged* slashed ornamentally (hence no longer 'seamless').

seamless coat reference to Christ's garment, 'the type of love' as Christ himself says in 'The Sacrifice', line 242.

17 *Love God, and love your neighbour. Watch and pray.* Luke 10:27, 'Thou shalt love the Lord thy God with all thy heart, and with all thy soul, and with all thy strength, and with all thy mind'; Matthew 22:37–40, 'Thou shalt love the Lord thy God with all thy heart, and with all thy soul, and with all thy mind. This is the first and great Commandment. And the second is like unto it, Thou shalt love thy neighbour as thyself. On these two commandments hang all the law and the prophets'; Matthew 26:41, 'Watch and pray, that ye enter not into temptation: the spirit indeed is willing, but the flesh is weak', and Mark 13:33, 'Take ye heed, watch and pray: for ye know not when the time is.'

18 *Do as ye would be done unto* Matthew 7:12, 'Therefore all things whatsoever ye would that men should do to you, do ye even so to them: for this is the law and the prophets.'

20 *Gordian knots* extreme difficulties, from the intricate knot tied by King Gordius of Phrygia. The oracle declared that whoever could loosen it would rule Asia; Alexander the Great overcame the difficulty by cutting through the knot with his sword.
25 *Epicycles* small circles having their circumferences in circles, a way of describing the movements of the planets in Ptolemaic astronomy.

Ephesians 4:30

Title After asking his audience to 'put on the new man' (Ephesians 4:24), St Paul urges that they 'grieve not the holy Spirit of God, whereby ye are sealed unto the day of redemption' (Ephesians 4:30).
1 *Dove* the Holy Spirit.
24 *bowels* tender feelings, with a paradoxical play on bowels (guts), the origin of lute strings being cat-gut.
30 *Crystal* a stone harder than ice.
35 *Lord* Patrides draws attention to the natural shift for a believer in the Trinity from the Holy Spirit of line 1 to God the Father here.

The Family

3 *puling* whining.
7 *wranglers* quarrellers, disputants.
10 *plays* brings (the soul) into tune.

The Size

Title rank, status, importance: an example of quantity semantically becoming quality.
4 *passing brave* Cf. Marlowe in *Tamburlaine the Great*, Part I, II, v, lines 51–4, on the zenith of political and emotional 'size':

> Is it not brave to be a king, Techelles?
> Usumcasane and Theridamus,
> Is it not passing brave to be a king,
> And ride in triumph through Persepolis?

7 *fraught* cargo.

12 *Isle of spices* not the East Indies but an allusion to the Song of Solomon, where the union of Christ and his Church takes place in a garden of spices and on a mountain of spices, 4:16, 8:14.

12–13 *spices . . . worlds* Cf. Donne, 'The Sun Rising', an earlier poem of colloquial instructive imperatives, 'Look, and tomorrow late, tell me,/Whether both th' Indias of spice and mine/Be where thou left'st them . . .' (lines 16–18).

13–14 *full . . . hungry* Cf. Luke 6:21, 25, 'Blessed are ye that hunger now, for ye shall be filled . . . Woe unto you that are full! for ye shall hunger.'

16 *Enact* MSB has 'Exact', but 'enact' follows from 'laws', line 15.

18 *Wouldst thou both eat thy cake, and have it?* wishing to have things both ways.

22 *on score* in debt or on credit.

24 *Sion's hill* the heavenly city, as in Hebrews 12:22, 'But ye are come unto Mount Sion, and unto the city of the living God, the heavenly Jerusalem, and to an innumerable company of Angels.'

29 *'tice* entice.

36 *pretender* suitor, wooer, with some inversion of the expected gender.

39 A line seems to be lacking after line 39; also in MSB.

40 *destroy* raze out of the calendar.

46 *meridian* 'a graduated ring (sometimes a semicircle only) of brass in which an artificial globe is suspended and revolves concentrically' (*OED*).

Artillery

12–14 *If . . . Then* even if . . . nevertheless.

17 *shooters* shooting stars.

31 *articling* arranging by treaty or stipulations.

Church-Rents and Schisms

In the title 'rents' means tears or rips, and 'schisms' are separations or divisions, usually over matters of discipline or hierarchy rather than belief.

1 *Brave* handsome, splendid.

rose Cf. Song of Solomon 2:1 where the Church identifies herself, 'I am the rose of Sharon, and the lily of the valleys.'

21 *start* break apart.

Justice (2)

2 *old* that is, as found in the Old Testament, compared with 'Christ's pure veil' (line 13), the New Testament doctrine of mediation.

7 *balance* scales.

9 *scape* tongue of a balance.

12 *Daunting* subduing.

13 *veil* Christ, in contrast to the veil of the Temple at Jerusalem, is described by St Paul as the vehicle by which man enters the holiest, 'By a new and living way, which he hath consecrated for us, through the veil, that is to say, his flesh' (Hebrews 10:20) and 'But their minds were blinded: for until this day remaineth the same vail untaken away in the reading of the old testament: which vail is done away in Christ' (2 Corinthians 3:14). The purity of the veil of Christ is contrasted with the colours of the veil of the Temple in Jerusalem, which were 'blue, and purple, and crimson' (2 Chronicles 3:14).

16–17 *buckets . . . descend* Hutchinson notes that Herbert is echoing the lines of the *soi-disant* Christ-figure Richard II at the moment of his deposition (*Richard II* IV, i, lines 184–9):

> Now is this golden crown like a deep well
> That owes two buckets, filling one another,
> The emptier ever dancing in the air,
> The other down, unseen and full of water
> That bucket down and full of tears am I,
> Drinking my griefs, whilst you mount up on high.

18 *well* The use of 'well' is striking because we expect 'vale'.

21 *harp on* harp to.

The Pilgrimage

4 *cave of Desperation* Cf. Spenser 'Cave of Despair', *Faerie Queene*, I, ix.
14 *wold* open country, rolling uplands.
17 *Angel* a gold coin worth ten shillings, as well as the usual meaning.
36 *chair* perhaps, a sedan chair, i.e., a covered vehicle for one person carried on poles by two men, clearly a place for relaxation.

The Holdfast

Title something that supports or keeps together (as in building with stones). It is ironic in that the speaker is pharisaically committed to self-achievement in obeying the law without a proper understanding of the essential role of Christ. Critics note St Paul's words to the Philippians 3:9, 'And be found in him, not having mine own righteousness, which is of the law, but that which is through the faith of Christ, the righteousness which is of God by faith.' Also, Psalm 73:27, 'But it is good for me to hold me fast by God, to put my trust in the Lord God: and to speak of all thy works in the gates of the daughter of Sion.'
1–2 See note to 'Divinity', line 17, p. 390.

Complaining

8 *silly* insignificant.

The Discharge

Title document conveying release from obligation (Hutchinson); Ecclesiastes 8:8, 'There is no man that hath power over the spirit to retain the spirit; neither hath he power in the day of death: And there is no discharge in that war . . .'
3 *licorous* having a keen desire for something pleasant, not necessarily, but often, sexual. Cf. Chaucer's Alisoun in *The Miller's Tale*, line 3244, 'And sikerly she hadde a likerous ye.'

6 *counts* accounts.

31 *provide* exercise foresight, to make adequate provision for the future, seemingly a virtue but not so here, where the lesson is that the current moment is all. Cf. Luke 12, especially 22 and 40: 'Therefore I say unto you, Take no thought for your life, what ye shall eat; neither for the body, what ye shall put on' and 'Be ye therefore ready also: for the Son of man cometh at an hour when ye think not.'

45 *And draw the bottom out an end* unravel a ball of thread to its ultimate length.

47 *And wake thy sorrow?* Cf. Shakespeare's 'Sonnet 30':

> Then can I grieve at grievances foregone,
> And heavily from woe to woe tell o'er
> The sad account of fore-bemoanèd moan,
> Which I new pay as if not paid before. (lines 9–12)

Praise (2)

Title The Psalms are divided into those of complaint, praise and thanksgiving, and penitence; this poem is made out of lines from a number of the Psalms of praise.

26 *enrol* to record with honour, to celebrate.

An Offering

9 *title* claim title to, give title in the legal sense.

11–12 *In public judgements one may be a nation,/And fence a plague, while others sleep and slumber.* 'Fence' is equivalent to 'ward off'. Herbert is alluding to 1 Chronicles 21:17, 'And David said unto God . . . even I it is that have sinned and done evil indeed; but as for these sheep, what have they done? Let thine hand, I pray thee, O Lord my God, be on me, and on my father's house; but not on thy people, that they should be plagued.'

19 *balsam* healing agent.

22 *All-heal* balsam or medicine that heals all wounds; a panacea.

39 *oblation* offering to God.

Longing

8–9 ... *ground/Which thou dost curse.* Cf. Genesis 3:17, 'And unto Adam he said, Because thou hast harkened unto the voice of thy wife, and hast eaten of the tree, of which I commanded thee, saying, Thou shalt not eat of it: cursed is the ground for thy sake; in sorrow shalt thou eat of it all the days of thy life.'

11 *giddy* Cf. Troilus' expression of his longing for a different kind of love (*Troilus and Cressida* III, ii, lines 18–22):

> I am giddy; expectation whirls me round;
> Th' imaginary relish is so sweet
> That it enchants my sense; what will it be,
> When that the wat'ry palates tastes indeed
> Love's thrice-repured nectar?

19 *Bowels* heart, bosom.

21 *Bow down thine ear!* Psalm 31:2, 'Bow down thine ear to me: make haste to deliver me,' and Psalm 86:1, 'Bow down thine ear, O Lord, and hear me: for I am poor, and in misery.'

35–6 *Shall he . . . hear?* Psalm 94:9, 'He that planted the ear, shall he not hear: or he that made the eye, shall he not see?'

52 *interlined* come between the lines, and thus found a place in the book.

53 *board* Communion table.

The Bag

Title Tuve argues that the title is a metaphor for Christ as the carrying pouch for requests to the Father. The poem is something of a response to the appeals of 'Longing'.

6 *close his eyes* as on board ship on the sea of Galilee, Matthew 8:24, 'And, behold, there arose a great tempest in the sea, insomuch that the ship was covered with the waves: but he was asleep.'

his heart Cf. line 36.

13 *tire* head-dress.

14 *fire* lightning.

24 *score* debt.
38 *the door* Cf. John 10:9, 'I am the door: by me if any man enter in, he shall be saved, and shall go in and out, and find pasture.'

The Jews

2 *scions* offspring.
3 *sluice* 'a dam or embankment, for impounding the water of a river, canal, etc., provided with an adjustable gate or gates by which the volume of water is regulated or controlled' (*OED*).

The Collar

Title the symbol of service and discipline, especially ecclesiastical; perhaps there is also a play on the words 'choler' as 'anger' and 'caller', as in Luke 5:32, 'I came not to call the righteous, but sinners to repentance.' Latent in the poem is the belief as expressed in the BCP that God's 'service is perfect freedom'.
1 *board* Communion table.
4 *lines* directions, in the sense of destiny, appointed lot in life (cf. Psalm 16:6 AV) perhaps with a pun on 'lines' of verse.
road sometimes spelled 'rode' in the seventeenth century, with a pun on 'rood' for 'cross'.
5 *store* plenty.
6 *still* (1) always and (2) silent, as he has been up to this moment of outburst.
in suit supplicating, petitioning (i.e., never having reward).
9 *cordial* (1) stimulating (2) enspiriting and (3) affecting the heart.
10–11 *Sure . . . corn* the material origin of the bread and wine of Communion.
14 *bays* leaves of the bay-tree, symbolic of triumph and fame (but perhaps with a reference to Psalm 37:36, 'I myself have seen the ungodly in great power: and flourishing like a green bay-tree').
21 *not. Forsake* The fifth edition changed the punctuation of 1633, 'not forsake thy cage' to that which appears in MSB, which is a logical correction.

35 *Child* Among the many scriptural references to believers as children, note especially Matthew 18:3, 'Except ye be converted, and become as little children, ye shall not enter into the kingdom of heaven.'

The Glimpse

13 *Lime* a powerfully caustic substance which, when combined with water, produces very great heat.
23 *heap* store.
24–5 *the droppings . . . the lock* some small amount of future good may fall to me without diminishing the pile of goodness or breaking the fastening.
27 *stay* absence.
29–30 *O make . . . court!* that is, 'Do not by thy absence give grief and sin an occasion to jeer at me, whereas *thy coming* would transform my heart into a court. The antecedent of *Who* is *me*' (Hutchinson).

Assurance

3 *Is such poison bought?* that is, may such poison be punishment?
4 *but* but only.
29 *indite* put into written words, possibly with reference to the Word, i.e., Christ.
35 *rock and tower* Psalm 61:3, 'O set me up upon the rock that is higher than I: for thou hast been my hope, and a strong tower for me against the enemy.'
39 *bone* cause of contention, as when two dogs fight for one.
40 *bounds* rebounds.

The Call

1 *Come, my Way, my Truth, my Life* The Christian speaker adopts the words of Christ, and makes Christ his audience: 'I am the way, the truth, and the life: no man cometh unto the Father,

but by me' (John 14:6) and 'Come unto me, all ye that labour and are heavy laden, and I will give you rest' (Matthew 11:28).
9 *Come, my Joy* Cf. the refrain from the Song of Solomon, 'Come, my beloved'.
10 *Such a Joy* John 16:22, 'your heart shall rejoice, and your joy no man taketh from you'.

Praise (3)

15 *Albion* Britain.
17 *Pharaoh's wheels but logs* in Exodus 14:24–5, 'And it came to pass, that in the morning watch the Lord looked unto the host of the Egyptians through the pillar of fire and of the cloud, and troubled the host of the Egyptians, And took off their chariot wheels, that they drave them heavily . . .'
23 *stint* limitation, restriction.
27 *bottle* a wineskin, a leather bag to contain liquids; cf. Psalm 56:8, 'Thou tellest my flittings; put my tears into thy bottle: are not these things noted in thy book?'
40 *use* interest.

Joseph's Coat

Title Jacob gave Joseph a special garment as a sign of his love, which exegetes read typologically as the human nature of Christ, the deepest sign of God's love. Cf. Genesis 37:3, 'Now Israel loved Joseph more than all his children, because he was the son of his old age: and he made him a coat of many colours.'
1 *indite* write, as in 'Assurance', line 29, with a play on 'indict'.
8 *both* 'grief and smart' are one and 'heart' is two.
9 *both* heart and body, the *loci* of emotional and physical grief.

The Pulley

Classical myth lies behind this poem in the story of Pandora's box, from which all grief escaped to trouble mankind, according to Hesiod, or all goods, in the minority view, leaving only hope in

the box as a gift. Here all virtues and goods are distributed, sufficient to make man independent of God, with the exception of rest, which man can find only with God. The poet puns on 'rest' as 'peace of mind' and 'rest' as 'remainder'.
5 *span* the width of an open hand from the tip of the thumb to the end of the little finger.

The Priesthood

5 *Fain* The mixture of humility and frustration echoes Donne, 'Holy Sonnet 14', 'Yet dearly'I love you, and would be loved fain' (line 9).

lay-sword secular weapon, as opposed to the sword of the Lord or the sword of the Spirit.
8 *earth and clay* God is several times likened to a potter working with clay, as in Romans 9:21, 'Hath not the potter power over the clay, of the same lump to make one vessel unto honour, and another unto dishonour?'
10 *compositions* physical and mental constitutions.
26 *serve him up* that is, in the eucharist.
32 *To hold the Ark* recalling the fatal presumption of one who had no right to touch the tabernacle of the Lord, 'Uzzah put forth his hand to the ark of God, and took hold of it; for the oxen shook it. And the anger of the Lord was kindled against Uzzah; and God smote him there for his error; and there he died by the ark of God' (2 Samuel 6:6–7).

The Search

3 *daily bread* Psalm 42:3, 'My tears have been my meat day and night: while they daily say unto me, Where is now thy God?' Herbert's change of 'meat' to 'bread' provides the eucharistic answer to his search, as well as echoing the appeal in the Lord's Prayer, 'Give us this day our daily bread'.
4 *prove* that is, prove or result in anything.
14 *Simper* twinkle, glimmer.

33 *of anything* above all.
43 *poles* each of the extremities (north and south) of the axis of the earth.
47 *charge* load, burden.
48 *case* grounds on which he rests his claim for mercy.
49 *lengths* distances.
59 *bear the bell* take the first place, have the foremost position, be the best.

Grief

Title Grief is remorse for something done; for its intensity, see for example its use in 'The Sacrifice'.
10 *less world* the little world of man, the microcosm.
15 *feet* This is a pun which combines reference to parts of human anatomy and to the division of verse.

The Cross

1 *uncouth* awkward, unpleasant, with the additional suggestion of 'strange'.
3 *some place* that is, Bemerton.
8 *wrestling* wrastling (*1633*)
dear end the vocation of priest.
9 *take away* Compare Job 1:21, '... the Lord gave, and the Lord hath taken away; blessed be the name of the Lord', in order to contrast the speaker's frustration and anger at his sickness.
10 *unbend* weaken.
18 *save ... sting* that is, weak in everything except seeing my weakness.
21 *turnest th' edge* as of a razor and, figuratively, of all things which have a sharp cutting side.
22 *Taking me up* Compare Herbert's formal differences, noted by Bloch, to both Psalm 102:10: 'thou hast taken me up, and cast me down' and Donne's final line in 'Hymn to God my God, in my sickness', a poem which refers to 'Christ's Cross' (line 22),

'Therefore that he may raise the Lord throws down' (line 30).
23 *be sped* have succeeded in obtaining fulfilment.
32 *cross actions* with a pun on 'cross' as 'contrary' and the Cross of Calvary.
35 *thy Son* Christ, and each Christian who takes up the cross of Christ.
36 *Thy will be done* Cf. Matthew 26:42 for Christ's words in the Garden of Gethsemane, 'O my Father, if this cup may not pass away from me, except I drink it, thy will be done.'

The Flower

3 *demean* bearing, but also 'estate' as in 'demesne'.
9 *recovered* Bloch suggests Job 14:7–9, 'For there is hope of a tree, if it be cut down, that it will sprout again, and that the tender branch thereof will not cease. Though the root thereof wax old in the earth, and the stock thereof die in the ground: yet through the scent of water it will bud, and bring forth boughs like a plant.'
16 *quick'ning* bringing to life.
18 *passing-bell* bell rung at the death of a person, as the soul passes from the body; cf. Donne in his verse letter 'To Sir Henry Wotton, At his Going Ambassador to Venice' (1604, lines 13–16):

> After those loving papers, where friends send
> With glad grief, to your sea-ward steps, farewell,
> Which thicken on you now, as prayers ascend
> To heaven in troops at a good man's passing bell.

The contrast is between a chime of bells ('chiming') which has several notes and the passing bell with a single note ('tolling').
21 *Thy word* the will of God.
spell interpret, with the secondary suggestion of a child learning his ABC.
25 *Off'ring at* aiming at.
30 *upwards bent* erect; the Renaissance made much of man's special posture as proof of his unique nature.
32 *pole* North or South Pole, the extreme of cold.

zone that is, the burning zone between the tropics of Cancer and Capricorn.

44 *glide* pass imperceptibly away.

45 *prove* have the experience of.

47 *Who would* Cf. Luke 14:11, 'For whosoever exalteth himself shall be abased; and he that humbleth himself shall be exalted.'

Dotage

Title Dotage is folly, not merely senility.

1 *glozing* flattering.

2 *night-fires* will o' the wisps.

3 *Chases* hunting scenes.

arras a rich fabric in which figures and scenes are woven in colours.

4 *in a career* at a gallop.

5 *nothing between two dishes* that is, concealed emptiness, a proverb favoured by Herbert. See Walton's *Life*, p. 307.

8 *in grain* ineradicable.

The Son

3 *coast* region, country.

8 *Chasing* putting to flight.

A True Hymn

9 *fineness* Tuve suggests both 'subtlety' and 'splendour'.

11–12 *all the mind . . . time* Cf. Luke 10:27, 'Thou shalt love the Lord thy God with all thy heart, and with all thy soul, and with all thy strength, and with all thy mind; and thy neighbour as thyself.'

14 *behind* lacking.

20 *Loved* Cf. 1 John 4:19, 'We love him, because he first loved us.'

The Answer

2 *ends* purposes.

3 *bandy* toss about.

4 *summer friends* fair-weather supporters.

6 *undertaking* bold.

8 *young exhalation* potential meteor believed to be formed from vapours arising from beneath the earth which were ignited by the sun. See *Romeo and Juliet* III, 5, line 13, 'It is some meteor that the sun exhal'd.'

10 *pursy* fat; cf. Hamlet to Gertrude, III, iv, lines 152–4, 'Forgive me this my virtue,/For in the fatness of these pursy times/Virtue itself of vice must pardon beg.'

A Dialogue-Anthem

2 *sting* 1 Corinthians 15:55, 'O death, where is thy sting? O grave, where is thy victory?'

10 *no more* Cf. Donne's 'Holy Sonnet 10', 'One short sleep past, we wake eternally,/And death shall be no more, Death thou shalt die' (lines 13–14).

The Water-Course

Title an artificial channel for the conveyance of water. The alternate rhymes in lines 5 and 10 suggest the turning of the pipes 'up' or 'down'.

Self-Condemnation

2 *Barabbas* the robber whom Pilate released from prison to the Jews instead of Christ.

12 *enchanting voice* M. E. Rickey (*Utmost Art*, pp. 51–2) notes the reference to the Sirens who were allegorised as 'worldliness' and 'the more specific vice of sensuality'.

18 *Judas-Jew* a traitor like Judas Iscariot.

19 *the last great day* of Judgement.

Bitter-Sweet

Title a kind of apple; cf. Mercutio in *Romeo and Juliet* II, iv, line 79, 'Thy wit is a very bitter sweeting.' Here there is the clear suggestion of the paradox of the *felix culpa*, a central principle in *The Temple*.
2 *Since thou dost love, yet strike* Various critics note the thematic and structural parallels with Hosea 6:1, '. . . he hath torn, and he will heal us: he hath smitten, and he will bind us up.'

The Glance

4 *Welt'ring in sin* wallowing, as rising and falling in tumult. Cf. Milton's *Lycidas*, 'He must not float upon his watery bier/Unwept, and welter to the parching wind' (lines 12–13).
12 *swing and sway* full control (Hutchinson).
16 *got* gained.

The Twenty-third Psalm

George Herbert was familiar with the BCP version, the AV translation, the two by Sternhold and Hopkins, as well as, almost certainly, that of Sir Philip Sidney; all follow here:

> The Lord is my Shepherd: therefore can I lack nothing.
>
> 2 He shall feed me in a green pasture: and lead me forth beside the waters of comfort.
>
> 3 He shall convert my soul: and bring me forth in the paths of righteousness, for his Name's sake.
>
> 4 Yea, though I walk through the valley of the shadow of death, I will fear no evil: for thou art with me; thy rod and thy staff comfort me.
>
> 5 Thou shalt prepare a table before me against them that trouble me: thou hast anointed my head with oil, and my cup shall be full.
>
> 6 But thy loving-kindness and mercy shall follow me all the days of my life: and I will dwell in the house of the Lord for ever. (BCP)

The Lord is my shepherd; I shall not want.

2 He maketh me to lie down in green pastures: he leadeth me beside the still waters.

3 He restoreth my soul: he leadeth me in the paths of righteousness for his name's sake.

4 Yea, though I walk through the valley of the shadow of death, I will fear no evil: for thou art with me; thy rod and thy staff they comfort me.

5 Thou preparest a table before me in the presence of mine enemies: thou anointest my head with oil; my cup runneth over.

6 Surely goodness and mercy shall follow me all the days of my life: and I will dwell in the house of the Lord for ever. (AV)

The Lord is onely my support,
and he that doth me feede:
How can I then lacke any thing,
whereof I stand in neede:
2 He doth me folde in coates most safe,
the tender grasse fast by:
And after drives me to the streames,
which runne most pleasantly.

3 And when I feele my selfe neare lost,
then doth he me home take:
Conducting me in the right pathes,
even for his owne names sake.
4 And though I were even at deathes dore
yet would I feare none ill:
For with thy rod and shepeheardes crooke
I am comforted still.

5 Thou hast my table richly deckt
in despight of my foe:
Thou hast my head with balme refresht,
my cup doth overflow.
6 And finally while breath doth last,
thy grace shall me defend:
And in the house of God will I,
my life for ever spend.

(Sternhold and Hopkins)

My shepeheard is the living Lord,
nothing therefore I neede:
In pastures faire with waters calme,
he let me forth to feede.
2 He did convert and glad my soule,
and brought my mind in frame:
To walke in pathes of righteousnesse,
for his most holy name.

3 Yea though I walke in vale of death,
yet will I feare none ill
Thy rod, thy staffe, doth comfort me,
and thou art with me still.
4 And in the presence of my foes,
my table thou shalt spread:
Thou shalt O Lord fill full my cup,
and eke annoint my heade.

5 Through all my life thy favour is
so frankly shewed to me:
That in thy house for evermore,
my dwelling place shalbe.
(Sternhold and Hopkins)

The Lord, the Lord my shepherd is,
And so can never I
Taste misery.
He rests me in green pasture his:
By waters still, and sweet
He guides my feet.

He me revives: leads me the way,
Which righteousness doth take,
For his name's sake.
Yea though I should through valleys stray,
Of death's dark shade, I will
No whit fear ill.

For thou, dear Lord, thou me besett'st:
Thy rod, and thy staff be
To comfort me;

Before me thou a table sett'st
Even when foes' envious eye
Doth it espy.

Thou oil'st my head thou fill'st my cup:
Nay more thou endless good,
Shalt give me food.
To thee, I say, ascended up,
Where thou, the Lord of all,
Dost hold thy hall. (Sir Philip Sidney)

J. C. A. Rathmell points out the likelihood that Herbert was familiar with the manuscript of the Sidneian Psalms, 'Donne, we know, was familiar with the collection, and there is an inherent likelihood that Herbert – who was related, and owed his living, at Bemerton, to the Pembroke family – also knew it' (*The Psalms of Sir Philip Sidney and the Countess of Pembroke*, New York, 1963, pp. xi–xii). Rathmell cites the opinion of Louis Martz that these Sidneian versions are 'the closest approximations to the poetry of Herbert's *Temple* that can be found anywhere in preceding English poetry'. Other critics find anticipations in the sonnets of William Alabaster.

In both the AV and the BCP versions, as well as that of Sidney, Herbert was drawn especially to the eucharistic focus of verse 5, 'Thou preparest a table before me in the presence of mine enemies' and 'Thou shalt prepare a table before me against them that trouble me', and Sidney's line 16, 'Before me thou a table sett'st.'

1 *love* Bloch notes 1 John 4:8, 'He that loveth not, knoweth not God; for God is love.'

3 *he is mine, and I am his* Bloch notes Song of Songs 2:16, 'My beloved is mine, and I am his: he feedeth among the lilies.'

9 *convert* 'cause to return' (*OED*).

10 *in frame* in appropriate attitude. Hutchinson cites *A Priest to the Temple* where Herbert writes of the congregation 'wallowing in the midst of their affairs: whereas on Sundays it is easy for them to compose themselves to order, which they put on as their holy day clothes and come to church in frame' (pp. 222–3).

24 *my praise* MSB has 'thy praise', a reading which loses the contrast with 'thy . . . love' of line 21.

Mary Magdalene

Here, as in Luke 7:37, Mary Magdalene is the sinful woman who washed and anointed Christ's feet at Simon's house. She stood by the cross at the crucifixion and learned from the angel at the tomb of the resurrection of Christ, who appeared to her later on Easter morning.

14 *dash* bespatter or splash.

Aaron

Title the brother of Moses, the archetypal priest and, as such, a type of Christ. In this poem Herbert plays on the 'perfect number' five (the sum of the first odd and even numbers): five-line stanzas, five rhymes throughout, five letters in 'Aaron', five stresses in line 3 of each stanza.

2 *Light and perfections* literal translation of Urim and Thummin, the symbolic stones on the breastplate of Aaron (Exodus 28:30).

3 *Harmonious bells below* On the title-page of the Authorised Version of 1611, Aaron appears with a tunic or chasuble, on the hem of which is a row of bells, partly illustrating the description of Aaron's dress cited in the note to line 10 of 'Decay', p. 374, and in the preceding verse: Exodus 28:33, 'And beneath upon the hem of it thou shalt make pomegranates of blue, and of purple, and of scarlet, round about the hem thereof; and bells of gold between them round about.'

5 *true Aarons* St Paul in the Epistle to the Hebrews, especially chapters 7–9, makes the distinction between Aaron and the new Aaron or Christ.

6 *Profaneness* impiety, with the etymology of *pro fanum*, before (or outside of) the temple.

8 *noise* consort of musicians.

23 *My doctrine* Galatians 2:20, 'I live; yet not I, but Christ liveth in me'.

25 *Aaron's dressed* that is, inside as well as outside – the appearance and the reality have become one. Note the importance of 'in' (line 21) as opposed to 'on' (line 1).

The Odour. 2 Corinthians 2

Title specifically, 2 Corinthians 2:14–17:

> Now thanks be unto God, which always causeth us to triumph in Christ, and maketh manifest the savour of his knowledge by us in every place. For we are unto God a sweet savour of Christ, in them that are saved, and in them that perish. To the one we are the savour of death unto death: and to the other the savour of life unto life. And who is sufficient for these things? For we are not as many, which corrupt the word of God: but as of sincerity, but as of God, in the sight of God speak we in Christ.

Bloch points out that burnt sacrifices to the Old Testament God are sweet to his nostrils, while Christ in the New Testament is himself the sweet odour, quoting Ephesians 5:2, 'And walk in love, as Christ also hath loved us, and hath given himself for us an offering and a sacrifice to God for a sweetsmelling savour.'

2 *Ambergris* waxy, odoriferous substance derived from the intestines of sperm whales, here a kind of perfume.

5 *oriental* 'eastern', and therefore 'rich' but also 'rising'.

9 *cordials* stimulants.

curious rare.

10 *fats* fattens.

16 *Pomander* a perfume ball, not only aromatic, but thought to be effective against disease.

The Foil

5 *foil* a thin leaf of metal placed behind a gem and designed to increase its brilliance. M. E. Rickey (*Utmost Art*, pp. 64–5) suggests that '"foil" also denotes a fencing weapon, here employed in a figurative engagement between virtue and sin'.

7 *toil* 'labour', but also 'fight'.

The Forerunners

1 *harbingers* forerunners, especially those in the advance of royalty or the main army, who also secure lodging for the king and officers; here death is to possess the speaker's body.
2 *my head* white with age.
3 *dispark* disperse, as deer from a park.
6 *Thou art still my God* 'still', in the sense of 'ever' and 'always'. It is Herbert's addition to the verses in Psalm 31:15–16:

> For I have heard the blasphemy of the multitude: and fear is on every side, while they conspire together against me, and take their counsel to take away my life. But my hope hath been in thee, O Lord: I have said, Thou art my God.

9 *pass not* don't care.
11 *ditty* not merely the song, but the lyric or theme of the song.
15 *stews* houses of prostitution.
stews and brothels This passage looks as if it might allude to the parable of the Prodigal Son (Luke 15:11ff.), but Bloch has shown the relevance of the prophets Ezekiel (especially 16:9–22) and Hosea, particularly the latter in his unsuccessful attempt to reform his 'wife of whoredoms' (Hosea 1:2) and his hope in a benign future: '. . . I will say to them which were not my people, Thou art my people; and they shall say, Thou art my God' (Hosea 2:23). Herbert repudiates the secular erotic verse with some frustration at its intractability.
21 *fond* foolish.
bane ruin, fatal mischief.
23 *broidered* ornamented with needlework.

The Rose

Title As in 'Church-Rents and Schisms', the rose is to be understood as the Church, following the traditional allegory of the Song of Solomon 2:1, 'I am the rose of Sharon, and the lily of the valleys.'

4 *size* portion.

6 *Coloured* feigned, misleading.

12 *my right* my claim upon worldly pleasures.

18 *purgeth* acts as a laxative. Cf. 'Providence', 'A rose, besides his beauty, is a cure' (line 78).

20 *forbearance* abstaining.

24 *biteth in the close* that is, you are pricked when you grasp it.

Discipline

22 *man of war* Cf. Exodus 15:3, 'The Lord is a man of war . . .'

25 *his bow* 'Perhaps also Herbert remembers that the Greek god of love has his bow' (Hutchinson). Note also for the continuation of the paradox of a loving God who is also wrathful the familiar opening verses of Psalm 38: 'Put me not to rebuke, O Lord, in thine anger: neither chasten me in thy heavy displeasure. For thine arrows stick fast in me: and thy hand presseth me sore.'

The Invitation

Title Bloch points out the Pauline generosity in Romans 14:13–14, and particularly 21,

> Let us not therefore judge one another any more: but judge this rather, that no man put a stumbling block or an occasion to fall in his brother's way. I know, and am persuaded by the Lord Jesus, that there is nothing unclean of itself: but to him that esteemeth any thing to be unclean, to him it is unclean . . . It is good neither to eat flesh, nor to drink wine, nor anything whereby thy brother stumbleth, or is offended, or is made weak.

3 *Save your cost* Cf. Isaiah 55:1–2, 'Ho, every one that thirsteth, come ye to the waters, and he that hath no money; come ye, buy, and eat; yea, come, buy wine and milk without money and without price. Wherefore do ye spend money for that which is not bread? . . .'

8 *define* characterise.
14 *arraign* indict on charges.
24 *As a flood the lower grounds* a reference to the practice of field cultivation recommended by Herbert in *A Priest to the Temple*, 'the improvement of his grounds, by drowning, or draining, or stocking, or fencing . . .' (Chapter 32, p. 250).

The Banquet

Title Holy Communion.
4 *neatness* elegance, tastefulness.
14 *Made a head* raised a body of troops.
25 *Pomanders* perfume balls, the scent of which is released by being squeezed or pressed. See 'The Odour, 2 Cor. 2', line 16.
49 *this pity* MSB has 'his pity', a reading that limits somewhat the broader tableau described in the poem.

The Posy

The word 'posy' may refer to a motto or a short poem. Cf. Hamlet to Ophelia on the brevity of the Prologue to *The Murder of Gonzago*, III, ii, line 152, 'Is this a prologue, or the posy of a ring?'
3–4 *Less than the least/Of all thy mercies* Cf. Genesis 32:10, 'I am not worthy of the least of all the mercies, and of all the truth, which thou hast shewed unto thy servant; for with my staff I passed over this Jordan; and now I am become two bands;' and Ephesians 3:7–8, 'Whereof I was made a minister, according to the gift of the grace of God given unto me by the effectual working of his power. Unto me, who am less than the least of all saints, is this grace given, that I should preach among the Gentiles the unsearchable riches of Christ.' Herbert made this phrase his own according to Ferrar and Walton; see Walton's *Life*, p. 311.

A Parody

Title Hutchinson quotes Dryden's definition of a parody as 'Verses patched up from great poets, and turned into another sense than their author intended them' and provides the parodied opening lines of a secular poem (once thought to be by Donne) by William Herbert, third Earl of Pembroke:

Soul's joy, now I am gone,
And you alone,
(Which cannot be,
Since I must leave myself with thee,
And carry thee with me)
Yet when unto our eyes
Absence denies
Each other's sight,
And makes to us a constant night,
When others change to light.

17 *awe* reverential fear.

The Elixir

Title the alchemists' or philosophers' stone, as in Chaucer's 'the philosophres stoon,/Elixir clept' (*The Canon's Yeoman's Tale*, lines 862–3). MSW provides an early version entitled 'Perfection'.
5 *rudely* irrationally.
7 *still* always, ever.
prepossessed foremost, with priority.
8 *his* that is, 'its' referring to the 'action' of line 6.
14 *Nothing can be so mean* Herbert states 'that nothing is little in God's service: if it once have the honour of that Name it grows great instantly' (*A Priest to the Temple*, Chapter 14, p. 224).
15 *tincture* quintessence, alchemical spirit, a word which looks back to 'The Elixir'.
20 *fine* rare and admirable.
23 *touch* test the fineness of the gold by rubbing it against a touchstone of quartz or jasper.
24 *told* reckoned up, counted.

A Wreath

5 *Life is straight* Cf. 'Colossians 3:3', line 3, echoed by this line.

Death

Title the first of 'the four last things'.
1 *uncouth* unknown, strange, as well as unpleasant.
9 *shooting short* erring.
11 *fledge souls* 'fledge' means 'fit to fly'. The image is of birds newly feathered having left the shell. Compare Donne, 'The Second Anniversary', where the images of the sick made ruddy, and fearsome death made useful is followed by the image of the soul as a newly hatched bird,

> She, she, embraced a sickness, gave it meat,
> The purest blood, and breath, that e'er it eat . . .
> And though he may pretend a conquest, since
> Heaven was content to suffer violence . . .
> Though he had right, and power, and place before
> Yet death must usher, and unlock the door.
> . . . this to thy soul allow,
> Think thy shell broke, think thy Soul hatched but now.
> (lines 147–8, 151–2, 155–6, 183–4)

For the direct address to Death, cf. Donne, 'Holy Sonnet 10', 'Death be not Proud' that concludes,

> One short sleep past, we wake eternally,
> And death shall be no more, Death thou shalt die.

18 *doomsday* the Day of Judgement.
24 *either down or dust* with a possible pun on eiderdown, although the *OED*'s earliest instance is 1774.

Doomsday

5 *member* limb.
12 *Tarantula's raging pains* Hutchinson: 'Tarantism, an hysterical malady, was supposed to be caused by the bite of the wolf-spider, or tarantula, and to be cured by music and wild dancing.'
14 *stay* stop; cf. Donne in his version of Doomsday graveside

hesitation, 'To make their souls, at the last busy day,/Meet at this grave, and make a little stay?' ('The Relic', lines 10–11).

15 *Let the graves make their confession* admit that they have no right to hold these bodies.

23 *noisome* noxious.

29 *consort* company of musicians.

Judgement

Title the second of the four eschatological last things.

5 *peculiar* own, personal.

peculiar book moral account record.

13 *Testament* The capitalisation directs us to St Paul's Epistle to the Hebrews, 9:14–15:

> How much more shall the blood of Christ, who through the eternal Spirit offered himself without spot to God, purge your conscience from dead works to serve the living God? And for this cause he is the mediator of the New Testament, that by means of death, for the redemption of the transgressions that were under the first Testament, they which are called might receive the promise of eternal inheritance.

Heaven

2 *Echo* not so much a particular classical reference as a term indicating a kind of verse in which one line is made to consist of a repetition of the concluding syllables of the preceding line so as to supply an answer to the question contained in it.

Love (3)

9 *unkind* undutiful.

17 *meat* food but also flesh, as it is when Christ speaks of the eucharistic meal. J. H. Summers points out that this is the final, heavenly communion of which each daily eucharistic banquet is an anticipation, 'Blessed are those servants, whom the Lord when he cometh shall find watching: verily I say unto you, that he shall

gird himself, and make them to sit down to meat, and will come forth and serve them' (Luke 12:37).

FINIS.

This is a firm sign of closure, separating the lyrics of *The Church* from the narrative survey of *The Church-Militant*.

THE CHURCH MILITANT

Title This refers to the body of Christians still on earth, as distinct from those in heaven. The style and tone of the poem reflect the influence of Donne's 'Second Anniversary' and Spenser's 'Mother Hubbard's Tale'.

9 *Spouse* Christ.

12 *endear* 'bind by obligations of gratitude' (*OED*).

15 *Noah's shady vine* Cf. Genesis 9:20, 'And Noah began to be an husbandman, and he planted a vineyard', the origin of the metaphor of Christ as the true vine, the pressed cluster of grapes and the sacrificial wine.

19 *Ark did rest* Herbert accepts the tradition that the resting place of the vessel which at the flood saved Noah's family and two of every living creature was the starting place of Abraham on his journey with the Ark of the Covenant to the Promised Land.

Abraham Hebrew patriarch, father of Isaac.

20 *the other Ark* the Ark of the Covenant, an ornamented rectangular box, the central sacred symbol of the presence of God.

Canaan the land subsequently called Palestine.

26 *partition-wall* previously separating gentiles from Jews but no longer, according to St Paul in Ephesians 2:14, 'For he is our peace, who hath made both one, and hath broken down the middle wall of partition between us.'

37ff. *Egypt* which once suffered plagues because of the refusal of the Pharaoh to release the people of God from their enslavement, now gives birth to Christian saints.

41 *Macarius* St Macarius of Egypt, a founder of monasticism, celebrated for his holiness.

great Anthony St Anthony of Egypt, one of the Desert Fathers.

42 *Made Pharaoh Moses* by freeing souls from the bondage of the Mosaic Law into Christian liberty, these Desert Fathers have from a new perspective turned Moses the liberator into a spiritual tyrant.

43 *Goshen* the fertile land in Egypt allotted to the Israelites in which there was light during the plague of darkness: Exodus 8:22.

44 *Nilus* the river Nile.

46 *For* instead of.

47–8 *How dear to me, O God, thy counsels are!/Who may with thee compare?* Psalm 139:17, 'How dear are thy counsels unto me, O God: O how great is the sum of them!' and Psalm 89:6, 'For who is he among the clouds: that shall be compared unto the Lord?'

51 *posed* confused.

set defeated.

52 *Sophisters* Sophists, i.e., Greek wise men who taught for money.

fisher's net alluding to the Apostles, several of whom were fishermen by trade, who were called by Christ to serve as fishers of men: Matthew 5:19.

53 *Plato* (427–347 BC) pupil of Socrates, teacher of Aristotle, the chief Greek philosopher; as Whitehead wrote, 'All Western philosophy is but a series of footnotes to Plato.'

Aristotle (384–322 BC) pupil of Plato, teacher of Alexander the Great, ancient philosopher second only to Plato in importance.

54 *spell Christ-Cross* learn a new alphabet of Christianity (Christ-Cross refers to an alphabet presented on a horn-book prefaced by the sign of the cross).

55 *syllogisms* logical arguments having two propositions called premises and a third proposition that is the conclusion which follows necessarily from the two premises.

56 *Ergo* Latin for 'therefore', the first word in the conclusion of a common syllogism.

Amen the word of assent at the end of prayer, which means 'so be it', in contrast to the 'ergo' of logic which suggests heresy; here the 'amen' implies humble acceptance of whatever God wills.

63 *The Warrior* A type rather than an individual, which represents external, pagan, military heroism that is inferior to Christian patience.

70 *Him in his members* The Roman soldier 'with a spear pierced his side' (John 19:34) but here the converted 'great heart' renounces violence ('quitting his spear') rather than wound Christ again in his followers, who make up the Mystical Body of Christ, 'his members'. There may be a play on words with 'members' meaning 'private parts'. Compare the death of Caesar as described by Plutarch.

72 *Giving new names and numbers to the year* that is, the calendar becomes Christian.

74 *Who were cut short in Alexander's stem* those frustrated by the death of Alexander are now pleased by another Greek Empire, as Constantine moved the seat of power from Rome to Byzantium/Constantinople and converted to Christianity.

76 *against* before.

78 *her throne* Religion's throne.

84 *harbingers* forerunners.

93 *Constantine's British line* Roman emperor, proclaimed so by his army in AD 306 at York. After the battle at the Milvian Bridge in AD 312 he favoured Christianity, eventually professing himself a Christian. His mother, St Helena, was in the Middle Ages believed to be English, indeed the daughter of Cole of Colchester.

95 *Within a sheet of paper* referring to the Donation of Constantine, a forged document purporting to grant special standing to the pope.

98 *old meridian* apogee, zenith. This might conceivably refer to the furthest west that we can see: the sun sets to the west, and the end of the known world was to the west.

108 *Gardens of gods* referring to vegetation deities, like Adonis and Tammuz (cf. Spenser's Garden of Adonis, *Faerie Queene*, III, vi).

110 *sallet* salad.

112 *Adoring garlic* Cf. Numbers 11:5, when the Israelites complained about their diet of manna in the desert: 'We remember the fish, which we did eat in Egypt freely: the cucumbers, and the melons, and the leeks, and the onions, and the garlic.'

118 *while he adores his broom* made as it is from the plants he worships as divine.

120ff. Although 'The Church Militant' as a survey of progress owes much to Donne's 'Progress of the Soul', these lines in particular echo its rhythms and diction.

127 *for* instead of.

130 *should befall . . . befell* a reference to pagan oracles, which were often duplicitous in their messages.

131 *Nay, he became a poet* Oracular wisdom was often expressed in verse. Sin has become an oracle. Milton vividly tells of the sinful angels finding employment as pagan deities and oracles (*Paradise Lost*, I, lines 364ff.).

132 *sublimate* a kind of arsenic; violent poison.
conserve confectionary preparation.

134 *pull* draw.

138 *braver* worthier.

147 *Disparking* throwing open, casting out.

149 *rogue* Muhammad (*c.* AD 570–629), the founder of Islam.

150 *coy* reserved.

151 *trim* neat.

153 *Mahometan* Muhammadan.

161 *extirpate* exterminate.

163 *Mitre* head-dress of a bishop.

174 *Christ's three offices* Prophet, King, and Priest.

186 *vizards* masks.

187 *anchorism* the practice of being a hermit.

194 *transmigration* removal from one country to another, with the suggestion of the transmigration of the Jews, the Babylonian captivity.

198 *fur* trim worn as a sign of high office.

204 *the Pope's mule* a coloured slipper worn in the manner of the classical Roman *magister*, here indicative of the near-total secular dominance of the papacy. There is a pun on 'beast of burden'.

205 *twist* combine into.

206 *Antichrist* title of the great personal opponent of Christ, frequently, as here, applied to the pope, originally meaning Satan.

207 *Janus* Roman god with two faces, the second at the back of his head. In seventeenth-century English the term 'Janus-faced' already denoted duplicity.
225–8 *The second Temple . . . tears* Hutchinson's gloss can hardly be bettered: '"The late reformation" fell as far short of the primitive Church as "The second Temple" did of the first, and is equally a matter for tears (Ezra 3:12).'
235–6 *Religion stands on tiptoe in our land,/Ready to pass to the American strand* Walton tells the story of how these celebrated lines led to a temporary awkwardness in the licensing of *The Temple*. Two years after the Vice-Chancellor licensed *The Temple*, following a momentary hesitation over these politically problematic lines, Archbishop Laud had the Puritan preacher Samuel Ward of Ipswich disciplined for an attack on alleged 'Popish' practices in which these very lines are quoted. See Dwight Levang, 'George Herbert's "The Church Militant" and the Chances of History', *PQ* 36 (1957), pp. 265–8.
250 *By carrying first their gold from them away* As did the Conquistadores, with the presumed beneficial effect on the natives of leaving them materially poor and spiritually rich.
256 *our ancient place* Europe.
265 *Spain hath done one* that is, used its power to Christianise Latin America.
268 *sound* haven, inlet.
275ff. The poem concludes with the image of a circle closed, the circle the figure of perfection.

L'Envoy

As the title states, this is the author's postscript with his parting words.
1 *King of Glory, King of Peace* cf. line 1 from 'Praise (2)'.
2 *war* MSW has 'wars' as does the scriptural reference, Psalm 46:9, 'He maketh wars to cease in all the world.'

Poems Not Included in The Temple

The Holy Communion

8 *bread* MSW requires considerable adjustment of confusing capitalisation. Here 'Bread' has been reduced to 'bread' in order to emphasise the eucharistic theme and the nature of divine presence.
12–18 *Concerneth . . . still* This apparent indifference to the manner of Christ's presence is illustrated by Hutchinson with a reference to Donne's sermon at St Paul's on Christmas Day, 1626, 'But for the manner, how the Body and Blood of Christ is there, wait his leisure, if he have not yet manifested that to thee: Grieve not at that, wonder not at that, press not for that; for he hath not manifested that, not the way, not the manner of his presence in the Sacrament, to the Church' (*Sermons*, ed. Potter and Simpson, VII, 11, 290–91).
25 *Impanation* In eucharistic theory, a local presence or inclusion of the body of Christ in the bread after consecration; one of the modifications of the Roman Catholic doctrine of real presence.
38 *Flesh (though exalted) keeps his grass* that is, its essential materiality; cf. 1 Peter 2:24.
41 *meres* landmarks.

Love

13 *when thou didst sleep* when Christ slept on a pillow in the stern of the boat that took him across the Sea of Galilee during a storm, which he later quelled. Cf. Mark 4:35ff.

Trinity Sunday

Title the first Sunday after Pentecost, a feast day celebrating the unity of Father, Son and Holy Ghost.
12 *the first Thief* Lucifer.

Evensong

Title Evening Prayer, Vespers.

The Knell

3 *wishly* longingly.
17 *Juleps and Cordials* sweet stimulants.

Perseverance

Title the continuing in a state of grace, guaranteed to the elect, according to Calvin, but dependent in part upon human effort in the judgement of non-Calvinists, as is clear from stanza 3.
7 *fowling-piece* light gun for shooting birds.
12 *banns* proclamation of marriage.
16 *rock* Cf. Psalm 18:1, 'I will love thee, O Lord, my strength; the Lord is my stony rock . . .'

Sonnet (1)

Title Walton tells us that this and the following sonnet were written when Herbert was not quite seventeen and sent to his mother as 'a New Year's gift' (Walton, p. 274).
2 *shoals* troops.
4 *Venus' livery* the uniform of a servant of the goddess of love.
5 *lays* verses, especially short lyric or narrative poems designed to be sung.
8 *dove* symbol of the Holy Spirit, with some irony, as traditionally Venus herself is attended by doves.

Sonnet (2)

2 *Deluge* Noah's Flood.
8 *crystal* the type of perfect transparency.
9 *invention* theme, topic.
14 *discovery* revelation, exploration, investigation, opening.

To My Successor

Walton describes (pp. 293–4) how Herbert had these verses engraved on the mantelpiece of the rectory at Bemerton.

To the Right Hon. the L. Chancellor (Bacon)

Title Hutchinson listed this poem among the doubtful works but recent scholarship has provided grounds for including it as authentic. See Fram Dinshaw, 'A Lost MS of George Herbert's Occasional Verse and the Authorship of "To the L. Chancellor"', *N&Q* 30 (October 1983), pp. 423–5. The text is a modernised version of British Library Additional MS 22602.

Sir Francis Bacon (1561–1626), statesman, philosopher, essayist, made Lord Chancellor in 1618 and convicted of taking bribes and forced into retirement from politics in 1621. Herbert had translated, at Bacon's request, *The Advancement of Learning* into Latin for inclusion in *De Augmentis Scientiae* (1623) and was the dedicatee, 'his very good friend, Mr George Herbert' of Bacon's *Translation of Certain Psalms into English Verse* (1625).

1 *diamond* that is, Bacon's gift to Herbert, probably the *Instauratio Magna*.

2 *blackamoor* that is, the Latin poem, '*Aethiopissa ambit Cestum Diversi Coloris Virum*' (see Appendix, p. 321), which Herbert sent to Bacon in return for the 'diamond'.

12 *factious* loyal to party rather than principle; i.e., the black ink which was drawn naturally to the theme of blackness.

To the Lady Elizabeth Queen of Bohemia

Title Modern scholars have argued convincingly that this and the following 'L'Envoy' are indeed by Herbert (cf. Kenneth Alan Hovey, 'George Herbert's Authorship of "To the Queene of Bohemia"', *RQ* 30 (1973), pp. 43–50, and especially Ted-Larry Pebworth, 'George Herbert's Poems to the Queen of Bohemia: A Rediscovered Text and a New Edition', *ELR* 9 (1979), pp. 108–20). Grosart made an imperfect transcription for his edition of

1870. I have modernised Pebworth's transcription with two changes (noted below). The Queen of Bohemia is Elizabeth, the daughter of King James, who married Frederick the Elector Palatine in 1613. The poems were written in late 1621 or 1622, when George Herbert was Public Orator at Cambridge.

1–2 *Bright soul . . . thine own* Elizabeth and her husband had lost Bohemia to the Archduke Ferdinand, Holy Roman Emperor and were fugitives.

3 *jointure* property assigned to a wife in lieu of return of her dowry at the death of her husband.

4 *pitch* zenith, the highest point in the flight of a falcon.

8 *two clods of earth* Bohemia and the Palatinate, i.e., instead of both lost kingdoms she has the sun and stars (lines 3–5).

ten spheres the universe, comprised of ten concentric circles surrounding the earth beginning with the sphere of the moon, extending through the planets to the sphere of the fixed stars, the crystalline sphere, to, finally, the Primum Mobile.

10 *brave* splendid.

11–12 *Maintain their . . . crystal sphere* These lines refer to Elizabeth and Ferdinand's visit to Holland in 1621, where they received a very warm welcome.

13 *optic* telescope.

14 *curious* exquisite.

16 *foil* setting of a jewel.

17 *that black tiffany* mourning garb worn in defeat.

18 *richer* The Cambridge MS has 'rich', but the meaning suggests and the metre requires the added syllable of the comparative. There is support for 'richer' in British Library Harleian MS 3910.

27 *hale* draw, tug, drag.

32 *self-thrall* the cause of the bondage of others to it.

33 *Of thousand hearts* Elizabeth was referred to as 'the Queen of Hearts'.

35 *misery cannot untwist* misery caused by the loss of her husband's dominions.

42 *Children for kingdoms* Elizabeth had five children by January 1621, and twelve by the time her husband died.

43 *frame* entire structure.

47 *wings* Logic and context suggest that this MS Harleian 3910 reading is correct. Cambridge MS has 'winds'.

48 *ravening* devouring, rapacious, with a pun on ravens.

harpies winged monsters, usually with female faces, that snatch food from people and, sometimes, snatch the people themselves.

49 *baiting-while* stop for refreshment or rest upon a journey.

51 *Paris Garden* the bull- and bear-baiting arena in Southwark; cf. the Porter in *Henry VIII* V, iv, lines 1–2, 'You'll leave your noise anon, ye rascals; do you take the court for Paris Garden?'

52 *Spanish* pejorative reference to relics, because the Hapsburgs, victors over Ferdinand and Elizabeth, ruled Catholic Spain.

saints with a play on 'scents'.

53 *untimed* eternal, with a secondary play on 'unthymed'.

58 *fain* gladly.

59 *Making a head* forming a rebellion.

64 *Rhenish* because the vineyards of the Rhine region are part of her political dominions.

66 *meet* fitting, condign.

Envoi To the Same. Another

Title The title is not in the Cambridge MS.

2 *David's tree* Hutchinson and others cite Psalm 1:3, where David sings of the blessed man who 'shall be like a tree planted by the water-side: that will bring forth his fruit in due season'. Pebworth draws attention to Psalm 137: 1–2, with its citation of the grief of the exiles by the waters of Babylon.

4 *Thy fruit* Your children.

their drops the tears of the grieving exiles in Babylon who were the fruit of David's tree, and who were also victims of exile whose banishment eventually ended.

8 *maugre* in spite of.

12 *our great sublunary ball* the earth; sublunary, under the sphere of the Moon. Cf. Donne, 'A Valediction: forbidding Mourning', 'Dull sublunary lovers' love' (line 13). Herbert's 'tears' (line 69) and 'compasses' (line 75) suggest that he was recalling Donne's

poem with its 'tear-floods' (line 6) and 'compasses' (line 26) when he was writing these consolatory verses to the defeated queen, with Donne's 'circle just' (line 35) becoming Herbert's 'that ring' (line 13) that weds eternity.

A PRIEST TO THE TEMPLE

The nature of *A Priest to the Temple* is indicated by the sub-title *The Country Parson, His Character and Rule of Holy Life*, for Herbert composed a work that belongs generically to the 'character sketch', a kind quite popular in the early seventeenth century. Deriving ultimately from the *Ethical Characters* of Theophrastus, the pupil and successor of Aristotle at the Lyceum, the English sketches of moral and eventually social and professional types best known in Herbert's lifetime were Joseph Hall's *Characters of Virtues and Vices* (1608) and John Earle's *Microcosmography* (1628). The special charm of *A Priest to the Temple* lies in its mixture of the typical with hints of the personal. Its value, apart from its picture of pastoral duty in the period, is as a gloss on words and phrases within *The Temple* itself. I have modernised those spellings from the first edition as it appeared in *Herbert's Remains, Or Sundry Pieces of that sweet Singer of 'The Temple', Mr George Herbert* (1652), edited by Barnabus Oley, that would cause confusion for the contemporary reader.

The Author to the Reader

1. *since our Saviour hath made that the argument of a pastor's love* Hutchinson cites John 21:15–17, in which Christ tells Peter to 'Feed my lambs . . . Feed my sheep . . . Feed my sheep.'
2. *pastoral* 'a book relating to the cure of souls', according to Dr Johnson, Hutchinson, and the *OED*; the text of the spiritual shepherd is himself and his fellow keepers of the flock.

Chapter 1: Of a Pastor

1. *reducing* leading back (to the right path).

2. *revoking* calling back.
3. *Colossians* Colossians 1:24.
4. *vicegerent* i.e., the representative of Christ endowed with some of his authority. This word was common in the sixteenth and seventeenth centuries and is best remembered in Don Armado's highflown address to the King of Navarre as 'Great deputy, the welkin's vicegerent . . .' (*Love's Labour's Lost* I, i, lines 219–20).

Chapter 2: Their Diversities

1. *cures* areas of spiritual responsibility.

Chapter 3: The Parson's Life

1. *patience* suffering without complaint.
2. *mortification* the killing of sensual desire, especially by such physically punishing tactics as fasting and abstinence.
3. *scandalise* shame or disgrace, but also to be the occasion by one's example of the sins of others. Cf. Donne's 'Hymn to God the Father' (1623): 'Wilt thou forgive that sin which I have won/Others to sin? and, made my sin their door?' (lines 7–8).
4. *I sat daily with you teaching in the Temple* Cf. Luke 22:53.
5. *dilating* itself increasing, spreading out into.

Chapter 4: The Parson's Knowledge

1. *sucks* i.e., takes knowledge and comfort from.
2. *if any do . . . doctrine* John 7:17.
3. *but with* i.e., without.
4. *collation of Scripture with Scripture* a critical comparison of passages which reveals the truth by mutual illumination.
5. *places controverted* i.e., the main areas of ethical and doctrinal debate.
6. *bear* i.e., produce, make.

Chapter 5: The Parson's Accessory Knowledge

1. *Fathers also, and the Schoolmen* i.e., the theologians of the early Church whose writings were considered to have special authority, and the thinkers of the medieval universities.
2. *bane* poison.

Chapter 6: The Parson Praying

1. *laver* a basin for washing, symbolic of spiritual cleansing.
2. *treatable* distinct, clear, easy to grasp.
3. *huddling . . . slubbering* bungled . . . careless.
4. *a reasonable service* Romans 12:1–2.
5. *presented* i.e., brought forward on arrival for dedication to God.

Chapter 7: The Parson Preaching

1. *character* quality, essence.
2. *Hermogenes* Second century AD rhetorician whose treatise on the seven excellences of style, best exemplified in Demosthenes, was influential as a textbook in the Renaissance.
3. *ravishing* enchanting, transporting.
4. *apostrophes* rhetorical gestures which involve both a stopping in the midst of an argument and an address to some one or some deity not immediately present.
5. *irradiations scatteringly* i.e., some devout comments addressed to God placed amongst the sermon itself.
6. *Isaiah 64 . . . Jeremy, chapter 10* Isaiah 64:1 and Jeremiah 10:23.
7. *And for the Corinthians* 1 Corinthians 1:4 'I thank my God always on your behalf, for the grace of God which is given you by Jesus Christ.'
8. *Revelations 1 . . . Hebrews 12* Revelation 1:15, Hebrews 12:29.
9. *. . . since the words apart are not Scripture* This is the basis for Herbert's opposition to the preaching style of discrete analyses made famous by his Westminster patron Lancelot Andrewes.

Chapter 8: The Parson on Sundays

1. *Thou art the man* the words used by the prophet Nathan to King David after the prophet's parable exposing the heinousness of David's crime in having Uriah the Hittite murdered (2 Samuel 12:7).
2. *hinds'* The BCP version of this phrase from the triumphal Psalm 18:33 is 'He maketh my feet like harts' feet: and setteth me up on high.'

Chapter 9: The Parson's State of Life

1. . . . *puts on the whole armour of God* . . . as St Paul urges, 'Put on the whole armour of God, that ye may be able to stand against the wiles of the devil . . .' (Ephesians 6:11ff.).
2. *for the human soul* . . . The soul has three faculties or powers, vegetative, sensitive, intellectual. Herbert here ignores the vegetative, but cf. Marvell, 'To His Coy Mistress', 'My vegetable love should grow/Vaster than empires and more slow' (lines 11–12).
3. *experiment* that is, experience.
4. *a wise and loving husband* Herbert's comments on marriage derive largely from the teachings of St Paul: see especially Ephesians 5:22–33.

Chapter 10: The Parson in his House

1. *His wife . . . winning her to it* Cf. 1 Corinthians 7:12–15.
2. *commonwealth-men* That is, good citizens of the country abiding by its laws and respecting its secular rulers. The 'Commonwealth' was a relatively new concept, expounded first by Sir John Fortescue in his treatise *The Governance of England* (written after 1471) in which sources of legal authority other than Canon and Roman law were presented. These alternative authorities were important for the emerging, and inextricably linked, sovereign church and state during the Reformation. This new identity was crucial to both the doctrinal and political positions of Herbert's beloved Church of England.
3. *the Chamber of London* the especially secure treasury of charitable donations at the City Chamberlain's office.

4. *101 Psalm* This psalm asks of God understanding, fidelity and humility and declares the psalmist's resolve to confound slandering, ungodly and proud people.
5. *fair table* attractive noticeboard.
6. *straitly* strictly, rigorously.
7. *boards a child* approximates the status of a child of the house.
8. *back-side* back garden.
9. *brook and bear* tolerate, endure.
10. *exinanition* exhausted condition.
11. *for meat was made for man* with an allusion to Christ's response to the Pharisees regarding work on the Sabbath (Matthew 12:10).

Chapter 11: The Parson's Courtesy

1. *but being not invited . . . hated* people not invited become convinced that the parson dislikes them.
2. *conceits* (negative) ideas.

Chapter 12: The Parson's Charity

1. *Matthew 25:35* The relevant verse is actually the one before: '. . . come, ye blessed of my Father, inherit the kingdom prepared for you . . .'.
2. *that excellent statute* the Poor Law Act of 1601.
3. *disseised* dispossessed.
4. *testimony* written certificate the better to distinguish a poor man (worthy of charity) from a vagabond (not worthy).

Chapter 13: The Parson's Church

1. *strawed* spread loosely over with rushes.
2. 1 Corinthians 14:26, 40.

Chapter 14: The Parson in Circuit

1. *receipts* prescriptions.
2. *carking* fretting, anxiety.
3. *he* i.e., the person the parson is visiting.

4. *as Nathan did* By the parable referred to in note 1 to Chapter 8, p. 430, Nathan the prophet proved to King David the error of his ways, and King David declared his own wrongdoing: 'And David said unto Nathan, I have sinned against the Lord.' 2 Samuel 12:13.

Chapter 15: The Parson Comforting

1. *lilies* an allusion to Matthew 6:28–9, 'Consider the lilies of the field, how they grow; they toil not, neither do they spin: And yet I say unto you, that even Solomon in all his glory was not arrayed like one of these.'

Chapter 16: The Parson a Father

1. *the opinion* that is, the opinion that he is father to the whole parish.
2. *he hateth him not* the priest does not hate the sinner.

Chapter 17: The Parson in Journey

1. *outlandish* foreign, as in the title of the collection of aphorisms ascribed to Herbert, *Outlandish Proverbs* (published 1640).
2. *buttery* a storeroom for provisions.

Chapter 18: The Parson in Sentinel

Title *in Sentinel* on guard.
1. *suppling* that is, supple-making.

Chapter 19: The Parson in Reference

1. *set at an armour* taxed or assessed for the cost of a suit of armour.
2. *respectively* with respect, in a respectful way.
3. *Diocesan* the bishop who has administrative control over the district.
4. *visitations* official visits by bishops especially to the clergy and parishes in their diocese.

5. *Philippians 4* This is the final chapter of St Paul's Epistle to the Philippians, in which he adjures the people of Philippi to joy in the holy life: verse 8 contains the passage quoted.
6. *brief* an official letter authorising a special collection.

Chapter 20: The Parson in God's Stead

1. *tester* a half-shilling.
2. *. . . as concerning this life, who hath promised that godliness shall be gainful* This is a doctrine espoused by Calvinists.

Chapter 21: The Parson Catechising

1. *regeneration* spiritual rebirth; 'born again'.
2. *give the word* spread the gospel.
3. *catholic* universally apt.
4. *1 Timothy 5:1* 'Rebuke not an Elder, but intreat him as a father, and the younger men as brethren.'
5. *silly* simple.
6. *hatchet* Hutchinson points out that this 'word in fact is not found in the AV, Geneva, or Bishop's Bible'.
7. *discover* reveal, but also the process of revealing; discovering, in the modern sense of the word, his own nature.

Chapter 22: The Parson in Sacraments

1. *wildly* possibly a misprint of 'widely'.
2. *Whitsuntide* Pentecost; the Feast of the Descent of the Holy Ghost, fifty days after Easter.

Chapter 23: The Parson's Completeness

1. *Dalton's Justice of Peace* Michael Dalton's *The Country Justice*, first published 1618, but sufficiently popular to have gone through four editions by 1630.
2. *tickle* difficult to deal with.

3. *physic* knowledge of medicine.
4. *anatomy* either an autopsy or, more probably, a skeleton.
5. *Fernelius* Jean François Fernel, court physician to Henri II of France, author of the *Universa medicina* (1554), a work especially valued by Herbert's brother Edward.
6. *mustard-seed and lilies . . . seed-corn and tares* The lilies appear in Matthew 7:28–9; the mustard-seed, seed-corn and tares are parables in Matthew 13:24–32.
7. *simples* medicinal herbs.
8. *bolearmena* Hutchinson gives 'an astringent earth from Armenia'.
9. *plaintain* a low herb with broad, flat leaves, good for curing a variety of ills, including, as Romeo reminds us, a broken shin, 'Your plantan leaf is excellent for that' (*Romeo and Juliet* I, ii, 51).
10. *hyssop* a small, bushy aromatic herb. Spenser tells us that 'Sharp isope is good for green wounds' (*Muiopotmos*, 190). *valerian* a variety of herbaceous plant used as a stimulant. *adder's tongue* a kind of fern. *yerrow* a common herb used as a tonic. *melilot* a kind of clover which when dried is useful for poultices. *mallows* a plant whose sticky leaves made a useful adhesive or plaster. *smallage* wild celery or winter parsley.

Chapter 24: The Parson Arguing

1. *schismatic* member of a sect separated from the Church.
2. *scandal* 'something that hinders reception of the faith', especially 'perplexity of conscience occasioned by the conduct of one who is looked up to as an example' (*OED*).
3. *exercise* testing.

Chapter 25: The Parson Punishing

1. *consters* construes, analyses.

Chapter 26: The Parson's Eye

1. *baned* tainted, spoiled.
2. *a prodigal* that is, someone who is extravagant and careless,

like the prodigal son in Luke 15:11–32. Note that Luke 14 tells the parable of the great supper with its meat, servants, salt and judgement, providing Herbert with the sequence of his own thoughts in this chapter.

3. *Gerson* Jean le Charlier de Gerson (1363–1429), Chancellor of the University of Paris, mystic and reformer, thought to be an author of the *Imitation of Christ*.

Chapter 27: The Parson in Mirth

1. *sad* sorrowful.

Chapter 28: The Parson in Contempt

1. *the Apostle's rule* Cf. 1 Timothy 4:12, 'Let no man despise thy youth; but be thou an example of the believers, in word, in conversation, in charity, in spirit, in faith, in purity.'
2. *bootless* useless.

Chapter 29: The Parson with his Churchwardens

1. *David says* i.e., Psalm 84:11, 'I had rather be a door-keeper in the house of my God: than to dwell in the tents of ungodliness.'
2. *the Canons* the principal body of Canon (church) a law passed by the convocations of Canterbury and York in 1604 and 1606 respectively. The Canons dealt with matters of practicality as well as doctrine, including the care of churches and how they should be furnished, which were the churchwardens' responsibility.

Chapter 30: The Parson's Consideration of Providence

1. *soil* manure.
2. *corn* grain.
3. *virtue* power.
4. *the sun stood still, the fire burned not* Cf. Joshua 10:12–13: 'Then spake Joshua to the Lord in the day when the Lord delivered

up the Amorites before the children of Israel, and he said in the sight of Israel, Sun, stand thou still upon Gibeon; and thou, Moon, in the valley of Ajalon. And the sun stood still, and the moon stayed . . . .' and Exodus 3:2: 'And the angel of the Lord appeared unto him in a flame of fire out of the midst of a bush: and he looked, and, behold, the bush burned with fire, and the bush was not consumed.'

5. *utter* sell.

Chapter 31: The Parson in Liberty

1. *emergent* unexpected.
2. *exigent* critical occasion.
3. *what he may* to the extent that he is able.
4. *resent . . . grief* that is, respond moderately to a moderate offence.

Chapter 32: The Parson's Surveys

1. *the necessity of a vocation* Cf. Donne in his *Letter to Sir H. Goodyer* (1608): '. . . But to be no part of any body, is to be nothing'.
2. *ingenuous* honourable.
3. *Men are either single or married* Note the dichotomous division in the manner of Peter Ramus, the influential simplifier of Aristotle.
4. *The Italian* not a particular Italian philosopher or poet, but a proverbial Italian expression.
5. *sessions* a continuous series of judicial meetings presided over by a Justice of the Peace.
   sizes assizes, meetings of a court of justice.
6. *great horse* a charger, a knight's war horse, the managing of which, as Herbert's brother Edward tells us in his *Autobiography*, was both demanding and essential.
7. *squared out* gave exact advice.
8. *even to soldiers* Cf. Luke 3:10ff., especially 14, 'And the soldiers likewise demanded of him saying, And what shall we do? And he said unto them, Do violence to no man, neither accuse any falsely; and be content with your wages.'

Chapter 33: The Parson's Library

1. *the Kingdom of God be first sought* Cf. Matthew 6:33, 'But seek ye first the kingdom of God, and his righteousness; and all these things shall be added unto you' and Luke 12:31, 'But rather seek ye the kingdom of God; and all these things shall be added unto you.'
2. *Romans 2* Romans 2:21, 'Thou therefore which teachest another, teachest thou not thyself? thou that preachest a man should not steal, dost thou steal?'

Chapter 34: The Parson's Dexterity in Applying of Remedies

1. *as he did our Saviour* i.e., during the Temptation in the wilderness, Matthew 4:11, 'Then the devil leaveth him, and behold, angels came and ministered unto him.'
2. *Job's admirable course* Cf. Job 1:4–5,

> And his sons went and feasted in their houses, every one his day; and sent and called for their three sisters, to eat and to drink with them. And it was so, when the days of their feasting were gone about, that Job sent and sanctified them, and rose up early in the morning, and offered burnt offerings according to the number of them all: For Job said, It may be that my sons have sinned, and cursed God in their hearts. Thus did Job continually.

3. *earing* ploughing.
4. *a careful Joseph* Cf. especially Genesis 41:48–9,

> And he gathered up all the food of the seven years, which were in the land of Egypt, and laid up the food in the cities: the food of the field which was round about every city, laid he up in the same. And Joseph gathered corn as the sand of the sea, very much, until he left numbering; for it was without number.

5. *Epicurean* a follower of Epicurus (341–271 BC), a hedonist denying any active role of the divine in human affairs.
6. *Isaiah 43:12* 'I have declared, and have saved, and I have

shewed, when there was no strange God among you: therefore ye are my witnesses, saith the Lord, that I am God.'

7. *Psalm 59:11* 'Slay them not, lest my people forget it: but scatter them abroad among the people, and put them down, O Lord, our defence.'

8. *Tertullian* Quintus Septimus Florens Tertullianus (*c.* AD 160–240), Carthaginian-born lawyer turned religious controversialist, the first Latin Churchman. *Chrysostom* Saint John Chrysostom (*c.* AD 347–407), Bishop of Constantinople whose name means 'golden-mouthed', one of the Doctors of the Church. *Tully* Marcus Tullius Cicero (106–43 BC), Latin lawyer, politician, philosopher and, most celebratedly, orator. *Virgil* Publius Vergilius Maro (70–19 BC), poet, author of *Eclogues*, *Georgics* and the *Aeneid*. *Livy* Titus Livius (59 BC–AD 17), Roman historian.

9. *Josephus's History* Flavius Josephus (*c.* AD 37–*c.* 100), Jewish historian, author of the *Jewish War*, to which he provides eye-witness accounts, and the *Antiquities of the Jews*.

10. *only not embraced* i.e., our rejection of God is the only way we can escape his love.

Chapter 35: The Parson's Condescending

1. *condescending* not a pejorative term here, rather 'acquiescing', 'accommodating', as in St Paul's admonition, 'Be of the same mind one toward another. Mind not high things, but condescend to men of low estate. Be not wise in your own conceits' (Romans 12:16).

2. *procession* 'During Rogation Days it was usual for priest and people to beat the bounds of the parish and to invoke the Divine blessing on the growing crops, the Litany and appropriate Psalms being sung in procession' (Hutchinson).

Chapter 36: The Parson Blessing

1. *Mark 10:16* 'And he took them up in his arms, put his hands upon them, and blessed them.'

2. *Numbers 6* i.e., verses 22–7.

3. *the Apostle* St Paul.
4. *ministration of condemnation* Cf. 2 Corinthians 3:9, 'For if the ministration of condemnation be glory, much more doth the ministration of righteousness exceed in glory.'
5. *Acts 8* Acts 8:20.
6. *Alexander the coppersmith* referred to in 2 Timothy 4 cited by Herbert in the previous sentence.
7. *Hymeneus and Alexander* object lesson in Paul's First Epistle to Timothy 1:20, 'Of whom is Hymeneus and Alexander, whom I have delivered unto Satan, that they may learn not to blaspheme.'
8. *Commination* 'the service drawn up by the compilers of the BCP for use on Ash Wednesday . . . and for other days appointed by the ordinary. It consists of an exhortation clearly intended for use by a non-preaching clergy (during which the Curses are solemnly recited), Psalm 51, suffrages, and prayers . . .' (*ODCC*).
9. *Benedicite* 'Bless ye (the Lord)', originating in the song of praise sung by Shadrack, Meshack and Abednego in Nebuchadnezzar's fiery furnace, it became part of Christian liturgy from the earliest days.
10. *Romans 12:14* 'Bless them which persecute you, bless, and curse not.'

Chapter 37: Concerning Detraction

1. *Romans 1:30* 'Backbiters, haters of God, despiteful, proud, boasters, inventors of evil things, disobedient to parents' are worthy of death, says St Paul.

A Prayer after Sermon

1. *hang in clusters* The grapes of the sacramental wine recur throughout Herbert's poetry and prose.

IZAAK WALTON'S *THE LIFE OF MR GEORGE HERBERT*

Izaak Walton (1593–1683), ironmonger, biographer and hagiographer, author of *The Compleat Angler* (1653), published his first edition of his *Life of Mr George Herbert* in 1670, collecting it with his biographies of Donne (1640), Wotton (1651) and Hooker (1655) in one volume. He would later add the life of a fourth Anglican divine, Robert Sanderson, in 1678. His *Lives* have as their goal spiritual edification. They are often unreliable in detail, but their author was clearly the recipient of information and anecdote that would otherwise have been lost. *The Life of Herbert*, revised in 1674 for use in the tenth edition of *The Temple* and again the following year for use in the second edition of the *Lives*, whatever its limitations in historical precision, is, after Herbert's works themselves, the chief source of subsequent interpretation of the poet's life and nature. I have used the 1675 edition, the last that Walton revised, modernising the spelling and capitalisation and adjusting Walton's now confusing usages of the colon to current expectations of comma, semi-colon and full stop. For the history of Walton's changes, see David Novarr, *The Making of Walton's 'Lives'*, especially Chapter 10 (pp. 301–61) and Appendix D (pp. 510–12).

1. *Saint Mary Magdalene* Mary Magdalene was a 'follower of Christ out of whom He is said to have cast "seven devils" and who ministered to Him in Galilee (Luke 8:2). Later she stood by His cross at the Crucifixion (Mark 15:40), with two other women discovered the empty tomb and heard the angelic announcement of His Resurrection (Mark 16:1ff.), and was granted an appearance of the Risen Christ early on the same day (Matthew 28:9, John 20:11ff.)' (*ODCC*).
2. *spikenard* a fragrant ointment.
3. *Dr Donne* John Donne (1572–1631), brilliant poet and preacher, Dean of St Paul's Cathedral.
4. *Sir Henry Wotton* poet and diplomat (1568–1639), Ambassador to Venice, notorious in his own day and celebrated in later times

for his definition of 'ambassador' as 'a man sent abroad to lie for his country'.

5. *wretches that were the cause of it* the Members of Parliament who in 1649 ordered the castle destroyed.

6. *High Ercall ... Salop* High Ercall, in what is now the county of Shropshire.

7. *late Prince Henry's* popular eldest son (1594–1612) of James I of England, whose unexpected early death (thought to be by poison) produced widespread grief.

8. *Lewis* Louis XIII, who reigned 1624–42.

9. *Duke de Luines* Charles d'Albert, Duc de Luynes, favourite of Louis XIII.

10. *Castle-Island* Castleisland.

11. *Dr Neale* Richard Neile (1562–1640), Bishop of Rochester (where he made Laud his chaplain), later Bishop of Durham and Winchester, and Archbishop of York (1631–40).

12. *the learned languages* Latin, Greek and Hebrew.

13. *Dr Nevil* Thomas Neville (d. 1615), Master of Trinity College, Cambridge, Dean of Canterbury.

14. *Edward her eldest son* Edward Herbert (1583–1648), later Lord Herbert of Cherbury, soldier, diplomat, poet and philosopher. He was the first English deist who held, in *De Veritate*, certain rational principles in religion, including the ideas that God exists, that virtuous conduct is a form of worship and that there is an afterlife where rewards and punishments are meted out.

15. *Paula* St Paula (AD 347–404), Roman matron, friend and disciple of St Jerome.

16. *Micham* Mitcham, town in Surrey where Donne lived with his rapidly growing family from 1606 to 1611.

17. *Bethina* Bethany, the village of Martha and Mary, where Christ stayed immediately before Passion week, at which time Mary Magdalene anointed the feet of Christ.

18. *Magdalo* By jointure (the estate given to a wife in lieu of her dower) Mary is called 'Magdalene'.

19. *those springs* of Helicon; cf. Milton, *Paradise Lost*, Book III, lines 27–9':

Yet not the more
Cease I to wander where the Muses haunt
Clear Spring, or shady Grove, or Sunny Hill.

20. *sonnets* short lyrics, not necessarily, as here, poems fourteen lines in length.

21. *heat* passion.

22. *dove* symbol of the Holy Ghost, in contrast to the similar birds attendant upon Venus.

23. *with God and man* Cf. Luke 2:52: 'And Jesus increased in wisdom and stature, and in favour with God and man.'

24. *1615* Walton is often inaccurate in his dating: Herbert became a fellow of Trinity in 1614.

25. *an earnest* a token of what is to come.

26. *gentleness* civility.

27. *Sir Robert Nanton ... Sir Francis Nethersoll.* Sir Robert Naunton (1563–1635) and Sir Francis Nethersole (1587–1659).

28. *Lady Elizabeth, Queen of Bohemia* daughter of James I of England, at whose wedding in 1613 to Frederick, Elector Palatine, Shakespeare's *The Tempest* was performed.

29. *Basilicon Doron* that is, *Basilikon Doron*, a manual of princely conduct written (1599) by King James for Prince Henry.

30. *Quid Vaticanam ... Liber* This translates as: 'How receptive the Vatican and Bodleian are to gifts sent to them! For us (this) one book is a whole library.'

31. *Andrew Melvin* Andrew Melville (1545–1622), Scottish Presbyterian controversialist, mildly satirised by Herbert in his *Musae Responsoriae* (1620), forty Latin epigrams on issues of Church liturgy.

32. *Causa tibi mecum ... mihi* This translates as: 'The reason you are here with me, Arabella, is prison; for you that's the reason. For me it is you, divine Arabella.'

33. *Dr Duport* James Duport (1606–79), Master of Magdalene College, Regius Professor of Greek at Cambridge, teacher of Isaac Barrow, John Ray, *et al.*

34. *Francis Bacon* (1561–1626) Lord Chancellor, first English essayist, spiritual founder of British experimental science, admirer and friend of George Herbert.

35. *Dr Andrewes* Lancelot Andrewes (1555–1626), Dean of Westminster, Bishop of Winchester, gifted in the ancient languages, one of the translators of the King James Bible (1611), brilliant preacher much given to wordplay.
36. *Crux mihi Anchora* 'The cross is my anchor.'
37. *Sine Cure* Literally a sinecure; an office or benefice without the responsibility of caring for souls.
38. *Sir Philip Sidney* (1554–86) Protestant champion, war hero, poet, critic, 'novelist', archetype of the Elizabethan courtier.
39. *prebend* a cleric who receives a stipend from a Church estate.
40. '*Affliction*' this is from the poem entitled 'Affliction (1)' on p. 41.
41. *Lodowick, Duke of Richmond* Ludovick, Duke of Lennox and Duke of Richmond.
42. *Leighton Ecclesia* Layton Ecclesia (Leighton Bronswold was the estate attached to the prebend).
43. *July 15 ... Lord Bishop of that see* Another example of Walton chronological vagueness – Herbert was installed on 5 July by Dr John Williams (1582–1650), Dean of Salisbury, of Westminster, Bishop of Lincoln, Lord Keeper (1621–5).
44. *Nicholas Ferrar* (1592–1637) founder of the religious community at Little Gidding in Huntingdonshire.
45. *goldsmith* at his shop called 'The Bunch of Grapes'.
46. *bottom* the core on which silk thread is wound.
47. *Goliath-like trouble* Cf. especially 1 Samuel 14:36–7.
48. *Psalm 55* verse 23, 'O cast thy burden upon the Lord, and he shall nourish thee: and shall not suffer the righteous to fall for ever' (BCP).
49. *1622* In 1674 Walton added this letter to Mrs Herbert, placing it at the time of a late illness in spite of the fact that the date reveals the composition as belonging to the period of Herbert's Oratorship. This is a clear instance of Walton's relative indifference to factual accuracy in the face of the needs of artistic design; the letter, 'placed where it is ... foreshadows Herbert's illness and his mother's death and coming just after the Leighton episode is further evidence of his holiness' (Novarr, *The Making of Walton's 'Lives'*, p. 257).

50. *1629* This looks to be a printer's error uncorrected by Walton. The '9' should be a '6', an inversion easy enough to make. 'In Walton's failure to pick up this error, we may find again his subsidiary interest in chronology' (Novarr, *The Making of Walton's 'Lives'*, p. 357).

51. *quotidian ague* an intermittent fever, returning daily. Mistress Quickly confuses this kind of fever with that which returns on alternate days when she describes Falstaff 'so shaked of a burning quotidian tertian' (*King Henry V* II, i, line 119).

52. *Sir Henry Herbert* (1595–1673) best known as Master of the Revels, 1623–42 and 1660–63.

53. *Dantsey* Dauntsey.

54. *inclining towards tallness* Walton does better by Herbert than Aubrey did by Milton 'He was scarce so tall as I am (quare: quot feet I am high)'.

55. *Bainton* Baynton.

56. *presentation* the power of nominating.

57. *only those that have endured them* as, for example, Donne, who hesitated long before accepting holy orders, not only because of the frustrations of his hopes for secular advancement, but also because he doubted his own spiritual worthiness.

58. *deacon* clerical rank just below that of priest.

59. *thirty-sixth* another example of Walton's faulty arithmetic: 1630 was Herbert's thirty-eighth year.

60. *St Chrysostom* Greek Doctor of the Church (*c.* AD 347–407), famed for his oratorical gifts.

61. *'The Odour'* Cf. p. 165.

62. *'The Pearl, Matthew 13'* Cf. p. 81.

63. *chancel* 'the entire area within the main body of the church east of the nave and transepts . . . the repair of the chancel, unlike that of the rest of the church, usually falls upon the incumbent' (*ODCC*).

64. *David's blessed man* that is, *Beatus vir* of Psalm 1, the blessed man who delights in the law of the Lord.

65. *Ember week* a week in which Ember days fall; Ember days are 'four groups each of three days, in the Church year, viz., the Wednesday, Friday and Saturday after St Lucy (13 Dec.), Ash Wed-

nesday, Whitsunday and Holy Cross Day (14 Sept.) respectively, which have been observed as days of fasting and abstinence in the Churches of the W.' (*ODCC*). The first Ember week between his induction (26 April) and his ordination (19 September) was that after Whitsunday.

66. *The Country Parson A Priest to the Temple: or The Country Parson His Character and Rule of Holy Life*, written 1632, first published in 1652: see pp. 199–263.

67. *Barnabas Oley* (1602–86) Fellow of Clare College, biographer and editor of *Herbert's Remains* (1652).

68. *his first sermon* Proverbs 4:23: 'Keep thy heart with all diligence; for out of it are the issues of life.'

69. *Epistle* 'In Christian worship, it was long customary for two passages of Scripture to be read or sung at the Eucharist; the former came to be known as the "Epistle", doubtless because it was normally taken from the NT Epistles, though occasionally from the OT, Acts or Rev.' (*ODCC*).

70. *collect* 'the short form of prayer, constructed (with many varieties of detail) from (1) an invocation, (2) a petition, and (3) a pleading of Christ's name or an ascription of glory to God' (*ODCC*).

71. *lauds* hymns, psalms and prayers of thanksgiving.

72. *the Blessed Virgin* Walton here refers in turn to the various psalms and canticles (biblical texts used in worship) that are appointed to be read at Morning and Evening Prayer: this first is the Magnificat, said or sung daily throughout the year at Evening Prayer: Luke 1:46–55.

73. *Simeon* When Jesus' parents presented him at the Temple for circumcision, the aged and devout man Simeon recognised Jesus as the Messiah and spoke the words used at Evening Prayer known as 'Nunc Dimittis' – part of which reads 'For mine eyes have seen thy salvation'.

74. *as Zacharias did . . . with them* This is a part of the 'Benedictus', from Morning Prayer, Luke 1:68–79.

75. *Doxology* 'an ascription of glory . . . to the Persons of the Holy Trinity' (*ODCC*). The 'shorter creed' is the lesser doxology, which begins 'Glory be to the Father'. It is used as a conclusion to almost

all psalms and canticles when they are said or sung in church.
76. *Mr Hooker* Richard Hooker (1554–1600), theologian who wrote *Of the Laws of Ecclesiastical Polity*, the classic statement of the principles that govern the Church of England.
77. *twenty-fifth day of March* Lady Day, the festival of the Annunciation of the Blessed Virgin Mary.
78. *Twelfth Day* the feast of the Epiphany, which falls on 6 January each year.
79. *circular commemoration* as is partly reflected in the order of the poems in *The Temple*.
80. *litany* 'the General Supplication, to be sung or said after Morning Prayer upon Sundays, Wednesdays, and Fridays, and at other times when it shall be commanded by the Ordinary' (BCP); a comprehensive form of prayer designed to give comfort in part by the involvement of the person at prayer in the series of alternating responses.
81. *like Joshua* Cf. Joshua 7:16–18.
82. *Saints Bell* the Sanctus, or sacring bell, was rung at Communion and at other important points in the Church service.
83. *Dr Lake* Arthur Lake (1569–1626), Warden of New College, Oxford, Dean of Worcester, consecrated Bishop of Bath and Wells 1616, described by Walton in his *Life of Sanderson* as 'a man of whom I take myself bound in justice to say, that he made the great trust committed to him [i.e., the bishopric] the chief care and whole business of his life'.
84. *the good Samaritan* Cf. Luke 10:30ff., the parable answering the question 'Who is my neighbour?'
85. *Emmaus* Cf. Luke 24:13ff., especially verse 27: 'And beginning at Moses and all the prophets, he expounded unto them in all the scriptures the things concerning himself.'
86. *almoner* one who dispenses charitable gifts for another.
87. *tithe* one tenth of a man's profit given to the upkeep of the Church and charity.
88. *deodate* a deodand, something forfeited to God; here a circular exchange in which God's gift to man is returned to him.
89. *Mr Bostock* Nathaniel Bostocke, Herbert's curate at Bemerton.

90. *Fuggleston* Fugglestone.
91. *chapel of ease* 'a chapel subordinate to a mother church, for the ease of parishioners in prayers and preaching' (*ODCC*).
92. *Fryer Barnet* Friern Barnet.
93. *Gidden* Little Gidding, where Nicholas Ferrar ran an Anglican community based on prayer and worship.
94. *John Valdesso* Juan de Valdes, Spanish-born student of the Scriptures and author of *Dialogo de Doctrina Christiana*, correspondent of Erasmus, who was briefly papal chamberlain to Clement VII and died in Naples in 1541, leaving behind an unpublished manuscript in Spanish of several hundred 'divine considerations'.
95. *Charles the Fifth* (1500–1558) Holy Roman Emperor celebrated for abdicating his throne in order to enter a monastery and the life of contemplation.
96. *Sir, I pray deliver . . . God's mercies* the most fascinating passage in the *Life*, both for those interested in the issue of the transmission of the text and the nature of *The Temple* itself.
97. *a Tip-toe* 'on tip-toe', *1633*, the first edition of *The Temple*.
98. *door* 'gate', *1633*; cf. p. 69, line 33.
99. *his last Enemy* the Devil.
100. *religion* fidelity.
101. *without any apparent disturbance* Cf. Donne, 'A Valediction: Forbidding Mourning':

> As virtuous men pass mildly away,
> And whisper to their souls, to go,
> Whilst some of their sad friends do say,
> The breath goes now, and some say, no (lines 1–4)

102. *blossom in the dust* lines adapted by Walton from the dirge in James Shirley's *Contention of Ajax and Ulysses*.

Appendix

Both the *Passio Discerpta* and *Lucus* were not published until 1874 when A. B. Grosart included them in *Complete Works: Verse and Prose of George Herbert*. They exist in the Williams

Manuscript, written in Herbert's own hand. References to Pope Urban VIII in *Lucus* and the rather overtly didactic nature of the verse in both groups allow for the relatively early dating of 1623, the year of the publication of the first folio of Shakespeare's works and of the naming of Sir Henry Herbert as Deputy Master of the Revels.

In Flagellum

Title The scourging of Christ is mentioned in Matthew 27:26, Mark 15:15 and John 19:1.

4 *virgae . . . umbra* Herbert alludes to Psalm 23:4–5, 'in medio *umbrae* mortis' (through the valley of the shadow of death) and, '*virga* tua et baculus tuus' (thy rod and thy staff).

In Vestes Divisas

Title The fullest description of the portioning of Christ's garments is given in John 19:23–4, 'Then the soldiers . . . said therefore among themselves, Let not us rent it, but cast lots for it, whose it shall be: that the Scripture might be fulfilled, which saith, They parted my raiment among them, and for my vesture they did cast lots.' The title alludes to the Scripture referred to (Psalm 21:18), '*diviserunt* sibi *vestimenta* mea, et super *vestem* meam miserunt sortem' ('They have parted my garments among them: and cast lots upon my vesture').

In Improbum Disertum

1 *pannusia Baucis* the rags of Baucis, the aged wife of the equally aged and equally poor Philemon. Their hospitality to the disguised gods Zeus and Hermes was rewarded by salvation from flood and their ultimate metamorphoses into intertwined trees. Baucis had only the most modest clothing. See Ovid's *Metamorphoses*, VIII.

4 *Charontis* Charon, the grim ferryman who brings the dead across the river Styx, normally receives as payment for his chore a

small coin, the obol, placed in the mouth of the deceased. Here the 'gilded', cheap words of the subject of the poem will guarantee passage to Hell.

Roma. Anagr. { *Oram, Maro*
Ramo, Armo
Mora, Amor

Title Herbert's interest in anagrams is of a piece with the enthusiasm of Lancelot Andrewes (his patron and putative tutor at Westminster School) for systematic analyses of rhetorically fragmented texts.

4 *MARO* Virgil (Publius Vergilius Maro), 70–19 BC, author of the *Aeneid*, the epic of Rome.

10 *Fabio* Quintus Fabius Maximus Verrucosus, surnamed 'Cunctator', the Delayer, d. 203 BC, the Roman commander in the Second Punic War whose strategy of avoiding pitched battles with Hannibal succeeded in wearing down the Carthaginians' strength, thereby saving Rome.

In Honorem Illustr. D.D. Verulamii, Sti. Albani, Mag. Sigilli Custodis Post Editam Ab Eo Instaurationem Magnam

12 *Idolum* In Book I of the *Novum Organum*, Bacon describes four kinds of false learning as the Idols of the Tribe (tacit agreement to preserve comfortable illusion), Idols of the Cave (errors of unconscious habit), Idols of the Marketplace (imprecise vocabulary) and Idols of the Theatre (traditional systems of thought).

14 *Brutus* Lucius Junius Brutus, consul 509 BC, founder of the Roman Republic, led the fight which expelled Tarquinius Superbus, the last Roman king.

17 *Atlas* the Titan who held up the sky. In mythology Atlas offered to help Hercules by fetching the apples of the Hesperides if Hercules would hold up the sky for him. After refusing to take back the duty of animated pillar, he is forced to accept the burden by Hercules. Herbert alludes only to the first part of the myth.

18 *Stagiritico* Aristotle was so called after Stagira, his birthplace in Macedonia.

Aethiopissa Ambit Cestum Diversi Coloris Virum

Uncharacteristic in its secular subject matter, but quite in keeping with Herbert's instinct for the paradoxical, this poem is the 'humble Blackamoor' referred to in 'To the Right Hon. the L. Chancellor', p. 196.

In Sacram Anchoram Piscatoris

Title Walton in his *Life of Donne* provided the first ten lines of the English version of this poem and a statement of the origin, the essence of which is repeated in the *Life of Herbert* where (p. 00) there is the added quatrain here labelled 'Another Version'. Herbert's Latin poems appear in *Herbert's Remains* (1652). Hutchinson points out that 'In all these editions [i.e., *Herbert's Remains* and in the *Poems* of Donne, eddn. 1650, 1654, 1669] the couplet beginning "Munde, fluas" ended the poem, and the corresponding English couplet was at the end of the Donne edition. In this form the Latin poem consisted of a set of seven lines, followed by two disconnected triplets and a final couplet; and this was represented in the English version by a set of eight lines, followed by two quatrains and a couplet. But in Walton's *Life of Donne* (1658), where Herbert's English lines appear, with the first two lines and a half only of the Latin, the couplet is attached to the first set, and is followed by the first quatrain only . . . the two disconnected stanzas "may or may not be by Herbert" [quoting Grierson]. The opening lines are addressed to Donne, but the additional stanzas seem to be written after his death on 3 March 1631.'

Helen Gardner, however, argues that Walton erred when he thought Donne's poem accompanied the gift of his seal ring. She believes that Donne's poem is about new, royal gifts that Herbert as a young man with political aspirations may yet receive, and that the verses were sent *under* Donne's new seal (of Christ upon his anchor), not *with* his new seal. Ms Gardner argues 'that separate poems written on two different occasions have been printed together'. That is, 'the first seven lines, the iambic trimeters, are the answer to Donne's poem . . . [Herbert's] poem is an obscurely worded conceit on the fact that Donne has "made assurance doubly sure" by sealing his letter with a seal, itself imprinted with an emblem of security, an Anchor . . . In both [of the following epigrams] Herbert speaks of Donne as dead. The final couplet . . . cannot be attached to the first seven lines in the Latin, for it is in a different metre', *John Donne, The Divine Poems*, ed. Helen Gardner (Oxford: The Clarendon Press, 1952), pp. 140, 145–6.

See the subtle analysis of the imagery in these poems of Donne and Herbert, pointing out how Herbert's poem develops the theme of fixity contained in Donne's poem, in Steven Berkowitz, 'Of Signs and Seals: The New Character of John Donne', *Fu Jen Studies* 18 (1985), pp. 1–30.

INDEX OF TITLES

INDEX OF FIRST LINES

READ MORE IN PENGUIN

In every corner of the world, on every subject under the sun, Penguin represents quality and variety – the very best in publishing today.

For complete information about books available from Penguin – including Puffins, Penguin Classics and Arkana – and how to order them, write to us at the appropriate address below. Please note that for copyright reasons the selection of books varies from country to country.

In the United Kingdom: Please write to *Dept. EP, Penguin Books Ltd, Bath Road, Harmondsworth, West Drayton, Middlesex UB7 0DA*

In the United States: Please write to *Consumer Services, Penguin Putnam Inc., 405 Murray Hill Parkway, East Rutherford, New Jersey 07073-2136.* VISA and MasterCard holders call 1-800-631-8571 to order Penguin titles

In Canada: Please write to *Penguin Books Canada Ltd, 10 Alcorn Avenue, Suite 300, Toronto, Ontario M4V 3B2*

In Australia: Please write to *Penguin Books Australia Ltd, 487 Maroondah Highway, Ringwood, Victoria 3134*

In New Zealand: Please write to *Penguin Books (NZ) Ltd, Private Bag 102902, North Shore Mail Centre, Auckland 10*

In India: Please write to *Penguin Books India Pvt Ltd, 11 Community Centre, Panchsheel Park, New Delhi 110017*

In the Netherlands: Please write to *Penguin Books Netherlands bv, Postbus 3507, NL-1001 AH Amsterdam*

In Germany: Please write to *Penguin Books Deutschland GmbH, Metzlerstrasse 26, 60594 Frankfurt am Main*

In Spain: Please write to *Penguin Books S. A., Bravo Murillo 19, 1°B, 28015 Madrid*

In Italy: Please write to *Penguin Italia s.r.l., Via Vittorio Emanuele 45/a, 20094 Corsico, Milano*

In France: Please write to *Penguin France, 12, Rue Prosper Ferradou, 31700 Blagnac*

In Japan: Please write to *Penguin Books Japan Ltd, Iidabashi KM-Bldg, 2-23-9 Koraku, Bunkyo-Ku, Tokyo 112-0004*

In South Africa: Please write to *Penguin Books South Africa (Pty) Ltd, P.O. Box 751093, Gardenview, 2047 Johannesburg*